D1103836

STATE FORMATION IN THE LIBERAL ERA

EDITED BY
BEN FALLAW AND **DAVID NUGENT**

STATE FORMATION

IN THE LIBERAL ERA

CAPITALISMS AND CLAIMS OF CITIZENSHIP
IN MEXICO AND PERU

THE UNIVERSITY OF
ARIZONA PRESS
TUCSON

The University of Arizona Press
www.uapress.arizona.edu

© 2020 by The Arizona Board of Regents
All rights reserved. Published 2020

ISBN-13: 978-0-8165-4038-9 (hardcover)

Cover design by Leigh McDonald
Cover art: *Port constructif avec ciel bleu*, 1930 by Joaquín Torres-García. Courtesy of de Torres, Cecilia and Susanna V. Temkin, Joaquín Torres-García Catalogue Raisonné. Collection: Gary Nader Art Centre.

Publication of this book is made possible in part by subsidies from Colby College and Emory University, and by the proceeds of a permanent endowment created with the assistance of a Challenge Grant from the National Endowment for the Humanities, a federal agency.

Library of Congress Cataloging-in-Publication Data
Names: Fallaw, Ben, 1966– editor. | Nugent, David, editor.
Title: State formation in the liberal era : capitalisms and claims of citizenship in Mexico and Peru / edited by Ben Fallaw and David Nugent.
Description: Tucson : The University of Arizona Press, 2020. | Includes bibliographical references and index.
Identifiers: LCCN 2019046598 | ISBN 9780816540389 (hardcover)
Subjects: LCSH: Nation-building—Peru—History—19th century. | Nation-building—Peru—History—20th century. | Nation-building—Mexico—History—19th century. | Nation-building—Mexico—History—20th century. | Peru—Economic policy—19th century. | Peru—Economic policy—20th century. | Peru—Politics and government—1829– | Mexico—Economic policy—19th century. | Mexico—Economic policy—20th century. | Mexico—Politics and government—1810–
Classification: LCC JL3420.S8 S73 2020 | DDC 320.10972—dc23
LC record available at https://lccn.loc.gov/2019046598

Printed in the United States of America
♾ This paper meets the requirements of ANSI/NISO Z39.48-1992 (Permanence of Paper).

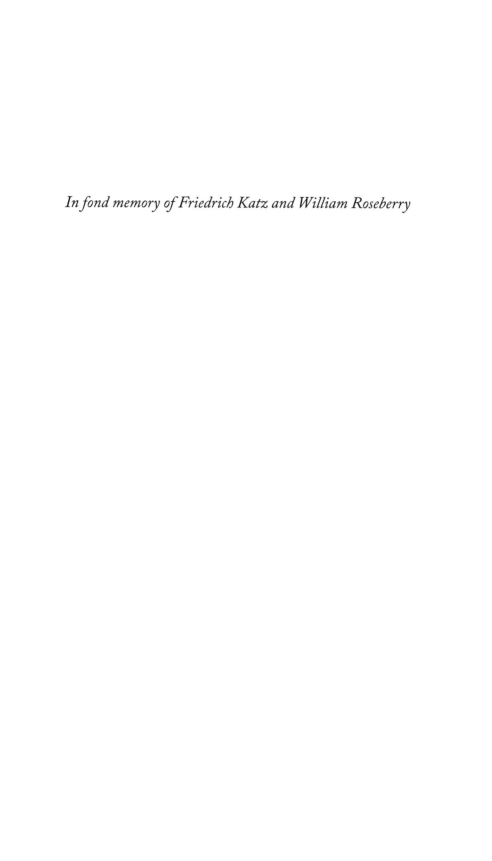

In fond memory of Friedrich Katz and William Roseberry

CONTENTS

PREFACE

Capitalisms, Citizens, and Claims of Statehood

I **N THIS** volume, we explore the processes that have variously worked for and against the organization of national societies in Mexico and Peru, two of the great centers of Latin American life. We focus on the era between 1850 and 1950—a century of nation-building activity that began in the aftermath of colonial rule, with the rise of "liberal" regimes, and ended with the onset of the Cold War. The 1850–1950 period was one of sweeping transformations in politics, economy, society, and culture—transformations that gave rise to an entire series of experiments in how to order social life. Collectively, these might be thought of as a succession of inevitably flawed, incomplete attempts to resolve what many regarded as among the era's central problems: that of defining and forming/actualizing national community by extending citizenship and integrating national economies into a global capitalist economy.[1]

Nation builders in Mexico and Peru experimented with a wide range of political forms in order to achieve these twin goals. Indeed, the century of liberal nation building was one that confronted all concerned with a bewildering and contradictory mix of political principles, processes, structures, and ideas. These ranged from monarchy (briefly) to parliamentary democracy, from dictatorship to indigenous forms of nationhood. The regimes of the era at times based the organization of national society on the unspoken codification of racial difference. At other times, however, they were outspoken advocates of the equal rights of all citizens. The era as a whole was one during which national governments formed and reformed their militaries and their police forces, their civil codes and their property regimes, their administrative structures and their fiscal bases. Each successive reformulation posited, implicitly or explicitly, a new version of national social order.

But the period was equally one of broad economic transformation. While long ensconced in the extended webs of economic dependence established under Spanish colonialism, during the century that is our focus, Mexico and Peru became drawn into—and Peruvian and Mexican elites often actively sought out—wholly new kinds of transatlantic economic relationships. Many of these were associated with the expanding centers of industrial capitalism found in the North Atlantic—where national governments were involved in their own protracted and contradictory efforts at nation building. The shadow cast over Latin America by Euro-American capitalism meant significantly different things for Mexico and Peru at different times during the study period, but the shadow itself was ever-present.

Depending on time and place, involvement in the economic networks associated with the North Atlantic could result in a huge influx of manufactured goods from the industrial centers of the Euro-American world. It might also mean, however, expanded markets for the goods produced in select regions of Mexico and Peru, especially primary agricultural goods and raw materials. During some periods, involvement with the north resulted in the availability of large quantities of loan capital for national governments (provided by private banks/investors, at varying rates of interest) as well as foreign direct investment in specific economic enterprises and activities within the two countries.

Investment from the north, and the new activities precipitated by that investment, could also compel national regimes and private interests alike to expand agrarian frontiers and to redefine property rights. It likely would also compel them to seek out new sources of generally forced labor, whether at home or abroad, and to place heavier demands on the working population already in place. Alternatively, the new flows of capital that came and went could also provide the impetus to do away entirely with long-standing conditions and categories of servitude (the end of slavery in Peru, for example).

The economic processes of the era that affected liberal nation-building efforts, however, were not limited to these. They also included debt, and at times default and bankruptcy. In the process of becoming independent republics, Mexico and Peru were compelled to borrow large sums of money from creditors in the North Atlantic. Thereafter, both countries were often capital-poor, in arrears on their standing obligations, and confronted with the prospect of imminent bankruptcy. These conditions could lead needy national regimes to take steps that seemed profoundly "denationalizing." In an effort to appease their creditors, these regimes were at times compelled to make deep concessions to foreign interests regarding the use of domestic resources. But concern about inordinate foreign influence in strategic sectors of the economy, or the desire to benefit more substantially from the foreign use of domestic resources, could lead governments to do the opposite—as reflected in Mexico's "nationalization" of its railroads and Peru's nationalization of its guano deposits.[2] In other words, struggles to define and affect national community during the liberal era were buffeted by a sea of evolving and contradictory forces, generating a range of incomplete and evolving efforts to address the national question. The nascent liberal states were defined in part by their contradictory relationship with global capitalism centered on North Atlantic countries, at times collaborative and at others conflictive.

The century that is our focus was similarly one of constant social transformation and upheaval. The instability of the era reflected the desire of diverse groups to intervene in and actively shape nation building—and to use instability to their advantage in the process. It is also indicated in the limitations of the era's successive experiments with that process. These upheavals were diverse in character and included civil wars, military coups, foreign invasions, and secessionist movements. They also precipitated the emergence (and generally the rapid destruction) of indigenous polities, which had their own conceptions of nationhood. These upheavals also included popular uprisings, both great and small, the most famous of which was the great conflagration known as the Mexican Revolution.

The upheavals of the century of liberal nation building point to the major lines of fracture within their respective societies during particular time periods. But they also indicate something more, something that is directly germane to the focus of the present volume. The era's ongoing social instability reflected the unwillingness of the various factions to be a part of the same national community—and also their willingness to take up arms, and to use force, to transform that community. The upheavals of the century of liberal nation making thus reflected expressions of profound dissatisfaction with the status quo, as well as deep commitments to changing it. In other words, the ongoing social unrest of the era reflected large-scale attempts to bring into being new forms of legitimate social order. Conflicts between different elements in society were often fought over citizenship—who was included, and who was excluded?

In sum, the social, economic, political, and cultural transformations that took place during the liberal era—and the successive experiments in nation building to which they gave birth—are our focus. We argue that a close examination of the various forms of socioeconomic and political life that came into being during this era, and of the transformations from one to the next, is an important and neglected topic of investigation. Such an examination will shed new light on the forces that have compelled the people of Mexico and Peru to go to such extraordinary lengths, to take such extraordinary risks, and to make such extraordinary sacrifices to make and remake their social worlds.

We find three broad analytical rubrics to be especially useful in analyzing the emergence of the era's successive experiments in nation building. As the title of our volume implies, these rubrics are capitalism, citizenship, and state. The way that we use these terms, however, and how we understand the relationships that obtain between them requires explanation.

The relationship between capital and the broad problematic we engage in this work—the forces that work variously for and against the organization of national societies—is a complex one.[3] Indeed, a great deal of academic discussion and debate has focused on the impact of capitalism on the societies of Latin America. We find two lines of argument within that scholarship to be especially fruitful. The first of these is work that disaggregates "capitalism" and distinguishes between different *forms* of capital (industrial, merchant, finance, etc.) that have operated in different combinations, in specific regions, depending on time and place.

If capital is above all else a social relationship, then it follows that different forms of capital imply distinct kinds of relationships. In our view, it is important to understand these relationships in all their particularity. In other words, it is important to distinguish between different forms of capital and to identify the distinctive combinations that are at work in any given context. It is equally important to analyze the impact of different forms and combinations of capital on everyday life.

The second line of argument about capital and its relationship to nation building that we find useful is scholarship that problematizes the spatial dimensions of accumulation processes. In our view, it is useful to think in terms of "circuits," or geographies of specific forms of capital. These circuits may be "opened" (i.e., initiated) in one locale, under one set of social conditions, and they may be "closed" (and accumulation completed) in an entirely different locale, in very different circumstances. In the course of defining their respective circuits or geographies of accumulation, however, each form of capital operates across multiple spatial scales. It also draws upon existing social relations of diverse kinds, and not uncommonly seeks to reshape those relations, often through extending or redefining citizenship.

In relationship to the problematic of our volume—understanding the forces that variously work for or against the organization of national societies—one point about capital and space is especially relevant.[4] The forms of investment that were of the greatest significance in Mexico and Peru during the century of liberal nation building, the circuits/geographies of accumulation defined by these forms of capital, and the spatial scales across which these circuits operated were only in rare cases national. Rather, in the vast majority of cases, capital "opened" the accumulation process by articulating with domestic activities at a subnational, regional scale. Capital was also able to "close" the process of accumulation by articulating across spatial scales that were supra- or subnational. The fact that capital was simultaneously sub- and transnational, we suggest, created real dilemmas for state officials seeking to legitimate the particular form of national society to which they had committed themselves. This was because regimes were faced with the daunting task of defending particular, regional, sectoral interests, even as they sought to represent them as general, national, universal concerns as implied by liberal aspirations of egalitarian citizenship.[5] The tension between the needs of the regime to accommodate the demands of interests linked to capital and the promise of universal citizenship was a recurring source of conflicts in the histories of both Peru and Mexico during this time.

This highlights the importance of another keyword in our title: "citizenship." This term has taken on a wide range of meanings, implicit and explicit, among scholars.[6] Because our focus is on the projects of nation building that characterized Mexico and Peru between 1850 and 1950, however, the point of departure for the discussion that follows is the meaning of citizenship that was embraced in the official charters of both countries. This was the liberal framing of citizenship. Liberal conceptions of citizenship draw upon Enlightenment principles of equality, democracy, and the inalienable rights of (wo)man. Many of these principles were articulated in the constitutions of revolutionary France and the United States in the late eighteenth century. They were included in the founding charters of independent Mexico and Peru a few decades later and were retained in the majority of the constitutions that followed.

Unlike the geographies of capital, which generally operate across multiple, simultaneously sub- and transnational scales, citizenship is an inherently nationalizing concept. Indeed, the kind of formal citizenship that is set out in the liberal charters of Mexico and Peru is meant to define the very essence of national community. It is meant to do so in part by defining the rights and duties that apply equally, to all individuals, who make up the nation.

As scholars have long noted, however, one of the most striking features of liberal citizenship is how very few people who live within liberal polities, and are entitled by law to its privileges and prerogatives, have enjoyed the rights and benefits of liberal citizenship.[7] This disjuncture between the theory of citizenship and the practices of everyday life certainly characterized the North Atlantic contexts that are regarded as having given birth to the liberal creed. So extreme was this disjuncture that, as Uday Mehta has shown, coded definitions of proper and improper personhood (defined on the basis of race, gender, class, and breeding) implicit in liberal discourse meant that its seemingly inclusive, universal principles in fact acted as mechanisms of broad and systematic exclusion for the vast majority of the population.[8]

It was not just in the North Atlantic, however, that only a tiny fraction of the people who lived within the territorial limits of the nation actually partook of the liberal rights, duties, and protections that were in principle available to all. The same applied to Mexico and Peru. Here, as in the North Atlantic, the exclusionary tendencies implicit in liberalism combined with everyday forms of political participation and informal codes of conduct inherited from the (colonial) past to "fracture" the universal rights and obligations set out in national charters.[9] Structured by contingent, context-specific combinations of race, gender, class, clientele, and so on, these alternative modes of participating in social and political life represented permanent and ongoing states of exception to what was articulated in national constitutions.[10]

As the foregoing suggests, we believe that it is important to distinguish between two forms of citizenship. The first of these is the formal and largely imaginary form of universal citizenship that is set out in political charters.[11] But there is also a second form of citizenship—one that is concrete rather than abstract, lived rather than imagined, active rather than passive. This active form of lived citizenship is not general, or uniform, across an entire national population, as is formal citizenship. It is instead particular. By the term *active (or lived) citizenship,* we refer to the concrete, tangible rights, responsibilities, and duties that accrued to specific categories of people (as a function of race, gender, class, clientele, etc.) and that structured their participation in everyday life, within specific regional domains. Furthermore, we suggest that it is this second form of citizenship that has been of the greatest importance in organizing the daily lives of the vast majority of the population in Mexico and Peru.

We also argue, however, that there was an intimate relationship between the era's active, lived expressions of citizenship and the various forms of capital investment that came and went during the period we consider. Indeed, the era's lived forms of citizenship were in many ways new, emergent phenomena. It was not just that Enlightenment-based notions of liberal citizenship were confounded by the complex realities of everyday life that Mexico and Peru had inherited from the past. The tensions were often compounded by new, developing forms of agrarian capitalism. In other words, the period's new forms and circuits of capital encountered these long-standing, habitual forms of participation and informal codes of conduct. It is equally true that new bundles of informal rights and obligations, new forms of active citizenship, emerged out of the encounter. Furthermore, these emergent forms of citizenship were extremely diverse. Overall, they gave expression to highly variegated national landscapes of citizenship. For the present purposes, however, what is significant about these active, lived forms of citizenship is the following: virtually none of them had any relationship whatsoever with official forms of liberal citizenship enshrined in national constitutions.

The outcomes of these encounters between capital and regional social orders thus produced regimes of capital accumulation and lived citizenship that were highly variable in time and space. This was in part because flows of capital from the north came and went, as it were. It was also because the terms under which foreign capital was allowed to enter Mexico and Peru and involve itself in different regions within the two countries were also highly variable in time and space. The encounters in question also produced such differing outcomes because capital investment came from a range of sources and found its way into different hands. These included different branches of government, each of which had its own plans for the funds made available to it. They also included private concerns of different kinds—from plantation to mine, from trading company to labor contractor. Here as well, those to whom investment funds became available had a range of intentions and uses for these funds.

Further contributing to the era's variegated landscape of lived citizenship was the fact that different forms of capital drew upon, sought to transform, and were transformed by a range of regionally specific, place-based social interdependencies. Indeed, foreign capital entered subnational fields of force in Mexico and Peru in which domestic interests pursued their own agendas, a fact that generated varying patterns of cooperation and competition between foreigners and nationals, each pattern having its own, peculiar dynamic.[12] As our case studies show, and as a broader literature confirms, foreign capital was (occasionally) a progressive, transformative force, as in the border area between Mexico and the United States during the Porfiriato.[13] Far more commonly, however, it had deeply conservative, even repressive, effects and helped consolidate profoundly illiberal relationships.[14] The overall effect was to generate patterns of deeply uneven development.

As the foregoing suggests, during the century of liberal nation building a great many emergent forms of everyday, active citizenship were being claimed, contested, disavowed, and denied across the socioeconomic and political landscape of Mexico and Peru. These ranged enormously in character—from the freedoms and dangers of "bandit citizenship," as described by Lewis Taylor (see chapter 5), to the coercive abuses endured by "conscript citizens," as analyzed by Sarah Washbrook (see chapter 3). To repeat, the vast majority of these forms of lived citizenship had little if anything to do with formal, liberal citizenship, as articulated in national constitutions. In fact, many of the era's active, emergent expressions of citizenship were in open conflict with their liberal counterparts. These contradictions between formal citizenship as a category of national belonging and the many forms of active citizenship as phenomena of lived participation form the context for our discussion of the final term with which we are concerned: the "state."

In much of the academic literature, the term *state* is used to refer to an institution, or a set of institutions, that enjoys a monopoly on the use of legitimate force within a given territory.[15] While useful as a normative construction, in our view it is unrealistic to attribute to an overarching institutional order the ability to monopolize the use of force across an entire national society—whether in Latin America or elsewhere. The history of Mexico and Peru (not to mention that of the United States) during the period under consideration would appear to lend support to our view.[16]

As our case studies show, and as an extensive academic literature confirms, during the century of liberal nation building, control of armed force was widely dispersed, and violence was wielded by a wide range of actors other than "the state." Indeed, negotiations and contestations over rights, responsibilities, and powers—which were played out in regional domains, as distinct forms of capital articulated with and reshaped place-based social orders—played a crucial role in the reproduction of inequality. Furthermore, these negotiations were often accompanied by the threat (or actual use) of violence, by all parties concerned. Even so, active citizenship relations were commonly renegotiated, and inequality was reproduced, in the absence of, or with minimal involvement by, armed representatives of a central authority. In addition, when those acting on behalf of central powers did become involved, the outcome was anything but a foregone conclusion. In other words, "the state" was not as all-powerful as it would have had people believe.

We prefer to regard "state" not as an institutional order that possesses a monopoly on the use of force but rather as a highly contested *claim* to the right to do so. The claim to the legitimate use of violence so as to maintain particular forms of social order, we assert, is made by highly specific and interested groups, who represent themselves as acting in a disinterested manner, on behalf of some common interest (i.e., on the basis of the nation, the people, the principles of popular sovereignty, etc.). In other words, following the work of Philip Abrams, Philip Corrigan, and Derek Sayer, we find it useful to regard the state as a mask of rule.[17]

We argue that there was an intimate relationship between the masking dimensions of the state and the aforementioned geographies of accumulation that were carved out by different forms of capital. As noted above, the key forms and circuits of capital that operated in Mexico and Peru during the century of liberal nation building operated at multiple spatial and social scales. Almost never, however, were these scales national.

As diverse forms of capital came to operate within and across national boundaries, they generated new forms of material inequality. They also challenged existing regimes of lived citizenship and their associated rights, duties, and obligations. The era's new flows of capital also called into being new regimes of lived citizenship, many of a highly repressive nature. These developments created real dilemmas for regimes with nationalizing aspirations. For although these diverse forms of capital operated within the national domains of Mexico and Peru, only rarely did they operate on behalf of their respective national communities.

Among the central problems faced by those who represented the state in Mexico and Peru were therefore the following. First, how was it possible to bring diverse, independent forms of capital, each with its own, separate, nonnational geography of accumulation, together in a broader coalition—one that was sufficiently coherent that the various forms of capital could coexist in the same national framework? Second, how was it possible for those who represented these nonnational coalitions to depict them, and the profoundly unequal and coercive relations that they so often sustained, as legitimately national? That is, how was it possible to present particular interests as general ones? As the constant social upheavals of the liberal era show, neither of these questions was even remotely hypothetical.

These are among the central questions we explore in the present volume. We are interested in how different national regimes did or did not succeed in bringing major fractions of capital and key regional powerbrokers together in a coherent coalition. We are equally interested in the forms of active citizenship that were claimed, undermined, asserted, and disavowed as government regimes struggled to form these coalitions—to establish what Antonio Gramsci called a historic bloc. Finally, we are concerned with the contradictions and dilemmas that the creation of active citizenship regimes created for the reproduction of capital and the maintenance of a historic bloc.[18]

In the remainder of the volume we offer a schematic comparison of the historical development of Mexico and Peru during the century of liberal nation building. Our goal in doing so is not to provide an exhaustive review of the broad literatures on these topics. Rather, it is to highlight the conceptual issues outlined above. These include the following: (1) the main forms of capital brought together in specific national coalitions; (2) the spatial and social scope of their circuits of accumulation; (3) the relations of coalition cores with regional elites not included within the core; (4) the forms of active, lived citizenship that emerge in the centers of accumulation; (5) the forms of active, lived citizenship that emerge in more peripheral regions; (6) the ways that core accumulation practices bend space, social relations, and the movement of goods and people in adjacent regions; and (7) claims that the subaltern make on the privileged and on the state.

In the introductions to parts I and II, we provide an analysis of the history of successive experiments in nation building in Mexico and Peru from 1850 to 1950. Before doing so, however, we offer some brief reflections on contrasts in the political geography of the two countries. These were contrasts that informed all the various efforts at nation building that we discuss.

In comparing citizenship and capitalisms in Peru and Mexico, we came to recognize that there are important geographic differences that profoundly shaped the historical trajectories of both nations. Regimes based in Mexico City seemed to enjoy significant advantages in attempting to govern national territory that regimes based in Lima attempting to govern Peruvian national territory lacked.

Bounded by the northern deserts, two oceans, and the impenetrable jungles, swamps, and mountains southeast of the Isthmus of Tehuantepec in the south,

Mexico's post-1848 national territory was coherent and difficult to disturb. In Peru, as in most of South America, on the other hand, international territorial conflicts flared until well into the twentieth century. The relationship between the capital and the rest of the national territory was profoundly different as well. The Spanish built their northern viceregal capital of Mexico City literally on top of the former Aztec capital, Tenochtitlán. The location was not far from the geographical center of the nation (in Cubilete, Guanajuato, to the north-west). Centrally located between the silver mines to the north and the ports of Acapulco and Veracruz to its west and east, respectively, Mexico City was at the intersection of three circuits of capital. It was also located in the center of some of the most densely populated indigenous complex societies in all of Mesoamerica. As a result, Mexico City was located at the very heart of, and could draw directly on, indigenous patterns of the production and circulation of wealth. These factors explain how Mexico City was able to exert a kind of gravity over Mexico's national territory, drawing in capital and political actors.

In Peru, the Spanish built their capital not in Cuzco in the southern sierra but on the coast. As a result, Lima was at a great distance from indigenous forms of the production and circulation of wealth. It was a nexus between the silver mines of Peru and Bolivia and the Pacific circuit of capital centered on the trade of Chinese silk and porcelain. It also provided a ready escape path should indigenous revolt break out. But Lima was the very definition of peripheral. Unable to act as a center of gravity, Lima simply could not draw in capital and political actors in the same way as Mexico City.

After independence, Peru seemed to be serendipitously endowed with a mir-acle export, guano. After its exhaustion, coastal valleys produced cotton and sugar for export from Pacific ports. Throughout the course of the nineteenth century, then, the Limeño elite could—and did—turn their backs on the sierra, where the nation's indigenous population was located. Furthermore, for better or worse, the United States took relatively little interest in Peru.

After independence, Mexico became painfully aware of a new geographical factor: its vulnerabilities in the north to hostile invaders. Belligerent indigenous groups that had resisted colonial rule, especially the Comanche and Apache, launched more frequent and larger raids as Mexico failed to replace Spain's fron-tier defenses. The loss of Texas (1836) and the disastrous invasion by the United States that resulted in the loss of half of Mexico's national territory (1846–48) were even more disastrous. At the same time, the threat of another U.S. invasion or intimidation would provide a centripetal force uniting Mexico's elites and convincing them of the need to chart a path of development that would convince the United States to respect Mexico's territorial integrity. Indeed, Mexico's northern neighbor supplied capital and technology for its railroad network, which stimulated booms in mining and commercial agriculture, industries that profited from proximity to U.S. markets.

Geography also forced elites based in Mexico City to incorporate the vast indigenous population surrounding them into their national projects. They simply could not turn their backs on the indigenous, as did Lima's elites. Mexican Liberals and their rivals the Conservatives competed for indigenous support, and the Liberals prevailed over Conservatives and the French in part because a powerful strain of popular liberalism developed among some indigenous communities, notably the Sierra Norte of the state of Puebla. During the armed phase of the revolution, the dominant faction, the Constitutionalists, had to seek popular support from agrarian leaders with a strong indigenous following (above all Emiliano Zapata) by offering them land, and in 1920 Álvaro Obregón brought the former Zapatistas into his ruling coalition.

Mexico is exceptional in Latin America because of popular elements' inclusion in national coalitions and the centrality of agrarian demands to national political struggles since the Conquest.[19] It is perhaps because of this that Mexico City elites were able to create an administrative apparatus with a presence in the regions, and negotiate with regional elites and popular elements. After Santa Anna, no Mexican regime could avoid a federalist arrangement that required compromise with local interests. The Porfirian regime, with all its fragility and weaknesses, seemed more robust compared to its Peruvian equivalent, the Aristocratic Republic. A cursory comparison of the success of Banamex in managing European investors explored by Thomas Passananti (see chapter 2) makes for an interesting contrast with Peru's disastrous financial arrangements with Auguste Dreyfus and Harry Meiggs, and brings out this contrast in stark terms.

The volume's nine chapters offer case studies of nation building in the liberal era that provide deeper, more nuanced discussions of the key concepts briefly explored here. To frame our contributors' case studies, we have divided the volume into two parts, taking 1900 as our watershed. We introduce each part with an original essay. Our goal is not just to provide historical context to nation building but also to provide a critical, comparative overview of Peru and Mexico's postcolonial eras as shaped by two persistent forces: capitalisms and claims of citizenships.

NOTES

1. We wish to make clear at the outset that we regard the attempt to form national community as a largely delusional activity. An extensive literature has shown that nations are imagined rather than real (see Benedict Anderson, *Imagined Communities: Reflections on the Origin and Spread of Nationalism* [New York: Verso, 1983]). Nonetheless, the fact that a wide range of political interests have staked their claim to the right to rule on the basis of such imagined communities makes them powerful constructs. As we argue at greater length below, it is important to distinguish between state formation, nation building, and the creation of regimes. We take the former to be a cultural process, rooted in violence, that seeks to normalize and legitimize the organized political subjection of large-scale societies. We regard the middle term as the imagined construct in the name of which such claims are so often made (David Nugent, "Phantom Pathologies: Regulating Imaginary Threats to the Common Good in Northern Peru," in *Social Wellbeing: New Pathologies and Emerging Challenges*, ed. Angela Hobart, Robert Muller, and David Napier [Herefordshire, UK: Sean Kingston Publishing, forthcoming]). We regard the latter as the coming together of coalitions made up of fragments of classes that control the formal apparatus of government during any given period and that seek to engage in state formation in the name of nation building.

2. As these two examples show, the consequences of nationalization for nation building were anything but a foregone conclusion.

3. For useful treatments, see John Coatsworth, "Los orígenes del autoritarismo moderno en México," *Foro Internacional* 16, no. 2 (1975): 205–32; John Coatsworth, "Comment on 'The United States and the Mexican Peasantry,'" in *Rural Revolt in Mexico and U.S. Intervention*, ed. Daniel Nugent (San Diego: Center for U.S.-Mexican Studies, University of California, San Diego, 1988), 61–68; Friedrich Katz, *The Secret War in Mexico: Europe, the United States and the Mexican Revolution* (Chicago: University of Chicago Press, 1981); Friedrich Katz, "The Liberal Republic and the Porfiriato, 1867–1910," in *Mexico Since Independence*, ed. Leslie Bethell (New York: Cambridge University Press, 1991), 49–124; William Roseberry, *Anthropologies and Histories: Essays in Culture, History and Political Economy* (New Brunswick, N.J.: Rutgers University Press, 1989); and Eric Wolf, *Europe and the People Without History* (Berkeley: University of California Press, 1982). As these authors, and a host of others, argue, capital is not inherently national. National regimes may seek to create conditions that are favorable to investment, and often do so in order to attract capital (witness the "race to the bottom," in which countries across the globe are currently engaged). But the capital thus invested does not in the process become national. Indeed, as dependency theorists (Fernando Henrique Cardoso and Enzo Faletto, *Dependency and Development in Latin America,* trans. Marjory Mattingly Urquidi [Berkeley: University of California Press, 1979]) and globalization scholars (Philip McMichael, *Development and Social Change: A Global*

Perspective, 6th ed. [Los Angeles: SAGE, 2016]) alike have argued, the opposite is often the case. One of the great puzzles pondered by a range of scholars of political economy focuses on precisely this issue: under what set of conditions does capital become national?

4. For influential work on the organization of space prior to the period that is our focus, see John Murra, *El "control vertical" de un máximo de pisos ecológicos en la economía de las sociedades andina* (Huánaco, Peru: Universidad Hermilo Valdizan, 1972); Carlos Sempat Assadourian, *El sistema de la economía colonial: El mercado interior, regiones y espacio económico* (Mexico City: Nueva Imagen, 1983); and Carlos Sempat Assadourian, "The Colonial Economy: The Transfer of the European System of Production to New Spain and Peru," *Journal of Latin American Studies* 24, S1 (March 1992): 55–68.

5. We suggest that the inability to reconcile particular, regional, sectoral interests with general, national, universal concerns gave birth to widespread concerns with "corruption."

6. For useful overviews, see Evelina Dagnino, *Meanings of Citizenship in Latin America* (Sussex, UK: University of Sussex, 2006); James Holston, *Insurgent Citizenship: Disjunctions of Democracy and Modernity in Brazil* (Princeton, N.J.: Princeton University Press, 2008); and Nancy Postero, *The Indigenous State: Race, Politics, and Performance in Plurinational Bolivia* (Berkeley: University of California Press, 2017).

7. Nancy Fraser, "Rethinking the Public Sphere: A Contribution to the Critique of Actually Existing Democracy," *Social Text* 25/26 (January 1990): 56–80.

8. Uday S. Mehta, "Liberal Strategies of Exclusion," *Politics and Society* 18, no. 4 (December 1990): 427–54.

9. Aihwa Ong, *Flexible Citizenship: The Cultural Logics of Transnationality* (Durham, N.C.: Duke University Press, 1999).

10. Giorgio Agamben, *State of Exception* (Chicago: University of Chicago Press, 2005).

11. In the case at hand, this is the form of citizenship associated with the era's more or less obligatory liberal discourse. See Karl Polanyi, *The Great Transformation: The Political and Economic Origins of Our Time* (Boston: Beacon, 1944); and Achille Mbembe, "Necropolitics," *Public Culture* 15, no. 1 (Winter 2003): 11–40.

12. We have found the work of William Roseberry ("Hegemony and the Language of Contention," in *Everyday Forms of State Formation: Revolution and the Negotiation of Rule in Modern Mexico*, ed. Gilbert M. Joseph and Daniel Nugent [Durham, N.C.: Duke University Press, 1994], 355–66) especially useful with respect to the notion of "fields of force." The concept has a long genealogy in anthropology and is strongly associated with the Manchester School. See Joan Vincent, *Anthropology and Politics: Visions, Traditions, and Trends* (Tucson: University of Arizona Press, 1990).

13. See Katz, *The Secret War in Mexico*, 7–21.

14. See Ben Fallaw and Terry Rugeley, eds., *Forced Marches: Soldiers and Military Caciques in Modern Mexico* (Tucson: University of Arizona Press, 2012); and David

Nugent, "Conclusion: Mexican State Formation in Comparative Perspective," in *Forced Marches: Soldiers and Military Caciques in Modern Mexico*, ed. Ben Fallaw and Terry Rugeley (Tucson: University of Arizona Press, 2012), 238–68.

15. Max Weber, *From Max Weber: Essays in Sociology*, ed. Hans Gerth and Charles Wright Mills (New York: Oxford University Press, 1958); Miguel Angel Centeno, "Blood and Debt: War and Taxation in Nineteenth-Century Latin America," *American Journal of Sociology* 102, no. 6 (May 1997): 1565–1605; James Dunkerley, ed., *Studies in the Formation of the Nation-State in Latin America* (London: Institute of Latin American Studies, 2002); Fernando López-Alves, *State Formation and Democracy in Latin America, 1810–1900* (Durham, N.C.: Duke University Press, 2000).

16. See Alfred W. McCoy, "Covert Netherworld: An Invisible Interstice in the Modern World System," *Comparative Studies in Society and History* 58, no. 4 (October 2016): 847–79.

17. Philip Abrams, "Notes on the Difficulty of Studying the State," *Journal of Historical Sociology* 1, no. 1 (March 1988): 58–89; Philip Corrigan and Derek Sayer, *The Great Arch: English State Formation as Cultural Revolution* (Oxford: Basil Blackwell, 1985).

18. The work of Antonio Gramsci has been the subject of many, varied interpretations. We are interested less in interpretations of Gramsci that focus on issues of cultural hegemony and more on interpretations that focus on his preoccupation with capitalism and the formation of historic blocs. See Antonio Gramsci, *Selections from the Prison Notebooks of Antonio Gramsci*, trans. and ed. Quintin Hoare and Geoffrey Nowell-Smith (New York: International Publishers, 1971). We found the following particular useful: Perry Anderson, "The Antinomies of Antonio Gramsci," *New Left Review* 100 (1976): 5–81; Perry Anderson, *The H-Word: The Peripeteia of Hegemony* (New York: Verso, 2017); Kate Crehan, *Gramsci, Culture, and Anthropology* (Berkeley: University of California Press, 2002); and Roseberry, "Hegemony and the Language of Contention."

19. Popular involvement and agrarian demands may have contributed to national struggles even earlier. See Friedrich Katz, "Rural Rebellions After 1910," in *Riot and Rebellion: Rural Social Conflict in Mexico*, ed. Friedrich Katz (Princeton, N.J.: Princeton University Press, 1988), 521–60.

ACKNOWLEDGMENTS

THIS VOLUME emerged out of a series of conference panels organized by the editors at the meetings of the Latin American Studies Association in 2012, 2013, 2014, and 2015. We would like to thank the panel participants and audiences for pushing us to refine and improve our arguments, in particular Chris Boyer, Liz Dore, José Galindo, Alan Knight, Chris Krupa, Thomas Passananti, and Pablo Piccato, In addition, we owe a debt of gratitude to Colby College and Emory University for providing crucial support, without which this volume would not have been possible. We would like to express our special gratitude to Alan Knight. Without his invaluable input, *State Formation in the Liberal Era* would have been a very different book. We would also like to thank anthropologist Constantine Hriskos, our mutual friend who has enriched our understanding of temporal and spatial relations.

Our families were unfailingly patient and understanding during our frequent and protracted absences working on this project, including long conversations in our backyard seminars dating back to 2000. The contributors to our volume were also remarkably understanding regarding the long fruition of the volume. Finally, we would like to express our deep appreciation to Kristen Buckles, our editor at the University of Arizona Press, and to the entire editorial team at Arizona. It has been a great pleasure working with them.

Our approach to Latin America's past was in many ways inspired by three remarkable mentors we were fortunate enough to study with: Friedrich Katz (for Ben), and William Roseberry and Eric Wolf (for David).

The usual scholarly disclaimers apply here: we are indebted to many colleagues and teachers over the years, but any errors are our own.

STATE FORMATION IN THE LIBERAL ERA

PART I

COMPARATIVE STUDIES IN NATION BUILDING, CA. 1850–1900

I **N THE** preface, we argued that understanding nation-building processes in Mexico and Peru requires locating these countries within the specific "globalizing" forces to which each, respectively, was subject. This led us to identify a range of sub- and transnational circuits of capital that operated within and across the national territories of Mexico and Peru, and to trace the way that these circuits changed through time.

In this, the introduction to the first half of the volume, we compare Mexico's and Peru's struggles to create liberal capitalist economies and forge liberal notions of citizenship during the second half of the nineteenth century. We explore the challenges involved for nation builders in attempting to aggregate these disparate circuits of capital into a coherent coalition, in part through the extension (or retraction) of formal citizenship rights to specific sectors of society—even as conditions of lived citizenship emerge that are in blatant contradiction with those rights. To the extent that these disparate geographies are separate and do not rely on one another, there is little to bring them together into the same "national" coalition. If there are forces at work that can aggregate these disparate geographies, on the other hand, different possibilities for coalition-formation emerge. Taking into account factors such as these, we identify a succession of path-dependent experiments in nation building.

THE TRAVAILS OF LIBERALISM IN MEXICO AND PERU, CA. 1850s–1870s

We begin our study in the 1850s—a decade that marked the rise of liberal regimes, and also the tentative end of several decades of fragmentation and economic decomposition. After the extensive destruction caused by decades of fighting during and after the Wars of Independence, ascendant liberal regimes in both countries reached similar conclusions: recovery, future prosperity, and even national survival hinged on infusions of capital from the industrialized world.

Mexico and Peru had used European connections to cover war expenses in past decades, and as a result were heavily in debt. Access to additional capital depended crucially on resolving existing obligations. There were important differences, however, in the resources that each country could draw upon to do so. The strategies chosen by Mexico and Peru to promote liberal policies, as each country utilized the resources available to it, produced the first two experiments in liberal nation building that we discuss.

PERU, CA. 1850–1879: NATION BUILDING AS AGGREGATION

Peru's efforts at nation building are a useful point of departure for our broader discussion because they represent one end on a continuum of strategies.[1] Despite its penury, the government was able to arrange for large, steady infusions of new capital over a period of decades while undertaking the most minimal of reforms. Indeed, Lima-based regimes were not compelled to challenge virtually any aspect of the existing distribution of wealth or legal and cultural norms.[2]

The reason that Lima's liberal regimes were able to borrow abroad without upsetting the domestic status quo had to do with guano, or dried bird dung, a natural fertilizer highly in demand in the North Atlantic. Guano was found in seemingly endless quantities on small, uninhabited islands off the coast of Peru. The decision to declare guano an official monopoly in 1841 allowed the government to borrow much-needed capital from foreigners against future guano deliveries.

This arrangement brought in large sums of money to the ruling liberal regimes of the era, year after year, like clockwork. It also allowed the government to consolidate in a way that had not formerly been possible. In the process, these regimes were able to end decades of social and regional strife associated with caudillos.

In their classic treatment of caudillo politics, Eric Wolf and Edward Hansen argue that caudillo rule was highly unstable and lacked any definite or stable center.[3] Because resources were found in small quantities and distributed over a wide area, the bands of armed men who sustained themselves from these resources were forced into a pattern of constant movement and dispersion. Rather than creating new sources of wealth through capitalist development, caudillos were locked in a zero-sum struggle to seize wealth. Finding new sources of wealth to plunder was an especially pressing matter for the leaders of these bands. For they could only retain a following as long as they were successful in locating and seizing new sources of wealth—and distributing the spoils among their followers. Because no one space could provide what was required in a reliable or consistent manner, no particular space was more important than any other. Rather, space as a whole was the objective and movement across it a necessity. Conditions of lived citizenship were a function of where one was located in this organization. Formal citizenship rights were of little consequence, as they could not be enforced even in the rare instances in which they were invoked.

Wolf and Hansen's model of caudillo conflict draws our attention to tendencies toward *dispersion* and to forces that prevented the creation of strong and stable centers. In so doing, Wolf and Hansen help us understand not only caudillo organization but also regional social orders. At midcentury, much of the sierra was composed of semiautonomous regional domains, where elite contenders struggled for dominance. Each contender jealously guarded his own privileges and sought to expand his powers by encroaching on the domains of his rivals. To prevail, each elite contender reluctantly entered into alliances with others in the region, which were intended to promote the position of the elite contender. As in caudillo bands, lived citizenship depended on where (and if) one was located within these elite-led, violence-wielding coalitions. Formal, liberal citizenship rights were of little consequence. Indeed, endless rounds of warfare were another force that nullified the promise of citizenship for the vast majority of the population.

The inherent weakness of these coalitions, held together only by unstable personalistic bonds and their inability to create as opposed to redistribute wealth, worked against permanent concentrations of wealth and power. Competition between evenly matched elite alliances ensured that no one alliance could permanently prevail over its enemies. Indeed, efforts to consolidate and expand were constant but were simultaneously undermined, resulting in a repeated pattern of dispersion and dissipation.

Bird dung did much to counteract these tendencies. Guano was available not in small amounts, whether scattered across a broad territory (as in caudillo organization) or the subject of contention among multiple elite contenders (as in regional organization). Rather, bird dung was to be found in enormous quantities in the same, fixed location.

This feature of guano drew a range of interests toward it. It resulted in the concentration rather than the dissipation or dispersion of forces and allowed guano to act as a fixed geographic or spatial center. Because large amounts of this valuable resource could be had in the same location over an extended period of time, it could act as a center not only in spatial but also in temporal terms. Indeed, the stability, consistency, and predictability of this resource generated forces not of dispersion but of *aggregation*.

Because guano was found on a series of uninhabited islands, the Lima government did not have to contend with competing claims for the era's most valuable resource. Nor did the exploitation of guano require elite groups to surrender property or position. To the contrary, guano was an unexpected windfall. Liberal governments could use the proceeds from guano to build up a coherent, ruling coalition in Lima without threatening entrenched elite interests. Indeed, they could afford to ignore the regions.

The peculiar geography of accumulation that was the basis of Peru's experiment in nation building brought together specific partners—government officials in Lima and investors in London's bond market—in relations of limited scope. Other than making regular payments, officials in Lima had virtually no accountability to their creditors in London. Nor did they have much accountability to constituencies at home, as the vast majority of the population was simply not considered. Indeed, a small number of Lima officials decided how the huge amounts of money (about $750 million) derived from the sale of a "nationalized" resource would be spent.[4]

This tale of two cities gave birth to an excessively narrow ruling coalition. Indeed, the tendencies toward aggregation inherent in guano exploitation helped generate a parallel aggregation of political power. The core of the coalition (see below) had little reason to disperse wealth outside its immediate circle, to caudillos or regional elites, or to challenge the oppressive conditions of lived citizenship faced by the majority of the population. Dispersing wealth outside guano's immediate circle would have strengthened tendencies toward dispersion and dissipation and would have undermined the coalition core. Challenging conditions of lived citizenship in the regions would have threatened place-based, rural powerholders, generating hostility toward the regime in Lima.

The regimes of Lima pursued a range of policies that were superficially liberal. In 1854 the government abolished Afro-descendants' slavery and eliminated the *contribución personal* (the Indian head tax), which suggested a concern with individual rights. The government also agreed to honor its debts, and thus appeared to be respecting the rights of property. Lima also committed vast sums of money to the mammoth Central Railroad project, which was intended to promote yet another liberal goal—the creation of a single, unified national market. Other policies pursued by the government, however, were not so liberal. These included a huge expansion of the bureaucracy and the army. The former was used to expand the constituency that was dependent on (and loyal to) the government. The latter was used to give the Lima regime the decisive edge over rival caudillos in the highlands.

Even when liberal in form, however, government policies were anything but liberal in content. Rather, these policies brought into being an exclusive ruling coalition, centered in Lima, which enjoyed enormous wealth and power. This coalition excluded from its ranks almost all the national population; citizenship remained a nominal category bereft of meaning for the vast majority of Peruvians. The coalition treated as irrelevant virtually the entire national territory. Indeed, the guano coalition denationalized, divided, and coerced in the name of a unifying, liberal, nation-building project.

The regimes of the guano era ignored the country's vast mountainous interior and redefined Peru in de facto terms as a narrow strip of land along the Pacific Coast. The regimes restricted substantive citizenship to the tiny plutocracy that emerged in relationship to the management and use of guano wealth. The interests of this coalition had little to do with Peru as a whole. Rather, the coalition's concerns were focused on maintaining the transnational circuit of capital that was based on guano and that linked Lima to London. The governments of the era spoke the liberal language of nation but pursued policies that belied the very language they spoke.

One of the superficially liberal policies pursued by guano-era regimes was to emancipate Afro-descendants. The government made no reparations to former slaves. It did, however, compensate slave owners (at 300 pesos per person) for the "loss" of more than twenty-five thousand human beings. The London-Lima circuit of capital thus introduced about 7.65 million pesos into a moribund plantation sector. Estate owners used the bulk of the funds to recruit a new, nonnational workforce: about one hundred thousand indentured laborers, who were brought to Peru from China. The conditions of lived citizenship they confronted closely resembled those of slavery.

The infusion of large quantities of capital and labor into the estate sector reversed the fortunes of export agriculture and contributed to the ascendance of its plantation elite. So did the reconciliation of outstanding debt.[5] Using guano wealth as collateral, liberal governments devised a restructuring scheme for their international creditors. They also established procedures for reimbursing those who held bonds for the internal debt. A key part of the guano coalition consisted of the domestic and foreign speculators who bought up the seemingly worthless bonds for the internal debt. The government distributed approximately $25 million to these individuals. Almost all lived on the coast. About one hundred people (out of perhaps two thousand) controlled almost two-thirds of the value of the bonds.

Settling the internal debt in this manner, however, did more than bring into being an immensely wealthy coastal elite. It also denied highland elites their share of the wealth that was dispersed to settle the internal debt. The resolution of the debt thus segmented and warped the national space. It made the coastal region a key center of gravity in national affairs and relegated the sierra to the margins of a new national geography of dynamic core and stagnant periphery.

The coastal elite of the guano era also included a small group of foreign merchant companies and their domestic partners, who provided European luxury goods for elite conspicuous consumption. The elite also included those who controlled the new banking sector, which emerged to manage the enormous quantities of wealth that were flooding into the coastal region. This included the huge amount of borrowed capital pumped into the coastal economy for the construction of the Central Railroad. Although it remained unfinished, liberal governments spent more than $130 million on this project.

The guano-era regimes took additional steps that turned the sierra into a periphery in a new geopolitics of nationhood. As Carlos Contreras explores in chapter 1, starting in the middle of the nineteenth century, Peru began to modernize its antiquated fiscal structure along liberal lines, a process both helped and distorted by guano wealth. Ironically, the War of the Pacific (1879–83), resistance from aggrieved social sectors, and fiscal shortfalls forced the restoration of abolished taxes.

The linchpin of the liberal fiscal reforms was the 1854 decision to abolish the *contribución personal* charged to indigenous Peruvians. The contribución had been administered by a government bureaucracy that spanned the entire national territory. It had also defined a form of lived citizenship in which indigenous cultivators were guaranteed rights over community lands in exchange for payment.[6]

With the elimination of the contribución, a huge proportion of the population lost their limited lived citizenship rights. Furthermore, the bureaucratic processes that had grown up around the administration of the contribución personal fell into disuse. Interdependencies between people who lived in the same region grew in importance. Regions became more autonomous, and the national territory became increasingly segmented. The surplus extracted from primary peasant producers in the countryside in the form of rents, fees, and interest stayed within regions. The distance between regional domains in the highlands and the Lima government increased.

A countervailing tendency was the creation of new corridors of capitalism, centered on the coastal plantations. These corridors extended inward, toward the Andes, for foodstuffs. Select regional domains in the highlands were incorporated into these corridors, bending space and social relations in those regions.[7] The corridors also looked outward: to East Asia for labor, to London for investment capital, and to the North Atlantic for markets.

The new geography of accumulation that formed around guano and speculative capital from London was thus subnational, transnational, and transoceanic. It allowed a small group of officials in one city (Lima) to pursue policies on behalf of "the nation." The policies in question, however, did much to dismember the nation and its territory, to undermine existing forms of lived citizenship for indigenous Peruvians, and to replace them with more oppressive forms. While liberal in form, the policies of the era's liberal regimes underwrote the formation of an exclusive, aristocratic elite on Peru's coast, centered in Lima. Liberal governments drew upon the wealth derived from guano to create a new national geography of core and periphery. Peru's vast mountainous interior, and the enormous population of the sierra, found itself relegated to the margins. The coastal region, and the tiny plutocracy that emerged in relationship to the management of guano-based wealth, took center stage.

Nation building as aggregation was thus based on a highly unusual set of circumstances. It relied upon government control of a single resource, guano, which acquired great value abroad, more or less overnight. Guano was available in huge quantities, and thus appeared to offer stability, reliability, and predictability for many years into the future—something that had been sorely lacking in previous decades.

MEXICO'S DISASTER CAPITALISM, 1854–1876: NATION BUILDING AS DISPERSION

Mexico provides a useful counterpart to Peru because it represents the other end of a continuum of nation-building strategies.[8] While Peru's initial experiment in liberal nation building was based on the principles of aggregation, Mexico took a very different path. Mexico's experiment was based on what we call dispersion.

Mexico began the liberal era with many of the same problems that plagued Peru. Both countries had been devastated by decades of conflict generated by predatory caudillos. Worse still, Mexico also suffered from the loss of about half of its national territory to the United States in 1848. Like Peru, Mexico was in dire need of new infusions of capital with which to rebuild war-torn societies. Despite facing similar problems, however, Mexican Liberals had a very different range of potential resources. One contrast in particular stands out as especially important. Mexico lacked a key resource like guano, over which the central government could easily establish monopoly control—and in the process, could resolve its outstanding debt problems and attract foreign capital. As a result, there was nothing that could act as a force toward aggregation—a force that could counteract the era's widespread tendencies toward dispersion. To the contrary, developing Mexico's potential mineral and agricultural exports, which were found widely distributed across national space and far from ports, meant intervening on an extensive scale in the regional social orders in which those resources were embedded. This in turn called for profound cultural, legal, and institutional reforms, which were deeply threatening to established elites.

Much like contemporary polities that have been exiled from global circuits of capital, Mexico was left to its own devices to resolve its many problems. In other words, with no possibility of attracting capital from abroad, Mexico was compelled to promote domestic capital accumulation (especially in agriculture) as a way out of the impasse in which it found itself. The difficulty was, however, that virtually all land, labor, and markets were already firmly embedded in deeply entrenched, noncapitalist social structures—a fact that represented a major obstacle to the emergence of new forms of accumulation. The only way to overcome this obstacle was to transform those social structures. This meant challenging the existing distribution of wealth and power. Moreover, because potential wealth in the form of labor and capital trapped in corporate relations was found in pockets distributed across the national territory, Liberals believed that the national territory had to be unified through a railroad network. Given the cost of such an undertaking, foreign capital would be necessary. But it was not available.

In an effort to promote the accumulation of agrarian and mineral capital—and create capital to eventually promote industrialization—the regimes of the era championed an ambitious project inspired by North Atlantic liberalism. The most important of these liberal reforms were the protection of private property rights (of specific groups) and the (selective) promotion of a "free" market. Indeed, so determined were Mexico's liberal regimes to promote new forms of accumulation that they resorted to highly illiberal practices. Liberals firmly believed that property was used for productive ends only when owned by rationally acting, self-interested individuals as defined by liberal constitutions. Consequently, land owned by corporate bodies and chartered by colonial governments had to be disentailed. Most notable in this regard was the Catholic Church, which was not only immensely wealthy and powerful but also maintained extensive, numerous clienteles across much of the country, among all social classes. Equally important was Mexico's indigenous population, which made up a majority in most of the central and southern states. In most cases, they had farmed their *ejidos* since before the Conquest, as well as using a range of corporately owned resources, including woods, pastures, and waters.

As the foregoing implies, faced with the necessity of having to overhaul domestic social structures, the liberal reforms in Mexico had an unfortunate consequence. They threatened the interests of the many different constituencies, humble and powerful alike, that were dependent upon the status quo. Indeed, the liberal reforms called for a major redistribution of wealth, power, and prestige. As a result, unlike the situation with guano in Peru, these reforms in Mexico provoked widespread resistance. Especially resistant to change were those who were committed to existing, noncapitalist social structures. Distributed as they were across the national landscape, and opposed as they were to reform, these groups represented powerful forces toward dispersion. Paraphrasing the title of a work on contemporary capitalism, we refer to the state of affairs precipitated by Mexican governments at this time as "all disaster, no capitalism."⁹ It is to the details of this process that we now turn.

In 1851, thirty years after Mexico achieved independence, a cohort of mostly young civilian leaders backed by regional caudillos seized power in the Revolution of Ayutla (named after the southern town where it was proclaimed). In so doing, they ended the last regime of Antonio López de Santa Anna, Mexico's dominant caudillo who headed a conservative, centralist regime. The victorious liberal "generation of giants" led by Benito Juárez radically transformed Mexico's legal and institutional framework during the Reform (1855–61) and Restored Republic (1867–77), with the goal of promoting agrarian capitalism and luring investment capital from Europe and the United States. Widespread forces toward dispersion, however, thwarted their efforts. Indeed, the number and range of groups whose well-being depended on maintaining the status quo meant that Liberals spent much of their time and energy battling foes, Liberals and Conservatives alike. The latter were especially threatened by liberal policies. So much so was this the case that, to safeguard their interests, the Conservatives supported invasion and occupation by a foreign power, the French, from late 1861 to 1867.

The many struggles in which the liberal regimes of the era were embroiled left them vulnerable to additional challenges that threatened further dispersion. Particularly important in this regard were raids by unvanquished indigenous peoples, which devastated the northern states and much of the southeastern Yucatán Peninsula. At the same time, liberal governments had to squelch smaller simmering social conflicts over land and local self-rule and also had to dislodge powerful regional caudillos. These wars kept Mexico's regions isolated and mired in poverty. The conflict, combined with daunting geographic barriers and a still archaic legal structure, made achieving social peace and political unity, and promoting agrarian capitalism, seem close to impossible.

Nevertheless, Mexican Liberals had faith in the ability of capitalism to unify and develop their nation's potential wealth. From the start, liberal rights and a free market were inseparable on the governing coalition's agenda. Success, they believed, would require a new cultural and legal framework centered on a liberal model of formal citizenship (implicitly gendered male and "raced" as white) and a political structure in which the federal government was limited constitutionally, congress overshadowed the presidency, and state governments enjoyed considerable autonomy. Like contemporary disaster capitalists, Mexico's Liberals hoped that the country's perpetual conflicts and its perennial economic decline would compel people to accept novel reforms aimed at creating a liberal capitalist economy. Given Mexico's travails, they believed, the unification of isolated regional economic circuits into a single market guided by a strong liberal state would integrate Mexico into global markets and give it access to foreign credit.

Mexican Liberals looked to the United States for their roadmap to the future. Like the Republicans of the United States, they advocated (in theory) universal male suffrage, free markets, and free labor. They despised European monarchies. They also craved U.S. capital investment and technology. Abolition ended U.S. territorial ambitions in Mexico, as southern white slaveholders no longer coveted more Mexican territory to carve up into new slave states. It also raised Mexican liberal hopes for resolving lingering claims and boundary disputes, which would in turn unleash U.S. investment. But it was not to be, despite the fact that the United States was beginning its life as a capital-exporting country at that very moment. Moreover, the proximity of the United States to Mexico meant that, in practice, some prominent Liberals feared that a tidal wave of dollars and U.S. control of the planned network of railroads would threaten national sovereignty.[10]

Without the transformative effect of foreign investment and technology, above all railroads, Liberals were unable to overcome the era's widespread tendencies toward dispersion and Mexico's geographic obstacles and thus promote agrarian and industrial capitalism and create a large domestic market. Further undermining their efforts to transform existing social structures was the Liberals' failure to make sweeping legal and institutional reforms. For instance, 1863 legislation did not systematically or energetically privatize public lands, which precluded efforts to increase agricultural productivity or to fill the coffers of the treasury. Not until 1872 did Liberals update their 1856 tariff on imports. Furthermore, the new draft was overly complex, encouraged corruption, and failed to remove the *alcabala* (internal sales tax) that retarded market growth.[11]

Despite official rhetoric to the contrary, the Liberals' political reforms failed to extend the right to vote to the majority of the (male) population, above all to poor and indigenous Mexicans. Furthermore, faced with widespread resistance to their policies, the leaders of the Restored Republic ended up retreating from supporting federalism and local elections. They were also compelled to embrace a strong executive branch and to build up a repressive political machine. Otherwise, they could not stifle dissent from disaffected Liberals and dissatisfied popular groups (or stave off the possibility of a conservative restoration). Centralization and repression compensated for lack of popular support. This was crucial for the Restored Republic's survival because its limited, tentative liberal reforms benefited so few.[12]

The privatization of corporate (predominantly Church) land benefited mostly urban middle-class speculators and those wealthy few who snapped up haciendas once owned by the Church. The sell-off of Church land, however, failed to free capital, create industry, or transform mestizo and indigenous peasants into a prosperous rural yeomanry. As a result, the core of the Liberals' base ended up being very narrow and was limited to a small, insecure bourgeoisie made up of industrialists, hacendados, and *agiotistas*, or predatory lenders to the government.

In light of the narrowness of their social base, and because of the era's ongoing conflicts, the survival of the Liberals came to depend on forming alliances with the very regional caudillos whose powers they were in principle trying to undercut. This was especially true during the War of the Reform and the French Intervention. Indeed, so compromised did the liberal regimes become that they were compelled to grant amnesty to many wealthy Conservatives. This outraged liberal veterans, who rarely benefited from the sale of Church or indigenous landholdings.

Ironically, and tragically, a great many of the rank and file that fought against Mexico's foes under liberal leaders were ignored when the fighting was over. It was not uncommon for them to have to resort to social banditry or to be forced into debt peonage on estates—to be subject to conditions of lived citizenship that were in blatant contradiction with liberal concepts. Indeed, the failure of the Restored Republic to enforce laws against debt peonage ensured that a great many people would be denied the benefits of formal, liberal citizenship. The fact that haciendas were able to expand at the expense of peasant communities contributed further to the growth of oppressive conditions of lived citizenship and spurred widespread agrarian conflict. Although municipal elections had been established, their integrity was compromised by extensive fraud and outright coercion, a fact reflected in the rapid growth in abstention. Finally, the government proved incapable of investing in infrastructure or promoting education, despite Liberals' belief in schooling as a panacea.[13]

Liberals protected the property rights of their predominantly privileged allies but ignored the rights of out-of-favor elites and the rural poor majority. Indeed, the latter found that their rights were continually ignored or violated. The result was political fragmentation and instability, which alienated many elites and most of the rural poor. Widespread social conflict discouraged investment, encouraged reliance on coerced labor, and discouraged innovation. It also reproduced widespread poverty, malnutrition, and illiteracy.

The attitude of the ruling elite toward indigenous Mexicans helps explain why they clung to their distorted liberal project even after its failures were manifest. When Liberals addressed the "Indian problem," they assumed privatization of land and improved transportation and communication would allow indigenous Mexicans to become active, productive members of society. Instead, in the face of extensive land loss and coercive labor practices, peasant revolts increased in number and became larger and longer lasting, especially in central and southwestern Mexico. In the end, government officials were unable to overcome the era's powerful forces toward dispersion—making the Restored Republic largely a disaster, with little in the way of capitalist development.

NEW CAPITALISMS AND NEW EXPERIMENTS IN NATION BUILDING, 1877–1919

Prior to the 1880s, Mexico and Peru had looked to Europe for the capital they believed they so desperately needed to pursue their respective projects of reconstruction and liberal nation building. Investment from the United States, on the other hand, had been of very limited importance, for either country. As the United States became a major industrializing power in the second half of the nineteenth century, however, its shift from being a capital-importing to a capital-exporting country transformed this state of affairs. New sub- and transnational geographies of accumulation took shape in the Global South as surplus capital from select U.S. industries sought out new outlets. These developments had major implications for both Mexico and Peru. Indeed, it was in this transformed global environment of the movement of capital that our next two experiments in nation building unfolded.

By the 1870s, industrial manufacturing processes in the United States were well into a major transformation—one that would have sweeping consequences for Mexico and Peru. The consequences differed, however, as a function of their timing and scale. The "great transformation" that took place in the U.S. economy had immediate, profound, and long-term implications on Mexico much sooner. While Peru came to feel some of the impact of this transformation, it came later, on a much-reduced scale. Furthermore, when the era's new forms of capital investment eventually did make their way to Peru in the 1890s, their impact was conservative rather than transformative. They tended to articulate with and reinforce existing geographies of capital—which were isolated and disparate—rather than transform those geographies.

Finally, for reasons to be discussed later in this section, by the time the new flows of capital reached Peru, government regimes were in no position to dictate the terms under which that capital would operate. Instead, while the country was desperate for foreign capital, it no longer had much to offer to attract investment. Indeed, Peru had been forced to declare bankruptcy in the 1880s and had defaulted on a huge loan to creditors in England. Although Peru subsequently renegotiated its debt, it did so on terms that were extremely unfavorable and made domestic capital accumulation very difficult.

In Mexico, on the other hand, the impact of the great transformation was much deeper. This was in part because Mexico's civil wars and defeat of the French Intervention had compelled Liberals to build up an extensive network of political alliances that reached across much of the national space—something that did not occur in Peru. On the one hand, this network of alliances facilitated the creation of entirely new geographies of accumulation rather than reinforced existing, disparate geographies, as in Peru. But on the other hand, the novel developments of the era in Mexico were not limited to the creation of new individual circuits of accumulation. The overall transformation was made more far-reaching because the existence of a broad network of political alliances, forged in the context of armed conflict against Conservatives and the French, made it possible to integrate a number of these separate circuits into a single, unified geography of accumulation. The fact that multiple circuits of capitalist development were integrated into a single, interdependent geography gave a wide range of constituencies a vested interest in the preservation of that emerging structure.

This in turn made the construction of a ruling coalition less challenging than it had been during the previous period, when elites had been pitted against one another, and the gain of one came at the expense of the other. The fact that formerly separate circuits of capital were integrated into a single, interdependent geography also resulted in the potential for a national market, which facilitated domestic capital accumulation. Finally, as we argue in the next section, Mexico was able to arrange access to foreign capital and credit from a range of sources, above all from the United States. Mexico also managed to work out a much more advantageous relationship with foreign capital in general—a circumstance that allowed much more latitude for domestic capital formation.

PORFIRIAN MEXICO: NATION BUILDING AS AGGREGATED DISPERSION, 1877–1910

It was in this new global context, in which sources of capital investment were diversifying and multiplying, that a new experiment in nation building unfolded in Mexico, under the direction of Porfirio Díaz. The Porfiriato was based on a coalition-building strategy very different from the guano-based approach of Peru. This was in part a function of differences in the way that natural resources were distributed in the two countries and the availability of investment capital to exploit those resources. Proximity to the United States proved to be a crucial variable determining access to investment capital, and for once a common border with the United States proved to be an asset for Mexico.

During the Porfiriato, Mexico continued to lack a single resource like Peruvian guano, which could be monopolized by the government and could act as an aggregating, consolidating force. At the same time, however, scattered across Mexico's national landscape were a range of resources that were in demand in the markets of the Global North. As Díaz's liberal predecessors had discovered, however, the ability to exploit these resources depended crucially on access to foreign capital. This is precisely what Mexico's liberal regimes had lacked in previous decades.

The strategy Díaz adopted to overcome these obstacles, and to overcome the tendencies toward dispersion that had so plagued earlier regimes, had several components. Díaz did little to promote the liberal political rights that he had championed during his campaign or revolt. He instead focused on instituting a range of sweeping legal and institutional reforms that were intended to attract foreign investment and in the process assemble a ruling coalition that (eventually) distinguished Mexico from Peru. His success hinged on gaining foreign capital investment. As noted earlier, however, the sources and kinds of capital available to the Díaz regime were more varied than they had been in the past. Mexico's new leader was careful to cultivate as many of these sources as possible.

In order to end the government's insolvency and encourage foreign direct investment, the Díaz regime reached out to the United States first, and then turned to the Europeans. He would consistently play one against the other, avoiding overdependence on the United States by setting aside key sectors—in particular banking and the Isthmus of Tehuantepec—for Europeans.[14] To convince potential creditors that Mexico was a safe investment, Díaz adopted a policy of strict financial austerity and responsibility. Under the guidance of the *científicos* (literally "scientific ones," Eurocentric intellectuals who provided Díaz technocratic expertise), he also sought to construct an image of Mexico as a rational, modern bureaucratic state—an endeavor that revolved around the creation of "capital fictions."[15]

The Porfirian search for foreign investment involved appeals both to reason and irrational "animal spirits" of investors from the Global North. Díaz and the científicos adopted the Global North's desire to know, measure, and quantify nature and natural resources by adopting the metric system, drafting censuses and surveys, and invoking positivism and science.[16] At the same time, Mexico and its foreign intermediaries also played to foreign investors' greed. Even though U.S. investors often failed to turn a profit—even after making huge capital investments—there was no shortage of new investors.[17] Mexico's integration into global circuits of capital required it to represent itself as transparent, legible, open, and pliant to outside investors and the governments that backed them. But the very same processes generated rampant deception, not to mention requiring force against Mexicans who impeded Porfirian progress.[18]

Beginning in the 1870s, the Díaz government took concerted steps to court U.S. capital using this strategy. What Díaz sought from the United States was not loans to support government expenditures but direct investment in production, in activities such as mining, where Mexican entrepreneurs were reluctant to venture.[19] U.S. investment flooded into agriculture, too, above all in the northern tier of states. Indeed, Mexico's leader created conditions in which it was possible for capital in production to spread across wide reaches of Mexico, where it was used to exploit a variety of export products.

Díaz thus succeeded in attracting unprecedented quantities of capital in production to support the development of primary goods exports. In the process, his regime helped create an entire series of new, individual corridors of capitalism, predominantly in mining, petroleum, and agriculture. Had these individual corridors been left strictly to their own devices, they probably would have acted as a force toward dispersion, as they did in Peru. As a crucial part of the government's experiment in nation building, however, Díaz managed to integrate a number of these key circuits into a single, interconnected geography in a process that we refer to as "aggregated dispersion." The overall effect was transformative.

It was the construction of a nationwide network of railroads, built with U.S. and British capital, that made it possible to transform Mexico's disparate, fragmented geographies of accumulation into a single, integrated whole. There were two steps to this process. First, Mexico's rail system helped break down the insularity of the country's semiautonomous regions, converting them into corridors of capitalist development. Second, having overcome the regional insularity that had so frustrated earlier liberal regimes, the Porfiriato's nationally integrated rail system helped ensure that the country's emergent corridors of capitalism did not become new forces for dispersion.

As we will see in the next section, this is precisely what transpired in Peru, where capitalist corridors began to form during the age of guano and expanded rapidly during the subsequent era of the Aristocratic Republic, the export boom of the 1890s–1919. Unlike their Mexican counterparts, Peru's corridors tended to be disparate and isolated. In terms of national space, they led in different, unrelated directions. Some of Mexico's corridors of capitalist development, especially coastal export agricultural enclaves, were isolated, but many led to the same place. That "place" was the aforementioned network of interconnected railroads. The network also directed the produce of various corridors to major centers of demand in the United States. Mexico's integrated rail network and the corridors of capitalism that it brought together also contributed to the emergence of a nascent home market for Mexican production—a development that facilitated domestic capital accumulation. Furthermore, the highly favorable conditions that the Díaz regime created for investment in production did not apply exclusively to foreign capital. To the contrary, the Díaz regime also created unprecedented opportunities for domestic elites to accumulate wealth (especially land), across an equally widespread, spatially dispersed national arena. The government did so in part by making available to elite Mexicans the landholdings of peasant and indigenous populations—which elites obtained through a combination of sale, plunder, and theft. Díaz also made "unused" land available for purchase to domestic and foreign elites.

By attracting capital in production in huge quantities, and by dispossessing subaltern groups of enormous amounts of land, Díaz initiated a widespread process of elite class formation. Unlike the situation in Peru, there was no single center, no one prized good (like guano) that could act as an aggregating, consolidating force. The absence of such a key resource, however, did not undermine coalition formation. To the contrary, the fact that elites and capitalist corridors were distributed across the national landscape but could nonetheless still be aggregated created the possibility for a more inclusive national coalition than Peru had been able to form with guano. Indeed, Díaz appears to have given enough members of the elite a way of benefiting from his policies—and by preying upon humble social elements rather than by threatening other members of the elite—that the coalition held together (as long as Díaz was on hand to pull the strings!).

Indeed, the Porfiriato's entire experiment in nation building was based on dispossession, proletarianization, and repression. These exceptionally brutal and coercive processes were focused overwhelmingly on subaltern populations—for the most part, indigenous and small-scale cultivators who were forcibly separated from their most basic means of livelihood. A great many became paupers and were forced to work as day laborers. Similar to the process of official decitizenship described by José Ragas in Peru (see chapter 4), others were declared vagrants and were compelled to work as labor conscripts, often in locations far removed from their communities of origin. A great many of those who objected to the era's violent processes of dispossession, or who sought to interfere, were shot, execution-style, by the Rurales, the national police.

Mexico thus went from insolvency to accumulation, from dispersion to aggregated dispersion. The Porfirian project in nation building occurred at a fortuitous moment in the history of industrial capitalism—one in which unprecedented levels of foreign capital were available for investment in productive activities. Among the most important of these activities in Mexico were mining, petroleum, and agriculture. In sharp contrast to new investment in Peru, this new investment in Mexico came to be distributed across much of the national landscape, geographically.

As capital in production poured into these regions, they rapidly lost their former insularity and were transformed into corridors of capitalist development. As corridors, they acted as centers of gravity, drawing labor power, foodstuffs, and so on toward them. In the process, the corridors transformed conditions of lived citizenship for large numbers of people, empowering some and marginalizing others. In other words, the growth of the corridors bent space and social relations across extensive hinterlands.

In regions where mining and petroleum were the focus, it was the time/space compression associated with railroad construction that made it possible for semiautonomous regions to become capitalist corridors. Although many gaps remained, the railroad network linked Mexico City directly with the United States' cities, mines, and factories. Exports (and labor) flowed northward, raising wages along the U.S. border in Mexico and allowing for relatively prosperous working and middle classes to flourish in the north (although the Mexican upper class were the clear beneficiaries of these developments). U.S. capital flowed south, buying ranches, mines, and haciendas, totaling an estimated $1 billion by 1910.[20]

Elite class and coalition formation during the Porfiriato did not revolve exclusively around the new corridors of capitalism and the elite interests that grew up around investments in mining and petroleum. Equally important was the enormous capitalization of agriculture in the Porfiriato. This was predicated on the alienation of land on a wholly unprecedented scale. Some of the lands that were privatized at this time had been "public" (*tierras baldías*), and some had been seized from vanquished indigenous groups who had zealously guarded their independence along the northern frontier. Other lands that were expropriated by elites had hitherto been held by peasant (and often indigenous) villages, in collective forms of tenure.

Most notoriously, in 1883, about the time Peru emerged a broken country after the disastrous War of the Pacific, the Díaz regime chartered domestic private survey companies to map and sell "unoccupied" public land, compensating them with one-third of the land declared vacant. In this manner, millions of hectares of public land were claimed, mainly in the relatively underpopulated north and south. While the alienation of some land was based on purchase, it was not uncommon for hacendados and speculators simply to seize land. Rather than a rational, legal transfer of land from tierras baldías and corporate indigenous villages to modern commercial farmers, the Porfirian surveys at times relied upon and encouraged extralegal, coercive forms of expropriation. As a result, they generated widespread conflict and distress in the landscapes they transgressed.[21]

As with mining, Mexico's network of railroads helped precipitate this agrarian transformation. The expansion of the country's rail system facilitated access to important new sources of market demand that could sustain production and export on an expanded scale, incentivizing privatization and seizure. It helped give birth to emergent national and transnational markets for agricultural produce and fostered domestic capital accumulation. As was true of regions transformed by mining and petroleum, agrarian domains become corridors of capitalist development, bending space and social relations across extensive hinterlands.

Mexico's mining, petroleum, and agricultural booms in some ways resembled Peru's: mining and ranching and cotton in Mexico's north, tropical forest products ranging from rubber in Oaxaca to vanilla on the Gulf Coast, agricultural exports ranging from sugar in numerous states across much of Mexico to vegetable oil in Guerrero, chocolate in Chiapas, and henequen (fiber) in Yucatán. Comparing the sheer number of corridors in Mexico to Peru's four (see next section) reveals the Porfiriato's "success" relative to the Aristocratic Republic. But more importantly, the Díaz regime was able to combine this strategy of export-based, aggregated dispersion with the development of some industry and banking.

Among the most important of the factors distinguishing the growth of capitalism in Porfirian Mexico from Peru was the emergence of a small but stable industrial sector. As the Porfiriato wore on, the Díaz regime pursued policies that anticipated import substitution industrialization. In particular, the government used tariff policy on imported manufactured goods to support nascent Mexican manufacturing. The result was the development of not just light but even heavy industry, which set Mexico apart not only from Peru but also from most countries in Latin America.[22]

Much of this industrial activity was centered in the northern city of Monterrey, which developed steel, beer, and glassmaking. Monterrey benefited from its proximity to the U.S. border, Mexico's rail network, and its linkages to producers of raw materials. Moreover, Monterrey's tightly knit regional elite provided its own (meaning Mexican) capital.[23]

The emergence of corridors of capitalism distributed across the national landscape—each with its own need for financial services—spurred the development of credit and banking institutions. Industries, commerce, and the most highly commercialized agricultural ventures were centered on a few dominant regional banks, which were controlled by a small number of politically connected elite families. The distribution of banks reflected Porfirian conditions of aggregated dispersion. Although most of Mexico's dispersed corridors of capitalism were loosely integrated into a broader structure, banking institutions had arisen autonomously in the larger corridors, limiting competition. Furthermore, even within a single corridor, those without social or political clout struggled to find credit.[24]

The national government sought to break its dependence on foreign sources of credit and to draw upon domestic sources of accumulation by establishing Mexico's first national banking system. The cornerstone was the Banco Nacional de México, or Banamex, whose origins are explored by Thomas Passananti in chapter 2. Passananti shows how Díaz used the creation of the bank to both defy and satisfy demands of international finance capital, even as he rationalized stifling internal dissent as a means to honor commitments to foreign lenders. Domestically, Banamex provided for the regime's own needs and also served as lender of last resort. The concessions to induce private investment in it, however, did not create a single, unified domestic market, as the Díaz regime hoped. Instead, the National Bank was unable to aggregate the capital that was dispersed regionally, in corridor-based banking institutions. As this suggests, there were limits to aggregation during the Porfiriato.[25]

The limits to aggregation, and the importance of guarding against and counteracting any residual tendencies toward dispersion, are further suggested by the following. Díaz found that he could not count on state governors—who were (in theory) elected officials and often represented dispersed localizing interests—to pursue his market-oriented, modernizing reforms with the zeal he required. As a result, Díaz felt compelled to introduce a new figure into the structure of his regime. This figure was the *jefe político* (literally, the political chief), who oversaw a district encompassing several towns. The jefes were appointed directly by the president, and at times the choice countered regional interests. The basic charge of these three-hundred-odd prefects was to keep the peace and ensure that state authority was respected. In practice, they carried out tasks that were intended to extend the national government's control over distant regions. These tasks were both "hard" (deputizing police, drafting conscripts, punishing vagrants, hunting down bandits, crushing peasant or labor organizing) and "soft" (regularizing tax assessments, organizing patriotic civic rituals, supporting schools, carrying out the census and vaccination campaigns, collecting information on Díaz's behalf).[26] Their power forced local elites to turn to Díaz to protect their economic interests. This in turn centralized power and afforded Díaz control over corridors of capitalist development like mines and haciendas. Jefes políticos, in theory, at least, were also agents of capitalist discipline because they were often on the local landowner's payroll, figuratively and at times literally.[27]

Not surprisingly, abuses were rampant, as jefes políticos used violence arbitrarily, extracted fixed rents, and generally undermined the rights of those seen as enemies of the public peace or resisters to Mexico's forward march.[28] The jefe político often called on the Rurales to enforce his authority. Díaz enlarged this national constabulary (it was founded by Juárez) and encouraged it to liberally apply the Ley Fuga (literally "law of flight," extrajudicial killing). This 1894 law criminalized interfering with rail or telegraph lines, mandating summary penalties of capital punishment. Recruitment of former bandits into the Rurales did little to improve discipline or improve their reputation among nonelite Mexicans.[29] Over the short run, the power of the jefe político and Rurales helped cow opponents and enforce the will of the Díaz regime. Over the long run, however, reliance on coercion increasingly generated forces toward dispersion and resistance.

The Porfirian preference for using repression to advance progress prevented most Mexicans from exercising even the most basic rights of formal citizenship. In the eyes of elites, Mexico's indigenous peoples—a majority in central and southern states and a substantial segment in the north—were not worthy of citizenship (although they debated the origins of inferiority). Indeed, when Porfirian leaders made education mandatory in 1892, they built few schools in indigenous regions. Their goal was to make Indians into workers, not citizens.[30]

Jefes políticos' bullying, toleration of unconstitutional debt peonage, and vagrancy laws coerced Indians into hacienda labor. In the minds of elites, the plantation was the best school. The seemingly modern forms of agrarian capitalism that grew rapidly in Porfirian Mexico were thus hybrid in nature. They combined technology, high levels of capitalization, and integration into global commodity markets with regressive labor regimes.[31] In chapter 3, Sarah Washbrook explores the creation of the hybrid coffee finca in the southeastern state of Chiapas during the Porfiriato. The autocratic, intellectual governor Emilio Rabasa and the Chiapan landowners claimed a deep knowledge of "their" Maya society legitimized with positivism and the "science" of race to rationalize Maya debt servitude and unpaid labor drafts. By tapping into Porfirian circuits of capital and monopolizing political office, Rabasa and his fellow oligarchs offered the Maya majority not liberal rights but subordinate status as "conscript citizens" valued for their docile labor on the "school" of the coffee finca.

While Peruvian elites shared prejudices regarding indigenous populations remarkably similar to those of the *finqueros* of Chiapas, there was a fundamental difference between Peru and Mexico in terms of the geography of capitalist expansion. With the exception of the *altiplano*, much of Peru's *mancha india* ("Indian stain," or heavily indigenous highlands region) was bypassed by the corridors of capitalism (see next section). In Mexico's center and south, however, the corridors often ran right through the heart of indigenous populations, as in the sugar zones in Morelos, which seized extensive areas of land and copious amounts of water from Nahua communities. Even in the less indigenous north, the Yaqui and Mayo peoples occupied fertile river valleys that made them the focus of genocidal campaigns of dispossession.

If the Porfiriato succeeded in generating new processes of accumulation, this came at a very high cost in human terms. Indeed, the conditions of lived citizenship that growing numbers of Mexicans were forced to endure had nothing in common with formal, liberal citizenship. This was in large part because the economic demands of the rapidly expanding agricultural and mineral sectors required a large, docile, poorly educated, and underpaid work force. These forces help explain the regime's need to develop consolidating and coercive mechanisms and institutions, including the Rurales.

Although the Porfiriato sought to create a centralized, repressive authoritarian system, it could not completely do away with long-standing tendencies toward dispersion. Nor could it disavow the liberal definition of citizenship enshrined in the country's constitution. Indeed, the brutal conditions of lived citizenship in the Porfiriato's corridors of capitalism created spaces for opposition to central policies. This is reflected in the spread of masonic lodges—something of a proxy for new sociabilities and ideologies that challenged conservativism and Catholicism. These lodges sprang up in the new corridors of capitalism created by railroads and ports along the Gulf Coast, from Tamaulipas to Yucatán, and along the Pacific Lowlands from Michoacán to Chiapas.[32]

In the autumn of the Porfiriato, rivalry for elected office could lead elites who had been excluded from power to mobilize working-class and peasant support. This "political baptism" of subalterns is clearly reflected in the Yucatán. Here, the candidate of one of the three main cliques of henequen barons and businessmen, Delio Moreno Cantón, challenged the dominance of científico Olegario Molina, Díaz's client. Moreno Cantón did so by allying with radical labor activists, who openly denounced Porfirian repression and debt servitude and invoked their rights as citizens under the 1857 Constitution. This case in the Yucatán was anything but an isolated one.[33] Indeed, in contrast to developments in Peru at this time, Mexico's more developed and geographically dense corridors of capitalism created new sociabilities—which were more secular and class-based—and free from the influence of traditional authorities. These new social spaces interacted with elite-led but popularly based political factions that jostled for power. This in turn created widespread opportunities for people long denied formal citizenship rights to voice sharp criticisms of the political order, and to imagine new forms of justice and belonging.

WAR AND "RECOVERY" IN PERU: NATION BUILDING AS DISPERSED AGGREGATION, 1885–1919

By 1885 Peru was much as it had been forty years prior on the eve of the guano revolution.[34] The country was deeply in debt and in desperate need of new infusions of capital. It had little, however, with which to attract foreign capital. A range of serious problems beset the country. The coastal plantation sector lay in ruins, mining was stagnant, and the banking system had been destroyed. Inflation was very high, and the paper currency almost worthless. Roads, railroads, and other basic infrastructure were in very bad condition.

Further contributing to the anxieties of elite nation builders were issues of "social control." Indigenous groups in the sierra had seized upon the elite crisis to propose alternative forms of polity and nationhood. In some instances, they threatened to segment or subdivide the national territory. Other groups did so as well. In much of the country the simple act of moving across the landscape had become problematic, as various interested parties (hacendados, caudillos, secessionists, bandits, etc.) all claimed the right to control and "tax" this process—and across the same spaces. Finally, escalating intraregional conflicts threatened to further segment and divide the national space. In sum, tendencies toward what we have called dispersion were broadly in evidence.

Before turning to postwar efforts at "recovery," we comment briefly on the half decade of invasion, defeat, and occupation by Chile followed by civil war, and what it suggests about the preceding experiment in nation building. Earlier in the chapter, we argued that these experiments differ according to the forces that encourage the formation of elite coalitions. We also identified three distinct sets of forces—aggregation, dispersion, and aggregated dispersion—each of which affects coalition building in different ways.

Finally, we proposed that paying attention to the exclusions inherent in different processes of coalition formation, and to conditions of lived citizenship, can shed light on the fortunes of different nation-building experiments. To these we add one additional assertion: in moments of crisis, the lines of fracture of any given experiment in nation building become more clearly visible. We illustrate this last point by examining what Chile did to defeat the national government of Peru, and how the Peruvians responded (or rather, were unable to respond) to foreign invasion.

As noted above, Peru's 1854–79 experiment in nation building was in many ways a tale of two cities. It was based on the ability of government officials in Lima to form a new, transoceanic geography of accumulation, based on guano, which tied their fate to the London bond market. The fact that the liberal regimes arose based on their ability to market guano abroad meant that their fortunes could fall should they fail to do so. This is exactly what transpired in the conflict with Chile. Using its naval superiority, Chile seized Peru's guano islands, cutting off the government from the key resource that was at the center of its aggregation-based coalition. Without guano, the center could not hold, and forces toward dispersion rapidly began to assert themselves.

Once the Chileans had seized the guano islands, Lima was denied funds with which to fight the war. Control of the sea lanes, however, gave the Chileans another strategic advantage in undermining Lima's guano-based, transoceanic experiment in nation building. As we have seen, the guano experiment was focused overwhelmingly on Peru's Pacific Coast, and from there looked outward, beyond the country's territory and population. The coalition sold not only its guano but also its estate-grown cash crops in the North Atlantic. By controlling the sea lanes, Chile prevented estate owners from marketing their goods abroad. In so doing, the Chileans denied their adversaries a second source of revenue with which to prosecute the war. They also further undermined the geography of accumulation that held the guano experiment together.

The Chileans did more than interfere with the marketing of cash crops. They also struck at the production process, attacking both the cotton estates on the central coast and the sugarcane plantations on the north coast. The Chileans' reception by the plantation communities is indicative of another weakness in the era's aggregation-based model of nation building—one that concerns the conditions of lived citizenship endured by the bulk of the estate population. When the Chileans threatened to destroy the estates, the plantation owners had no formal army units to protect them.[35] They did, however, have a potential "army" at their disposal—their numerous Chinese laborers. Those workers did indeed become a military force. The problem was, they fought for the wrong side.

The Chinese indentured laborers did not come to the aid of their masters. Nor did they simply stand aside. Instead, the workers embraced the enemy with open arms. On the central coast, more than one thousand conscripts abandoned their plantations and joined the Chileans. In the north, the laborers also greeted the invaders as liberators, joined the invading army, and helped them destroy the great estates. The Chinese were noted for having been especially destructive.

As noted earlier, aggregation is based on exclusivity. It encourages the formation of a narrow constellation of coalition members, who develop ways of accentuating their distinctiveness. Aggregation tends to construct divisions within the social body and develop mechanisms for reinforcing those divisions and policing them with great care. Whoever is not needed is treated as superfluous, regardless of their class or rank.

The exclusionary aspect of aggregation-based models was clearly reflected in the coastal plantations, where Chinese conscript laborers faced conditions of lived citizenship hardly distinguishable from slavery. They were also treated like a deviant, criminal population. At night, they were locked into crude, crowded dormitories. Because only men had been brought to Peru from China, homosexuality became common. Some plantation owners sold their workers opium, increasing their indebtedness and lengthening the terms of their indenture.

Examples from other contexts suggest that there was nothing inevitable about the Chinese joining forces with the Chileans. Indeed, examples where disadvantaged populations have helped defend against foreign aggressors are as instructive as those in which they have not.[36] In sum, had the workforce not been systematically humiliated and excluded, they might not have assisted the enemy. The conditions of lived citizenship the indentured workers had been forced to endure, however, were so intolerable that they wanted to tear the system down.

Similar problems undermined efforts to protect Lima when the Chileans laid siege to the capital. Had the guano-based coalition been more inclusive than it was, the defense of Lima might have been very different. As we have seen, however, that coalition was exceptionally narrow. Indeed, it excluded almost the entire national population and the bulk of the country's territory. Outside of a small circle of privileged coastal elites—who came together around the exploitation, commercialization, and management of guano and its profits—virtually no one had any stake in the reproduction of the coalition.

As a result, when it came time to defend Lima, the effort was weak and ineffectual. The Chilean army seized the capital on January 15, 1881, and proceeded to burn and pillage. As had been the case on the coastal estates, not everyone appears to have entirely disapproved of the actions of the Chileans. Indeed, poor and disenfranchised groups who had been excluded from the benefits of the guano bonanza engaged in activities that paralleled those of the invading army. Lima's working poor went on destructive rampages of their own, venting their anger about their conditions of lived citizenship. They did so by destroying the homes and businesses of the small group of families who had become so fabulously wealthy as members of guano's inner circle.

The guano elite had treated Lima's laboring poor as if they were a superfluous population. The working poor found their needs completely ignored as the inner circle of the guano coalition amassed fortunes the likes of which had never before been seen—and as they indulged in the most opulent, public displays of conspicuous consumption. In terms of the era's Lima-London-based geography of accumulation, it was no accident that these families protected themselves from the wrath of their working-class compatriots by taking shelter in the British Embassy.

To engage again for a moment in counterfactuals, what if the hacendados of the highlands had been given a stake in the guano experiment in nation building? What if the highland peasantry, and/or Lima's working population, had been granted a seat at the table that was set with guano? Had the era's ruling coalition been more national in scope, it is not at all unlikely that the Chileans would have confronted a far more daunting challenge in seeking to take control of the national capital. As it was, the Chileans were able to defeat "Peru" despite having seen little of it.

When the conflicts of the 1880s came to an end, in 1885, the victor, General Andrés Avelino Cáceres, embarked upon a new effort at nation building. To overcome the era's widespread and powerful forces toward dispersion, Cáceres sought to attract foreign capital. By 1885 Peru's foreign debt was approximately £50 million—£10 million more than on the eve of the guano era. Cáceres would be unable to bring any more capital to Peru from abroad without first settling the foreign debt. But he had no tangible resource like guano to offer as collateral.

The regimes of the guano era had mortgaged the future to foreigners but in return for a limited right—access to a valuable resource that was outside normal processes of elite competition. This agreement limited foreigners' spatial intrusion to a group of uninhabited islands, keeping them out of the national territory as a whole. The agreement also allowed the government to use guano proceeds as it chose. The geography of accumulation that emerged with respect to guano thus afforded the government a kind of spatial and political "autonomy."[37]

The same could not be said of the post-1885 geography of accumulation. Because Cáceres had no collateral for new infusions of capital, he was forced to surrender a "resource" that was far less tangible and far less spatially circumscribed than guano. What he ended up offering Lima's foreign creditors was not a space apart, like the guano islands, but rather space itself. Cáceres mortgaged the future not in return for access to a few deserted islands on the extreme margins of the national territory. Rather, he mortgaged the future in return for access to *all* the national territory. From that point forward, foreigners had open access to virtually every corner of Peru.[38]

In a complete reversal of guano's geography of containment, Cáceres denationalized the national territory, offering to suspend sovereignty in a bid to restore solvency. He canceled the foreign debt by bartering rights of access to—and movement through, and out of—the national space. Cáceres's agreement with foreign creditors, called the Grace Contract (because of the prominent role of Irish North American entrepreneur and adventurer Michael Grace), gave the Peruvian Corporation, which represented foreign bondholders, control over all of Peru's railroads for a period of sixty-six years.[39]

The Cáceres regime thus opened up the national territory to foreigners in a way that stood in marked contrast to the guano age. Rather than being relegated to the margins, as it were, foreigners would now be at the very center of economic life. Furthermore, they would be centrally involved in the most modern sectors of the economy (some of which were highly capitalized, had advanced technology, and were integrated into global markets). In particular, foreign-owned rail transport would bend space and redefine lived citizenship in new ways.

Once the Grace Contract was signed in 1889, foreign capital began pouring into Peru. Unlike the guano era, however, the new flows of capital largely bypassed the government. Furthermore, rather than coming from a single source, such as the London bond market, incoming capital had diverse origins and flowed directly into a range of export-oriented activities. Foreign investment thus formed a series of diffuse geographies and separate corridors of capitalist development. The new flows of investment also created novel, corridor-specific political coalitions and forms of lived citizenship, which empowered a few and marginalized many.

The new domains into which foreign capital flowed included railroads, petroleum, mining, sugar, cotton, rubber, and cotton manufacturing. These domains were found scattered across virtually the entire landscape, from coast to sierra to jungle, from remote rural hamlet to large industrial center. In other words, Cáceres made it possible for multiple, diverse forms of capital to disperse unimpeded across much of the national landscape. From 1889 onward, the geography of accumulation that took shape was no longer a tale of two cities. It was, rather, a tale of diffuse geographies, denationalized territories, embedded investments, and transnationalized connections. That said, much of Peru's national territory remained left behind, above all the interior of the country where most indigenous citizens resided.

During the Aristocratic Republic, one may identify four main corridors of accumulation, each with its own separate transnational circuit of accumulation. These circuits defined distinct and isolated corridors of capitalist development, each with its own aggregating effects, in the sense that each drew a range of social forces toward it. Each corridor thus acted as a kind of "center of gravity" with respect to the surrounding space, bending space and social relations in and around the corridor. In ways that differed from one corridor to the next, each of the new circuits of capital investment implied not only fixity in space but also continuity through time, so that some (but not all!) of the forces that were drawn toward the emergent centers of gravity tended to remain there.

While the new corridors of capitalism had aggregating effects, this was a new kind of aggregation. During the Aristocratic Republic, capital was no longer invested in domains that were outside, socially or spatially, existing sets of social arrangements, as had been the case during the age of guano. Rather, the era's new infusions of capital had to force their way into already densely populated social landscapes, and therefore tended to disrupt and transform the relationships in those landscapes.

As foreign capital poured into plantations, mines, and oil refining centers, modernizing and expanding them, it disrupted in situ forms of lived citizenship.[40] Some people were drawn toward the new developments while others were repelled. Still others found themselves wholly displaced by the consolidation of the corridors, and the ways that they bent space and transformed lived citizenship in adjacent hinterlands. Each corridor of capitalist development was thus a force for aggregation *and* dispersion.

A comparison of the coalitions of the guano era and the Aristocratic Republic will help bring out the distinctiveness of each. During the former, a ruling coalition emerged that was based on the control of a single resource—one that overcame the era's widespread tendencies toward dispersion and made it possible to organize political life around a kind of center. The government had a monopoly on that one resource and used its monopoly to dole out benefits to a highly restricted group of clients. Everything radiated outward from a single point, allowing the center to dictate.

During the Aristocratic Republic, it was no longer the case that a single resource, monopolized by the government, acted as the country's sole aggregating force, drawing all interests toward a single center. Rather, multiple capitalist corridors emerged to take the place of that single center. Unlike guano, these corridors were anything but highly localized and neatly circumscribed. Nor were they easy to monitor and control. To the contrary, the new corridors stretched across extensive areas, had vague and porous boundaries, and bent the surrounding space in corridor-specific ways. In the process, the various corridors generated a variegated landscape of lived citizenship.

Not only were there four aggregating corridors, but these corridors were also widely dispersed in space. Corridor I focused on the export of cash crops (sugar and cotton) and was located on the north and central coast. Corridor II was organized around the export of minerals (and secondarily, petroleum) and was located in the central sierra (with petroleum located on the north coast). Corridor III focused on the export of wool and was located in the southern highlands. Corridor IV was organized around the export of rubber and was located in the remote northeast, in the Amazon rainforest. Each individual corridor was a force toward aggregation, pulling in a different direction. As a group, however, the corridors acted as a powerful force of dispersion. Furthermore, unlike the guano era, during the Aristocratic Republic the government in Lima had no direct control over any of the corridors. To the contrary, because Lima relied on revenue from the corridors, the health of the government came to depend on the health of the dispersed corridors of capitalism.

The independence of the corridors from Lima inverted the relations of dependence between government and nongovernment. During the guano era, Lima had controlled the country's sole aggregating resource and had doled out benefits to supplicants as it chose. With the demise of guano, however, and the rise of the independent corridors of capitalism, it was the government that became the supplicant. And it was the capitalist corridors that doled out resources to the government.[41]

Finally, the conditions of the Aristocratic Republic also transformed the landscape of "autonomy" of the guano era. During the Aristocratic Republic, it was not the national government that was autonomous of foreign capital but rather the capitalist corridors that were autonomous of the national government. During the age of guano, the challenge of forming a more inclusive, national coalition had been how to overcome the overly narrow concentration of wealth and power that resulted from having a single, aggregated center. During the Aristocratic Republic, however, the problem was how to overcome the tendencies toward dispersion inherent in having four separate centers of aggregation. A key question for would-be nation builders was how to bring these different corridors together without threatening the interests of any of them. As the foregoing suggests, unlike in Mexico, in Peru there were no incentives to curb or limit the power of foreign capital—after the Grace Contract the power of foreign capital was difficult to contest.

These differences are reflected in the kinds of government regimes to which each era gave rise. The regimes of the export boom were the opposite of the bloated bureaucracies of the guano era. Indeed, the Aristocratic Republic took a "minimalist" approach to government, despite mounting pressures from below to do otherwise.[42] The elites of each corridor were anxious to retain their autonomy and were distrustful of "outside" interference. They were equally concerned to restrict the benefits of their labor-repressive accumulation practices as narrowly as possible. In general, the conditions of lived citizenship that emerged in and along the corridors of capitalist development violated the principles of liberal citizenship in the most egregious of manners. For instance, as Ragas describes in chapter 4, elites of the Aristocratic Republic sought to identify Andean migrants to Lima and Afro-descendants not in order to extend liberal citizenship to them but to exclude and marginalize them, by classifying them as partially undocumented populations and "ignored." Eventually, expanded collection of demographic information in overwhelmingly indigenous Andean regions facilitated the military and road-building drafts.

Like its guano-era predecessor, the national coalition that emerged during the Aristocratic Republic was an exceptionally narrow one. Indeed, virtually every important position in government were monopolized by the elites of Corridor I. As long as the export economy thrived, each corridor could reproduce itself independent of Lima, and the excluded corridor elites were willing to participate in a single national coalition. As we will see, however, when the export economy faltered, cracks in the coalition began to reveal themselves.

The willingness of elites to participate in a single coalition was also due to the actions of the Partido Civil (Civilista Party), which provided a framework within which elite groups could settle their differences. This was no small matter because of the number and range of elites that had been excluded from positions of real power in the Aristocratic Republic. In addition to the leadership of Corridors II–IV, this included the hundreds of highland estate owners who were not involved in any of the four aggregating corridors. The Civilista leadership worked out marginal power-sharing arrangements with these individuals. But highland elites were largely ignored during the Aristocratic Republic—just as they had been during the age of guano. As a result, this elite had little real stake in the preservation of the regime.

During the Aristocratic Republic, it was therefore a political party that sought to do nationally what capital investment was doing in the corridors— act as an overarching force of aggregation. The party did so in an effort to counteract the many powerful forces toward dispersion generated by the Aristocratic Republic's experiment in nation building. These forces were both sub- and transnational. They included the above-mentioned corridors of capitalism, which were focused outward, toward the transnational arena. The corridors confronted nation builders with the challenge of managing powerful forces that were *centrifugal* in nature—each of which pulled in a different direction.

The era's forces toward dispersion also included an extensive class of regionally based hacendados. Unlike their counterparts in the corridors—who looked outward, toward the transnational arena—these elites looked inward, to their own regions (and thus had powerful centripetal tendencies). They confronted would-be nation builders with the challenge of managing a large number of independent, region-specific forces, each of which was *centripetal* in nature. The Civilista Party tried to hold the center in the face of these centrifugal and centripetal forces. But its ability to overcome these multiple, contradictory tendencies toward dispersion—forces that pushed and pulled simultaneously, in many different directions—was ultimately limited, because the forces the party sought to integrate did not wish to be integrated.

In the aftermath of World War I—after almost thirty years of growth in the export economy—the contradictions in this experiment in nation building came to a head. These contradictions stemmed in part from the exclusions inherent in the era's structure of dispersed aggregation. They resulted as well from the oppressive conditions of lived citizenship generated by that experiment. We turn to a consideration of these contradictions in the second half of the volume.

CONCLUSION

This introduction to part I has afforded us the chance to make a few brief reflections about broad similarities and differences between the nation-building experiments undertaken in Mexico and Peru in the second half of the nineteenth century.

Between 1850 and the War of the Pacific, Peru seemed to overcome the challenges to implementing a liberal capitalist economy but failed to offer a liberal notion of citizenship to its population. Yet Peru's guano-dependent elites clustered in Lima had neither the need nor the means to unify the country's disparate geography and create a truly national coalition. Mexico's troubled mid-century liberal regimes sought to foster an identical project of liberal capitalism and citizenship but had even less success because it also failed to overcome the highly dispersed nature of its project of coalition building.

After the disastrous outcome of the War of the Pacific (1879–83) for Peru and Porfirio Díaz's rise to power in Mexico in 1877, the trajectories of liberal nation building in the two countries altered substantially. During Peru's so-called Aristocratic Republic, the regime successfully promoted isolated pockets of capitalism (agrarian, mining, oil) but never bridged the country's disparate geographies. The coalition of elites ruling Peru was a loose one held together by relatively weak ties. In Mexico, on the other hand, Díaz's regime provided a degree of coordination and the possibility of integration for regionally fractured zones of intensive capitalist development that Peru could only envy.

NOTES

We would like to clarify that rather than a historiographical review with extensive (if not exhaustive) endnotes, we offer our readers two interpretative essays prefacing the first and second parts of the volume. The originality of these essays lies in comparisons using the analytical categories sketched in the preface. The historical events and processes mentioned here for the most part lie in the public domain and have been extensively treated in the scholarly literature. We do cite particularly original and novel research that was central to our interpretation and offer readers several explanations of the major historiographical influences in endnotes.

1. We have found the following works to be especially useful in framing this section of the introduction: Heraclio Bonilla, *Guano y burguesía en el Perú*, 3rd ed. (Quito: Facultad Latinoamericana de Ciencias Sociales, 1994); Gregory T. Cushman, *Guano and the Opening of the Pacific World: A Global Ecological History* (Cambridge: Cambridge University Press, 2013); Paul Gootenberg, *Imagining Development: Economic Ideas in Peru's "Fictitious Prosperity" of Guano, 1840–1880* (Berkeley: University of California Press, 1993); Shane Hunt, *Growth and Guano in Nineteenth-Century Peru* (Princeton, N.J.: Princeton University Press, 1973); Alfonso W. Quiroz, *La deuda defraudada: Consolidación de 1850 y dominio económico en el Perú* (Lima: Instituto Nacional de Cultura, 1987); Alfonso W. Quiroz, *Domestic and Foreign Finance in Peru, 1850–1950: Financing Visions of Development* (Pittsburgh: University of Pittsburgh Press, 1993); Javier Tantaleán Arbulú, *Política económica-financiera y la formación del estado: Siglo XIX* (Lima: Centro de Estudios para el Desarrollo y la Participación, 1983); Rosemary Thorp and Geoffrey Bertram, *Peru, 1890–1977: Growth and Policy in an Open Economy* (New York: Columbia University Press, 1978); and Catalina Vizcarra, "Guano, Credible Commitments, and Sovereign Debt Repayment in Nineteenth-Century Peru." *Journal of Economic History* 69, no. 2 (2009): 358–87.

2. The main exception would be the Civil Code of 1852. See Jorge Basadre, *Historia de la República del Peru, 1822–1933*, 6th ed., 17 vols. (Lima: Editorial universitaria, 1968–69).

3. We draw on Wolf and Hansen's work (see Eric R. Wolf and Edward C. Hansen, "Caudillo Politics: A Structural Analysis," *Comparative Studies in Society and History*, no. 2 [1967]: 168–79) as an ideal type, to point to tendencies in forms of organization rather than to refer to any specific historical formation.

4. Discussions with economic historians of nineteenth-century Peru have helped us appreciate the difficulties involved in converting currency figures from the nineteenth century into contemporary equivalents. These scholars rarely attempt such conversions, and discouraged us from trying to do so. We have therefore decided to follow their suggestion, and have not attempted conversions. Economic historians also stress that the figures we quote are best understood as rough estimates, and are useful for heuristic purposes.

5. On the eve of the guano revolution the foreign debt amounted to approximately $40 million; the internal debt, about $25 million. Internal obligations were largely the result of a series of forced loans, imposed during Peru's postindependence civil wars, by caudillos in need of funds with which to fight their adversaries.

6. Brooke Larson, *Trials of Nation-Building: Liberalism, Race, and Ethnicity in the Andes, 1810–1910* (Cambridge: Cambridge University Press, 2004).

7. See Lewis Taylor, this volume, chapter 5.

8. Our understanding of the Restored Republic and Porfiriato has been shaped by Friedrich Katz, "The Liberal Republic and the Porfiriato, 1867–1910," in *Mexico Since Independence*, ed. Leslie Bethell (New York: Cambridge University Press, 1991), 49–124, as well as William Beezley, "Kaleidoscopic Views of Liberalism Triumphant, 1862–1895," in *The Divine Charter: Constitutionalism and Liberalism in Nineteenth-Century Mexico*, ed. Jaime E. Rodríguez O. (Lanham, Md.: Rowman & Littlefield, 2005), 167–79; John Coatsworth, "Los orígenes del autoritarismo moderno en México," *Foro Internacional* 16, no. 2 (1975): 205–32; Laurens B. Perry, *Juárez and Díaz: Machine Politics in Mexico* (DeKalb: Northern Illinois University Press, 1978); Richard Sinkin, *Mexican Reform, 1855–1876: A Study in Liberal Nation-Building* (Austin: University of Texas Press, 1979); Mark Wasserman, *Pesos and Politics: Business, Elites, Foreigners, and Government in Mexico, 1854–1940* (Stanford: Stanford University Press, 2015); Allen Wells and Gilbert M. Joseph, *Summers of Discontent, Seasons of Upheaval: Elite Politics and Rural Insurgency in Yucatán, 1876–1915* (Stanford: Stanford University Press, 1996); and Paul Vanderwood, *Disorder and Progress: Bandits, Police and Mexican Development* (Lincoln: University of Nebraska Press, 1981).

9. Naomi Klein, *The Shock Doctrine: The Rise of Disaster Capitalism* (New York: Metropolitan Books / Henry Holt, 2007).

10. Michael Matthews, *The Civilizing Machine: A Cultural History of Mexican Railroads, 1876–1910* (Lincoln: University of Nebraska Press, 2014), 37–44.

11. John Coatsworth, "Obstacles to Economic Growth in Nineteenth-Century Mexico," *American Historical Review* 83, no. 1 (February 1978), 80–100; Robert Holden, *Mexico and the Survey of Public Lands: The Management of Modernization, 1876–1911* (DeKalb: Northern Illinois University Press, 1994); Sandra Kuntz Ficker, "The Import Trade Policy of the Liberal Regime in Mexico, 1870–1900," in *Constitu-*

tionalism and Liberalism in Nineteenth-Century Mexico, ed. Jaime E. Rodríguez O. (Lanham, Md.: Rowman & Littlefield, 2005), 308–13.

12. Our analysis in this and the following paragraphs relies above all on Katz, "The Liberal Republic and the Porfiriato."

13. Perry, *Juárez and Díaz.*

14. See Thomas Passananti, this volume, chapter 2.

15. Ericka Beckman, *Capital Fictions: The Literature of Latin America's Export Age* (Minneapolis: University of Minnesota Press, 2013).

16. Lucero Morelos Rodríguez, "A peso el kilo: Historia del sistema métrico decimal en México," *Investigaciones Geográficas*, no. 69 (August 2009): 132–35.

17. Wasserman, *Pesos and Politics*, 10, 77, 81.

18. Vanderwood, *Disorder and Progress*, esp. 89–104.

19. Wasserman, *Pesos and Politics*, 7–9, 15, 19, 24.

20. Wasserman, *Pesos and Politics*, 7.

21. Holden demonstrates, however, that despoliation of land by survey companies has been overestimated by some historians, and that Porfirian institutions and laws did not reflexively serve the interests of large landowners. This is yet another case where the Porfirian regime was more autonomous than commonly recognized. Holden, *Mexico and the Survey of Public Lands.*

22. Edward Beatty, *Institutions and Investment: The Political Basis of Industrialization in Mexico Before 1911* (Stanford: Stanford University Press, 2001), 7, 20–22, 37–39.

23. Alex Saragoza, *The Monterrey Elite and the Mexican State, 1880–1940* (Austin: University of Texas Press, 1988), 29–49.

24. Noel Maurer, *The Power and the Money: The Mexican Financial System, 1876–1932* (Stanford: Stanford University Press, 2002), 115–17, 131.

25. Maurer, *The Power and the Money*, 70–71, 85–91.

26. Romana Falcón, "Force and the Search for Consent: The Role of the Jefaturas Políticas de Coahuila in National State Formation," in *Everyday Forms of State Formation*, ed. Gilbert M. Joseph and Daniel Nugent (Durham, N.C.: Duke University Press, 1994), 107–34.

27. Vanderwood, *Disorder and Progress*, 124–27.

28. Alan Knight, *The Mexican Revolution*, 2 vols. (Lincoln: University of Nebraska Press, 1986), 1:24–30.

29. Vanderwood, *Disorder and Progress*, 51–60, 67, 130.

30. Richard Weiner, *Race, Nation, and Market: Economic Culture in Porfirian Mexico* (Tucson: University of Arizona Press, 2004), 33–41.

31. Wells and Joseph, *Summers of Discontent*, 144–46.

32. Benjamin Smith, "Anticlericalism, Politics, and Freemasonry in Mexico," *The Americas* 65, no. 4 (2009): 559–88, esp. 564.

33. Wells and Joseph, *Summers of Discontent*, 156–65; Vanderwood, *Disorder and Progress*, 129–31.

34. We have found the following works to be especially useful in framing this section: Jorge Basadre, *Reflexiones en torno a la Guerra de 1879* (Lima: F. Campodónico,

1979); Heraclio Bonilla, "The War of the Pacific and the National and Colonial Problem in Peru," *Past and Present*, no. 81 (1978): 92–118; Manuel Burga and Alberto Flores Galindo, *Apogeo y crisis de la República Aristocrática* (Lima: Rikchay Perú, 1979); Paulo Drinot, ed., *La Patria Nueva: Economía, sociedad y cultura en el Perú, 1919–1930* (Chapel Hill: University of North Carolina Press, 2018); Steven Jay Hirsch, "The Anarcho-Syndicalist Roots of a Multi-Class Alliance: Organized Labor and the Peruvian Aprista Party, 1900–1933" (PhD diss., George Washington University, 1997); Nelson Manrique, *Campesinado y nación: Las guerrillas indígenas en la guerra con Chile* (Lima: Centro de Investigación y Capacitación, 1981); Rory Miller, "The Making of the Grace Contract: British Bondholders and the Peruvian Government, 1885–1890," *Journal of Latin American Studies* 8, no. 1 (1976): 73–100; Quiroz, *Domestic and Foreign Finance in Peru*; Steve J. Stern, ed., *Resistance, Rebellion, and Consciousness in the Andean Peasant World, 18th to 20th Centuries* (Madison: University of Wisconsin Press, 1998); Denis Sulmont, *El movimiento Obrero en el Perú, 1900–1956* (Lima: Pontífica Universidad Católica del Perú, Fondo Editorial, 1980); and Thorp and Bertram, *Peru, 1890–1977*.

35. Civilian regimes of the 1870s reduced the army from 12,000 soldiers (in 1870) to 4,500 soldiers (by 1875). They did so due to their fear that the army would seize power. Peter Klarén, *Peru: Society and Nationhood in the Andes* (New York: Oxford University Press, 2000), 183.

36. Sieges in which working populations refused to ally with foreign aggressors but instead joined forces with domestic powers include the following: most of Latin America during the Wars of Independence; China during the Japanese invasion of the 1930s; and the German siege of Leningrad in World War II. In addition to what is discussed above in the text, examples of contexts in which laboring populations sided with invading powers include much of Southeast Asia during World War II, when laboring groups greeted the Japanese as liberators from European colonialism; and in the U.S. South during the Civil War, when some white and many black southerners supported the Union Army against the Confederacy.

37. Our use of *autonomy* is distinct from the use of that term in the debates about the autonomy of the state. See Timothy Mitchell, "Society, Economy, and the State Effect," in *State/Culture: State Formation After the Cultural Turn*, ed. George Steinmetz (Ithaca, N.Y.: Cornell University Press, 1999), 76–97.

38. It is difficult to avoid thinking of Gabriel García Márquez's novel *The Autumn of the Patriarch* (New York: Harper & Row, 1976), in which the aged ruler of a Caribbean island leases the entire Caribbean to the gringos.

39. Miller, "The Making of the Grace Contract." The Grace Contract also granted foreign bondholders rights to guano deposits as well as an extensive area of land in the montaña region of the central sierra.

40. Less commonly, the formation of the new corridors of capitalism spurred the growth of middle-sector groups (as in the Mantaro Valley, and in the hinterlands that formed in the margins of Corridor II, which focused on the huge mining center at Cerro de Pasco). In an alternative pattern, new forms of dispersion-

based lived citizenship emerged on the margins of the corridors and allowed those involved in them "freedoms" that were highly unusual for the time (see Taylor, this volume, chapter 5).

41.   We use the term *doled out* intentionally. In general, the Lima government acquiesced to receiving only a fraction of what it was entitled to by law. One might think of this as a form of "corruption" that mirrored that of the guano age—but also turned it on its head.

42.   For an important analysis of the emergence of the "labor state," which helped mediate relations between the government and the emergent working populations of the era, see Paulo Drinot, *The Allure of Labor: Workers, Race, and the Making of the Peruvian State* (Durham, N.C.: Duke University Press, 2011).

1

STATE FORMATION AND FISCAL ORGANIZATION IN PERU, 1850–1934

CARLOS CONTRERAS

THIS CHAPTER seeks to describe the fiscal dimensions of Peruvian state formation during the decisive hundred-year period between the midpoints of the nineteenth and twentieth centuries. Every regime requires a fiscal organization that assures it of the considerable revenues required to meet the costs of rule. Such organization can take different forms, including state ownership of natural resources or economic assets, receipt of taxes paid by inhabitants of the country, or periodic confiscation of the wealth of citizens (or of neighboring countries). The formula chosen will have a profound impact on the nation's social, economic, and political structure. There is no such thing as a neutral fiscal structure, so there is a need to further explore the fiscal development of Latin American countries during their republican history.

The fiscal organization of a country is difficult to change in the short term. The economic and political costs of fiscal reform are generally high. Because the elements of a country's fiscal organization are intimately intertwined with the other political, economic, and social structures, change is difficult. If the population has grown accustomed to paying a certain tax, it is utter folly to replace it with a new one that might be more suitable in theory. Fiscal arrangements constitute social and political pacts, to which any alteration will provoke reactions by those affected.[1]

Republican Peru inherited a fiscal structure from its colonial past and attempted to adapt it to the principles embraced at independence. But it was not only political ideology that decided the reforms to be adopted; the national and international economy, marked by cycles of growth and recession, also had a bearing. So too did the social and political alliances and commitments that the governing groups upheld with different sectors of the population.

The years 1854 and 1880 bookended the first period in the finances of Peru to be considered in this chapter. This period was dominated by the guano revolution, which did more to transform the country's fiscal organization than did independence itself. The public economy grew like never before during these years, despite the abolition of most taxes, as a result of the government's appropriation of the guano deposits and the income they generated. The period came to an abrupt end with the Saltpeter War—also known as the War of the Pacific—whose outcome determined the loss of sources of state revenue and led to a forced reform in the final decades of the nineteenth century.

A second period, between 1880 and 1915, was characterized by fiscal reform and the search for a new form of organization that could replace the revenues lost following the Treaty of Ancón (1883) and would furnish the government with the resources necessary to promote economic growth and social modernization. These were years when the idea of competition between nations prevailed, whereby survival would only be attained by those with large standing armies. Given this impetus, work began in 1915 on a new public economy that would give a more central role to the government and call upon social sectors that, until then, had played the political game in rather more obscure ways. This new era extended to the middle of the twentieth century, when the start of a new capitalist growth cycle necessitated an overhaul of public finance. By the time Peru's first century of independence drew to a close, the progression from an ancien régime fiscal structure to liberal or modern taxation, based on direct levies such as income tax, had hardly started.[2]

PUBLIC FINANCES IN THE MID-NINETEENTH CENTURY: THE POWERLESS REGIME

The 5.5 million pesos that comprised the Peruvian government's annual revenues in 1850 were drawn from customs duties and the so-called contributions, the most important of which was paid by the indigenous population. In the biennial budget for 1850–51, customs duties accounted for 42 percent of government revenues. The lion's share (80–90 percent) came from the entry of imported goods, followed by the levies on the exportation of silver. This basic fiscal regime, hinging on foreign trade, has prevailed throughout the history of the republic. Today, however, it is exported rather than imported products that account for the largest proportion.

Fiscal revenues based on foreign trade did nothing to forge citizenship, in that they did not foster an exchange of rights and responsibilities between the government and the population. The contributions (introduced by Viceroy Fernando de Abascal in 1815), however, were geared toward forging the citizenship so cherished by the fiscal policy makers of the nineteenth century. The contributions consisted of providing the government with a proportion of a person's earnings from their properties, trade, or industry. The rates were low from today's perspective and fluctuated between 3 and 5 percent of net income or earnings. There were four types of contributions: homeowners and landowners paid "property" contributions (urban or rural), traders and business owners were subject to "license" contributions, artisans paid "industry" contributions, and indigenous persons shouldered "indigenous" or "personal" contributions.

The indigenous contribution was a fixed sum applied to peasants without title deeds to their land, or to those whose landholdings were so small that they escaped the rural property tax.[3] The budget for 1850 forecast the collection of 1.408 million pesos per year from the indigenous contribution, which accounted for 26 percent of all revenue projected by the government. The literature has not yet consolidated the incomplete, nineteenth-century registers of contributors, but the number of payers of this tax can be estimated at some 250,000 peasants, representing around half of the adult male population of Peru. After import duties (which accounted for 37 percent of takings), it was the most fruitful tax. The customs levy was fairly straightforward to collect, concentrated as it was at the country's limited number of ports. The payers of the contributions, on the other hand, were dispersed throughout the country and could plead poverty or victimhood of droughts or other misfortunes. As a result, there was a considerable gap between the amount that should have been collected and the amount that actually was collected. The few treasury figures available for this period indicate that the effectiveness of collection was situated at around 70 percent.[4]

The situation was no better in the other contribution categories. To begin with, the sums raised were far below those of the indigenous contribution. White and mestizo owners possessed the best cropland in the country but were taxed at a rate that was not even a tenth of the indigenous levy. Furthermore, the properties registered were few in number, and the values assigned to them (and thus the tax to be paid) were low. The sum of all projected nonindigenous contributions did not even equate to a quarter of the indigenous levy, which accounted for 80 percent of all contributions. The collection of nonindigenous contributions was thus no more effective than that of the indigenous one.[5] Indeed, it was landowners who proved the most reluctant to pay.[6]

The task of collecting the contributions fell to the local authorities appointed by the central government: prefects, subprefects, and governors, who were charged with the political governance of the departments, provinces, and districts, respectively, into which the national territory was divided. The subprefects frequently resorted to hiring assistants, oftentimes local police officers on their days off, for the collection operations. The assistants were mestizo men who were frequently accused of committing abuses against the Indians. To compel peasants to pay, they threatened them with imprisonment, whipped them, or confiscated their animals.[7]

The fiscal income system institutionalized a kind of division of work whereby indigenous persons paid the direct taxes while whites and mestizos paid the indirect ones, such as customs duties. Indeed, it was they who consumed most of the imported goods, or the products made using imported goods, such as clothing or books. The beneficiaries of this system were the landowners, who, despite possessing large expanses of cropland, accounted for just 2 percent of the budgeted revenue. And since half of them shirked the tax, the figure can be whittled down to 1 percent.

Customs duties and the contributions made up three-quarters of government revenues in the budgets of the mid-nineteenth century; the remaining quarter was composed of a motley assortment of taxes, income, and fees. The most important in terms of the amounts raised were the income from guano, classified as state property; collected debt arrears; and municipal and police revenues.[8] The municipalities collected certain taxes or tolls, obtained revenue from the lease of properties that they owned, and used these revenues to fund public works and services in their localities. Municipal revenues, however, were always too meager to meet the many needs of the population (paving and cobbling roads, building bridges and water systems, etc.). As a result, in 1848 the government of Ramón Castilla made provisions to absorb the municipal treasuries. In so doing, the government hoped that the departmental subprefects would have access to more resources, from central treasury transfers, than the mayors.

Even if the centralization of revenues was justified as a means of enabling more equal distribution of spending, it still undermined the formation of a fiscal culture. It hindered the population from relating the taxes they paid to the public goods and services they received. This created little incentive to ensure that the authorities engaged in effective and transparent spending practices.

Government spending circa 1850 was concentrated on the armed forces, which consumed 44 percent of the budget, and on public administration, which accounted for 21 percent. The rest was invested in tax collection and public spending control (13 percent), the administration of justice (6 percent), and the upkeep of foreign affairs and the Church (3 percent), and a supplementary category serviced the public debt and financed public works (13 percent).[9] With such a small budget—less than three pesos per person—the government's capacity to guarantee public order, enforce the law, protect property, promote economic growth, and develop infrastructure was extremely limited. Indeed, the government's limited tax base rendered it unable to raise large amounts in fiscal contributions for virtually any purpose. But with guano came the possibility of overcoming these problems.

A REPUBLIC WITHOUT TAXES

Guano is an agricultural fertilizer that comes from seabird excrement. The islands and peninsulas of Peru's desert coast contained enormous quantities of guano, which was first exported by private Peruvian business interests in partnership with European technicians and entrepreneurs. Beginning in the 1840s it became possible to sell Peruvian guano on the markets of Europe and elsewhere. And because viable guano deposits could not be found anywhere else, Peru was free to impose monopoly prices.

Guano was declared state property from an early stage, allowing the treasury to capture the earnings from its exportation. Extraction, transportation, and marketing rights were granted in the form of concessions, in exchange for a commission, to private interests known as "consignees."[10] Guano allowed the Peruvian government to increase its revenues exponentially, from 5.4 million pesos in the 1850 budget to 20.8 million pesos in 1861 and to 41 million pesos (32.8 million soles) in 1875.[11]

If the quarter century that followed independence was marked by dwindling fiscal revenues, the next twenty-five years were quite the opposite. However, from the 1850s onward this was hardly a tax burden per se. The bulk of government revenues no longer came from taxes paid by inhabitants of the country but from earnings on guano (and secondarily, saltpeter). This trend was accentuated because the authorities abolished or cut existing taxes. As guano revenue increased, the government abolished the indigenous contribution, the agricultural tithe that farmers paid to the Church (from which government officials skimmed off a ninth), and the tax paid by the mining industry for the extraction of pastes. The remaining contributions (those pertaining to property, licenses, and industry) remained in place. In 1873 President Manuel Pardo assigned two-thirds of these contributions to the municipal councils (rehabilitated in 1861), which would increase to all contributions after the Saltpeter War.

The abolition of the indigenous contribution proved most controversial because it meant reducing the tax base to a small minority and also because this was the most stable of all fiscal revenues (it was less dependent on the ups and downs of commerce). The arguments in favor of abolition stressed its inequitable character: what the Indians paid was out of all proportion to their resources. Moreover, collection went hand in hand with abusive practices and personal mistreatment of Indians. The liberal deputy Santiago Távara argued that the despondent and impassive disposition of the Indian was a consequence of the fiscal burden that had weighed him down for centuries.[12] Another argument against the indigenous contribution was its colonial and feudal origins: it came into being during the age of absolutism, when the villeins or *pecheros* had to show submission to a powerful lord.

The arguments against abolition called for the tax to be reformed, so that it could be turned into a "personal contribution" levied upon all men of productive age regardless of "race." This would, of course, have continued to apply to the Indian population, the rationale being that it was important they remain subject to some form of taxation. Cutting the only tie that bound them to the authorities could, it was believed, have negative repercussions, such as weakening their connection with the republic or stirring up fears in them about the legality of their landholdings. The requirement to pay the tax compelled Indians to be hired by mines or estates on a seasonal basis to earn the wages they needed, thus alleviating the labor shortfall that afflicted the economy.

In addition, some feared that abolition would plunge the departments into fiscal deficit—because the contribution was used to cover the costs of public administration—and render them dependent on transfers from the central government. Guano wealth would allow the governing regimes to plug the hole left in the public purse by the abolition of the tax, but what would happen when this temporary bounty disappeared? Peru's integration into the world economy on the strength of guano ultimately severed the fiscal cord that had tied peasants to the governing classes.[13]

After the tax abolitions of the 1850s, agricultural and mining producers ceased to be treasury contributors altogether, while the propertied class continued paying a few paltry taxes for their rural estates and urban residences. Customs duties, on the other hand, increased fourfold. Thus, the guano boom did not facilitate tax collection and did not translate into significant revenue increases for any tax besides the customs duty, which was an indirect tax that was easy to collect.

On the spending side, an important transformation occurred during the guano era. Although a not-inconsiderable proportion of government expenditure continued to go toward the military (10 percent in the national accounts of 1870), an even greater proportion was allocated to efforts to integrate the national territory. Indeed, spending under the "governance" field rose to a third of the total by the early 1870s. Part of this total was invested in expanding the police presence, from less than 1,000 in 1849 to more than 6,000 by 1875. New departments and provinces were also created, with their respective prefect's and subprefect's offices. By 1875 public employees numbered more than 15,000 men, of whom 1,231 were unarmed civilian personnel.[14] Another part was allocated to construction of the new communications infrastructure: railroads, steam, and telegraphs. The country went straight from the mule to the steam locomotive without any interim infrastructure such as roads or stagecoaches.

Without specialized professionals or an existing freight flow with which to orientate the lines to be constructed, the railroads were designed based on political impulse rather than economic need. Peru's geography and the shortage of inputs such as wood and labor pushed up the cost of the works, producing a bloated external debt. The government also promoted, albeit tentatively, greater knowledge of the national territory and culture through the hiring of foreign geographers, artists, and engineers, culminating in 1875 in the foundation of a School of Engineers. In terms of their spending and "stimulation" of production, national regimes were more akin to liberal European polities, constructing modern infrastructure and establishing professions such as engineering to furnish the industries with qualified personnel. But when it came to revenues, the regimes of the era did not hold their population to account through taxes. Nor were they aware of the country's forms of production or income. Neither were these regimes held to account by a population seeking to know how its taxes were spent. As proposed by Pedro Gálvez, one of the ideologues of tax liberalism, Peru was a country whose population was the recipient of public spending but not the source of its revenues, in that each inhabitant cost the government ten soles per year but contributed no more than two soles to the national budget; the remaining eight soles came from guano, a resource that cost no one anything and therefore did nothing to create a "fiscal contract" between the population and the government.[15]

Between 1872 and 1876, the government of Manuel Pardo attempted to reform this fiscal regime by setting it on a more republican and liberal course, so that the treasury could avail itself of taxes paid by the population rather than depending on an ephemeral, unstable income of external origin. Although Pardo's endeavors did not succeed, they served to demonstrate where the difficulties lay in reforming the fiscal structure of the nation. On the one hand, Pardo sought to decentralize public finances by transferring tax collection and the bulk of spending to departmental councils. On the other hand, he dramatically raised the contributions, signaling to the propertied class that from that point on, their tax burden should be more in line with their wealth.

In the biennial budget for 1873–74, the forecast takings from the urban property and license contributions quadrupled in value from four years earlier, to 523,448 soles in the former case and 432,000 in the latter; meanwhile, revenue from the rural property contribution doubled to 227,000 soles.[16] To the same end, during his earlier spell at the Ministry of Finance under the dictatorship of Mariano Ignacio Prado (1865–67), Pardo implemented the stamp duty, which was the only element of his fiscal reform that would survive through to Pedro Diez Canseco's revolution. The fiscal stamp had to be placed on any written contract in which the contracting parties sought the arbitral backing of state power, and the value of the stamps depended on the amount of money involved in the contract. Clearly, it was a tax intended to come from the pockets of businessmen and the landed class in general. As of 1873, the stamp duty raised some 300,000 soles per year—more than any other contribution.[17]

Pardo's other aim was to ring-fence the guano proceeds and turn them into an extraordinary revenue that could not be used to cover ordinary spending but would instead be reserved for rail infrastructure or cropland expansion. It was not easy, of course, to change what the president called "the special organization of our society," which was accustomed to everyday expenses being covered by raw-material monopolies rather than taxation.[18] No advances were made in education, entrusted to the departmental and provincial councils, which demonstrated for a long time that the transfer of responsibilities from central to local government came at the cost of public-spending efficiency. Meanwhile, efforts to raise taxes did not readily translate into an increase in collection. In 1873 the contributions, including stamp duty—budgeted at 1.5 million soles—yielded revenues of just 593,435 soles.[19] Nor was Pardo able to implement a personal contribution that would turn every male of productive age into a taxpayer.

The most significant event in Pardo's failed fiscal reform was the nationalization of saltpeter between 1873 and 1975. After guano revenues plummeted, having been used to service the external debt acquired in Europe for railroad construction, the dilemma arose of how to fill the gap left in the budget: with new taxes or by dipping into the earnings from another government asset? It is fair to say that Pardo made an effort to pursue the former option, which was more attuned to his ideas about how a republic should function, but it proved to be a solution that would only bear fruit in the long term. In the meantime, he gave in to the temptation to prolong the established system of state dependence on income from natural resource exports. In this variant of the resource curse, governing oligarchies postpone fiscal modernization, safe in the knowledge they can obtain their income through ownership of natural resources.

Saltpeter was another agricultural fertilizer, but it also had other uses, such as in the production of explosives and iodine. Unlike guano, saltpeter in its naturally occurring state required some form of processing or refining; it had to be removed from the subsoil, after which the caliche was extracted and separated into its useful parts, and then transported on animals or carts (or by train starting from the 1870s) to the nitrate works, where it was pulverized for leaching. Leaching involved leaving the pulverized caliche to stand in tubs of boiling water, which further broke it down. Then, the resultant parts were exposed to sunlight in order to crystallize the nitrate, before packaging and transportation to the port. The deposits were the property of the state—a throwback to the Spanish colonial era when all natural resources belonged to the king—but the refinement works were run by private firms whose owners were businessmen from the south of Peru, as well as Lima, Chile, and several European countries. Expropriation carried a cost, both financial and political: the former because it was necessary to compensate the owners, especially foreign nationals, whose claims were often backed by their powerful governments; the latter because the businessmen repudiated government appropriation of an activity initiated by private enterprise. This had already happened with guano in the 1840s, and the experience was repeated thirty years later with saltpeter. Was there anything that private interests could turn to without the threat, if their endeavors were successful, of the authorities having their fill? The creation of the saltpeter monopoly in 1873, and the government's expropriation of the industry two years later, showed that once underway, the dependence of public finances on income from a natural resource was difficult to arrest.

The guano boom availed the treasury of greater resources, but the population had very little scope with which to challenge the government through fiscal disobedience given that taxes had steadily been abolished. The regimes of the guano era invested the proceeds in expanding the government's presence throughout the country. The idea that judicious application of this income would enable an increase in tax revenues in the future—by improving the cadastres and the statistics on trades, professions, and industrial production, as well as increasing the number of production centers through better infrastructure for economic activity—was only partially borne out.[20] The propertied class made moves to ensure that the guano money was used to improve communications as well as to create a gendarmerie and a judicial and government bureaucracy (which had been depleted severely following independence) but did little to increase government surveillance over economic activity.

In the 1870s, there were efforts to improve statistics. A national population census was conducted and the first statistics on mining claims and foreign trade were published. The outbreak of the Saltpeter War, however, and the resultant impoverishment set the country back many years in this endeavor. It was only in the twentieth century that foreign trade statistics reemerged and as late as 1940 before another census was carried out. During the guano era, the propertied class and the small population residing in the cities were the only payers of the precious few taxes that remained. By virtue of the increase in the contributions and reinforced by the emergence of a stamp duty, property owners and businessmen regarded themselves as the sole fiscal partners of the nation, propagating a "censitary republic" model in which citizenship was restricted to treasury contributors. Meanwhile, the Indians were now condemned as a "dead weight" for the nation.[21] Customs duties increased from a little over 2 million pesos in 1850 to the equivalent of 10 million pesos (more than 8 million soles) in 1873. The sum of customs duties, contributions, and certain additional taxes and income came to almost 10 million soles in ordinary revenues (as opposed to income from natural resources, which was roughly twice as much) in the mid-1870s, for a population of slightly more than 2.5 million. Almost a century on from the rebellion of Túpac Amaru, the tax burden had yet to equal that achieved by the viceroyalty that executed him. The Saltpeter War (1879–83), in which Peru, in alliance with Bolivia, lost to Chile, forced the country to undertake an important reform that would put an end to the republic that was liberal in its spending but archaic in its fiscal revenues.

THE RETURN OF TAXATION

Paradoxically, the nationalization of saltpeter in 1875, which might have been expected to prolong the tax-free republic for a few decades more, ended up precipitating its demise. The Peruvian government intended to neutralize the competition that had emerged on the world market for saltpeter from Bolivian coastal territory, and the Peruvian national saltpeter company gradually gained control of its neighbor's saltpeter works, which until then had been run by Chilean firms.[22] In 1873, in parallel to the creation of the saltpeter monopoly, a mutual defense agreement was signed in secret between the governments of Peru and Bolivia in case of aggression by another nation.[23] In 1878 Bolivia's application of a levy on saltpeter exports from its coast was resisted by the Chilean companies still based there. The following February, the Chilean army responded to Bolivian government threats to expropriate these firms by invading its coastline. Bolivia called upon its ally to activate the secret agreement, and Peru was dragged into the conflict.

This war underlined the difficulties that the South American nations faced in building fiscal regimes fit for economic and social modernization. The need for an infrastructure of railway and telegraph lines, ports able to accommodate steamships, services for the expansion and improvement of urban life, and training of the population for paid employment all required a dramatic increase in public revenues. It soon became evident that governments lacked information about the economy, the capacity to gather it, and the political clout required to register potential taxpayers and impose a more aggressive fiscal regime.[24] Given these circumstances, it is unsurprising that governments opted for direct or indirect nationalization of natural resource exports, and that they were even prepared to resort to war when these resources came under threat or needed to be secured. The Saltpeter War was just such a conflict over fiscal resources.

The Treaty of Ancón, signed on October 1883, ratified Peru's temporary loss of its guano deposits and the permanent loss of its saltpeter. Now that this route to tackling its fiscal predicaments had been closed off, governments were pushed onto the slow and complex path of creating taxes. In the postwar years, the economic oligarchy, having long since built its fortune on guano and saltpeter exports, began seeking out other natural resources to exploit. The most readily obtainable—those that involved no more than collecting the product, shaking off the dust, and putting it on a ship—had been lost with the war, but agriculture and metal mining, sectors overlooked during the guano boom, remained. In November 1890, the government of Remigio Morales Bermúdez signed a commitment pledging not to trouble the mining sector with new taxes, nor to resurrect old ones, for a period of twenty years.[25] In practice, this consideration was extended to agriculture and the entire export sector. In the years that followed, exports of sugar from the coast and silver—later joined by copper—from the highlands began flowing from Peruvian ports, a trend that accelerated with the arrival of foreign capital in the new century.[26]

Denied the opportunity to live off the taxes or earnings left by the export economy, governing regimes took advantage of the full suite of sales taxes: customs duties were reformed in 1886 to their fiscal maximum—that is, to the point at which they yielded the greatest tax revenues, which in Peru was a high ad valorem percentage of around 40 percent—while taxes were placed on the sale of several locally or foreign produced articles that were not readily substitutable and were widely consumed across the population, such as alcohol, tobacco, opium, sugar, salt, and matches.[27] These taxes yielded significant sums in the coastal region, where the ports and most bustling cities were located, but very little in the highlands, where trade was limited and a subsistence economy predominated. To cover fiscal spending in the region, the personal contribution was restored alongside a fiscal decentralization regime. However, collection of the contribution was limited, exposing the transformations in the relationship between the governing and the governed that had taken place since independence.[28]

The personal contribution was set at two soles per year for the highland region and at four soles per year for the coast; although these rates were lower than the indigenous contribution up until 1854 or the labor wage contribution between 1865 and 1867, they had to be paid by the entire male population aged between twenty and sixty and not just by Indians. The revenues collected were accumulated in the departmental treasuries and were used to meet their own running costs. Collection was initially entrusted to the local authorities (subprefects and governors); a subsequent attempt to create a specialized fiscal bureaucracy failed.

The voices that opposed this contribution denounced it as the restoration of the indigenous tax. But why was it that a "foreign" king from a far-off metropolis managed to impose a tax levied at a higher rate and used for general expenses when the republic could not repeat the experience at a lower rate, and when the takings were to be used to finance public services in the localities themselves? It was quite apparent that in their more than half a century of existence, postindependence regimes were unable to match the legitimacy of the colonial monarchy in the eyes of the population, particularly after the Saltpeter War. Moreover, postcolonial regimes, which sought to defend the exclusive authority of their functionaries, dismantled the network of indigenous authorities that had facilitated collection of the indigenous levy under the colonial regime. With neither the collaboration of the Indian caciques nor the charisma of the distant monarchs to draw upon, the republic was powerless to raise the personal contribution.[29]

Moreover, the punitive methods employed by the Spanish *corregidores* to collect the tax, including lashings, imprisonment, and the seizure of animals or harvests, were morally and politically unworkable at the end of the nineteenth century. A republic that styled itself as liberal could not very well send its tax debtors to jail, nor beat them with whips in the plazas. And any legitimate forms of pressure that there were, such as expropriation of assets, did not work in a society in which no property registers were kept and owners went unidentified. In fiscal terms, the Peruvian republic was in a fix, since this new framework of dominant ideas—at least in the capital—only allowed for the forms of pressure that were legitimate under liberalism; but the economy, especially in the interior, was a throwback to the ancien régime in which there was only room for taxes of a similar ilk.

During the period 1883–1915, government revenues were limited (or more so than during the guano era, at least) but secure; though they amounted to just 5 percent of GDP, they grew in tandem with an ever-expanding economy. Indeed, revenues increased from an average of 7 million soles per year throughout the 1880s to 35 million soles in 1913.[30] Exports of sugar, silver, copper, petroleum, cotton, wool, and rubber were crammed into the ports and gave employment to more than one hundred thousand operators, especially in coastal agriculture. The exporters did not pay taxes on their earnings and only very little on their properties, but they did consume imported goods that were subject to customs duties—as did their employees and workers as well as the public servants and salespersons. This was the fiscal model of an oligarchic republic in which a regime of limited scope provided the basic services the oligarchy required, based on a limited but effective sales tax regime.

From 1890, tax collection was assigned to private interests. The process began with specific taxes, such as those on alcohol or tobacco consumption and a stamp duty, until in 1896 the government of Nicolás de Piérola opted to hire a single private firm—of which the government became a shareholder, although its management was left in private hands—to collect a large package of taxes. The company's shares had high unit prices that only the economic elite could afford; in fact, the firm was controlled by the largest banks from the capital, such as the Banco del Perú y Londres and the Banco Popular del Perú.[31] The information these banks gathered as part of their tax collection endeavors was bound to have been useful to their financial operations. The efficiency attained by the tax collection company helped establish sales taxes in the interior, where there were no major stores or factories that could evade its control.[32]

The concession of tax collection to a private company allowed the local tax authorities to unburden themselves of what until then had been one of their primary responsibilities. But this approach was applicable chiefly to indirect taxation, and to some extent it upset the fiscal relations between the government and the population—to whom it seemed immoral that tax collection could become a profit-driven business. Yet the collection company grew and "became almost a monster," in the words of the finance minister of 1914.[33] Its actions helped centralize taxation, even though the firm's services were also procured by departmental councils and municipalities.

The oligarchy's economic power was based on control of the export-oriented natural resources, and they paid little to no taxes on their usufruct. For instance, the landowners paid the rustic property contribution to the municipal councils, set from 1879 at 5 percent of their presumed earnings. This, in turn, was esti-mated as one-tenth of the commercial value of each property, which was set at a modest level below the market value. Mining entrepreneurs paid government officials a "mine contribution" of 30 soles per year for each "belonging," which equated to about two months' wages for an unskilled mine worker, and that was all. Based on the 1890 agreement, no duties or royalties were paid for the use of natural resources, nor taxes on the proceeds from their exportation.

The downside to such low taxation was that it restricted the population's political and economic rights: the export capitalism that now reigned in the country did not involve any expansion of citizenship, at least during this first stage. In 1895 an electoral reform was introduced with the aim of putting an end to the chaotic and discredited system that predated the Saltpeter War. The reform excluded most of the population from the vote, granting suffrage only to men over the age of twenty-five (as well as married men below that age) who knew how to read and write. This was the first time that the latter restriction was expressly applied, even if it had been implicit since independence.[34] The population of literate adults at that time was estimated at just 20 percent and was largely concentrated in the coastal cities.[35]

THE PARTIAL REFORM OF OLIGARCHIC TAXATION

At the start of the twentieth century, in a country with a population of some 4 million, the electorate comprised as few as 150,000 people—less than 4 percent of the total.[36] This state of affairs came under increasing attack from an intellectual and political current that advocated the "integration of the Indian" into national life. Through the end of the nineteenth century, social Darwinist ideas held sway, whereby indigenous peoples occupied one of the lower rungs in the ranking of the "human races" and were not deemed worthy of investment in education or health care; conversely, foreign immigrants from the "superior races" should be attracted. Later, counterarguments began to emerge in defense of the Indian's capacity for education and integration into the modern commercial and industrial economy. Their current prostration was no more than the result of their historical exploitation and marginalization from national life. It therefore fell to government officials to begin to "regenerate" the Indian through public instruction and aggressive health, nutrition, and "urbanity" programs.[37]

The rise in fiscal revenues on the strength of the export boom during those years allowed successive regimes to embark upon public education and health programs. Starting in 1905–6, these services, previously in the hands of local governments, became part of the remit of the central government. This was in keeping with the continued predominance of indirect taxation as a source of fiscal revenue since it placed most of the resources in the state coffers. By 1912 government spending on education, health, and production and transportation infrastructure—almost nonexistent in the 1880s—accounted for 12 percent of the total expenditure.[38] The categories of Treasury (29 percent), War and Navy (23 percent), and Governance and Police (17 percent) continued to come off best in the distribution of the budgetary pie.

During the 1910s, it became apparent that the ostensibly modest goal of running a primary school, a basic health center, and a justice of the peace in the capital of each of the country's one hundred provinces, and a secondary school, a hospital, and a court of justice in the twenty departmental capitals, required regimes that were better equipped in economic and bureaucratic terms. The oligarchic fiscal regime was found wanting. The emergence of a specialized bureaucracy, initially in tax affairs but later in fields such as public education, health, and communications, reached critical mass on the eve of World War I and went on to became a public actor that challenged the political and intellectual dominion of the oligarchy.[39] Men like José Manuel Rodríguez, Fernando Tola, Ricardo Tizón i Bueno, Enrique León García, Jorge Polar, Alberto Ulloa, Alejandro Garland, and Hernando de Lavalle, among others, published journals, books, and newspaper columns calling for a more active official presence in the formation of citizens. These citizens could not be conjured out of thin air: it was incumbent on the government to deploy a cadre of teachers and nurses to "regenerate" the population in the interior, after centuries of isolation under a brutal feudal regime.[40]

The outbreak of the Great War lifted the prices of the raw materials exported by Peru to a vertiginous height. This coincided with the end of the twenty-five-year period of tax relief on mining exports. The pressure for greater public investment in education and health care, ratcheted by the mood of a public that had witnessed the succulent windfall profits enjoyed by the exporters—notably the major foreign firms—culminated in exports being restored as one of the nation's fiscal pillars. This came despite the head of state at the time being José Pardo, son of the founder of the civilism movement and a prominent member of the group of exporters.

In November 1915, Pardo passed a law that reintroduced export duties. The levy would be activated when the price of the export products exceeded the threshold that covered the costs of production and transportation, plus 10 percent. It was purposely not legislated as an income tax, given that under the provisions of the fiscal centralization law, the administration of income tax, as a form of direct taxation, corresponded to the departmental treasuries rather than the central coffers. The tax was considered a customs duty that was paid on each unit of weight exported. In 1916, the year that this tax came into effect, it generated almost 5 million soles, more than 10 percent of the total fiscal revenues for the year. In 1920, revenues from the tax totaled 24 million soles, a sizable third of the budget for the year. But in the years that followed, the international prices of raw materials dropped, taking down the revenue from this tax with it.

It might have seemed that this renewed dependence on foreign trade levies meant a return to a fiscal pattern that hinged on customs duties, of the kind that characterized Latin American countries between the middle of the nineteenth century and the first third of the twentieth century.[41] But the differences lay on the fiscal spending side. The indigenous population had ceased to be taxpayers and instead became recipients of "social spending" by the central government in the form of programs to boost literacy and tackle infant mortality.[42] Since Peru had not received the desired numbers of immigrants to address the lack of manpower for agriculture and mining, policy makers looked to eugenics or self-eugenics to turn Andean Indians into modern laborers for the country's new economy.[43]

In 1920, however, the government of Augusto Bernardino Leguía enacted the so-called road conscription law, which was condemned by the political opposition as a restoration of the indigenous tax. The law obligated the entire adult male population to work on Sundays to build roads in their home provinces, though it was possible to gain exemption by paying the equivalent of a day's wage. The need for roads to connect the settlements of the interior was critical, as was the lack of manpower to build them. The tax was repealed in 1930 after the fall of the Leguía regime, when the international crisis saw the labor shortage give way to a job shortage.[44]

The indigenous communities, which had developed a distrust of government authorities over centuries, refused, at least to begin with, the schools, teachers, and nurses that were provided. They feared that the service, then free, would later be subject to an onerous levy from which there would be no escape. They were also disinclined to submit their wives and children to the care of strangers who would exercise great authority over them. They presumed that the introduction of the schools and health programs would effect grave changes in their everyday lives and their household economy. As a result, it was the mestizos based in the villages of the interior who became the main users of the new government services.

The lengthy government of Leguía (1919–30, known as *el Oncenio*) was highly active on the fiscal front. On the one hand, it centralized the fiscal administration, rolling back the decentralization implemented in the years that followed the Saltpeter War. On the other hand, it extended the use of the stamp duty and created new levies on the export economy, including a tax on petroleum production and on the area occupied by the exploitation operations, as well as on a wider range of agricultural and mining products, and the sales taxes. In 1926 the government introduced a tax on excess profits, payable when these exceeded 10 percent of the capital invested, and a progressive tax on salaries and income whose rates ranged between 1 and 7 percent, depending on level of income.[45] In 1929 the different forms of income tax accounted for 6.3 percent of all government revenues. The "progressive tax" on wages and income contributed only 0.8 percent.[46] For that year, official revenues, not counting loans, totaled 104 million soles. The lack of GDP data for those years means that the slice taken by the government cannot be calculated, or compared with the start of the century, with any certainty. But as far as can be inferred, 1929 appears to have been similar to the years preceding World War I in this respect.[47]

As to public spending, on the cusp of the Great Depression of the 1930s, one-third was consumed by the Ministry of Finance and Commerce, especially on servicing the debt that had been used to finance the ambitious public works program during el Oncenio; another third went toward the military and internal order; and the remaining third was allocated to education, health care, development (roads, railways, docks, telegraphy, irrigation works, and urban sanitation), and the administration of justice. Thus, the expenditure corresponding to the government's social and political project had increased. In the 1930s, this trend was consolidated with the creation of the ministries of Education and Health.

El Oncenio extended public infrastructure with the aid of loans from the U.S. banking sector. The administration was also strengthened fiscally, but this came at some cost to the economic oligarchy, sparking a confrontation that culminated in the crisis of Leguía's government in 1930, and the legal proceedings the oligarchy pursued against him and his collaborators in the years that followed. Leguía had removed the oligarchy from control of key activities such as issuing money and collecting taxes, through the creation of the Reserve Bank in 1922 and the Caja Nacional de Depósitos y Consignaciones (National Deposits and Allocations Fund) in 1927, replacing the Junta de Vigilancia del Cheque Circular (Circular Note Oversight Board) and the Compañía Nacional de Recaudación (National Collection Company), respectively. His government also pestered them with taxes that reduced their earnings, especially in the export sector.

The Great Depression caused a contraction in foreign trade and in the flows of foreign capital that had been financing public works over the last decade. The governments of Luis Sánchez Cerro (1930–33) and Óscar Benavides (1933–39) turned their attention back to domestic taxes levied on sales and income. In 1934 Law 7904 provided for an income tax on the basis of the property contribution and the tax on movable capital (which taxed earnings on mortgage bonds, public debt securities, and credit operations in general) created during the Saltpeter War, as well as the excess profits tax and the progressive tax on salaries and income introduced by Leguía. In the five-year period from 1930 to 1934, customs duties, which at the onset of World War I made up 40 percent of fiscal revenues, totaled "just" 26 percent, of which one-third came from export levies—and in truth constituted an income tax, or at any rate a form of direct taxation. The sales taxes, having contributed similar revenue levels as customs duties before the war, now accounted for 28 percent, and direct taxes 10 percent.[48] Sparked by the world economic crisis, direct taxation had started to displace indirect forms in Peru.[49]

This transformation was a fiscal expression of the social changes prompted by the expansion of paid work on estates and mining camps in highland and coastal areas, and of the emergence of an urban "middle class" made up of the state bureaucracy and employees of banks and trading houses.[50] The policies implemented to avert the effects of the Great Depression served to reinforce the tools of the central government. In 1931 a new law strengthened its control of the Central Bank, while the abandonment of the gold standard opened the floodgates to fiat currency, an instrument turned to with frequency over the next two decades to alleviate the chronic fiscal deficit. A development banking sector was created alongside new ministries with responsibilities for the social project, thereby divesting the Church of this function. In 1936 the civil registry was made obligatory—it had been created in 1876 but only as an optional alternative to its ecclesiastical counterpart—and government power was further bolstered. The prolonged battle between the civilian and religious powers that dated back to the Bourbon era appeared to have ended with the victory of the former.

During its first century of independence, in fiscal terms Peru went from being an ancien régime based on customs duties and the indigenous levy to one of transition to the liberal model where sales tax prevailed and glimpses were caught of modern direct taxation, levied upon income in its multiple forms. The government began to assume direct control of collection operations, giving up the program of concession to private companies that characterized the period Jorge Basadre called the "aristocratic republic" (1899–1919).[51] Meanwhile, government spending was no longer confined to the military or to fiscal and political order, becoming more oriented toward investment in infrastructure and health and education services for the majority of the population. This transformation occurred in response to changes on the economic front, whereby raw materials went from a period of momentum to one of depression; on the political front, whereby the government lost its direct control over natural resources (to return during the period 1968–92); and on the social front, whereby an indigenous population in demographic and social ascent exerted pressure for more effective routes to integration.

Insofar as the fiscal reform was partial, with indirect taxation continuing to account for most government revenues throughout the twentieth century, and direct taxation still gravitating around raw material exports, whose swings from boom to bust remained highly marked following the Great Depression, the treasury was unable to position itself as a decisive or leading element in national integration. From the 1930s onward, spells of expansionary and contractionary government spending alternated based on the peaks and troughs of raw materials trading, conditioning the rise and fall of social movements in pursuit of improved welfare and social and political rights.

NOTES

1.   Gabriel Ardant, "Financial Policy and Economic Infrastructure of Modern States and Nations," in *The Formation of National States in Western Europe*, ed. Charles Tilly (Princeton, N.J.: Princeton University Press, 1975), 164–242; Richard Bonney, *The Rise of the Fiscal State in Europe, c. 1200–1815* (Oxford: Oxford University Press, 1999); John Campbell, "The State and Fiscal Sociology," *Annual Review of Sociology* 19 (1993): 163–85.

2.   See Harley Hinrichs, *Una teoría general del cambio de la estructura tributaria durante el desarrollo* (Mexico City: Centro de Estudios Monetarios Latinoamericanos, 1967); Marcello Carmagnani, *Estado y mercado: La economía pública del liberalismo mexicano, 1850–1911* (Mexico City: Fondo de Cultura Económica, El Colegio de México y Fideicomiso Historia de las Américas, 1994).

3.   Those homes and lands whose net income or earnings were presumed to be below fifty pesos per year were exempt from paying the contribution. Santiago Távara, *Emancipación del indio decretada en 5 de julio de 1854 por el libertador Ramón Castilla* (Lima: Printed by J. M. Monterola, 1856), 92.

4.   Estimated on the basis of the tables included as annexes to Manuel del Río, *Memoria que presenta a las Cámaras reunidas en Sesiones Extraordinarias en 1849 por el Ministro de Hacienda [Manuel del Río] sobre la situación actual de esta y las causas que la han motivado* (Lima: Imprenta de Juan Masías, 1849).

5. The exception was for the levy on licenses paid by traders, who numbered less and were more susceptible to being penalized by the authorities.

6. Some observers of the postindependence era, such as José María Córdova y Urrutia, painted a depressing picture of the state of the economy, especially agriculture in the department of Lima. Córdova y Urrutia calculated the earnings of owners from their properties at just 2 percent and explained: "Everyone laments the lack of capital, slavery, and the ills they suffer because of the war"; "The War of Independence has made American capitalists disappear, so that their wealth has been reduced to the property they have, to the rural and urban estates, with whose little earnings they sustain their families." José María Córdova y Urrutia, *Estadística histórica, geográfica, industrial y comercial de los pueblos que componen las provincias del Departamento de Lima* (Lima: Imprenta de Instrucción Primaria, 1839), 19, 39. All translations are mine unless otherwise indicated.

7. Juan Bustamante, *Los indios del Perú* (Lima: Printed by J. M. Monterola, 1867), 32, 50–51.

8. José de Mendiburu, *Presupuesto calculado del producto de las rentas de la República en un año, que forma la Dirección Jeneral de Hacienda, conforme a los datos que existen en ella* (Lima: Ministerio de Hacienda, 1849).

9. José Fabio Melgar, *Memoria que presenta á la Lejislatura Ordinaria del Perú del año de 1849, el Oficial Mayor del Ministerio de Hacienda encargado de su despacho* (Lima: Imprenta de Eusebio Aranda, 1849).

10. William Mathew, *La firma inglesa Gibbs y el monopolio del guano en el Perú* (Lima: Banco Central de Reserva del Perú; Instituto de Estudios Peruanos, 2009).

11. Pedro Dancuart and José Rodríguez, *Anales de la hacienda pública del Perú: Historia y legislación fiscal de la República*, 24 vols. (Lima: Ministerio de Hacienda, 1902–26), 6:225, 10:177–204; Miriam Salas, *El presupuesto, el Estado y la Nación en el Perú decimonónico y la corrupción institucionalizada, 1823–1879* (Lima: Instituto de Estudios Histórico Marítimos del Perú, 2014), 45–46.

12. Távara, *Emancipación del indio decretada*, 6.

13. According to Jorge Basadre (quoting Pedro Gálvez): "Following elimination of the indigenous and caste contributions, all departments in the republic with the exception of Lima and Moquegua were left without sufficient funds to meet the needs of their interior services. The suppression of the indigenous tax deprived the treasury of an annual income calculated at 1,400,000 pesos, at the same time as it faced the expenses of the freedom of slaves and those arising from civil strife." Jorge Basadre, *Historia de la República del Peru, 1822–1933*, 17 vols., 6th ed. (Lima: Editorial Universitaria, 1968–69), 4:323.

14. Carlos Contreras, *La economía pública en el Perú después del guano y el salitre: Crisis fiscal y elites económicas durante su primer siglo independiente* (Lima: Banco Central de Reserva del Perú; Instituto de Estudios Peruanos, 2012), 392–93.

15. Gálvez, quoted in Pedro Dávalos y Lissón, *La primera centuria: Causas geográficas, políticas y económicas que han detenido el progreso material y moral del Perú en su primera centuria*, 4 vols. (Lima: Librería e Imprenta Gil, 1926), 4:186–87.

16.   Dancuart and Rodríguez, *Anales de la hacienda pública del Perú*, vols. 7 and 9; Salas, *El presupuesto, el Estado y la Nación*.

17.   Dancuart and Rodríguez, *Anales de la hacienda pública del Perú*, 9:58; Salas, *El presupuesto, el Estado y la Nación*.

18.   See Carmen McEvoy, "Estudio preliminar, recopilación y notas," in *La huella republicana liberal en el Perú: Manuel Pardo; Escritos fundamentales*, ed. Carmen McEvoy (Lima: Fondo Editorial del Congreso del Perú, 2004), 224.

19.   Dancuart and Rodríguez, *Anales de la hacienda pública del Perú*, 9:72; Salas, *El presupuesto, el Estado y la Nación*.

20.   See Távara, *Emancipación del indio decretada*. In the 1870s, there was some development of sugar and cotton production along the northern and central coast, as well as mining in the highlands of Lima, boosted by the start of work on the railway line to La Oroya. Javier Tantaleán Arbulú, *Política económica-financiera y la formación del estado: Siglo XIX* (Lima: Centro de Estudios para el Desarrollo y la Participación, 1983); Alfonso W. Quiroz, *Domestic and Foreign Finance in Peru, 1850–1950: Financing Visions of Development* (Pittsburgh: University of Pittsburgh Press, 1993).

21.   See Carlos Milla Batres, *Cartas a Piérola: Sobre la ocupación chilena de Lima*, introduction and notes by Rubén Vargas Ugarte (Lima: Ediciones Milla Batres, 1979), 13–14.

22.   See Ronald Crozier, "Guano y salitre: Las causas económicas de la guerra de Perú y Bolivia contra Chile en 1879" (paper presented at the Congreso de Historia de la Minería, San Luis Potosí, 1997).

23.   See Oscar Bermúdez, *Historia del salitre desde sus orígenes hasta la Guerra del Pacífico* (Santiago de Chile: Universidad de Chile, 1963); and William Sater, *Andean Tragedy: Fighting the War of the Pacific, 1879–1884* (Lincoln: University of Nebraska Press, 2007).

24.   Miguel Angel Centeno, "Blood and Debt: War and Taxation in Nineteenth-Century Latin America," *American Journal of Sociology* 102, no. 6 (1997): 1565–1605.

25.   Dancuart and Rodríguez, *Anales de la hacienda pública del Perú*, vol. 21, annexes, p. 60; Salas, *El presupuesto, el Estado y la Nación*.

26.   Rosemary Thorp and Geoffrey Bertram, *Peru, 1890–1977: Growth and Policy in an Open Economy* (New York: Columbia University Press, 1978).

27.   Dancuart and Rodríguez, *Anales de la hacienda pública del Perú*; Salas, *El presupuesto, el Estado y la Nación*.

28.   See Carlos Contreras, "El impuesto de la contribución personal en el Perú," *Histórica* 29, no. 2 (2005): 67–106.

29.   Between 1886 and 1895, the take never exceeded 30 percent of the projections (see Dancuart and Rodríguez, *Anales de la hacienda pública del Perú*), and riots and rebellions broke out in multiple places—a notable example being the Revolution of Atusparia in the Callejón de Huaylas. William Stein, *El levantamiento de Atusparia: El movimiento popular ancashino de 1885* (Lima: Mosca Azul, 1988).

30.   Paul W. Drake, *The Money Doctor in the Andes: The Kemmerer Missions, 1923–1933* (Durham, N.C.: Duke University Press, 1989), 308; Augusta Alfageme et al., *De la*

moneda de plata al papel moneda: Perú: 1879–1930 (Lima: Banco Central de Reserva del Perú, Agencia para el Dasarrollo Internacional, 1992), 129, 260–61.

31. Alfonso W. Quiroz, *Banqueros en conflicto: Estructura financiera y economía peruana, 1884–1930* (Lima: Universidad del Pacífico, 1989).

32. Luis Ponce, "Banca libre y empresas privadas de recaudación," *Revista Peruana de Ciencias Sociales* 3, no. 3 (1993): 9–41.

33. Basadre, *Historia de la República del Peru*, 7:388.

34. Gabriella Chiaramonti, *Ciudadanía y representación en el Perú (1808–1860)* (Lima: Universidad Nacional Mayor de San Marcos, 2005).

35. The 1876 census, the closest to that date, recorded an illiteracy rate of 82 percent among those over the age of six, while the 1902 school census estimated it at 77 percent. Carlos Contreras, "Maestros, mistis y campesinos en el Perú rural del siglo XX," in *El aprendizaje del capitalismo: Estudios de historia económica y social del Perú republicano* (Lima: Instituto de Estudios Peruanos, 2004), 214–72, esp. 257–58.

36. Víctor Peralta, "Los vicios del voto: El proceso electoral en el Perú, 1895–1929," in *Historia de las elecciones en el Perú: Estudios sobre el gobierno representativo*, ed. Cristóbal Aljovín de Losada and Sinesio López (Lima: Instituto de Estudios Peruanos, 2005), 78–79.

37. Francisco Graña, *El problema de la población en el Perú: Inmigración y autogenia* (Lima: Tipografía El Lucero, 1908).

38. República del Perú, *Liquidación del presupuesto de 1911 al 31 de mayo de 1912: Anexo á la Cuenta general de la república* (Lima: Ministerio de Hacienda, 1912).

39. Osmar Gonzales, *La academia y el ágora: En torno a intelectuales y política en el Perú* (Lima: Universidad Nacional Mayor de San Marcos, 2010), 72, 202; Marcos Cueto, *Excelencia científica en la periferia: Actividades científicas e investigación biomédica en el Perú, 1890–1950* (Lima: Grupo de Análisis para el Desarrollo, 1989), 181–90.

40. For an example of this type of manifesto, see Víctor Andrés Belaunde, *La crisis presente, 1914–1939*, 7th ed. (Lima: Ediciones "Mercurio Peruano," 1940).

41. Víctor Bulmer-Thomas, *La historia económica de América Latina desde la independencia* (Mexico City: Fondo de Cultura Económica, 1998).

42. Marcos Cueto, *El regreso de las epidemias: Salud y sociedad en el Perú del siglo XX* (Lima: Instituto de Estudios Peruanos, 1997).

43. Paulo Drinot, *The Allure of Labor: Workers, Race, and the Making of the Peruvian State* (Durham, N.C.: Duke University Press, 2011).

44. On road conscription, see Mario Meza Bazán, "Estado, modernización y la Ley de Conscripción Vial en Perú," *Revista Andina* 49 (2009): 165–86.

45. Sociedad Nacional Agraria, *La tributación directa en el Perú: La nueva legislación y las disposiciones legales anteriores* (Lima: Sociedad Nacional Agraria, 1935).

46. Drake, *The Money Doctor in the Andes*.

47. Bruno Seminario (*El desarrollo de la economía peruana en la era moderna: Precios, población, demanda y producción desde 1700* [Lima: Pontificia Universidad Católica del Perú, 2015]) has reconstructed GDP series starting from 1700, but he expresses figures in indexed dollars and not in nominal figures for each year, which compli-

cates the calculations. In any case, it can be deduced from his data that between 1913 and 1929 the national GDP at constant prices had more than doubled (increasing from 4.434 million to 10.292 million Geary-Khamis dollars). Meanwhile, the soles of 1929, taking into account the price index, were worth little over half of those of 1913 (Alfageme et al., *De la moneda de plata al papel moneda*, 276). The 140 million soles collected by the state in 1929 would be equivalent to 79 million soles in 1913, which was slightly more than double the fiscal revenues of that year (35 million soles).

48. Carlos Boloña, *Políticas arancelarias en el Perú, 1880–1980* (Lima: Instituto de Economía de Libre Mercado, 1994), 90, 103.

49. Ali Díaz Gálvez, "La política tributaria en el Perú de 1930 a 1948: De los impuestos indirectos a los impuestos directos" (undergraduate thesis, Pontificia Universidad Católica del Perú, Lima, 2007).

50. David Parker, *The Idea of the Middle Class: White-Collar Workers and Peruvian Society, 1900–1950* (University Park: Pennsylvania State University Press, 1998).

51. Basadre, *Historia de la República del Peru*, 11:5, 321; Banco de la Nación, *50 años llevando la Banca a donde tú estás* (Lima: Banco de la Nación, 2016).

2

BANKING ON FOREIGNERS

Conflict and Accommodation Within Mexico's National
Bank, 1881–1911

THOMAS PASSANANTI

THIS CHAPTER examines the evolving relations between the Mexican
state and the nation's primary financial institution, the Banco Nacional
de Mexico (hereafter Nacional), during the long dictatorship of Porfirio
Díaz. The Porfirian state oversaw a massive transformation of Mexico, and as
scholars have increasingly recognized, the Nacional, founded in 1881, long played
a crucial role in supporting the state's ambitious agenda until revolutionary
forces toppled the regime in 1911. Most of the initial research was heavily empir-
ical and provided a rich basis for reconsidering the importance of Nacional in
the history of the Porfiriato.[1] However, recent scholarship has suggested that an
explicit cronyism pervaded the state and bank relations, and that this cronyism
compromised the state's autonomy, restricting its ability to promote development and thereby distorting the economy's development along the narrow lines
of its financial elite. In short, cronyism, or "vertical political integration" between
domestic financial elites and the Porfirian state, meant that the state traded its
independence for financial resources.[2] This chapter offers a more nuanced view
of the Porfirian state's relations to Nacional, arguing that the state was not captured by financial elites but instead used the bank and its bankers as instruments
to pursue its own independent agenda.[3]

Rather than attempting a general survey of state–bank relations, this chapter
focuses on the fascinating but little-known relations between the Porfirian state

and the Nacional's dual boards of directors, one foreign—the so-called Paris Committee—and one local, the Mexican board. The reasons for the creation of this unusual, dual board will be explained below, but to anticipate the argument that follows, the archival evidence supports several noteworthy claims. First, the foreign board persistently sought to pressure the Porfirian state to adopt policies, assume debt obligations, and pass and enforce legislation that reflected the bankers' own narrow (and often immediate) financial goals. Second, the European bankers' preferences were often blocked by the local, Mexican board, either because it feared reprisals from Porfirian officials or because it held opposing viewpoints. Third, Porfirian officials took advantage of these differences, often manipulating internal bank rivalries to maintain greater autonomy and flexibility in pursuit of its strategic goals. Fourth, Porfirian officials, while preserving a "special relationship" with the Nacional and its foreign patrons, persistently sought alternative sources for public finance and a more competitive domestic banking system. Finally, the Porfirian state's relative autonomy from these powerful financial elites, both foreign and domestic, helps make explicable its political resilience, its economic achievements, and its remarkable longevity.

After a short section that reviews the unusual founding of a national bank with European capital and the creation of its hybrid dual board, this chapter will briefly analyze three financial episodes taken from the 1880s, the 1890s, and the early 1900s. The first two episodes explicitly involve disputes between the dual boards and the Porfirian state. The third episode involves the Paris Committee's longtime president, Edouard Noetzlin, and Mexico's finance minister, José Yves Limantour.

A NATIONAL BANK WITH FOREIGN OWNERS

The Nacional was founded largely with foreign capital. The bank was designed to provide both public finance to the Mexican state and private finance to the general economy. Although Nacional was a Mexican corporation, domiciled in Mexico, it had two boards of directors, one in Mexico and one in Paris (the so-called Comité de Paris), an arrangement demanded by its initial European founders.[4] In an effort to preserve control over their substantial investment, the European financiers imposed a bank statute stipulating that both boards needed to be consulted when a decision involved more than one million pesos.[5] In practice, however, especially in the bank's first twenty years of existence, the two boards were in close contact, exchanging scores of letters and telegrams annually. Over time the divided management structure, with overlapping foreign/Mexican boards, created tensions and conflicts usually resolved in favor of local control.

Both boards, in effect, relied on foreigners to advance their collective interests. The Paris board provided Mexican bankers with valuable and personal access to capital, markets, information, and networks. Likewise, the Mexican board provided the European board with direct access to information and networks in close proximity to the Mexican state. In general, the two boards cooperated to effectively build a profitable financial institution. But as this chapter will suggest, the two boards repeatedly wrestled over the bank's relations with the state, and it was the Mexican board and even more so the Mexican state that determined the outcomes of these conflicts. Interestingly, some of the same European financiers who promoted Nacional had founded other similar banks, foremost in the Near East (in the Ottoman Empire and Egypt) but also in Latin America and the European periphery.[6] The foreign boards, in addition to providing a supervisory role, pursued another role, largely hidden from public view. Since these banks served governments, their overseas boards were privy to insider information.[7] Access to inside information was exploited on European bourses by trading, speculating, and manipulating a range of securities such as public debt bonds, railroad stocks, and currencies.

One European financier, Edouard Noetzlin, grew to dominate the Paris board. In 1881 Noetzlin had traveled to Mexico to negotiate the founding of the original Banco Nacional Mexicano, and he remained active in Mexico finances until the regime's end. Given his centrality to the history of Nacional, the Paris board, and Mexican finances more generally, I provide a brief biographical sketch. Noetzlin was born in Basel, Switzerland, in 1848 and died in Paris, France, in 1935. Except for recurrent business travel, Noetzlin spent his entire career in Paris, where he rose from relative obscurity in the late 1860s to become, in 1911, the president and chairman of Banque de Paris et des Pays-Bas, one the world's largest banks. His rise was owed to several factors: being part of the extensive banking network of Bischoffscheim and Goldschimdt, his own acumen and industry, and impeccable timing since he came of age in Europe's heyday of overseas banking. Finally, I argue that he was also lucky to have become involved in Porfirian finances just as the country emerged from a half century of financial morass and began to grow rapidly.

In the late 1860s, Noetzlin worked at Banque de Paris and continued there when it merged to become Banque de Paris et des Pays-Bas in 1872. In 1875 he moved to a smaller, associated bank called Banque Franco-Egyptienne. In both banks he was a colleague of Ernest Cassel, a German émigré (who settled in London and would later become the banker and adviser to King Edward VII) with whom he worked closely for decades on international financial operations. His friendship with Cassel proved the most valuable in his early career. Both Banque Franco-Egyptienne and Banque de Paris et des Pays-Bas sought to establish overseas banks dedicated to lending mainly to sovereign governments.[8] Noetzlin's key career break came when he was selected to represent Banque Franco-Egyptienne in its efforts to create just such a national bank for Mexico, along the lines of its previous investment in Egypt. His successes in Mexico, and the social capital he acquired by partnering with major European bankers (Gerson Bleichroder in Berlin and Ernest Cassel in London) to form lending syndicates for the Mexican government, enabled him to become a major banking figure by the mid-1890s. When Noetzlin was appointed as an officer of Banque Paribas in 1895, he helped create affiliated banks in Russia, Italy, Spain, and Indo-China. These banks put European bankers at the center of both public and private businesses in peripheral economies, just as an expanding world economy created new demand for capital and raw materials. Noetzlin leveraged his growing European network to raise capital for these markets and he formed social ties with financial elites and governments abroad.

But we are getting ahead of ourselves. During Nacional's first five years, from 1881 through 1885, its European founders were repeatedly frustrated in their attempts to achieve their two core objectives: first to obtain a banking monopoly in Mexico, and second to shepherd the Mexican state's return to international capital markets. On the one hand, local banking competitors thwarted Nacional's monopoly aims (eventually in 1884 Nacional merged with its chief rival, Banco Mercantil Mexicano, in a complex arrangement overseen by the Mexican state). On the other hand, wily and independent Mexican officials preferred postponing debt accords until the Treasury was on stronger footing. Noetzlin, representing Nacional's European board, was a key participant in both the bank merger and the infamous 1884 foreign debt debacle.

FIRST EPISODE: 1880S

In June 1886 the Mexican government finally concluded negotiations with the English bondholders, settling the English debt in default since the 1820s. But rather than relieving Mexico's financial challenges, on the contrary the settlement increased Treasury deficits and forced the government to service growing semiannual remittances. In the months before the first coupon was due, Finance Minister Mañuel Dublán secured an agreement from Nacional whereby the bank would advance the government the $616,000 necessary to meet the first coupon of the English debt due in December 1886. Nacional's actions drew a sharp rebuke from its Paris committee, which criticized the local board for not consulting it before concluding the advance, for not exacting better terms from the state, and in general for providing the state with funds and thereby reducing the financial pressure on the state. The manner in which Nacional had handled the advance to cover the English debt coupon signaled one of the earliest conflicts between the two boards. It also signaled the growing will and capacity of the Mexican board to act independently.

Nacional did not treat this lightly; on the contrary its local directors met and decided to create a small three-man commission to answer Paris's criticisms, thoughtfully and at length. The three delegates named—Gustavo Struck, Nicolás de Teresa, and Félix Cuevas—were leaders of Nacional. The message they conveyed is worth examining at length because it provides a window into the evolving relations not only between the foreign and local boards of Nacional but also into the ongoing changes between the national bank and the state. Throughout the seven-page letter, Nacional's commission sought to underline the bank's special relationship to the state, explain the effect that harsh conditions would have on both the bank and the regime, and describe the political environment in Mexico.

> No doubt it would have been better if the advance of December 3 had not been made, but here we have taken into account what you would do well to recall; our character as the banker to the State, to help the Government to fulfill its commitments abroad, and at the same time not to impose onerous conditions that, if they were not accepted, would put the bank in a bad predicament, and if they were, would put the Government in a bad predicament, because once the agreement was publically known, what the Government earned in credit for the fact of the payment, it would also lose in credit, for the ruinous loan terms that the Government would have had to accept in order to make the payment.[9]

Specifically, the Nacional commission discussed the terms of the loan proposed by Paris in January 1886. The commission members wrote, "If the loan was presented to the public on the bases of that contract, it would give a rude blow to the Government's credit, from which it would take several years of prudent and ordered administration to recover."[10] The bank reviewed what the government would pay and receive. Mexico would receive "$6,500,000 in funds and $1,000,000 in paper and it would pay in London £5,00,000 [$25,000,000] in the course of thirty years. The sole fact of making this loan would be evident proof that the Government was bankrupt, because only Governments in that desperate situation could make deals manifestly so ruinous." Nacional admitted that if the bank was in charge of the loan, "the affair could be profitable, but with the gravest difficulties of another sort. In the first place, a reckoning of the profits would be calculated and presented before the press as one-sided and unjustly benefiting the Bank, which would provoke an atmosphere of hatefulness; and in the second place the Government would cite those profits to make them seem enormous and thus justify not complying with the stipulations of the loan agreement." The local board recognized that neither its long-term nor its short-term interests would be served by such a loan.

Nacional then indirectly confronted the behavior of the European board. The commission asked Paris: "Should the Bank take advantage of any urgent trouble the Government has in order to squeeze things to the extreme? We believe not: we believe that excessively advantageous businesses, although attractive at the beginning, always have so many stumbling blocks, so many difficulties and so many pitfalls in the execution, that the real advantages are outweighed by the problems caused, and even more so for a permanent establishment like ours which has to be in daily and constant contact with the Government."[11] Nacional's commission concluded by correcting the Paris committee's idea of the government's comfortable situation. The commission acknowledged that "the Government has a regularized march, makes its ordinary payments, fulfills religiously its assignments made to its creditors; but to do so it solicits short-term advances at high rates, and its situation is very far from being comfortable, nor could it be rationally, having received the Public Treasury in such a grave state."[12] This letter provides a rare early window into the divisions that split the Paris and Mexican boards. The Paris board had banked on its Mexican partners cooperating with it to pressure the Mexican state to accept a loan with onerous conditions. The Mexican board's reaction reflected changes afoot inside Mexico's financial elite. The Mexican directors of Nacional were distancing themselves from their European counterparts; the majority were identifying themselves with the general interests of the regime. Yet Nacional's advances were useful because they allowed the Mexican state to raise its credit standing in international markets by demonstrating its ability to meet its foreign obligations.

SECOND EPISODE: 1890S

In the mid-1890s, confrontations between the Nacional and the Mexican state intensified, as a new finance minister, José Yves Limantour, on the strength of an improving economy and public treasury, successfully diversified the state's sources of public finance and created a more competitive banking system. This underlined the regime's growing activism and autonomy, especially as it confronted the powerful foreign and domestic interests found in Nacional. A key to the regime's successful confrontation was its subtle and clever manipulation of conflict between the bank's dual boards of directors.

The Porfirian state's financial activism frustrated Nacional and its foreign board, with both boards detecting a disturbing pattern. Yet the two differed on how to respond to the state. In early January 1897, the Paris board suggested that the bank forthrightly confront the government with a laundry list of grievances. However, the local board cautioned discretion because "to submit to the Minister of Finance written claims about infractions, difficult to specify and justify with documents, will expose us to vague blows and predispose the spirits against us when neither the times nor the circumstances favor us to assume a firm attitude in asserting our rights."[13] Almost six months later, in June 1897, faced with stronger recriminations from Paris, Nacional's director, Carlos Varona, sought to explain the government's recent hubris and hostility toward the bank. First, Varona declared that "our conduct has not changed, even though indeed the circumstances have changed, which have created a delicate situation." Second, he reviewed recent history and circumstances.

It will suffice to express that, since two years ago when the Bank refused to raise the Government's debit balance to $5,000,000, preventing, as it wished, to rescue all its Mint houses at once, we understood that we had provoked the Finance Minister's antipathy, which, although concealed, has since translated into acts aimed at circumscribing our prerogatives, reducing emoluments and favoring other credit institutions. Encouraged by the relief he imagines he is given by the millions he now has in our boxes and by the greed of others who are competing with us, the Government imposes and makes its will prevail; and

we, placed in a false and delicate position, must temper ourselves to it, trying not
to provoke conflicts in which we will surely get the worst part.[14]

Thus, the bank recognized that its old alliance with the government was subject
to serious revision since both the state and the private sector had grown financially stronger and more assertive.

Although preliminary discussions about bank reform occurred in early 1896,
the reform became law in March 1897. Nacional quickly felt the effects of the
reforms, especially the newly competitive environment. For example, in the
booming northern state of Chihuahua, Nacional began to lose deposit accounts
to local banks. All Chihuahuan banks, including Nacional's chief competitor,
Banco Minero, offered interest-bearing checking accounts. At the end of 1897,
writing to Paris, Nacional observed disdainfully that "excited, by the banking
reform, the greed of those who believe that the country will lend itself to the
development and prosperity of many financial institutions, which will earn them
fat profits, have obtained concessions that they have begun to put into operation."[15] Yet Nacional was not above joining the competitive battle for the "fat
profits" in an anticipatory way, advising Paris that "in order not to appear forced
by competition, our bank has dropped to 6 percent annual the discount price in
all its branches, a measure that has been applauded and put it on good ground
to face the coming events."[16]

By means of the bank reform and associated initiatives, the Porfirian state
reordered relations between itself and the financial elite, upsetting old alliances,
nurturing new ones, and creating a more hospitable legal framework for financial entrepreneurs. The state's conduct, not inadvertently, also sparked a new era
of relations between Nacional and its foreign board. The conflict grew out of an
evolutionary change in the loyalties of the Mexican directors and in the balance
of power between the two boards. The divided loyalty of Nacional's directors
was foreshadowed in the 1880s by the early tension between Nacional and Mercantil before the two merged. As the Porfirian state strengthened, Nacional's
domestic directors began to identify themselves less as discrete bankers (or as
Paris's junior partners) and more as supporters of the regime's general interests.
This evolution formed part of the process of the making of a national economic
elite, nationalist to the extent that its formation occurred in confrontation with
foreign partners and in support of its national government when the latter
found itself in conflict with those same foreign partners. Nacional's leaders had
extensive and growing stakes in many economic sectors, which depended on

political stability and a hospitable climate for external investment. They more readily acceded to banking reforms because they were well placed to exploit the opportunities created by legal and institutional change. Moreover, they recognized that opposing the reforms was futile and might threaten their remaining privileges.

For its part, the state was aware of divisions between the local and foreign boards of Nacional, recognized that local bankers were more likely to be swayed by appeals to the national interest, and sought to exploit those divisions and make those appeals. Thus, the state pursued one tactic repeatedly: to pressure Nacional to quickly decide on a business proposal without conferring with its foreign board. The state had learned that the foreign board was more likely to postpone unfavorable deals indefinitely. However, as alternatives to Nacional grew, like the Barcelonette-invigorated Banco de Londres or the private Scherer house with extensive financial relations in the lower Rhine, the government increasingly brought propositions to Nacional with effective urgency. The Paris board criticized Nacional for acting unilaterally and for not apprising it of important business affairs with the state. Nacional sought to defend itself by asserting: "We hope that you will understand easily that, whenever a business is proposed to us by demanding an immediate reply, we have to accept or refuse it flatly, as we deem advantageous or disadvantageous to the interests of the Bank, without resorting to consulting you." In April 1897, Nacional tried to explain why it acted to sell government bonds for the completion of the Tehuantepec Railroad to Paris by pointing to Limantour's pressure, noting that it had acted "for the urgency with which Minister Limantour wanted our answer, in order to demonstrate our constant willingness to provide the services he needs."[17] Cuevas concluded that the native directors were convinced that it was a sound operation, especially "in light of the good circumstances of the Public Administration."[18]

In the following years, the rift between the Paris and Mexican boards widened. The two boards continued to disagree sharply over the bank's relations with the Díaz government. The French board criticized the aid Nacional lent the state—aid Noetzlin deemed unwarranted given the government's hostility. In late 1898, Noetzlin sharply criticized Nacional's use of bank reserves to support the value of Mexico's debt. On behalf of the European board, Noetzlin complained that employing reserves in such a speculative maneuver exposed the bank to ill-advised risk and that such "favors" were especially unnecessary since the Mexican government had been working "to facilitate the establishment of the other competing banks and their undercover and constant actions of reducing our operations with their Treasury." The domestic directors admitted that "the favors that we lend to this to the government, to credit their finances, is not reciprocated in the proportion due." Yet they continued aiding the state because "we will avoid responding to one inconsistency with another." And thus "we will prolong the good understanding that we are maintaining with the current Minister of Finance, whose insight and expertise recognizes the correctness of our conduct and usefulness of our services."[19] Nacional recognized that it needed to tread carefully in its relations with the government, and its behavior bespoke a fine regard for the subtleties of dealing with a Treasury whose financial strength and options were growing and whose capacity to punish (or reward) was far-reaching.

The Mexican board's forbearance frustrated Noetzlin, and the frustration erupted into recriminations unusually candid in the formal culture of international finance. He charged that the reason why the state had adopted a hostile attitude toward Nacional lay in the fact that the local board had neglected its relations with Finance Minister Limantour. Nacional's domestic board fired back that "very significant reasons and in which you bear some responsibility explain—even if they do not justify" the finance minister's behavior toward the bank.[20] The Mexican leadership of Nacional distinguished its relations with Limantour, which "have been frequent and cordial," from Noetzlin's relations, which were not "as friendly as they had been in the past." As proof, Nacional's domestic board offered Noetzlin an example of its intimate relations with Limantour. Nacional's Mexican director wrote to Noetzlin that Limantour had read to him "some letter from you and his reply. This fact would suffice to demonstrate to you that our Board of Directors has not been that distant from the Finance Minister as you suppose." The Mexican board gave further proof of its close relations with the minister. For example, Limantour had asked it to intervene "very directly and efficiently" in the selling of Mexican bonds on the Frankfurt market, which the director did "in order to reinforce our good relations with the Minister." The bank explained that "we did not say anything to you or the Paris Board about this interesting business deal because the Finance Minister asked our director to be discreet."[21]

The Mexican directors' growing independence was echoed in private banking affairs, which also drew Noetzlin's ire. Again Nacional retorted, "You should not think that everything done is your work or that to manage the bank's business we need to be driven by your valuable initiative. We have done some work ourselves, and the best business deals made recently were done by us."[22] Specifically the bank questioned Noetzlin's advice that it be drawn into more aggressive banking business, arguing that "it would not be prudent nor bring good results to risk capital and prestige looking for and entering into business deals that are outside the scope of banks of emission."[23]

These incidents were not simply personal and ad hoc. Rather, they reflected the limits and contradictions of Nacional's hybrid foreign/domestic composition. More importantly, they reflected that state's clever manipulation of those divisions and its appeal to national sentiment.[24]

THIRD EPISODE: 1900S

Edouard Noetzlin, as a founder of Nacional, and president of the Paris Committee for more than twenty years, represented himself in Europe as the ultimate insider both of Mexico's financial elite and of Mexico's finance minister, Limantour. In short, if cronyism defined the Porfirian regime, then Noetzlin defined and embodied Porfirian cronyism as well as any foreigner could. Given this, I will briefly review here Noetzlin's striking failure in 1904 to secure the forty-million-peso loan that he and his bank had worked to obtain for more than two years. Instead, Mexico's finance minister Limantour awarded the loan to a rival syndicate, led by the U.S. banking house of Speyer Brothers.

I will touch only on the 1904 loan negotiations affair as it relates to Noetzlin's striking failure to leverage his personal and professional networks in Mexico, and more specifically his relations with Minister Limantour to win the loan deal. The results underline the explanatory limits of cronyism and the centrality of politics and political economy to decoding Porfirian economic diplomacy. Indeed, in this case, the apparent cronyism was an artifice used by officials, specifically Minister Limantour, to stimulate greater competition among foreign lenders and thereby extract more advantageous terms and conditions. Space constraints allow me only to suggest how political goals worked to undermine the putative value of financial networks.

I begin by reviewing the contemporary analysis of the loan negotiations written by Noetzlin's colleague at Banque Paribas, Emile Moret, who had traveled to Mexico City to negotiate the loan with Finance Minister Limantour. On October 17, 1904, just after learning of his bank's failure, Moret wrote to the bank's chairman, Henri Thors, blaming Noetzlin. In uncharacteristic language for a banker, Moret exclaimed, "I am leaving immediately. I'm dreadfully sorry, angry, and profoundly distressed. After so much effort, after three weeks of fighting, after having twice had the affair in hand, and failing at the last moment due to a persistent misconception of things in Paris, is a severe test for nerves in the best temper."[25] Moret insisted that the persistent misconception was Noetzlin's fault.

> The central idea persistently found in all of Noetzlin's telegram correspondence is this: "My relationship with Limantour is so old, my negotiations with him in 1893, while Mexico was on the verge of a suspension of payment, have created in us such a friendship, if not a recognition on his part, that if I come across almost affectionately in my correspondence to him in offering my support and that of my friends, he is somehow bound to give preference to me over all others." That's a mistake. . . . Mr. Limantour only refers to 1893 to remember what he did, to take credit for the entire recovery of the finances of his country, and I am not convinced that the very friendly tone of correspondence of Noetzlin, instead of appearing affectionate, does not seem, on the contrary a little too familiar. . . . This initial error of Noetzlin, so regrettable, resulted in a false conception of things from the beginning of negotiations.[26]

We might paraphrase Moret that while Noetzlin believed that the Mexican finance minister owed him the loan business because of earlier favors and because they were cronies, Limantour did not share that belief. Instead, as Moret continued, Limantour "wanted above all to obtain a good price for the loan, as a way of showing that an uninterrupted cycle of progress has continued since he took control of Mexican finances, such that in 1893 Mexico borrowed at nine percent, and in 1899 at 5.31% and he can now contract at an effective rate slightly below five percent."[27] Indeed, Limantour played the two syndicates off against each other, and he obtained a better price than had the competing bankers cooperated. But these financial gains, as Moret recognized, served a larger political purpose. By demonstrating financial progress, Finance Minister Limantour was seeking to legitimize the policies of the Mexican state, and more specifically his policies as finance minister. Viewed from this perspective, Limantour's friendly correspondence with Noetzlin over many years can be interpreted, perhaps, as "faux-cronyism," in an effort to stimulate and increase lending alternatives for Mexico. Not all bankers were taken in by these sorts of ploys, or at least they could only be fooled once. Kuhn Loeb's Jacob Schiff, having been party to Limantour's manipulations in 1899, balked at joining the 1904 negotiations on the side of Noetzlin. In September 1904, after Moret visited his offices in New York before traveling to Mexico, Schiff wrote to his friend Cassel that "in the end all of these gentlemen will play into the hand of the very sly Mr. Limantour who will play [Bleichroeder and Banque Paris et des Pays-Bas] off against Speyers and Deutsche Bank, and obtain an unjustifiably high price which will leave a very small profit to the contractors."[28]

Moret also criticized Noetzlin's assumption that Limantour would do virtually anything to open Mexican debt to the Paris Bourse, in part because of his pronounced French affinities. Moret wrote, "Do not forget that he [Limantour] is not considered in the country as a true Mexican, and regardless of his distinguished merits, his French name, his ancestry, his habits are very French, which has been raised by some detractors who have managed to keep him away from the Vice-Presidency."[29] Moret then suggested that Limantour may have not wanted to give more fodder to these detractors and thus opted against a French bank. Finally, because Noetzlin's syndicate partner was the Bleichroeder firm, which had long controlled Mexico's debt, Limantour had diversified the state's credit exposure by concluding the loan with a U.S.-led syndicate. As we have seen, the Mexican state's effort to diversify its foreign creditors was foreshadowed in the 1890s as it established local counterweights to Nacional in public finance. Credit diversification at home and abroad allowed the state to improve the terms and conditions for its debt and provided the regime greater flexibility to pursue its financing options.

CONCLUSION

Over succeeding years, the conflicts continued between the foreign and domestic boards of Nacional in part over banking strategies and partly over confronting the Mexican state. In both cases, the Mexican board adopted the stance of acting in the broadest interests of the country. Indeed, in December 1910, in a letter written to the Paris board, Nacional invoked quite clearly its class and national interests.

Let me remind you that the National Bank of Mexico plays and has always played a role in Mexico that is not simply that of an institution that, without worrying about general circumstances and being inspired only by selfishness, tries only to make a profit, but that, being at its foundation an important regulator of national, public and private credit, in its broadest sense, it has high duties to fulfill, although without ever sacrificing its shareholders and with the aim of having and conserving for them, as it has always had and preserved, the enlightened protection and the benevolent support of public authorities.[30]

It seems clear that the Mexican directors were more easily swayed by nationalism or considerations of the "national interests" than were its foreign directors. The former recognized that the regime generally acted in its long-term interests—in what may be called its class interests. Only when one considers political interests that are not explicable in terms of efficient markets or discrete benefits can one understand the different responses among Nacional's local and foreign shareholders. Issues having to do with the maintenance of state power were important. This suggests that what Hubert Bonin has written about French financiers with respect to their own government was also true of their Porfirian counterparts: "Private interests showed themselves to be strangely malleable and submissive, when, in the name of the general interest, public authorities appropriated for themselves a proportion of the controllers of wealth's inheritance."[31]

As the Díaz regime matured, Nacional's domestic directors identified themselves less as discrete bankers (or as Paris's junior partners) and more as supporters of the regime's general interests. This evolution formed part of the process of the making of a national economic elite, nationalist to the extent that its formation occurred in confrontation with foreign partners and in support of its national government when the latter found itself in conflict with those same foreign partners. Nacional's leaders had extensive and growing stakes in many economic sectors, which depended on political stability and a hospitable climate for external investment. They more readily acceded to the state's wishes and reforms because they were well placed to exploit the opportunities created by legal and institutional change. Moreover, they recognized that opposing the reforms was futile and might threaten their position and privilege.

Similarly, when Noetzlin negotiated with Mexican officials, he was not dealing with business partners per se but public officials whose alleged friendship was always subject to other priorities, concerns, and goals. Among these competing concerns figured the goal of getting the best terms and conditions possible, which meant that these officials often sought competing offers. A second concern was broadly political in the sense of seeking to determine how financial accords might affect political stability and political legitimacy. Often the concern was one of controlling the timing of debt servicing or legislative enforcement, and here bankers and public officials could differ widely. A third concern was more narrowly political in how any negotiation might affect the political standing of the president (or minister) in power.

The conflicts that erupted between the two boards of Nacional were not unique or isolated during the Belle Epoque. Instead they were inherent in the overlapping, hybrid administrative structure that foreign banks sought to impose on the overseas progeny. In fact, Edouard Noetzlin, as a member of various other Comités de Paris for satellite banks in Italy and Russia, faced strikingly analogous confrontations and disputes over local control.[32] It may be that the experiences of Nacional are representative of how far-flung formal and informal networks of credit, mediated through politics, knitted together the global economy in the long era of expansion before World War I. What is certain is that the push of foreign control and pull of local autonomy that defined Nacional's first thirty years of existence continues today at Nacional (now called Banamex) as disputes rage between it and its current foreign patron, Citibank.[33]

NOTES

1. Leonor Ludlow, "El Banco Nacional Mexicano y el Banco Mercantil Mexicano: Radiografía social de sus primeros accionistas, 1881–1882," *Historia Mexicana* 39, no. 4 (1990): 979–1027; Leonor Ludlow and Carlos Marichal, eds., *Banca y poder en México, 1800–1925* (Mexico City: Grijalbo, 1986); Leonor Ludlow and Carlos Marichal, eds., *La banca en México, 1820–1920* (Mexico City: Instituto Mora, 1998).

2. Stephen Haber, "Industrial Concentration and the Capital Markets: A Comparative Study of Brazil, Mexico, and the United States, 1830–1930," *Journal of Economic History* 51 (September 1991): 559–80; Noel Maurer, "Banks and Entrepreneurs in Porfirian Mexico: Inside Exploitation or Sound Business Strategy?," *Journal of Latin American Studies* 31, no. 2 (1999): 331–61; Noel Maurer and Stephen Haber, "Institutional Change and Economic Growth: Banks, Financial Markets, and Mexican Industrialization, 1878–1913," in *The Mexican Economy, 1870–1930*, ed. Jeffrey Borzt and Stephen Haber (Stanford: Stanford University Press, 2002), 23–92.

3. See, for example, some of my earlier work: "Financial Conflict and Cooperation in the Belle Epoque: German Banks in Late Porfirian Mexico, 1889–1910," in *México y la economía atlántica (Siglos XVIII–XX)*, ed. Sandra Kuntz Ficker and Horst Pietschmann (Mexico City: Colegio de México, 2006), 173–203; "Nada de Papeluchos: Managing Globalization in Early Porfirian Mexico," *Latin American Research Review* 42, no. 3 (October 2007): 101–28; "Dynamizing the Economy in a façon irrégulière: A New Look at Financial Politics in Porfirian México," *Mexican Studies / Estudios Mexicanos* 24, no. 1 (Winter 2008): 1–29; "The Politics of Silver

and Gold in an Age of Globalization: Mexico's Monetary Reform of 1905," *América Latina en la Historia Económica*, no. 30 (July–December 2008): 67–95. On the relative autonomy of the Porfirian vis-à-vis economic elites, see Paolo Riguzzi, "From Globalisation to Revolution? The Porfirian Political Economy: An Essay on Issues and Interpretations," *Journal of Latin American Studies* 41, no. 2 (2009): 347–68; Mark Wasserman, *Pesos and Politics: Business, Elites, Foreigners, and Government in Mexico, 1854–1940* (Stanford: Stanford University Press, 2015); John Coatsworth, "Inequality, Institutions and Economic Growth in Latin America," *Journal of Latin American Studies* 40, no. 3 (2008): 545–69; Robert Holden, *Mexico and the Survey of Public Lands: The Management of Modernization, 1876–1911* (DeKalb: Northern Illinois University Press, 1994); Donald Stevens, "Agrarian Policy and Instability in Porfirian Mexico," *The Americas* 39, no. 2 (October 1982): 153–66; and David Walker, "Porfirian Labor Politics: Working Class Organizations in Mexico City and Porfirio Diaz, 1876–1902," *The Americas* 37, no. 3 (January 1981): 257–89.

4. See Leonor Ludlow, "La construcción de un banco: El Banco Nacional de México (1881–1884)," in *Banca y poder en México, 1800–1925*, ed. Leonor Ludlow and Carlos Marichal (Mexico City: Grijalbo, 1986), 299–345.

5. In addition, the European board was designed to bolster public confidence when the bank's shares were traded on the Paris Bourse.

6. On the activities of the Bischoffscheim group in the Ottoman Empire, see James Thobie, "European Banks in the Middle East," in *International Banking, 1870–1914*, ed. Rondo Cameron and V. I. Bovykin (New York: Oxford University Press, 1991), 406–40, esp. 406–13. On the joint-stock banks promoted by Bischoffscheim and Goldschmidt, see Stanley Chapman, *The Rise of Merchant Banking* (Boston: Allen & Unwin, 1984), 133–34. On the interests of these bankers in the 1864 Maximilian debt, see Philip L. Cottrell, "Anglo-French Financial Co-operation, 1850–1880," *Journal of European Economic History* 3, no. 1 (1974): 75–86; and Philip L. Cottrell, "The Coalescence of a Cluster of Corporate International Banks, 1855–75," *Business History* 33, no. 3 (1991): 31–52, which considers the reach of these banks into Latin America. The general story is well known, and is especially well told by David Landes. Beginning in France in the 1850s but steadily gaining momentum in the 1860s (with its arrival to England) and 1870s was a new type of financial institution, the joint-stock bank. See the classic depiction by David Landes in *Bankers and Pashas* (Cambridge, Mass.: Harvard University Press, 1958), chapters 2 and 3, as well as David Landes, "The Old Bank and the New: The Financial Revolution of the Nineteenth Century," *Revue d'Histoire Moderne et Contemporaine* 3 (1956), reprinted in *Essays in European Economic History, 1789–1919*, ed. F. Crouzet, W. H. Chaloner, and W. M. Stern (London: Economic History Society, 1969), 112–27.

7. For a provocative reconsideration of the role that information asymmetries play in inducing capitalists to invest capital in otherwise prohibitively risky political and legal environments, see Philip Keefer, "Protection Against a Capricious State: French Investments and Spanish Railroads, 1845–1875," *Journal of Economic History* 56, no. 1 (1996): 170–92.

8. Cassel, for example, was attached to the London Bischoffscheim group, which had used such tactics to gain access to Ottoman state debt.

9. De Teresa, Struck, and Cuevas to Comité en Paris, March 1, 1887, Archivo Histórico Banco Nacional de México (hereafter AH BNM), Correspondencia del Banco con el Comité de Paris, vol. 1. All translations are mine unless otherwise indicated.

10. De Teresa, Struck, and Cuevas to Comité en Paris, March 1, 1887, AH BNM, Correspondencia del Banco con el Comité de Paris, vol. 1.

11. De Teresa, Struck, and Cuevas to Comité en Paris, March 1, 1887, AH BNM, Correspondencia del Banco con el Comité de Paris, vol. 1.

12. De Teresa, Struck, and Cuevas to Comité en Paris, March 1, 1887, AH BNM, Correspondencia del Banco con el Comité de Paris, vol. 1.

13. Carlos Varona to Comité en Paris, February 15, 1897, AH BNM, Correspondencia del Banco con el Comité de Paris, vol. 2.

14. Carlos Varona to Comité en Paris, June 7, 1897, AH BNM, Correspondencia del Banco con el Comité de Paris, vol. 2.

15. Carlos Varona to Comité en Paris, Cartas al Comité de Paris, December 24, 1897, AH BNM, Correspondencia del Banco con el Comité de Paris, vol. 2.

16. Carlos Varona to Comité en Paris, Cartas al Comité de Paris, December 24, 1897, AH BNM, Correspondencia del Banco con el Comité de Paris, vol. 2.

17. Carlos Varona to Comité en Paris, Cartas al Comité de Paris, December 24, 1897, AH BNM, Correspondencia del Banco con el Comité de Paris, vol. 2.

18. Carlos Varona to Comité en Paris, Cartas al Comité de Paris, April 17, 1897, AH BNM, Correspondencia del Banco con el Comité de Paris, vol. 2.

19. Nacional to Comité en Paris, Cartas al Comité de Paris, January 17, 1899, AH BNM, Correspondencia del Banco con el Comité de Paris, vol. 3.

20. Carlos Varona to Edouard Noetzlin, October 14, 1899, AH BNM, Correspondencia del Banco con el Comité de Paris, vol. 3.

21. Carlos Varona to Edouard Noetzlin, October 14, 1899, AH BNM, Correspondencia del Banco con el Comité de Paris, vol. 3.

22. Carlos Varona to Edouard Noetzlin, October 14, 1899, AH BNM, Correspondencia del Banco con el Comité de Paris, vol. 3.

23. Carlos Varona to Edouard Noetzlin, October 14, 1899, AH BNM, Correspondencia del Banco con el Comité de Paris, vol. 3.

24. The links between financial politics (and more broadly economic policies) and nationalism have been explored by other scholars of the Porfiriato. For a lively and provocative example of how financial diplomacy shaped and was shaped by nationalism, see Steven Topik, "When Mexico Had the Blues: A Transatlantic Tale of Bonds, Bankers, and Nationalists, 1862–1910," *American Historical Review* 105, no. 3 (2000): 714–738. For a broader perspective that also examines nationalist ideology, see Richard Weiner, *Race, Nation, and Market: Economic Culture in Porfirian Mexico* (Tucson: University of Arizona Press, 2004).

25. Emile Moret to Isaac de Camondo, October 17, 1904, Archive Historique Paribas (hereafter AHP).

26. Emile Moret to Isaac de Camondo, October 17, 1904, AHP.

27. Emile Moret to Isaac de Camondo, October 17, 1904, AHP.

28. Jacob Schiff to Ernest Cassel, September 18, 1904, American Jewish Archive, Schiff Papers.

29. Emile Moret to Isaac de Camondo, October 17, 1904, AHP.

30. Sebastián Camacho to E. Huard, December 20, 1910, AH BNM, Correspondencia del Banco con el Comité de Paris, vol. 4.

31. Hubert Bonin, "The Political Influence of Bankers and Financiers in France in the Years 1850–1960," in *Finance and Financiers in European History 1880–1960*, ed. Youssef Cassis (New York: Cambridge University Press, 1992), 239.

32. Writing about relations between Russo-Asiatic Bank's domestic head and its two French directors (one of whom was Noetzlin), V. I. Boykin and Boris Anan'ich observed that "from the outset [they] were at odds over various matters. Part of the problem was the system of the bank management—'Board-Paris Committee,' which proved to be very unwieldy." Various conflicts ensued, with the Russian head alternatively "threatening resignation and demanding greater freedom of action." Ultimately the French bankers "continued to exercise control over the [Bank's] shares, but in its practical activity [it] was guided by its own program." See V. I. Boykin and Boris Anan'ich's superb "The Role of International Factors in the Formation of the Banking System in Russia," in *International Banking, 1870–1914*, ed. Rondo Cameron and V. I. Boykin (New York: Oxford University Press, 1992), 155. For the foreign/domestic board dispute in Italy, also involving Noetzlin, see Antonio Confalonieri, *Banca e industria in Italia, 1894–1906*, vol. 3, *L'esperienza della Banca Commerciale Italiana* (Milan: Banca Commerciale Italiana, 1980).

33. As a March 11, 2014, *New York Times* story (Michael Corkery and Jessica Silver-Greenberg, "Banamex Fraud Exposes Challenges for Citi in Mexico") points out, one of the central issues with Banamex has been its autonomy from Citibank oversight:

> Through his long career as one of Mexico's top bankers, Mr. Medina-Mora has proved adept at navigating the political challenges, according to his former and current associates.
>
> But the bank he built has been considered something of a "black box"—a highly profitable but not especially transparent unit that was run with great autonomy by its leader, according to current and former bank executives. Sometimes, though, that autonomy rankled other executives in New York, the people said.
>
> Ever since Citigroup acquired Banamex in 2001, Mr. Medina-Mora made it clear that "I will take care of Mexico," said one of the former executives who, like the other current and former executives interviewed for this article, declined to be identified. Through a spokesman, Mr. Medina-Mora declined to comment.

"We dispute assertions that the management team is autonomous," a bank spokesman said in a statement. "While Banamex is a subsidiary of Citigroup, it is absolutely subject to the same risk, control, anti-money laundering and technology standards and oversight which are required throughout the company."

The relationship has worked well for more than a decade for Banamex, Citigroup and Mr. Medina-Mora personally.

3

ORDER, PROGRESS, AND THE MODERNIZATION OF RACE, STATE, AND MARKET IN CHIAPAS, MEXICO, 1876–1911

SARAH WASHBROOK

THIS CHAPTER examines the relationship between capitalism, citizenship, and state formation in the southern Mexican state of Chiapas during the regime of Porfirio Díaz (1876–1911). It seeks to highlight how positivist political ideology, scientific racism and racialized practices of state rule, along with political centralization and export-led development contributed to the spread of *caciquismo* and the intensification of coercive practices of labor recruitment, particularly after 1891. It also highlights the coexistence of liberal republican and colonial forms of state rule within the territory of the nation and analyzes how these interacted to aid the consolidation of the state and the development of export agriculture. It concludes that "traditional" ethnic relations and political and economic institutions, such as corporate patriarchy, the Indian community, labor drafts, and debt peonage, were no impediments to export development and "modern" state formation (although they may have hampered the development of market capitalism). Instead, transformed by liberalism, reinterpreted through the lenses of positivism and scientific racism, and managed through a centralized state apparatus, "traditional" colonial forms of rule, rent seeking, and labor control increasingly became the instrumental means to achieve export-led modernity in the last quarter of the nineteenth century.

From 1867 until 1891, the authority of the central state remained weak and Chiapas was divided into a number of powerful *cacicazgos* ruled by military leaders from the Reform period. After 1876 they owed their power to loyalty to Porfirio Díaz's Plan of Tuxtepec.[1] By the late 1880s, though, these caciques were increasingly perceived by many local agricultural and commercial elites, outside investors, and the federal government as obstacles to modernization because they impeded political centralization and undermined investor security in order to further their own local political and economic interests.[2] After Governor Manuel Carrascosa (1888–91) failed to tackle the issue, Emilio Rabasa was appointed state governor by President Porfirio Díaz in 1891. Rabasa rose to prominence in Mexico City, but he was a Chiapaneco from the Central Valley, drawn from the same commercial elites who petitioned the federal executive for a strong centralized government to aid capitalist modernization in Chiapas.[3] He believed Chiapas could become one of the richest commodity-exporting states in Mexico, based on the production of coffee, cacao, and hard woods.[4] In order to end the political intrigues that he perceived were "retarding" economic development, he overhauled the entire bureaucratic and political apparatus.[5] After deftly neutralizing the power of regional caciques, Rabasa replaced customs officials, judges, tax collectors, and office workers with loyal candidates and staffed many of the most important posts with personal appointees from Oaxaca. He also directly named the *jefes políticos* (district governors) for the first time. Finally, he transferred the state capital from the colonial city of San Cristóbal to the growing commercial center of Tuxtla Gutiérrez in the Central Valley.[6] In so doing he strongly favored the economic and political interests of liberal elites in the Central Valley, above all Tuxtlecos with whom he was closely associated, over those of Conservatives in the central highlands.

Between 1891 and 1894, when he stepped down as governor to return to Mexico City, Rabasa improved communications, established a public security force, oversaw education and fiscal reform, and abolished communal property. He centralized and rationalized tax collection, raising revenues and at the same time undermining municipal autonomy vis-à-vis the state and federal governments.[7] Two significant aspects of Rabasa's fiscal reform were the strict enforcement of the head tax and the implementation of a new education tax. The latter instituted a contribution of one peso per year for public education to replace the 1880 *ley de prestación personal*, which had demanded four days of public works from all males (except debt peons) between the ages of sixteen and sixty.[8] However, in practice labor drafts continued and intensified after 1891. Rabasa also abolished communal land tenure and decreed the division of the towns' ejidos into individual parcels to be sold at auction to the highest bidder.[9] These reforms were intended to increase state revenues, stimulate the demand for cash among peasants, thereby contributing to the development of a plantation labor force, and make land available to investors who wished to develop commercial agriculture.

A *científico* and successful jurist, Rabasa was one of Porfirio Díaz's most erudite governors, who eloquently encapsulated in his writings much of the essence of Porfirian political ideology. Perhaps the cornerstone of Rabasa's political thought was the belief that Mexico's 1857 Constitution was fundamentally flawed because it included universal male suffrage, a principle that he opined was based on "abstract," "scientific lies" and not suitable for Mexico's "peculiar conditions."[10] For Rabasa, popular sovereignty was "without value," a mistake derived from conceptual and semantic confusion over the word *pueblo* (the people). In public life, in decisions over a country's destiny, the pueblo could not include "the masses" or "the lower classes" but instead only "the 'active' part of the population," "the sum of those individuals capable of exercising their political rights," "that part of society conscious of national life."[11] It was only possible for the popular will to triumph if every citizen was capable of free will and that, he opined, was impossible without positive knowledge.[12] Suffrage then was not a right but a function that required a certain aptitude, education, or culture.[13] Only a minority of the population were capable of pondering issues of political significance or realizing their electoral potential. The majority, by contrast were "infantile" and "immature."[14] In such a context, universal suffrage was "the enemy of effective government, order [and] progress."[15]

At the heart of this political vision were the issues of race and nation. According to Emilio Rabasa, Mexico was "a new nation being built upon the difficult formation of a race."[16] At independence, he argued, there was "a superior class" born to lead, endowed with the learning of the age and knowledge of contemporary political and philosophical ideas, and an enormous majority, "the lower class," unable to comprehend them.[17] This latter group was "pre-national," "passive," destined to be no more than cannon fodder, and "primitive" in its stage of evolution, able only to follow a leader and not equipped to exercise democracy.[18] It was principally composed of Indians who had not formed part of the "colonial nation" or constituted "part of the people [*el pueblo*] or society" at independence. Instead, national consciousness was exclusive to the creoles and a portion of the mestizos, which together made up the "rational part" of the population.[19] By contrast, the Indian population constituted "three million [inhabitants], morally and intellectually inferior to the Indians of Moctezuma [i.e., the Aztecs], without personality or any idea of it, without any idea or common sense that links them with the conscious part of the population."[20] This "colonial legacy" lacked aspirations of autonomy and a conception of emancipation, was immune to feelings of nationality, and was prone to participate in popular political movements associated with disorder, violence, and religious fanaticism, protagonized by a seductive leader.[21] Indians, then, constituted one of the great "national problems," "the enormous burden of another people [*pueblo*] equal in number [to the whites and civilized mestizos] but without any preparation for adaptation." This was an obstacle unmatched by any other nation but one that could not be dodged, owing to the "inflexible imperative of the moral of modernity."[22]

In the United States, Rabasa argued, giving blacks the vote was now considered "a grave error that ha[d] placed the great nation under the threat of very serious dangers," which "of course ha[d] made it necessary for politicians from the South to have recourse to tricks in order to deceive the colored people and mock their electoral rights."[23] Thus, in Mexico he opined:

> It would seem incredible to have to even discuss the political exclusion of men who are because of their ignorance as incapacitated from voting as madmen and idiots. Men who have not entered into the community of consciousness; for whom there is no epoch; who have not experienced any evolution, whether the government is to blame or not. Among this group there are entire populations; ignorant of the national language, they have not even had contact with the civilized world and they have today the same notion of national government as they had of the privileges of the Crown in the sixteenth century.[24]

There was no abstract equality and Indians should not be entitled to rights of citizenship that they were unable to fulfill due to their "lack of active capacity."[25]

According to Rabasa, racial improvement was to be achieved through a Darwinist process of natural selection. For that reason, he favored "the colonizing invasion of civilized families into regions or towns of isolated Indians."[26] It was only through the survival of the fittest that races could "arrive at human dignity."[27] Consequently, Rabasa was highly skeptical about the power of schooling to civilize Indians and believed that educational resources should be concentrated instead on "the part [of society] already prepared for national life . . . since they are the ones who will give stability and strength to the nation."[28] Indeed, it was contact with "superior castes" that would transform the mentality of the Indian rather than formal schooling, and only after he had acquired a new mentality would the Indian be capable of taking advantage of school instruction.[29] In this respect, better communications, commercial expansion, and the development of mining and agriculture, all of which would increase dealings between "the backward race" and national society, were the best means for civilizing Indians, although progress would be slow, difficult, and painful.[30]

In practice both positivists such as Rabasa and more conservative elites supported debt servitude and obligatory labor for economic and racial reasons. However, while the latter favored peonage because of the key role that it played in the maintenance of social and racial hierarchies and because they believed that it afforded the appropriate paternalistic means by which to educate and discipline the Indian population, those who subscribed to positivism and social Darwinism tended to view Indians instrumentally and to believe that debt servitude and forced labor in general were justified because Indians were neither fit to exercise their constitutional rights nor able to meet the demands of modernity, which required labor for national and international commodity markets. Therefore, as Richard Weiner notes, liberals in the Porfiriato increasingly "championed legal forms of coercion such as vagrancy laws, mandatory consumption, and employing labor contractors."[31] The idea that Indians were a "little-evolved race that could not be propelled forward by market forces . . . opened up the possibilities of coercion."[32] In Chiapas, this point of view served as an ideological justification for the forced trafficking of Indian workers to export-oriented plantations and logging camps, which grew rapidly after 1890.

Such practices were increasingly denounced in the opposition highland press after 1900, although most articles principally blamed the Indians themselves for their "ignorance" and alcoholism that made them prone to such abuses.[33] An alternative position, though, was expressed in opposition newspapers such as the Catholic weekly *La Voz de Chiapas*, which circulated at the beginning of the revolutionary period. This newspaper directly blamed Porfirian political centralization for forced labor recruitment and other abuses committed against Indians. The jefes políticos, who were appointed by the state governor after 1892, were singled out as the key elements in a government that ruled "without law or justice . . . sustaining its authority with an iron hand and incredible despotism."[34] They were said to be

worse than a plague, hard and despotic with the humble, they do nothing more than exploit them and fill their own bottomless pockets with the sweat of the[ir] brow . . . but if the[y] [the people] complain worse things will happen to them; because in Chiapas the jefes políticos are sacred [along with] all the other authorities . . . [who are] able to tyrannize at will, assured of impunity and [guaranteed] that whoever so dares to complain will be severely punished. Forced labor [*el batallón*], the security force, police service . . . all absolutely unpaid, prison or other shameful alternatives, these are the methods used by those who govern to achieve obedience and silence their critics.[35]

The power of the jefe político stemmed from the complete lack of oversight of his activities by other branches of government, a situation that was institutionalized by a system of personalist political centralization that undermined electoral politics and tightly controlled dissent.

The jefe político, omnipotent in his power, has more authority than [the emperor] Negus Menelik of Ethiopia; and the [district] judge has more than the Supreme Court. They are two authorities appropriate to the rule of Nero and what is most serious . . . is that if one complains to the governor he does not believe what one says; but instead that one is insulting such good men; and if one does the same with the [state] Supreme Court the procedure is a farce that leaves things how they are or in a worse state for the complainant who [finds] no alternative but to emigrate.[36]

Thus, *La Voz de Chiapas* argued, only the executive had a voice because it was the governor who chose the judiciary, the legislature, and the administration on the basis of loyalty and cronyism.[37]

The result, according to the newspaper, was an especially cruel variant of "caciquismo," motivated by extortion and sustained by force, in which the jefes políticos were the prime culprits.[38] Indians were the principal victims—deprived of all rights—and exploited shamefully for financial gain by state officials, who made them work "like animals" and "slaves," unpaid in public services and private properties owned by the officials and their friends. Many Indian towns, such as Cancuc, Bachajón, and San Andrés, had been desolated because the municipal secretaries, following the orders of the jefe político, had sold numerous inhabitants to labor contractors (*enganchadores*).[39]

The abuse of state power was systematic in Porfirian Chiapas, most notably in the predominantly Indian districts, which were considered by politicians and investors as the principal source of labor for the export sector. In 1904 the opposition newspaper *El Clavel Rojo* accused the jefes políticos of Chilón and neighboring Palenque of being at the heart of a "trade in human flesh" associated with all the "horrors of slavery," and in 1911 *La Voz de Chiapas* directly blamed the Rabasas for the "crimes" and "slavery" of the logging camps (*monterías*) of Chilón.[40] Indeed, both *La Voz de Chiapas* and another Catholic newspaper, *Mas Allá*, agreed that such impunity and "caciquismo" were the direct product of rule by the Rabasa family, which governed the state as a "hereditary fief," doling out positions of authority to favorites in its circle, which were drawn from members of the Tuxtleco camarilla and sympathetic lackeys from the neighboring state of Oaxaca.[41] Archival evidence strongly suggests that *enganche* (labor contracting via wage advances) to the large coffee and rubber plantations and monterías in Chilón and neighboring Palenque was not just the result of ad hoc corruption at the municipal or even district level but was instead a deliberate policy born of the personal, political, and financial links between big investors, the federal government, and Rabasistas in Chiapas.[42]

Throughout Mexico during the Porfiriato, the jefes políticos were increasingly appointed from the center. They served to control electoral politics, undermine municipal autonomy, and enable the national government or select regional interests to impose their will in the provinces.[43] However, as agents of modernization the *jefaturas políticas* (district governments) were highly problematic, for as Romana Falcón points out, the office was one that "concentrated any number and variety of functions," thus betraying "its primitive character and its position as an obstacle to the processes of modernization and administrative and political rationality."[44] The "extensive legal functions" and "greater authority" of the jefaturas "fostered extended networks of patronage and clientele" and in practice "the jefes políticos imposed their dominance through traditional, personalist, petty, corrupt, and inefficient means, often to the detriment of the formal image and capacity of the state."[45] They were thoroughly unaccountable entities, which institutionalized arbitrary behavior, encouraged personal domination, and invited clientelism. Furthermore, "the political and military machinery at the jefaturas'" disposal led them almost naturally to shape an extremely authoritarian and closed structure of power.[46] On the one hand, their "combination of legal functions[and personal dominance . . . enabled the[m] . . . to run relatively efficient political machines, and to utilize them for integrating, channeling or repressing those who made demands or who refused to accept the rules of the game."[47] But, on the other hand, "the jefes' very excesses, their corruption, ineptitude, and inflexibility translated into structural weaknesses for the old regime."[48]

In Chiapas, as in the rest of the republic, the powers of the jefe político were wide-ranging, multifaceted, and authoritarian. One of the principal legislative tools at the jefe político's disposal was the 1880 Regulation of Police and Good Government. This document facilitated increased state control over rural, and specifically Indian, labor through the tighter regulation of vagrancy and alcohol consumption. Thus, alcohol could be legally sold in Indian towns only during fiestas and on Sundays and on haciendas with the permission of the *finquero*, and domestic servants and debt peons were prohibited from leaving their masters "to give themselves over to leisure or drunkenness." The municipal presidents and rural judges were to send a register of all those in their area of jurisdiction who lacked goods or income, along with a list of any ladino men, to the jefatura política so that "jefes políticos and municipal presidents [could] . . . provide a suitable profession, art, post or occupation to each depending on class and condition and to the Indians who do not have regular employment."[49]

The jefes políticos principally governed in the countryside by means of unelected municipal agents and municipal secretaries, many of whom were also schoolteachers, and, increasingly after 1900, via municipal presidents appointed from above. The jefe político usually chose these subordinates from among one or two ladino families in each municipality, who were paid with a share of the profits from tax collection, alcohol monopolies, and labor contracting. Indeed, according to a government circular of 1903, many of the individuals who operated as municipal agents and committed numerous abuses in Indian towns had no legal authority and were simply clients of the jefe político.[50] As the opposition *La Voz de Chiapas* highlighted, such caciquismo had its roots in the patrimonial nature of centralized state authority: "Here a jefe político ignorant and despotic; there an alcalde or municipal president inflated and cruel; over there an agent of the jefatura as pretentious and tyrannical as he is stupid and ruffian, and still . . . they are caciques with no more authority than that of *compadrazgo*, friendship or family relationships with 'those above.'"[51] Thus, although the municipal authorities were supposed to be chosen by and accountable to the local population, the centralization of power meant that they were appointed by and responsible to the jefe político and ultimately the state and federal governments.[52] These caciques acted as mediators between the towns and an increasingly centralized government apparatus, by "controlling and manipulating the channels of communication, especially of the system of authority."[53] They also, crucially, used their power to control land and labor in a context of rising market demand and commercial opportunity.[54]

This system was not invented during the Porfiriato but constituted an intensification and adaptation of earlier state-building efforts, now given greater direction and impulse by the expansion of export markets and the growing hegemony of the federal government throughout the republic. In Chiapas, secular state building had resumed following the end of the Caste War of 1869–70, with ladino schoolteachers at the forefront of the drive to reestablish the authority of the state government.[55] After 1871 schoolteachers often filled the unelected post of municipal agent or were appointed municipal secretary in Indian town governments. They oversaw tax collection, recruited laborers, and frequently monopolized trade, above all the sale of alcohol, as they had done in the past. But now they did so with less oversight and competition from priests.[56] Indeed, the power and authority of liberal public authorities derived in part from the usurpation of the "traditional" monopolies and caste privileges formerly enjoyed by priests.

This particular process of secular state building is well documented in the predominantly Indian districts of Palenque and Chilón in northern Chiapas. There, after the end of the Caste War, the declining power of the Catholic Church was accompanied by accelerating agrarian commercialization. In 1874 the priest of Tumbalá, José Fernando Macal, complained to the bishop that the local population had lost interest in the Catholic religion and that instead of paying church dues to him, they were paying "tribute" to the Protestant schoolteacher.[57] By 1880 the inhabitants of Tila and Yajalón were also apparently "completely subject" to the will of their schoolteacher, Don Carmen Trujillo. In Petalcingo, Sabanilla, and Moyos it was a similar story. Throughout the region civil marriage had come to replace church unions and the only baptisms were in Tumbalá. Yet in that town the priest had been marginalized from ritual life, which was now organized by Indian men and women, and he no longer received rations or unpaid labor.[58]

However, this was no golden age for Indian peasants. The waning of ecclesiastical power provided finqueros as well as secular officials with the opportunity to strengthen and exploit their authority as paternal mediators between Indians, the state, and the expanding market. Thus, observed the priest of Tila in 1878:

> The indigenous class has been converted into an article of speculation for the jefe políticos and their subalterns, and the consequence of this has been the extinction of many parishes, because, lacking free men able to meet their own needs, there are [even] fewer to undertake the ritual observances and unpaid

services [*prestaciones*] of the parish. . . . [Instead] the miserable wretches have become trapped on the properties of foreigners [, which] has been the kiss of death for their religious beliefs . . . and what's more unfortunate [in] those towns that have lost part of their ejido, such as Chilón and Yajalón, [the inhabitants] not having anywhere to work anymore, go to the foreigners, but to become corrupted. Now we have taken away your prestige, a young German said to me in conversation, now they obey us more than their priest; we marry them, we call the man and the woman and we say that they are married: go to live happily together.[59]

Growing secularization, like land privatization, became associated with greater landlord power and the expansion of unfree labor. For example, just two years later, the municipal president of Tila complained to the jefe político that demands for porters had reached a level that was now unsustainable for the community. The trader Segundo Trujillo (very likely a relative of the schoolteacher) was contracting Indians against their will to transport large quantities of goods to Tabasco, and besides being inadequately paid, the Indians were forced to abandon their own agricultural activities for the duration of the trip.[60]

However, despite being increasingly pressed into working as porters (*cargadores*) between San Cristóbal and the Gulf Coast, the Chol Indians of Tila and Tumbalá still retained community lands on which they produced maize, cacao, and pigs for market.[61] That changed when those lands were acquired by foreign coffee planters in the early 1890s. Shortly afterward the government put the schoolteachers in charge of recruiting plantation labor. Thus, in a letter of 1892, President Porfirio Díaz instructed Chiapas's state governor, Emilio Rabasa, to "protect" the interests of coffee cultivators in Palenque. He suggested that the German planters should approach the local authorities, in particular the schoolteachers, so that "by means of intelligent and opportune advice and encouragement" a labor force could be mobilized for coffee.[62] Rabasa, in fact, had already given German businessmen in San Cristóbal letters of recommendation to show to the local authorities in Palenque several months earlier.[63] Indeed, in 1891 the inhabitants of Tila accused the schoolteacher, who was employed by the Körtum brothers of the coffee plantation Mumunil, of destroying their communal cacao plantations and replacing them with private plantings of coffee and rubber.[64] Four years later, according to the priest, a new, particularly "vicious" schoolteacher arrived in Tila; this teacher controlled labor contracting more tightly than his predecessor, even charging the priest twenty-five cents a day per laborer for repairs to the church. The Indian government also objected to the new ladino schoolteacher from Ocosingo. They tried to burn down his house and managed to destroy the thousand coffee trees that he had planted in the town.[65]

Initially, there were also troubles in the relationship between foreign investors and ladino schoolteachers. In 1893, for example, German planters in the municipality of Tumbalá complained that the schoolteacher-municipal agent, who was also the jefe político's cousin, was making excessive profits at their expense.[66] His official salary was only 120 pesos per year, but he was taking 250–300 pesos a month from the enganche of workers to foreign coffee plantations.[67] To smooth out such problems and ensure that the Germans got a better deal, Emilio Rabasa enlisted the services of the president of the Superior Tribunal of Justice in San Cristóbal, Ausencio Ruíz, who mobilized the schoolteachers to recruit Indian laborers more in accordance with the needs of the export sector.[68]

Thus, schoolteachers overseen and coordinated by the jefe político became agents of Porfirian economic and political modernization in Palenque and other regions of Chiapas. Paradoxically, these public officials were considered by the government to be contributing to the positivistic progress of the state. Yet much of their authority rested on and reinforced colonial relations of paternalism, caste, and graft. For example, in the case of the schoolteacher of Tumbalá, as well as earning money from enganche, he took a cut of the fees that he charged for services such as funerals and baptisms, the taxes he levied on transport, the slaughter of livestock and the sale of meat, and fines for an assortment of misdemeanors, as well as receiving free rations of maize, beans, eggs, and chickens, and the services of a woman to grind maize (*molendera*) and of schoolchildren who served him as *mozos* on a weekly basis, just as had the priests before him.[69]

Of central importance to the shape and success of state building and labor recruitment in Chiapas after 1892 was taxation. According to François-Xavier Guerra, Chiapas fell among the Mexican states with the highest fiscal burden in 1910, more than four pesos per inhabitant.[70] The state budget also was in the category of highest growth nationally—600–900 percent—between 1878 and 1910.[71] The centerpiece of taxation in Chiapas was the revamped colonial head tax (*capitación personal*), which had been reintroduced by the state government in 1869. In 1892 Emilio Rabasa revised the existing law to increase the coverage and enforcement of the tax. In so doing he converted personal taxation into the principal means by which the jefes políticos, and through them the executive, exerted authority in the countryside. The jefe político, civil registrar, and municipal president were made responsible for deciding who should be on the tax rolls.

The jefes políticos were rewarded with between 8 and 12 percent of the income they received, while the municipal presidents were allowed to keep 4 percent, from which they paid those subordinates who actually collected the tax. The jefes políticos and their agents were also authorized to use coercion when contributors did not pay, and defaulters were considered to be vagrants who could be consigned by the respective authority for judgment and correction, including the sale of their debt to a third party such as a labor contractor.[72] Officially, if the authorities were found to have charged the head tax arbitrarily, they were severely fined. However, as a government circular of 1896 noted, the lack of an independent system of oversight meant that such infractions were systematic.[73] The result, according to the Catholic opposition, was a "feudal" tributary system in which the jefe político, chosen directly by the state governor after 1892, re-created the role of the *encomendero* (a Spaniard granted Indian tributaries), aided by private helpers who dispossessed Indians of goods and resources far beyond the official rate of taxation.[74] The modern state, then, rested on what were perceived by many as premodern fiscal practices and the systematic abuse of power.

Guerra also notes that Chiapas was one of the three Mexican states with the lowest levels of primary schooling in 1910, and the state stood in the bottom three in terms of literacy, along with Oaxaca and Guerrero, all of which had a rate of less than 15 percent.[75] It seems, therefore, that little of the state's increased fiscal revenue was spent on schools, a policy consistent with Emilio Rabasa's beliefs concerning the low value of educating Indians, who made up the majority of the population. Rabasa did, nevertheless, introduce a new education tax in 1892, which like the head tax was paid by all men between the ages of sixteen and sixty. Indeed, in 1894 Rabasa claimed to have established more than one hundred primary schools in the state. But, on taking office in 1895, his successor, Francisco León, complained of the "shocking void" that he found in public education, "the strangest thing being that even after investing considerable quantities in this area, the practical result has remained virtually nil. . . . In Chamula, for example, there has always been a schoolteacher there, and one cannot find even three individuals who know how to read."[76] In 1911 *La Voz de Chiapas* commented that Indians paid thousands of pesos in public education tax, but even the luckiest Indian towns had only a rundown school attended by eight to nine pupils, who were "taught" by a teacher who was often illiterate himself.[77] The budget for 1901 shows that state expenditure on public education heavily favored the district of Tuxtla. Predominantly Indian districts, such as Comitán, Simojovel, Chamula, Chilón, and Palenque, by contrast, paid more of the education tax but received much less of the budget.[78] Thus, the education tax of 1892 principally served to tax Indian peasants and laborers, to pay for limited public education in ladino towns in the central valley and the Pacific Coast, and to subsidize improvements in infrastructure that would further the reach of the state and aid the development of the export economy.[79]

The politics of the education tax are well illustrated in the case of the district of Chamula, which attracted the attention of Governor Francisco León in 1895. Chamula had the lowest literacy rate and highest proportion of Indians in the state. In 1904 there were 8,276 taxpayers who paid the state around 8,000 pesos per year in education tax.[80] In 1901 the state spent 1,140 pesos on teachers' salaries in the six schools and in 1902 rented buildings in San Andrés and Chamula for 60 pesos per year.[81] Although there were approximately 9,500 children under the age of fourteen in the district, there were only 204 children enrolled in school.[82] In 1901 Rafael Pimentel began work on the Escuela Regional de Indígenas in San Andrés in the district of Chamula. He planned that 200 pupils would attend the school to learn reading, writing, and arithmetic and that the best would go on to study at the Normal school.[83] The records of the jefatura show that the state government provided thousands of pesos to fund the construction of the school. However, the Indians who built it were not paid for their labor. Instead, as the jefe político, Manuel J. Trejo, explained to the governor in 1904, fifty men per week were requisitioned for "tequio," a pre-Columbian term that meant "unpaid community service," and sent by the municipal presidents of the different towns within the district to work on the school.[84] In his memoir, the former priest of Chamula remembered how Manuel Trejo

> had been rich, but he was almost bankrupt owing to a number of bad business deals when he received the post [of jefe político]. Of course, he dedicated himself to recouping his capital by thousands of means, but his favorite system was that of public works. He built a huge building for regional schooling and did so by imposing enormous demands on the unlucky Indians, whom he made work without rest. By means of various agents he exploited the towns, Chamula being the worst hit.[85]

Apparently, by 1910 the school building stood abandoned, having never been used for teaching.[86]

As the example of the Escuela Regional de Indígenas illustrates, although Rabasa's public education tax of 1892 officially replaced corvée labor, the district authorities continued to consign Indians to public works while levying the new tax. Indeed, public works drafts seem to have become more common after 1891. For example, in 1910 members of the Indian population of Ocosingo complained to the governor that for the previous twenty years they had been obliged to work unpaid on public works such as the construction of a church, the municipal palace, two bridges, and a school, even though such "customs" were unconstitutional and the municipality, rich with cash from the logging business, could afford to pay them. In addition, although one-third of the population was ladino, they had never been called upon to labor on public works.[87] The municipal presidents of other towns in Chilón, including Bachajón, Cancuc, Oxchuc, and San Martín, also sent men on a weekly basis to public works in Ocosingo, as well as engaging them in public works in their own towns.[88]

The increase in unpaid public works was only in part due to budgetary constraints. Corruption also played a large part. As the priest of Chamula observed, public works were often a "favorite" means through which public officials could profit from their post. Consequently, they were very inventive in the schemes they employed and the justifications they made. For example, in 1904, when faced by a request from the governor for men to work on the road from San Cristóbal to Comitán for the wage of twenty-five centavos per day, Manuel Trejo perversely argued was that it would be "unfair" for some Indians to receive a salary for public works when others had already worked unpaid on the construction of the school—thus in the interests of justice it would be better that none were paid! The more practical reason was that such differences would test the limits of his authority—all the men wanted to work on the road and consequently the municipal presidents were unable to recruit workers for the school unless that work too was salaried.[89]

Frequently, as in Chamula, when money was available for public works, the local authorities took the cash and forced the local population to work unwaged. For example, in 1910 the inhabitants of San Pedro Remate in Mariscal complained that the 800 pesos sent by the state government to cover the costs of road building had been pocketed by the schoolteacher and the municipal president, who were lending the money out privately at 5 percent interest per month and forcing the population to work unpaid on the road.[90] In 1910 the residents of the town of Ixtapangajoya in Pichucalco complained to the state governor that the municipal president, authorized by the jefe político, was forcing the town's inhabitants to work on the national road for half the official wage—the other half of which was kept by the authorities. The salary was not sufficient to buy food and pay taxes, they were badly treated by the overseers, and only Indian peasants were summoned for public works.[91] The municipal president of Juárez, Pichucalco, went even further. The residents of the municipality complained to the state Superior Tribunal of Justice in 1910 that not only did the municipal president oblige them to work for twelve days on the road unpaid, but he charged them twelve pesos each! Alternatively, they were forced to sign a token so that he could claim the money from the federal government. Those who refused to sign were imprisoned and denied food or water until they did so.[92]

Much of the power of the jefes políticos and their subordinates stemmed from the authority to enforce public order and vagrancy statutes as well as tax collection. They thus fined and imprisoned the population for a number of poorly defined misdemeanors, including drunkenness, disobedience, lack of respect toward authority, assault, verbal assault, and drunken and scandalous behavior.[93] Most of these fines were never reported or handed over to the state treasury by the jefes políticos.[94] Furthermore, in addition to the education and head taxes, municipal transit taxes (*alcabalas*) continued to be collected by the local authorities long after their abolition in 1889, as did numerous other arbitrary contributions.

For example, in Oxchuc in the district of Chilón, a number of inhabitants had complained to the governor about the municipal agent, Margarito Penagos, in 1898. They alleged that he had altered the tax rolls in order to overcharge the head tax; he fined the inhabitants five pesos each for drunkenness and for not attending saints' day celebrations (where they would be obliged to participate in ritual alcohol consumption); and he taxed them one peso for entering the town square. Even though he was not qualified to oversee the civil register, he charged between one and ten pesos for each death certificate and eight and twelve pesos for a marriage certificate. Penagos had a monopoly on the sale of alcohol and groceries and severely punished any commercial rivals. He confiscated many people's lands and demanded unpaid labor on his properties. Finally, he contracted workers for local finqueros on a commission basis, asking twelve reales (1.5 pesos) per week for each worker and paying only six reales (0.75 pesos). The Indians had previously complained about Penagos's "greed and arbitrary actions." But their complaints had led only to greater abuse. Indeed, authorized by the jefe político and the district magistrate, he had jailed fifteen of their children and siblings and undertaken "cruel attacks" against their families in retaliation for their "cry[ing] out against such injustice."[95] Similarly, in 1910 the inhabitants of San Pablo in the neighboring district of Simojovel complained to the governor about the "abuses committed daily" by the municipal secretary, Pomposo Martínez.

> He is today the terror of the town; for without the least consideration and without hearing pleas or cries, he treats our poor families with cruel despotism, imposing unjust fines and taxes that we never had to pay before, such as 2 reales [25 centavos] for each death certificate, 1 real [12.5 centavos] alcabala for each pig that we sell, and under the pretext of the construction of the *cabildo*, he fines all those who do not go to work on it, even though he does not pay them even a single cent. After getting the poor Indians of the town drunk [due to his alcohol monopoly] he arrests them and frees them only after they have paid a fine of at least 2 pesos.[96]

Martínez had succeeded his brother in the post after the latter was dismissed by the jefe político "for abuse of power."

Ideas of race, racialized practices of state rule, patrimonialism, political centralization, and rising market demand for labor constituted key factors in the growth and consolidation of caciquismo in Chiapas during the Porfiriato. Power, however, was not solely exercised by ladinos. Instead, as Greg Grandin has argued for Guatemala, patriarchal power within the Indian community and the divisions of power and wealth that this engendered were crucial for determining ethnic relations and state formation.[97] In Chiapas, too, political and kinship institutions within Indian society were both the means through which Indian society negotiated state rule and the way in which the state was able to coerce and elicit conformity with its demands. State officials mobilized the patriarchal authority of the Indian cabildo and the civil-religious hierarchy of male elders—*principales*—as well as rivalries between lineages and barrios to better repress dissent, extract forced labor and taxation, and enforce debt contracts.[98] Select Indian authorities also used the power of the central state to bolster their own hegemony within the community vis-à-vis factional rivals. Thus, the caste and class power of loyal Indian political elites played a key role in the formation of the state and the hegemony of the Porfirian regime throughout Chiapas.

Congruent with Porfirian centralization, municipal presidents in Indian towns were increasingly appointed by the jefe político. Other members of the town government often had to pay a fee to the municipal agent in order to "triumph in the elections."[99] But this policy served to co-opt as well as to coerce. For example, in 1898 a number of Indians from Oxchuc who wrote to the governor for a second time complaining about the abuses of the municipal agent, Margarito Penagos, observed that "our [previous] complaints gave rise to greater abuses. . . . Many of us were imprisoned, others persecuted *and a few flattered with the posts of municipal president and regidores.*"[100]

Further evidence highlights the role played by the Indian political authorities as key intermediaries between the state and the Indian population. In 1904 the jefe político of the district of Chamula, Manuel Trejo, explained to the governor that he collected taxes, requisitioned labor, and policed the communities through the municipal presidents of the Indian towns, who made the population comply by deploying the *mayores* or *comisionados*.[101] Seven years later *La Voz de Chiapas* remarked that the municipal presidents who, "invested with limitless power, consider themselves sultans . . . look on the citizens as defenseless, insignificant beings," and implemented their orders by deploying native police known as "comisionados" or "mayores."[102] A comisionado, according to the newspaper,

> was a poor individual . . . named from above . . . obliged to police [the town] on certain nights during one whole year; who receives an arbitrary number of blank tax receipts that he must get rid of using his talents as best he can; who will be sent to prison if he does not keep a good watch; who will have to send to the jefatura the money to cover the number of head and education tax receipts he was given; and in case of [a shortfall] . . . he will be held personally responsible for paying the outstanding balance . . . on pain of imprisonment.[103]

These obligations were detested by many Indians, but they were imposed primarily by the native hierarchy—both the cabildo and the principales—rather than the state government, and dissent was discouraged by tradition as much as by force.

A legal case from 1906 further illustrates the point. That year, the ladino Mariano Franco, a shoemaker and trader from San Cristóbal, brought a criminal case against the Indian municipal president of Oxchuc, Martín Luna, for the "premeditated" abuse of authority. Franco claimed that even though he had presented Luna with a permit from San Cristóbal guaranteeing him the right to sell alcohol during the period of carnival, the alcaldes, under orders from the municipal president, had confiscated his merchandise—180 liters of aguardiente—and forced Franco's porters to take it to the town hall of Oxchuc.[104] As Juan Blasco notes, the 1880 law of policing and good government that prohibited the sale of alcohol in roadside hamlets and in Indian towns on days other than Sundays and feast days was honored in the breach and virtually never the observance, because almost all the ladino municipal secretaries and schoolteachers and traditional Indian authorities participated in the business.[105] However, the law did serve as an instrument to keep competitors out during most days of the year.

The case gives us an insight into the politics of the alcohol sector and the way in which state regulation and taxation were used to prop up arbitrary power and monopoly profits. It also shows the ways in which Indians could use deference to the norms of the dominant society to defend themselves and their interests. Playing to ladino prejudices, the Indian authorities presented their illiteracy and ignorance as an excuse for refusing to accept Franco's permit—even though they had to be familiar with such receipts in their capacity as tax collectors. Furthermore, to counter Franco's accusations that the municipal authorities had purposefully sought to impede his commercial activities, they justified their unusually rapid and zealous enforcement of public order legislation by invoking the stereotype of the Indian man—susceptible to the vice of alcoholism and, once drunk, prone to violence, vagrancy, and disrespect for authority. It was therefore better to be safe than sorry.

Finally, and crucially, the case illustrates that, far from being outside the state, the Indian authorities constituted an integral part of state power that reached deep inside the communities—constituting and constituted by a hierarchy of patronage and entrepreneurial activity—from the governor to the jefe político, through the municipal agent, secretary, or schoolteacher, to the municipal authorities, civil-religious hierarchy, and the Indian police, known as mayores or comisionados, who helped the members of the town government collect taxes, recruit workers, and enforce the "superior orders" dictated from above. This structure, then, was highly centralist, subverting the principle of municipal autonomy through a combination of "modern" Porfirian authoritarianism and patriarchal colonial institutions; and it was highly corrupt. However, it was also a structure that depended on the cooperation of some Indians and rewarded their complicity in the exploitation of their neighbors. In Chiapas coercion was undeniable, but complicity and the consent of a privileged few were also necessary.

NOTES

1. Thomas Benjamin, *El Camino al Leviatán: Chiapas y el estado mexicano, 1891–1947* (Mexico City: Consejo Nacional para la Cultural y el Arte, 1990), 44.

2. Antonio García de León, *Resistencia y utopía: Memorial de agravios y crónica de revueltas y profecías acaecidas en la provincia de Chiapas durante los últimos 500 años de su historia*, 2 vols. (Mexico City: Era, 1985), 1:171; Thomas Benjamin, *A Rich Land, a Poor People: Politics and Society in Modern Chiapas* (Albuquerque: University of New Mexico Press, 1989), 30; Colonel Telesforo Merodio to P. Díaz, July 11, 1888, Archivo General Porfirio Díaz (hereafter AGPD), La Universidad Iberoamericana, Mexico City, leg. XIII, exp. 7025.

3. Benjamin, *A Rich Land*, 40.

4. "Discurso por el Licenciado Emilio Rabasa, Gobernador del estado, ante la Legislativa XVIII para abrir su primer periodo de sesiones ordinaries, Tuxtla Gutiérrez," September 16, 1893, Instituto Nacional de Arqueología e Historia (hereafter INAH), Bibilioteca Manuel Orozco y Berra, Archivo Chiapas, roll 9.

5. E. Rabasa to P. Díaz, November 30, 1892, AGPD, leg. XVII, exp. 19861.

6. Benjamin, *A Rich Land*, 42–44.

7. Benjamin, *A Rich Land*, 46.

8. "Congressional decree," November 29, 1892, INAH, Museo de Antropología, Serie Chiapas, roll 84.

9. "Congressional decree," August 11, 1892, INAH, Museo de Antropología, Serie Chiapas, roll 78, vol. XXVIII.

10. Emilio Rabasa, *La organización política de México: La constitución y la dictadura* (Madrid: Editorial América, 1920), 93–95. All translations are mine unless otherwise indicated.

11. Rabasa, *La organización política de México*, 4.

12. Rabasa, *La organización política de México*, 184.

13. Rabasa, *La organización política de México*, 183.

14. Rabasa, *La organización política de México*, 171, 184.

15. Rabasa, *La organización política de México*, 173.

16. Rabasa, *La organización política de México*, 165.

17. Rabasa, *La organización política de México*, 64.

18. Rabasa, *La organización política de México*, 191, 58, 190.

19. Emilio Rabasa, *La evolución histórica de México* (Mexico City: Imprenta Franco-Mexicana, 1920), 29, 241.

20. Rabasa, *La evolución histórica de México*, 241.

21. Rabasa, *La evolución histórica de México*, 241, 37, 39.

22. Rabasa, *La evolución histórica de México*, 235.

23. Rabasa, *La organización política de México*, 186.

24. Rabasa, *La organización política de México*, 189.

25. Rabasa, *La evolución histórica de México*, 244.

26. Rabasa, *La evolución histórica de México*, 270.

27. Rabasa, *Evolución histórico de México*, 270.

28. Rabasa, *La evolución histórica de México*, 265.

29. Rabasa, *La evolución histórica de México*, 269.

30. Rabasa, *La evolución histórica de México*, 280.

31. Richard Weiner, *Race, Nation and Market Economy: Economic Culture in Porfirian Mexico* (Tucson: University of Arizona Press, 2004), 39.

32. Weiner, *Race, Nation and Market Economy*, 39.

33. See, for example, *El Clavel Rojo*, October 2, 1904; and *Periódico Oficial de Chiapas*, November 1, 1889.

34. *La Voz de Chiapas*, February 12, 1911.

35. *La Voz de Chiapas*, March 12, 1911.

36. *La Voz de Chiapas*, May 14, 1911.

37. *La Voz de Chiapas*, February 12, 1911.

38. *La Voz de Chiapas*, March 12, 1911.

39. *La Voz de Chiapas*, April 9, 1911.

40. *El Clavel Rojo*, October 2, 1904; *La Voz de Chiapas*, March 12, 1911; *La Voz de Chiapas*, February 19, 1911.

41. *La Voz de Chiapas*, April 2, 1911; *Mas Allá*, November 19, 1910.

42. See Sarah Washbrook, *Producing Modernity in Mexico: Labour, Race and the State in Chiapas, 1876–1914* (Oxford: Oxford University Press, 2012), 181–85.

43. Romana Falcón, "Force and the Search for Consent: The Role of the Jefaturas Políticas de Coahuila in National State Formation," in *Everyday Forms of State Formation*, ed. Gilbert Joseph and Daniel Nugent (Durham, N.C.: Duke University Press, 1994), 109, 117–18, 122, 127–29.

44. Falcón, "Force and the Search for Consent," 126.

45. Falcón, "Force and the Search for Consent," 110.

46. Falcón, "Force and the Search for Consent," 107.

47. Falcón, "Force and the Search for Consent," 110.

48. Falcón, "Force and the Search for Consent," 112.

49. "Reglamento de policía y buen gobierno," June 1, 1880, Biblioteca Na Bolom, San Cristóbal de Las Casas.

50. "Circular 18, Secretaría de Gobernación de Chiapas," August 25, 1903, AGPD, leg. XXVIII, exp. 15736.

51. *La Voz de Chiapas*, February 2, 1911.

52. "Circular 20, Secretaría de Gobernación de Chiapas," November 18, 1903, AGPD, leg. XXVIII, exp. 15736.

53. Louise Paré, "Diseño teórico para el estudio del caciquismo actual en México," *Revista Mexicana de Sociología* 34, no. 2 (1972): 338, quoted in William Taylor, *Magistrates of the Sacred: Priests and Parishioners in Eighteenth-Century Mexico* (Stanford: Stanford University Press, 1996), 384.

54. Alan Knight, *The Mexican Revolution*, 2 vols. (Lincoln: University of Nebraska Press, 1986), 1:112–13.

55. Juan Blasco, "Producción y comercialización del aguardiente en los Altos de Chiapas en la segunda mitad del siglo XIX" (master's thesis, Universidad Autónoma de Chiapas, San Cristóbal de las Casas, 2001), 22, 65.

56. Blasco, "Producción y comercialización del agudiente," 66–68.

57. José Fernando Macal to the Bishop of Chiapas, November 23, 1874, Archivo Histórico Diocesano de Chiapas (hereafter AHDC), Ref. Palenque, IV, d. 1.

58. José Fernando Macal to the Bishop of Chiapas, November 1880, no. 3.991, AHDC, Ref. Palenque, IV, d. 1.

59. Manuel G. Trujillo to the Bishop of Chiapas, August 1878, AHDC, Ref. Tila, IV, d. 1.

60. "Comunicaciones de varias presidencias municipales," 1880, Archivo Histórico de Chiapas (hereafter AHCH), Fondo Documental Fernando Castañón Gamboa (hereafter FDFCG), exp. 596.

61. November 1887, Archivo General de la Nación (hereafter AGN), Fomento, Agricultura, C. 17, exp. 29.

62. P. Díaz to E. Rabasa, November 20, 1892, AGPD, leg. XVII, exp. 17728.

63. E. Rabasa to P. Díaz, December 20, 1892, AGPD, leg. XVII, exp. 19860.

64. García de León, *Resistencia y utopía*, 1:164.

65. "Promovido por Juan de Dios Guillén contra Sebastián, Manuel Felipe y Fernando López por abuso de autoridad, ultrajes, amenazas de incendio y destrucción de casa ajena," 1895, AHCH, FDFCG, exp. 865.

66. Moisés González Navarro, *Historia moderna de México*, vol. 4, *El Porfiriato: La vida social* (Mexico City: Editorial Hermes, 1957), 230.

67. "Promovido por Juan de Dios Guillén contra Sebastián, Manuel Felipe y Fernando López . . . ," 1895, AHCH, FDFCG, exp. 865; González Navarro, *Historia moderna de México*, 4:630.

68. Ausencio M. Ruiz to Porfirio Díaz, June 3, 1894, AGPD, leg. XIX, exp. 8554.

69. González Navarro, *Historia moderna*, 4:231.

70. François-Xavier Guerra, *México: Del antiguo régimen a la revolución*, vol. 1, 3rd ed. (Mexico City: Fondo de Cultura Económica, 1995), 315. Rates between municipalities varied greatly, though—from a high of 4.39 pesos per inhabitant in Tapachula to 0.23 pesos in the Lacandón region. Guerra, *México del antiguo régimen*, 4:318.

71. Guerra, *México del antiguo régimen*, 4:315.

72. "Reglamento para el cobro del impuesto de capitación," November 1, 1892, INAH, Museo de Antropología, Serie Chiapas, roll 84.

73. "Circular del secretario de hacienda a los jefes políticos," February 4, 1896, INAH, Museo de Antropología, Serie Chiapas, roll 84.

74. Enrique Camberos Vizcaíno, *Francisco el Grande: Mons. Francisco Orozco y Jiménez, biografía*, 2 vols. (Mexico City: Editorial Jus, 1966), 1:206.

75. Guerra, *México del antiguo régimen*, 1:414, 417.

76. F. León to P. Díaz, June 10, 1896, AGPD, leg. XXI, exp. 9401.

77. *La Voz de Chiapas*, April 9, 1911.

78. R. Pimental to P. Diaz, May 22, 1901, AGPD, leg. XXVI, exp. 5770.

79. The jefes políticos were authorized to hand over funds for public improvements, including the education tax, to "groups of solvent and honorable people" such as

prominent finqueros. "Reseña de las atribuciones y deberes de los jefe políticos de Chiapas,"Tuxtla Gutiérrez, 1897, Biblioteca Na Bolom, San Cristóbal de Las Casas.

80. "Minutario de Correspondencia Oficial," December 22, 1904, Archivo Municipal de San Cristóbal de Las Casas (hereafter AMSCLC), Jefatura Política de San Andrés, Chamula, exp. w/n.

81. "Escuelas en el *partido* de Chamula," 1902, AMSCLC, Jefatura Política de San Andrés, Chamula, exp. w/n.

82. Gobierno Federal, *Censo y división territorial del estado de Chiapas, año 1900* (Mexico City: Secretaría del Fomento, 1905). In Chamula twenty-seven pupils were ladinos. In San Andrés twenty-four of the thirty-five schoolchildren were ladinos. "Escuelas en el *partido* de Chamula," 1902, AMSCLC, Jefatura Política de San Andrés, Chamula, exp. w/n.

83. R. Pimentel to P. Díaz, May 22, 1901, AGPD, leg. XXVI, exp. 5768.

84. AMSCLC, Jefatura Política de Chamula, 1904, exp. 11.

85. Instituto de Asesoría Antropológica para la Región Maya A. C., *Boletín del Archivo Histórico Diocesano de San Cristóbal de Las Casas* 4, no. 4 (November 1991): 31.

86. *Adelante*, August 21, 1910.

87. AHCH, Gobernación, 1910, vol. XIV, exp. 46, n.d.

88. AHCH, FDFCG, 1908, exp. 1060.

89. AMSCLC, Jefatura Política de Chamula, 1904, exp. 11.

90. AHCH, Gobernación, 1910, vol. XIV, exp. 46.

91. Gobernación Mexico City to state governor, May 9, 1910, AHCH, Gobernación, 1910, vol. II, exp. 10.

92. Correspondencia con el Tribunal Superior de Justicia, 10175, no. 493, Tuxtla Gutiérrez, October 26, 1909, AHCH, Gobernación, 1909, vol. IV, exp. 15.

93. AHCH, Gobernación, 1909, vol. VII, exp. 35.

94. Secretary of Government, circular no. 4, Tuxtla Gutiérrez, April 17, 1895, INAH, Museo de Antropología, Serie Chiapas, roll 78, vol. XXVIII.

95. "Indígenas de Oxchuc contra el Agente Municipal, Margarito Penagos," 1898, Archivo General del Poder Judicial (hereafter AGPJ), Ocosingo Ramo Penal, exp. 1674.

96. AHCH, Gobernacción, 1910, vol. XIV, exp. 46.

97. Greg Grandin, *The Blood of Guatemala: A History of Race and Nation* (Durham, N.C.: Duke University Press, 2000), 5, 15, 26, 38, 41, 48–50, 74.

98. For example, in 1896 the jefe político of the district of Chamula told the ladino municipal agent of San Andrés not to send him fifty men from the town to work on the public road but fifty men from each barrio. Such arrangements were worked out between the municipal agent, the Indian cabildo, and the principales, who represented the different barrios. AMSCLC, Jefeturas políticas, Partido Chamula, Presidentes Municipales, October 3, 1896.

99. "Diligencias de unos delitos documentados en contra de Pedro Gómez," 1914, AGPJ, Ocosingo, Ramo Penal, exp. 3154.

100. "Indígenas de Oxchuc contra el Agente Municipal, Margarito Penagos," 1898, AGPJ, Ocosingo, Ramo Penal, exp. 1674, emphasis added.

101. AMSCLC, Jefatura Política de Chamula, 1904, exp. 11.

102. *La Voz de Chiapas*, May 14, 1911.

103. *La Voz de Chiapas*, May 2, 1911.

104. "Contra el presidente Municipal Martín Luna por abuso de autoridad," 1906, AGPJ, Ocosingo Ramo Penal, exp. 2461.

105. Juan Blasco, "La industria aguarentera chiapaneca, 1900–1940" (manuscript in author's possession, n.d.), 39.

4

THE OFFICIAL MAKING OF UNDOCUMENTED CITIZENS IN PERU, 1880–1930

JOSÉ RAGAS

IN THE last two decades, Latin America went through one of its most radical albeit silent transformations: hundreds of thousands of people were taken out of the shadows and into visibility due to several ambitious identification campaigns carried out by national governments with the technical and financial support of international organizations.[1] Although it is difficult to establish with accuracy how many people were registered and received an identity document, the simultaneous efforts displayed by governments in such a short period of time represent a watershed in the expansion of government registration since the rupture with the Spanish Empire in the early nineteenth century. The massive expansion of government registration using the discourse of liberal citizenship and legitimized by social science was possible due to an extraordinary articulation of resources, logistics, and human power in order to provide legal papers and an official identity to vulnerable populations, allowing them (in principle) to enact social and political rights. In some countries these identification campaigns adopted the form of "social crusades." The Bolivarian Revolution, for instance, implemented "Misión Identidad" to reduce the undocumented population in Venezuela, estimated at 70 percent, with the distribution of eighteen million ID cards through 2006.[2] Inspired by this accomplishment, the Bolivian government carried out similar efforts to eradicate the undocumented population through a "technological revolution," which consisted of the nationwide distribution of biometric personal documents that (again, in theory) extended citizenship.[3]

Peru was one of the countries that mobilized significant human and technical resources to distribute ID cards in urban areas as well as in remote rural areas of the country. Two major factors converged in the 2000–2015 period that made possible the expansion of identity documents nationwide.[4] The first was the existence of the Registro Nacional de Identificación y Estado Civil (RENIEC, National Registry of Identification and Civil Status), a special government entity in charge of the design and execution of identification programs. Created in the early 1990s as part of the neoliberal adjustment carried out by President Alberto Fujimori (1990–2000), RENIEC rapidly became an "island of efficiency" within the state apparatus, developing key initiatives using modern technologies to combat high rates of undocumented populations.[5] In addition, the return of democracy after the fall of Fujimori's authoritarian regime was accompanied by extraordinary economic growth that was the result of a commodity export boom. The revenues thus obtained were channeled through the government to different areas with one significant purpose: to reduce poverty in a reasonable length of time. After the transition, democratic governments committed themselves to the creation of social programs designed to facilitate the redistribution of financial resources throughout the country. The initial projects, which focused on effectively redistributing cash through a conditional cash transfer (CCT) program to the most vulnerable groups, exposed the existence of a significant number of undocumented people. Therefore, the alliance between successive government regimes and neoliberal capitalism in the Peruvian highlands during the last decade and a half provided a formidable machinery of personnel and technology. This machinery of civil registration did more than provide an identity card to a great many formerly undocumented individuals. It also became the basis upon which basic services were expanded, and had a major impact on health, education, and political participation within communities and at a national scale.

Undocumented populations posed particular challenges not only for policy makers but also for scholars. Obscured in both official records and scholarly research, unregistered individuals have been ignored for decades, constituting anonymous and amorphous groups living outside the official grid of recognition of national governments. In this chapter, I examine the construction of undocumented populations in modern Peru by analyzing three key institutions: the Civil Register, the Congress, and the National Jury of Elections. Whereas a robust scholarship emerged in the 1990s among Latin Americanists to analyze the complex development of "citizenship" in the region in the aftermath of independence, I take a different route, bringing the undocumented population back to the center of the narrative on inclusion.[6] By reversing the focus of analysis from those who were known and recognized by official entities and (in principle) enabled with social and political rights and duties (voters, taxpayers), I aim to highlight understudied aspects of the intersection between market, government, and majority/minority relations in postcolonial Peru. Whereas in the 2001–16 period governing regimes and the market converged as a major driving force to expand civil registration and documentation, in the period between the War of the Pacific (1884) and the 1931 presidential election, after the fall of Augusto Bernardino Leguía, these same forces actively sought to maintain the population in a subaltern position, depriving them of any opportunity to claim political and civil rights.

Between 1880 and 1930, successive national regimes officially excluded the vast majority of the national population by labeling them as "undocumented." This deliberate segregation was a conscious and meticulously crafted plan by policy makers and authorities. It invoked scientific background, technical knowledge, religious beliefs, and ongoing prejudices toward the indigenous population to provide a framework to justify a segregationist project. This operation took place at a moment when a national debate about the essence of the republic and the place of the indigenous population in the nation raged.[7] The end of the War of the Pacific brought the role of the indigenous population back into the public sphere discussion in Peru. The once-romantic vision of the indigenous population as a crucial part of Peruvian nationhood or as subjects that could be redeemed through education was replaced by a view that considered them as exogenous agents opposed to progress. Intellectuals, politicians, and writers emphasized the gulf between urban coastal areas and other developed areas— which looked overseas—and the underdeveloped rural highland in the mountains. Identity documents helped legitimate this gap by creating a paper divide between individuals bearing official personal documents, who lived primarily in coastal areas, and anonymous populations lacking identity cards, who resided in the rest of the country as well as in pockets of Lima.

Policy makers in Peru embraced an exclusionary identification system to bring together different instruments used in the past to manage social divisions, but they faced poor results. Personal identification and identity documents played a key role in providing the necessary logistics and framework to authorities and policy makers to justify the exclusion of hundreds of thousands of individuals from the official records and to deprive them of government protection and services. The potential benefits of being recognized by official entities were then redirected to those who fulfilled the narrow criteria designed by authorities: male, white, older than twenty-one years old, and literate. Those who did not fulfill the criteria designed by the government were denied the right to vote and to obtain a *libreta electoral* in 1931. The concept of the "undocumented" was then used by policy makers to mark a clear division between those individuals who fulfilled these strict requirements and those who should not be granted the right to vote. By granting (or not) identity documents to majority groups and by denying to minority groups full registration in official records, Peruvian policy makers were actively contributing to perpetuate the plight of marginal populations. Whereas the dividing lines between social (class and race) groups had been amorphous earlier in the nineteenth century, authorities in the early twentieth century were tightening these definitions and excluding the vast majority from the category and benefits of citizenship.

Focusing on the undocumented population is also a helpful tool to reverse and challenge traditional perspectives on citizenship and state building in the Andes and Latin America. In recent decades, scholarship has provided original insights about efforts to build national regimes, both from above and from below.[8] Scholars have examined the human and territorial contours of state governance, based largely on access to official data and sources. Yet the exploration of both territory and population abandoned by policy makers and authorities can offer a crucial reinterpretation behind the motifs and projects of governments to centralize or expand the state apparatus. In this new light, what other scholars have posited as the seemingly progressive and unstoppable trajectory of centralized governance and the irreversible expansion of voting rights are shown to be problematic. What the presence of the unregistered and undocumented population suggests is a state apparatus that chose to confine itself to certain parts of the national territory (especially the coastal areas) and categories of the population (white, literate males over the age of twenty-one) at the very moment when other Latin American countries were deploying aggressive policies of internal colonialism to expand to the borders and to subjugate native populations. As scholars have shown, the trajectory of governance in Peru was characterized by cycles of high centralization and failed attempts of decentralization since the mid-nineteenth century. The surrender of the central government and the seizure of basic services and infrastructure by regional elites in the nineteenth century and part of the twentieth century is another feature that explains the erratic genealogy of governance in the Peruvian Andes.[9]

In order to examine the construction of undocumented populations in Peru, I focus on two specific areas. First, I use the statistics published by the Civil Register in its *Boletín Municipal* to assess the size of the population of "ignored" individuals and to explain their social profile with respect to those who were properly registered. The personnel of the Civil Register included specific information pertaining to the categories in which the "ignored" population appeared, leaving several questions about the methods employed to obtain it and the subsequent policies to address this problem. The second part of the chapter moves to the conjuncture of 1931 and the public debates held in the Congress to determine which individuals should be granted voting rights and which not. I explore such debates and the arguments exchanged between those who supported the inclusion of illiterates as voters and those who sought to justify denying the vote to illiterates.

REGISTERING THE UNKNOWN POPULATION

By the late nineteenth century, the personnel of the Civil Register had invested a significant amount of resources, efforts, and energy to implement a comprehensive system addressed to obtain vital information from the local population. The initial years of the entity were devoted to strengthening the institution itself, by reorganizing its internal structure and replacing employees with those who could do better work in the collection and analysis of the data extracted from the population. The efforts were crystallized with the accumulation of personal information once gathered by the parishes, and were now transformed into quantified data that could help policy makers establish the necessary policies to augment births and reduce deaths in the aftermath of the War of the Pacific. While expanding the size of the population registered in the municipality, registrars encountered anonymous citizens whose identities escaped the sophisticated methods developed by the civil registers to record personal information. This unknown population lacked some or many categories of their personal data, like civil status or race. Registrars recognized their incomplete nature as being statistical abnormalities, labeling them as "Ignored."

The personnel coined the category "Ignored" to address any missing information from this obscure and invisible group. In the past, the "Ignored" population had not necessarily been a major issue for those statisticians who started to develop modern censuses and techniques in the second half of the nineteenth century. For many years, the information submitted by regional authorities included whole numbers obtained from the jurisdictions of their population.[10] In some cases, statisticians lacked full demographic information from specific areas, having to extrapolate the scarce information gathered in order to have the best guess of the demographic trajectory of the country or of a specific region. Even when statisticians considerably reduced the scale of inquiry, it did not guarantee that they were going to capture the total number of inhabitants of such an area. For instance, when Hildebrando Fuentes, an expert on statistics, sought to trace the trajectory of the statistical knowledge in the world for his handbook, he expressed optimism by acknowledging that some of the major errors made by the experts in the past would be reduced in the future with "the education of the masses, which will reduce their suspicion and mistrust" toward censuses and census takers.[11] But until that happens, there were more immediate and urgent problems that the Civil Register had to confront in order to improve its mission.

Unknown demographic and social information was the inevitable result of the growing presence of registration in society. Civil registration was an expanding project that authorities were taking seriously. There had been some remarkable improvements in the decades before the War of the Pacific, and both statisticians and technocrats were less reluctant to use new instruments and methods to cover a larger number of the population. Hence missing demographic information was expected to be a temporary by-product of civil registration in Peru. Unlike our current forms and censuses that respect one's personal decision to not fill in some particular or sensitive boxes pertaining to race or gender, the inquiries carried out by the personnel of the Civil Register sought to extract as much information as they could from the people who approached their offices. The forms and certificates used by the Civil Register in the late nineteenth century exhibited a strong tendency toward simplification, a mandatory step to the standardization of information and its transformation into data. Every birth, wedding, and funeral offered multiple possibilities to refine the already circulating criteria. Once published in the *Boletín Municipal*, demographic reports confirmed that the new version of the Civil Register was as good if not better than its mid-nineteenth-century predecessor or its Latin American counterparts.

The unknown population posed several dilemmas and opportunities for the registration system. Certainly, registrars might have tried to hide or dismiss that category, as they did in the past. They also could have redistributed those whose information was unknown within the already existing categories, avoiding any discrepancies in the estimations. After all, only the registrars managed the information gathered. Only after the drafts of demographic data and the tables were designed and approved by the head of the office did the director of the *Boletín Municipal* have the green light to make them public. Otherwise, they were read and managed only by the staff of the Civil Register and no one else. The existence of a problematic category such as the unknown population might raise suspicion about the professionalism of the Civil Register and provide ammunition for potential criticism toward the institution. The inclusion of this new human group as a statistical category was, above all, a confirmation of the professionalism and transparency the institution aimed to project.

The "Ignored" category was both an invention and the acknowledgment of a problem. Peruvian registrars were active agents in the making of new categories and methods to measure the population. They took the basic information recorded by priests and expanded it in unlimited ways by adding subfields within each original category and crossing the new information with other data, generating endless options that could help them determine further actions. As a field of inquiry, the "Ignored" box did not exist before the late nineteenth century in Peru. Parish records did not have the problem of having missing information since their categories were limited to a basic number of entries, and because the person who collected the information, the priest, knew the people whom he baptized, married, or buried. Furthermore, ecclesiastical superiors were not concerned if the information filled in each certificate was incomplete. The priest was the only one who managed both the documents and the information contained in them.

Registrars and technocrats behind civil registration, nonetheless, had a particular attitude toward missing information. They had created and added that category to data analysis, but they were not able to intervene and modify it. Whereas registrars had significantly expanded the knowledge of the vital cycle of the population in Lima, they limited themselves to document the missing information and the population suffering this vacuum in their records. Experts in the Civil Register were not able to replace the empty boxes with new data, and nobody could do it, not even the people themselves. Unless the population could prove otherwise, they were incapable of changing their own missing personal categories, even their children's missing information. More than only documenting the "unknown" births, marriages, and burials, registrars also sought to protect the lack of information—which was as valuable as the existing data—to monitor and trace the demographic evolution of Lima. If they had wanted, they could have filled the empty boxes or dismissed them by analyzing only the complete data. As the tables published in the *Boletín Municipal* show, authorities compared the "Ignored" population over the years, portraying its growth or decline.

Who belonged to the anonymous and abstract group whose information eluded the experts of the Civil Register? The first group designated as "Ignored" appeared in November 1886—almost two years after the new phase of civil registration—and continued appearing with some interruptions for the following years until the first decade of the twentieth century.[12] In terms of numbers, it was a small size of the total registered population. For a modern statistician, the group of the unknown population that appeared in the tables published by the official bulletin should be considered more as a sampling error than as a category itself. For instance, the unregistered births in 1904 in the province of Lima were 66 out of 3,754.[13] In terms of gender, female babies without information outnumbered male newborns by 16 percent in the same year. In another table, the Civil Register offered a more extended version of the births registered in 1912, focusing on the civil status of the newborns ("Legitimate," "Illegitimate," and "Ignored").[14] "Ignored" babies numbered 84 (barely 2.14 percent of the total sum) whereas there were 1,800 legitimate births and 2,041 illegitimate ones. In a third chart, published in 1923, the percentage of "Ignored" infants was even smaller: 62 out of 6,992 registered births, or 0.88 percent.[15] Even though the "Ignored" box reached in some occasions only 1–2 percent of the total population (or even less), registrars did not discard it just as an anomaly or an error. Conversely, they incorporated those with missing information and crossed the information with those fully registered. The blank box had been so established in the analysis that synonyms like "sin datos" (without information) and "sin clasificación" (without classification) were added to accompany the original "Ignored" box.[16]

Missing information is crucial in order to reveal some analytical inner patterns used by registrars and experts that otherwise are hidden to scholars. The closer examination of race and how it was registered may allow us to understand the internal mechanism of the making of certain categories by the employees of the Civil Register. Citizens, either alive or dead, should fit into one of the boxes that registers had established for racial category: "white," "mestizo," "Indian," "black," and "yellow."[17] If the personnel of the Civil Register were responsible for the proper identification of citizens and their personal information (even physical features), why were some of them considered to be "raceless"? Was "race" an objective or subjective category that could be easily established by the experts or that they preferred to abstain from? The simplification of racial categories by the civil registers sought to prevent any "misreading" of the registered population by employees by reducing the distance between one category and the next one.

In the first months after the reopening of the register, the demographic data along with the tables generated from the information collected were still in an embryonic form, and the categories used to organize the population were still incipient. Authorities included the "Ignored" category since the very beginning but with empty information since all the births had complete information.[18] On the contrary, those who passed away were more likely to be considered as "raceless" than newborns. In some cases, deaths exhibited an unusual rate of people whose race was unknown, with 144 out of 589 people whose race was unidentified in December 1885.[19]

Based on the records published by the Civil Register in the *Boletín Municipal*, we can conclude that the group whose personal information was unknown was at the bottom of the social ladder. The evidence collected by the nascent institution suggests that once a person was sent to the "Ignored" box, that person remained trapped in such category and probably had very few chances to move upward in the social structure. What made the "Ignored" category more ominous is that it was transmitted from parents to children and probably across generations, condemning their offspring to a vicious cycle. For instance, in 1904 the children born of both parents whose race was unknown made 86 out of 88 of the total births whose race was unknown by the registrars.[20]

The "Ignored" population was far from being a statistical enigma for the Civil Register. It reflected a problem that had started to appear and that continued for the rest of the century. According to the data disseminated by authorities, there was a particular segment of the population whose records were not complete and who continued to live in the same city, get married, have children, and die. How did missing data affect them? It is most likely that at least in the first decades of the twentieth century they did not encounter any trouble by not having their race or part of their personal information entered in the Civil Register. In their daily lives, their friends, their community, and other authorities would fill in the identity that registrars could not. As the state implemented the libreta electoral in the 1930s and registration displaced parishes as sites of registration, those "Ignored" citizens encountered difficulties in obtaining certificates and identity documents. In the following decades, they joined another significant group of the population excluded for political reasons: the indigenous population.

ILLITERATES, VOTES, AND *LIBRETAS ELECTORALES*

In December 1931, recently appointed legislators met to discuss the new constitution. The moment was not the most propitious for a quiet and long debate, given the particular circumstances in which congressmen had been called to join the Constituent Assembly and draft a new constitution to replace the one approved by President Augusto Leguía in 1920. The country was still shocked due to the rapid fall and disintegration of the "Patria Nueva" as well as the Great Depression. Elections for the Constituent Assembly provided the necessary yet temporary legitimacy to design a new body of laws. The Constituent Assembly sessions were open. Accompanying the congressmen was an enthusiastic audience who witnessed how the new constitution was in the making. The audience vividly expressed their approval or disagreement in the chamber, applauding their leaders and interrupting them while they were presenting their arguments and rebuttals. For months legislators discussed the nature of the Constitution and its political and social influences. In terms of the number of representatives, the Assembly was composed mainly of the right-wing Unión Revolucionaria (Revolutionary Union) (67 congressmen), the Alianza Popular Revolucionaria Americana (APRA, American Popular Revolutionary Alliance) (27), the Partido Descentralista (Decentralist Party) (20), the Partido Socialista (Socialist Party) (4), and some other independents.[21] The Assembly performed its duty in a bubble, alien to the turmoil that was taking place in the rest of the country. However, tension was present during the debates, especially when political groups had to determine the inclusion (or not) of illiterates, eighteen-year-olds, and women as citizens.

The debates of 1931 provided an opportunity to confront and revoke the restrictions approved in 1896, which impeded the indigenous population from being granted the right to vote and therefore obtain a libreta electoral. Identification played a key role in these debates. Conversely to other groups excluded from the universe of voters (i.e., women and youngsters), the inclusion or not of illiterates directly shaped the identification of the official apparatus that was operating at that time in the country. The potential inclusion of (il)literates involved the change of voting tickets, censuses, and categories in identification papers. It also implied major changes among the population by closing the gap between those who knew how to read and write from those who did not. In this section I will trace the trajectory of the illiterate population to highlight how illiterates actively engaged in the political life of the nineteenth century until a bill passed in 1896 that officially excluded them from voting. I will demonstrate that by 1931 what was at stake was the formal recognition of illiterates as citizens, given their active participation as workers and soldiers during an aggressive expansion of the state in the highlands in the previous decades.

The 1931 election confirmed the sudden increase by twofold of the number of voters between 1919 and 1931 from 163,882 to 392,363 but threefold in the percentage of the population, from 2.5 percent to 7.1 percent.[22] It was not only a quantitative increase but a change in the social profile of voters with respect to the 1920s. The architects of the Estatuto Electoral (Electoral Statute) had taken advantage of the momentum soon after the fall of Leguía and the subsequent political vacuum to open the electoral body to the urban groups without encountering significant resistance.[23] Now the Assembly had to confirm that decision or purge those whose participation was not deemed as legitimate: women, illiterates, and youngsters below twenty-one years old. Therefore, this section will focus on the debates surrounding the potential inclusion—and further rejection—of illiterates as citizens. The 1931 debates marked a point of no return for the presence of illiterates in the national discussions about their nature as citizens. From then on, illiterates became a sensitive topic for policy makers, some of whom unsuccessfully sought to include them for decades until a new constitution in 1979 finally recognized them as citizens.

Literacy then became the battlefield to delineate the frontier between "civilization" and "barbarism" in modern Peru. One of the earliest documents to report the size of the literate population in the country stated that in 1845, 20 percent of the school population in Lima (men and women) learned to read but not to write.[24] The first serious inquiry to measure the capacity of reading and writing among the population took place with the 1860 census of Lima. Carried out door to door in a moment of high mobility and migration toward the capital city, the census of 1860 was the first modern census. It provides one of the first and comprehensive pictures of the social transformations that were taking place soon after the abolition of slavery and the Indian head-tax in a context of relative political stability and economic takeoff. Census takers extended their inquiry about literacy to capture the nuances of the practices and complexity of reading and writing by asking if people just read, both read and write, or neither read nor write. The method used by census takers to confirm literacy among the population remains obscure, yet the data obtained is revealing about the varieties of practices, considering that they were carried out in an urban milieu with high affluence of people from the highlands. The census shows that approximately 5 percent of Limeños knew how to read, 55 percent to read and write, and 40 percent were illiterate. The 1876 national census revealed that the literacy rate in Lima was below the national illiteracy average of 84.4 percent, where 2,699,106 citizens were illiterate.[25]

The prevalent political discourse managed to push them away from obtaining political rights. There were strong opponents to grant illiterates citizenship and the right to vote. The most vocal opponent of the illiterate vote and of illiterates in general was Bartolomé Herrera. Born in Lima in 1808, he decided to become a priest at a very young age and his reputation soon led him to obtain various positions in conservative governments. In 1841 he delivered a sermon at the funeral of President Agustín Gamarra, who had been shot in the back during a military campaign against Bolivia. The sermon, and particularly his claim to end political instability, turned him into a public figure and the most visible member of the Conservative Party. In the late 1840s he took an active part in an intense debate with liberal congressman Pedro Gálvez on whether illiterates should vote.[26] Liberals supported a bill that enabled illiterates to vote without restrictions for one more decade whereas Herrera, as we can anticipate, fiercely resisted any possibility that this could happen. For him, citizenship derived not from sovereignty and political participation but from God's "natural law." Given that "nature" had deprived illiterates from the necessary capacity to think rationally, granting them the vote, Herrera argued, could be counterproductive: allowing them to vote would further cement their role as the instruments of those in power due to their lack of judgment.[27]

Illiterates had also been a significant component of the public sphere and of political debates throughout the nineteenth century. Independently from the efforts displayed by authorities, liberals, and *indigenistas* to promote education and schools nationwide, illiterates had been active participants in political life since the Cortes de Cádiz. The political culture of the nineteenth century enabled the local participation of illiterate voters. Various rituals and practices such as political banquets, rallies, and reading aloud served as platforms to expose people to recent local, national, and global news, disseminated mouth to mouth, through gossip, and in print material. Elections boosted the circulation of print material and meetings. As of the second half of the nineteenth century, we witness an ongoing growth of print material disseminated in the highlands: newspapers, political catechisms, pamphlets, leaflets, and so on.

The illiterate vote, especially in the highlands, was not an issue for policy makers in the aftermath of independence. The indigenous population had been exercising the vote since the Cortes of Cádiz in the 1810s, and postindependence laws were permissive. In the 1820s, voters were able to be accompanied by an adjunct to the polling station to assist them in reading the documents, voting, and signing the acts on their behalf. As Gabriella Chiaramonti has described, electoral laws prior to 1896 privileged other criteria (like ownership, marriage, or being older than twenty-one rather than literacy itself). Following European examples adapted to an Andean setting, ownership, for instance, was deemed to be a key element to determine citizenship and the right to vote, since it granted autonomy and rationality to the citizen, in contrast to those who lacked individual property, like slaves, domestic servants, and Indians. In 1851 those who paid their taxes could vote even if they were illiterates.[28] Other countries in Latin America had to postpone calling for literacy to be the only requirement to participate in elections and bring legitimacy to the postcolonial political system. In Venezuela, for instance, 60 percent of the total population was illiterate. Although Chile possessed a more extensive school system in a more compact territory, its government delayed the demand of literacy to voters in 1833 for seven more years, authorizing signatures as valid proof of literacy. Some early political parties sought to counter illiteracy among potential voters by distributing preprinted tickets with the name of the candidate or permitting illiterate voters to be assisted by somebody else who read the tickets and wrote the name of their candidates.[29]

The 1896 electoral reform brought a double transformation to the country. First, the bill confined the universe of voters only to those older than twenty-one (or married if younger) and those who knew how to read and write, breaking a long tradition of tolerance toward illiterates.[30] The idea that "the man who does not know how to read and write is not and cannot be a citizen in modern society," as expressed by one proponent of the law, prevailed over its opponents.[31] The Congress ended up passing a law that obliged voters to cast ballots in direct and public suffrage, signing in a double "cédula."[32] Second, the exclusion of illiterates from the voting stations consolidated the transference of political power from the highlands to the coastal areas. The process had begun five decades earlier, when the revenue from guano suddenly dwarfed any other internal source of revenues, making them obsolete. By canceling the indigenous tribute and other taxes, regions stopped receiving the income source that gave the necessary autonomy to manage their own financial resources in order to pay local bureaucracy and develop public works.[33] Since the mid-nineteenth century, the central government sent money to the interior and kept the lion's share for the capital city.[34] By the end of the century, a cultural barrier loomed in the country between "white," urban, literate, and developed "citizens" on the coast and "indigenous," rural, illiterate, and underdeveloped "noncitizens" in the sierra.

The seeming social and cultural divide was soon bridged, at least partially, by an unstoppable force—the capitalist state. In a powerful parallel, Alberto Flores Galindo suggested that the twentieth century was the "century where the encounter of the 16th century between the Andean world and the West was repeated again."[35] Certainly, the metaphor encapsulates the rapid process that started in the first decades after the War of the Pacific and that privileged the export of natural resources, such as oil, agriculture, livestock, and mining. These years also witnessed the expansion of state authority over the national territory, a phenomenon acknowledged by Congressman Alberto Arca Parró in his speech to the National Assembly. For him, the expansion of the state in the highlands had taken place through two specific institutions: the army and the Conscripción Vial.[36] Both branches had incorporated the indigenous population coercively by pulling them out from the control of rural landowners and damaging their capacity to manage the indigenous labor force exclusively.

Both mechanisms boosted the coerced integration of the Andean population, whether they were literate or illiterate. Although they underwent a process of modernization in the late nineteenth century, both the army and the office in charge of public works relied more on archaic and traditional mechanisms to retain the Andean population and oblige them to serve as soldiers and workers. The army had been literally obliterated in the war against Chile in the 1880s. The government hired a foreign mission to implement the modernization of the army.[37] These reforms, however, masked an ongoing problem: the recruitment of soldiers through the "leva" (forced recruitment). In the last century, the highlands were the natural reservoir where caudillos could obtain fresh recruits for their military adventures. Authorities suspended the recruitment due to harsh criticism in the late nineteenth century, but it remained the easiest way to fill the barracks given the absence of modern strategies of recruitment.

In a similar manner, the "Patria Nueva" of Augusto Leguía started a vast program addressed to build and maintain roads nationwide in the 1920s. The Conscripción Vial was an ambitious program that for more than ten years forced the male population between eighteen and sixty years old to work twelve days per year. This extraordinary amount of human labor was intended to modernize the country by building a new road system and connecting the highlands with the coastal areas, seeking to break the isolation and foster the circulation of both commodities and the population.[38]

If there is something that the modernization of postwar state building may have influenced in both the Conscripción Vial and the army, it was the relevance of personal registers and the issuance of identity documents: the *libreta militar* and the *libreta de conscripción*. Both documents were necessary for several reasons: to keep a record of those who were enrolled whether as soldiers and workers, those who fled the barracks or their posts, those who were exempted from service, and those who had fulfilled their service and were allowed to leave the army or the Conscripción. The army kept personal records of officers and soldiers where they noted varied information about their ranks, leaves of absence, promotions, and so on. These records were centralized in Lima and were the basis for the libreta militar that people carried during the 1931 election. The libreta militar contained very comprehensive data about its holder. It required two photos, fingerprints, signature, information about personal health and major organ condition, "filiación," and information from the civil register. The Conscripción Vial also issued its own document, which was delivered when a person registered for the first time. According to the legislation, people serving in the Conscripción Vial should receive a libreta with "all the information regarding their registration" and "to prove their condition at any time."[39]

The effective enrollment of the Andean population in both activities, regardless of whether they knew how to read and write, was a powerful argument invoked by Congressmen Arca Parró to support the vote of the illiterate sector in the 1930s. Along with the Church, the army was the institution with the highest enrollment of the population. We lack the exact number of people registered by the army, but we should consider that it was one of the few nationwide institutions that had existed since independence. Given the existence of this ample database within the state, it is not surprising that the architects of the Conscripción Vial relied on the Military Register to complete their own list of people who should serve as workers.[40] The Conscripción Vial, on the contrary, only lasted a decade and the practices and elements associated with it—including its libreta—were rapidly dismissed as oppressive and as a symbol of the Leguía administration.

By stressing the contradiction between the role of illiterates serving as soldiers and workers for the state yet being denied as citizens, Congressman Arca Parró was exposing the hypocrisy and prejudices of authorities toward this group of citizens. More importantly, he was demonstrating that illiterates had been registered in the past, and that this process did not encounter any trouble by including literates and illiterates alike. Hence it should not be difficult, he concluded, to add them to the register and issue a libreta electoral to each one. Some congressmen expressed how important it was to secure the vote of illiterates and made suggestions on how to push forward ongoing reforms and adapt the current system to incorporate them. The collective and oral nature of the vote in rural towns allowed for the participation of illiterates in the past, but this was no longer the case. Furthermore, the logic of the secret ballot went against the possibility of a second person joining the illiterate voter in the secret booth. As in India, with a literacy rate as low as 16 percent in 1952, finding new strategies to allow illiterates to vote was not an option, especially after India gained its independence from the British Empire. A special Election Commission decided to incorporate electoral symbols on the ballot, and political parties demanded to determine their own symbols. Lions, hands, elephants, bikes, boats, stairways, and even camels emerged on the new ballot papers seeking to create a link between the voter and the Indian political parties.[41] Similarly, in Peru in 1931 Arca Parró proposed the use of colors to distinguish political parties, a direct precedent of the current use of party iconography on ballot papers.[42]

Not surprisingly, some congressmen fiercely opposed this initiative. Instead of refuting these ideas with technical arguments, they appealed to social prejudices like the fear of potential rebellions if illiterates were granted citizenship. "It would be a serious menace to national security to grant the vote to the illiterate Indigenous race," claimed Congressman Gamarra.[43] Peasant rebellions that took place in the southern highlands in the 1920s, distant from the capital city, served as a reminder, in the eyes of some, of what could happen if indigenous populations were encouraged to engage politically. Actually, rebellions were a symptom of the penetration of capitalism and the brutal conditions imposed on the local peasant communities by hacendados, officers, and merchants.[44] When the news about those riots reached the capital, the Limeño press demonized the rebels and their demands as being part of an alleged "caste war" against the white population. Congressman Gamarra sought to revive those memories of "plundering, fires and murder" to rally opposition to the illiterate vote.[45]

CONCLUSION

The 1931 presidential election represents a turning point in the convoluted trajectory of citizenship claims in Peru. The crisis accelerated the emergence of mass politics and created an opportunity for political parties to construct electoral machines in a short time, pushing the boundaries of the franchise, including subaltern groups that otherwise would likely have remained excluded from voting. The inclusion of such a vast number of people in the electoral arena required the possession of an identity document, the libreta electoral, which eventually would become the national identity card. Nonetheless, the optimistic view of an expanding citizenship is contradicted by the fact that despite the extraordinary number of new voters there were still large segments of the population who remained undocumented for decades. This did not substantially change until two other political ruptures took place: the 1955 extension of suffrage to women and the Constituent Assembly of 1978–79, which revoked the ban on illiterates voting.

Between 1880 and 1930, market and government operated in multiple directions, competing for a labor force and perpetuating racial, gender, and social barriers to maintain social order. Landowners, soldiers, investors, and policy makers developed legal and informal strategies in their own realms that confined government recognition to a small segment of the population and left the majority undocumented. In this chapter, I have analyzed the making of those who were considered "Ignored" by the Civil Register and were denied the ability to obtain a voting card by an electoral entity. In studying two institutions that were part of the government apparatus, I have compared and contrasted two rationales that would combine to create a political, social, and cultural divide between the documented and undocumented populations in two different moments.

This chapter also suggests that the examination of the undocumented population provides an alternative means of examining the expansion and contraction of the franchise in Latin America. As the Peruvian case proves, this process occurred in different areas and had distinct implications. Both the Civil Register and the National Jury of Elections operated separately during the period between 1880 and 1930, and only with the subsequent integration of bureaucratic functions would both databases be combined. Nonetheless, the analysis of both entities demonstrates that vulnerable populations were prone to remain invisible from the government and were forced to carry on the ominous feature of being undocumented to the next generation.

NOTES

1. Wendy Hunter and Robert Brill, "Documents, Please: Advances in Social Protection and Birth Certification in the Developing World," *World Politics* 68, no. 2 (2016): 191–228.

2. José Ragas, "A Starving Revolution: ID Cards and Food Rationing in Bolivarian Venezuela," *Surveillance & Society* 15, nos. 3/4 (2017): 590–95.

3. "SEGIP socializa nueva cedula de identidad inteligente," *Cambio*, July 6, 2016, http://www.cambio.bo/?q=node/10254.

4. Katia Vega Bendezú, "Relación entre el Estado y las poblaciones vulnerables a través del acceso a los documentos de documentación e identificación (de cómo ven la identificación los sectores vulnerables)," *Nombres* 1, no. 1 (2013): 39–78.

5. Eduardo Dargent, "Islas de eficiencia y reforma del Estado: Ministerios de Economía y de Salud 1990–2008" (report, Consorcio de Investigación Económica y Social, Lima, September 2008).

6. A succinct review of this subject can be found in Marta Irurozqui, *La ciudadanía en debate en América Latina: Discusiones historiográficas y una propuesta teórica sobre el valor público de la infracción electoral* (Lima: Instituto de Estudios Peruanos, 2004).

7. Manuel González Prada, "Discurso en el Politeama (1888)," http://evergreen.loyola .edu/tward/www/gp/libros/paginas/pajinas6.html.

8. The bibliography on this subject is vast, and some prominent titles include Gilbert Joseph and Daniel Nugent, eds., *Everyday Forms of State Formation: Revolution and the Negotiation of Rule in Modern Mexico* (Durham, N.C.: Duke University Press, 1994); James Dunkerley, ed., *Studies in the Formation of the Nation-State in Latin America* (London: Institute of Latin American Studies, 2002); Fernando López-Alves, *State Formation and Democracy in Latin America, 1810–1900* (Durham, N.C.: Duke University Press, 2000); and Vincent C. Peloso and Barbara A. Tenenbaum, eds., *Liberals, Politics, and Power: State Formation in Nineteenth-Century Latin America* (Atlanta: University of Georgia Press, 1996).

9. Carlos Contreras, *Centralismo y descentralismo en la historia del Perú independiente* (Lima: Instituto de Estudios Peruanos, 2000).

10. Paul Gootenberg, "Population and Ethnicity in Early Republican Peru: Some Revisions," *Latin American Research Review* 26, no. 3 (1991): 109–57.

11. Hildebrando Fuentes, *Curso de estadística* (Lima: Impr. de "La Revista," 1907), 53.

12. "Nacidos inscriptos en la Seccion de Registros Civiles, del 31 de octubre al 6 de noviembre de 1886," *Boletín Municipal* 117 (November 26, 1886): 950.

13. "Nacimientos, matrimonios y defunciones ocurridos en el año 1904, clasificados por distritos," *Boletín Municipal* 329 (April 20, 1907): 2550.

14. "Nacimientos inscritos en 1912: Clasificados por distritos, razas, condición civil y sexos," *Boletín Municipal* 670 (November 1913): 5283.

15. "Natalidad: Resumen general de la natalidad de la ciudad de Lima durante el año 1923; Clasificación por meses, condición civil y sexos," *Boletín Municipal* 166.

16. "Nacimientos en el año 1904, clasificados según la edad de los padres," *Boletín Municipal* 342 (July 20, 1907): 3657.

17. The category "yellow" to denote the Asian population was added later.

18. "Nacidos inscriptos en la Sección de Registro Civil: Del 13 al 19 de diciembre de 1885," *Boletín Municipal* 74 (January 16, 1886): 600; "Nacidos inscriptos en la Sección de Registro Civil: Del 3 al 9 de enero de 1886," *Boletín Municipal* 75 (January 23, 1886): 615.

19. "Defunciones en el mes de diciembre de 1885," *Boletín Municipal* 75 (January 23, 1886): 617.

20. "Clasificación de los nacimientos en 1904, según la raza de los padres," *Boletín Municipal* 342 (July 20, 1907): 2658.

21. Fernando Tuesta Soldevilla, "Las elecciones de 1931 (II)," *Polítika* (blog), March 10, 1998, http://blog.pucp.edu.pe/blog/fernandotuesta/1998/03/10/las-elecciones-de-1931-ii/.

22. Jorge Basadre, *Elecciones y centralismo en el Perú* (Lima: Centro de Investigación de la Universidad del Pacífico, 1980), 153, 161; Sinesio López and Milagros Barrenechea, "Peru, 1930–1968: Competencia y participación en el estado oligárquico," in *Historia de las elecciones en el Peru: Estudios sobre el gobierno representativo*, ed. Cristóbal Aljovín de Losada and Sinesio López (Lima: Instituto de Estudios Peruanos, 2005), 119.

23. Steve Stein, *Populism in Peru: The Emergence of the Masses and the Politics of Social Control* (Madison: University of Wisconsin Press, 1980), 196.

24. "Plan de los colegios y escuelas de instrucción primaria existentes en esta capital en el año de 1845," Archivo General de la Nación (AGN), Prefecturas, legajo 120.

25. Gabriella Chiaramonti, "La redefinición de los actores y de la geografía política en el Perú a finales del siglo XIX," *Historia* 42, no. 2 (2009): 332.

26. This debate has been extensively covered in recent years by Gabriella Chiaramonti, "A propósito del debate Herrera-Gálvez de 1849: Breves reflexiones sobre el sufragio de los indios analfabetos," in *Historia de las elecciones en el Peru: Estudios sobre el gobierno representativo*, ed. Cristóbal Aljovín de Losada and Sinesio López (Lima: Instituto de Estudios Peruanos, 2005), 325–58; Roberto Katayama, "Bartolomé Herrera y su debate con los liberales," in *Bartolomé Herrera y su tiempo*, ed. Fernán Altuve (Lima: Sociedad Peruana de Historia, 2010), 223–35; and José Francisco Gálvez Montero, "Herrera y los Hermanos Gálvez," in *Bartolomé Herrera y su tiempo*, ed. Fernán Altuve (Lima: Sociedad Peruana de Historia, 2010), 237–48.

27. Chiaramonti, "A propósito," 329; Katayama, "Bartolomé Herrera," 232; Gálvez Montero, "Herrera y los hermanos Gálvez," 243.

28. Chiaramonti, "A propósito," 339.

29. Richard Warren, *Vagrants and Citizens: Politics and the Masses in Mexico City from Colony to Republic* (Wilmington, Del.: Scholarly Resources, 2001), 39.

30. Basadre, *Elecciones y centralismo*, 53.

31. Gabriella Chiaramonti, "Construir el centro, redefinir al ciudadano: Restricción del sufragio y reforma electoral en el Perú de finales del siglo XIX," in *Legitimidad, representación y alternancia en España y América Latina: Las reformas electorales, 1880–1930*, ed. Carlos Malamud (Mexico City: Fondo de Cultura Económica, 2000), 232.

32. Chiaramonti, "Construir el centro," 252.

33. Contreras, *Centralismo y descentralismo*, 16.

34. The transformations of the political structure between 1850 and 1880 have been studied by Ulrich Mücke, "Estado nacional y poderes provinciales: Aspectos del sistema político peruano antes de la Guerra con Chile," *Anuario de Estudios Americanos* 56, no. 1 (1999): 173–94.

35. Alberto Flores Galindo, *Dos ensayos sobre José María Arguedas* (Lima: Casa SUR, 1992), 16.

36. *Diario de Debates del Congreso Constituyente de 1931*, n.d., p. 894.

37. Peter Flindell Klarén, *Peru: Society and Nationhood in the Andes* (New York: Oxford University Press, 2000), chapter 8.

38. The most comprehensive study of the Conscripcion Vial is the thesis of Mario Meza Bazán, "Caminos al progreso: Mano de obra y política de vialidad en el Perú; La Ley de Conscripción Vial, 1920–1930" (master's thesis, National University of San Marcos, Lima, 1999). I want to thank him for sharing his thesis and for his help with my questions on this road project and the documents generated in this process.

39. Despite all our efforts, we could not find any "Libreta de Conscripción" in the archives. Mario Meza Bazán, who conducted research on this topic, confirmed my suspicion since he could not find any of them either. Mario Meza Bazán, email, July 2014.

40. Ley 4113, Conscripción Vial, art. 2.

41. Christophe Jaffrelot, "Voting in India: Electoral Symbols, the Party System and the Collective Citizen," in *The Hidden History of the Secret Ballot*, ed. Romain Bertrand, Jean-Louis Briquet, and Peter Pels (Bloomington: Indiana University Press, 2006), 78–85.

42. *Diario de Debates*, n.d., 766.

43. *Diario de Debates*, n.d., 746.

44. José Luis Rénique, *La batalla por Puno: Conflicto agrario y nación en los Andes peruanos* (Lima: Instituto de Estudios Peruanos, 2004).

45. *Diario de Debates*, n.d., 746.

PART II

COMPARATIVE STUDIES IN NATION BUILDING, CA. 1900–1950

I **N THIS,** the introduction to the second half of the volume, we compare the trajectories of Mexico and Peru during (roughly) the first half of the twentieth century to provide a context for the following five chapters. The two countries' trajectories seemed to diverge radically when Mexico's revolution exploded in 1910, demolishing the Porfirian regime and ultimately forging new forms of citizenship. This in turn provided the postrevolutionary regime a popular base, which enabled it to radically reform certain aspects of Porfirian capitalism, most notably via the nationalization of foreign-owned oil companies and many highly capitalized estates producing export crops. In Peru, on the other hand, the Oncenio ultimately failed to replace the Aristocratic Republic with an enduring regime, and after its collapse in 1930 a series of undistinguished, relatively brief administrations staved off revolutionary change in part by making cautious, halting concessions to popular forces.

MEXICO IN REVOLUTION

Although the Porfiriato had been infinitely more successful than the Civilistas in aggregating disparate regions into a single coalition, it proved fragile when beset by political, economic, and (to a lesser extent) international crises.

If opposition to the Porfirian policies of dispossession and repression unified the opposition behind Francisco Madero, then Porfirian forms of capitalism also created significant geographic differences that would weigh heavily on the origins, process, and outcome of the revolution. Most importantly, the success of the Porfiriato in transforming, as Friedrich Katz famously put it, the frontier into a border created a large, wealthy, and much more socially dynamic north.[1] The north's growth was based on the creation of a vast railroad network that allowed rebels ready access to arms across the border and to move troops and supplies south. And northern landowners were more willing to head cross-class alliances in revolt, while *norteño* rancheros, laborers, and peasant military colonists proved to be superb self-taught soldiers.[2]

The revolution began with a democratic challenge to the reelection of Porfirio Díaz in 1910. Although Madero's challenge to the Porfiriato is often compared to Guillermo Billinghurst's reformist campaign, he also resembled Augusto Bernardino Leguía, who posed as a reformer who would replace a corrupt, self-serving elite with a government that recognized the rights and the interests of poor majorities. Like Leguía, Madero toppled the ancient regime relatively quickly and with little bloodshed. However, the forces unleashed by the collapse of the Porfiriato, attempts by powerful institutions and interests to restore it, and the proximity to the United States help explain why the armed phase of the revolution dragged on for ten years and proved immensely costly in human lives and economic devastation.

The strength of military foes in Mexico forced the faction that emerged the winner—Álvaro Obregón's wing of the Constitutionalists—to build a new army in order to completely defeat remnants of the Porfirian army and rival revolutionary armies. Popular demands forced Obregón to adopt a more radical program of land reform, unionization, and concessions to middle-class reformers. The contrast between Obregón's and Leguía's coalitions is quite sharp: Leguía's was forged in a few brief months of political crisis, which was largely resolved bloodlessly, and Peruvian popular forces never came close to seizing the national capital.

Although Peru's elites were bitterly divided, neither the Civilistas nor Leguía sought to arm and militarily mobilize Peru's workers and peasants. In Mexico, however, the coalition headed by Obregón that took power in 1920 coalesced after a decade of armed conflict, which has often been called Latin America's first social revolution. It included *agraristas* who once followed Emiliano Zapata and self-identified communists, anarchists, and socialist organizers. Key supporters of Obregón authored the most radical elements of the Constitution of 1917 that guaranteed (in theory) workers' rights, agrarian reform, and a modern welfare state.

Although the Peruvian Constitution of 1920 drew heavily on its 1917 Mexican counterpart, in practice, the contrast with Peru could not be sharper. Not surprisingly, Leguía's relatively fragile Oncenio collapsed under the stress of the Great Depression and was displaced by a military coup, while the Obregón coalition survived its leader's 1928 assassination in part through its "institutionalization" as the Partido Nacional Revolucionario (PNR, National Revolutionary Party; now the Partido Revolucionario Institucional [PRI, Institutional Revolutionary Party]). Just as importantly, most of Mexico's restive generals remained loyal. The relative strength of the postrevolutionary regime in Mexico that grew out of Obregón's coalition allowed it to move left after the Great Depression. It adopted deficit spending; extended agrarian reform to agricultural capitalist zones of henequen, cotton, and sugar; and nationalized foreign oil during the tumultuous 1930s without profoundly alienating either the United States or all of its own upper class. The same ideological flexibility and enduring unity then allowed the postrevolutionary coalition to tack right during the 1940s, reversing land reform, stifling strikes and wage increases, and favoring domestic industry without completely losing peasant and worker support. By the mid-twentieth century, the Oncenio was long forgotten, while Mexico's postrevolutionary regime, now headed by a new generation of civilian technocrats, was overseeing sustained economic growth, accelerating industrialization, and a mushrooming middle class.

PERU'S ONCENIO AND ITS DEMISE: REAGGREGATION, CONSOLIDATION, AND COLLAPSE

As noted earlier, in times of crisis the lines of fracture of nation-building experiments become more readily visible. The Aristocratic Republic entered into just such a crisis in May 1919. At this point the era's unresolved tendencies toward dispersion revealed themselves. At this same moment, the inability of the Partido Civil (Civilista Party) to aggregate these disparate forces became apparent.

The crisis of 1919 unfolded in the context of presidential elections. Despite growing labor militancy and social unrest in the capitalist corridors, the Civilistas expected to continue their decades-long control of the presidency, for they controlled virtually all positions in government, including those that "organized" the electoral process. This gave them a huge advantage in determining electoral outcomes. But the Civilistas had failed to grasp the enormous changes in the national social structure they themselves had precipitated, as Peru's dispersed corridors of capitalism surged to meet international export demands.[3]

Civilista leaders failed to grasp, for example, not only how narrow but also how internally divided their coalition was. They also failed to grasp the breadth and depth of the "new" social forces that were arrayed against them—the poor, working-class, and marginalized groups that had grown exponentially during three decades of growth in the capitalist corridors. If we are to understand the crisis that shook the Aristocratic Republic in 1919, we must attend to the multiple contradictory roles played by Lima in the era's experiment in nation building. One of Lima's roles was denationalizing in nature. The national capital was a key node on the central corridor of capitalist development, which brought foreign capital together with domestic labor power to draw huge quantities of mineral wealth out of the country.

But Lima also played nationalizing roles. As the seat of national government, the Senate and the Chamber of Deputies were located in Lima. Positions in Congress were an essential part of the power- and wealth-sharing arrangements that Civilista leaders made with regionally based, highland hacendados—to give the latter a stake in the ruling coalition in the highlands. But these positions left the highland elite peripheral to key Civilista decision-making processes. The parliament thus brought together in a single, nationalizing institution (Congress), in a single locale (the national capital), regional elites who were relegated to the margins of the power structure. Many were highly resentful at having been so marginalized. Having been peripheralized, their primary concerns were highly localized and powerfully centripetal in nature.

Lima had an additional nationalizing role, but not one intended by elite nation builders. The national capital also brought large numbers of internally displaced persons into one, shared urban environment. Indeed, Lima acted very much like the narrow end of a national funnel, which channeled people from across a broad sweep of the national territory toward a single destination. Viewed as uncouth Indians, they descended upon Lima in very large numbers during the Aristocratic Republic. By the time the Aristocratic Republic entered into crisis, they represented the majority of the population in the national capital.

The working populations of the Aristocratic Republic had played a key role in enabling elite prosperity. But they were treated as a "superfluous population" and were systematically denied the ability to share in the benefits of the era's prosperity. As the backward, uncouth highland hordes descended upon the "City of the Kings" (as Lima was called), the stage was set for a confrontation between the Aristocratic Republic's oligarchic, coastal elite and the multitude gathered at their doorstep.

The presidential elections of 1919 thus occurred in a social context that had been radically transformed, and to a degree that the Civilista elite had failed to grasp. Particularly important was the following: the vast majority of the displaced highland migrants who had relocated to Lima were outside the systems of social and electoral control that had proven so effective in ensuring elite dominance. As a result, even though the Civilistas did indeed control the entire apparatus of government—which in times past would have helped ensure success at the polls—times had changed.

As the voting results came in, it became clear that the Civilista candidate would lose to outsider Augusto Leguía. The Civilistas had promised a continuation of existing policies. Leguía, on the other hand, had promised a "new nation"—a radical break with the corrupt, elitist practices of the "Forty Families."[4] The Civilistas made a feeble attempt to prevent Leguía from taking power, compelling him to launch a preemptive coup. In so doing, he drew upon the support of people from humble, often working-class social backgrounds.[5] His nationalizing call for a new, more egalitarian society—one that brought an end to the inherited, aristocratic privileges of the past and that offered a more prosperous future—had a powerful appeal to these groups.

Leguía's coup was not only successful but also bloodless. Indeed, despite the fact that he challenged a powerful, entrenched elite coalition, very little organized opposition ever materialized. Considering that the Civilistas controlled virtually the entire government, on the face of it, it makes little sense that Leguía prevailed so easily. His nearly seamless rise to power makes more sense, however, in relation to the key lines of fracture of the era's elite coalition.

While the Civilistas did indeed control the government apparatus, this statement conceals more than it reveals, for it makes that apparatus seem far more coherent than it was. There were deep divisions within the party that controlled the government—divisions that reflected the party's only partially successful efforts to overcome the many powerful forces toward dispersion that were at work during the era. Perhaps the key weakness in the ruling coalition, however, was that its core was excessively narrow.

It would have been a simple matter for a stronger, more inclusive elite coalition to close ranks against Leguía. But the leaders of the three capitalist corridors that had been excluded from the coalition core had little stake in the preservation of the ruling coalition. Neither did the regionally based hacendados, who had marginal positions in the coalition as members of Congress. As a result, when a challenge finally came, these factions failed to aggregate around the coalition core and protect it from its enemies. Instead of protesting or resisting, these peripheralized elites responded in ways that reflected their particular, marginal position in that coalition. Each dispersed (literally or figuratively) to his own, semiautonomous domain—whether corridor or region—to attend to his own, independent affairs.

Upon seizing power, Leguía moved quickly to weaken and divide the opposition. He did so by striking at both the core and the periphery of the Civilista power structure. Soon after Leguía assumed office, government officials announced that they had discovered an elaborate plot intended to depose the new president. Many powerful members of the coastal oligarchy were implicated. Leguía responded by having these people banished from Peru. Because those implicated were the elites of the coastal corridor, who dominated Civilista leadership positions, his actions had a devastating effect on the party as a whole. Without its leadership, the party could not hope to reaggregate the disparate elements of the Aristocratic Republic's coalition. Indeed, these elements were left dispersed and divided, each having to fend for itself.

The president used a different strategy to strike at the periphery of the Civilista power structure—the regionally based, highland hacendados, who occupied the positions of senator and deputy for their respective regions. After taking office, Leguía dissolved the entire Civilista legislature, called for new elections, and declared members of the Partido Civil ineligible. The new, pro-Leguía legislature was filled with estate owners who were the adversaries of the recently dismissed ex-congressmen. These newly ascendant regional elites kept a close watch on the deposed Civilistas, making organized activity on their part extremely difficult.

Leguía took systematic steps to dismantle the elite coalition of the Aristocratic Republic. While doing so helped protect him from his enemies, it also exacerbated the tendencies toward dispersion that ruling elites of the Aristocratic Republic had been forced to confront. Leguía responded to these problems, however, in a way that had little in common with his immediate predecessors.

The president's approach to overcoming dispersion had strong similarities to the strategy employed by the regimes of the guano era, more than a half century prior. As had been true of the leaders of those earlier regimes, Leguía forged a new transnational circuit of capital to acquire the resources necessary to form a national coalition. He also drew upon these connections to establish monopoly control over a windfall—a valuable resource that was outside the bounds of elite competition. To form his national coalition Leguía also employed a highly intangible form of wealth: speculative capital. During the Oncenio, the president arranged to borrow $100 million from U.S. banks.[6]

Because these loans were made to the government, Leguía ensured that the distribution of all funds would radiate outward from a single point. The experiment in nation building he oversaw thus had much in common with its guano-era predecessors. It generated powerful forces toward aggregation. It also established Leguía as the key mediator between the international and the national arenas. Occupying this position allowed him to build a national coalition by supporting projects that were entirely of his own choosing.

As was true of guano-era leaders, Leguía used a large proportion of these funds to form clienteles that would be dependent on his regime. These included the government bureaucracy. Leguía reversed the Aristocratic Republic's minimalist approach to government and oversaw a fivefold increase in the size of the officialdom. The most important criteria for being given a position in the Leguía government were neither qualifications nor credentials but loyalty to the president.

Leguía also used speculative capital from transnational sources to build up additional forces that would defend his regime from its enemies. Among these were the armed forces. Leguía spent lavishly on the military. At the same time, however, he was aware that the coastal oligarchy he had just deposed had much influence among military officers. To guard against reprisal, in 1919 Leguía reorganized and expanded the national police (renamed the Guardia Civil, reflecting its Spanish origins), which was national in scope and had no ties to the coastal elite. By the time the Oncenio came to a close, this police force was almost equal in size to the army.

Leguía also used the funds acquired from transnational sources to subsidize a project that was intended to be productive in nature. Combining loan money with a new program of forced labor (the Conscripción Vial), he undertook a national project of highway construction. The president's goal in doing so was to overcome the inward-looking nature of Peru's many, semiautonomous regional domains and to involve as much of the country as possible in market relations. This was part of a broader strategy to deepen the international export orientation of the country as a whole.

Building roads between Peru's many inward-looking regions, between the sierra and the coast, and between the corridors of capitalist development, however, did not have the integrating, catalyzing effect that Leguía had hoped for. This was in part because many of Peru's regions continued to be inwardly focused. Connecting them via highways facilitated movement between them but did not change what transpired within the regions. They had little to offer to one another, or to urban manufacturing, in terms of demand. As a result, highway construction did not produce a national market.

While the growth of the capitalist corridors did not create prosperity in domains hitherto at a distance from market relations, it did bend space and social relations in those domains. In the process, corridor growth created insecurity and hardship for untold numbers of people. Many became internally displaced and followed the national funnel to Lima (or moved to other urban centers). Indeed, capitalist growth generated widespread instability in the relationships between the corridors and their hinterlands.

In chapter 5, Lewis Taylor examines how the German-owned Empresa Agrícola Chicama (EACh) in Cajamarca department found itself increasingly unable to suppress growing popular resistance and manage supposedly co-opted state agents seeking to enforce the Conscripción Vial (labor draft). Low-level bureaucrats willingly accepted bribes from the upper class, but they were influenced by the spread of indigenism and populism, and so proved increasingly willing to rule in favor of labor and peasants. That said, Peru's working poor continued to see the political authorities largely as takers (labor, revenue, the military draft) and not givers (social benefits, justice, or education), but their ability to migrate and squat on hacienda land meant that the authorities could neither compel loyalty nor use coercion.

Leguía (and subsequent regimes) could never overcome what Taylor usefully terms "obstructive ambiguity" among the lower rungs of officialdom in the labor state; it proved far more adept at destroying the elite coalition of the Aristocratic Republic. Constructing a new one proved much more vexing. Although Leguía succeeded in distributing borrowed funds to dependent constituencies, the alliances thus formed remained viable only as long as the transnational circuit of capital Leguía had established remained intact. The onset of the Great Depression, in October 1929, severely compromised Leguía's position as broker between these transnational sources of speculative capital and the national arena. In August 1930, he was deposed by a military coup, and the coalition that he had gathered around him collapsed. The Oncenio's aggregation-based experiment in nation building thus proved to be as short-lived as Leguía's tenure in office.

Leguía's rise and fall represented two successive moments in the breakdown of elite unity. The first moment came when Leguía rose to power and mounted a frontal assault on the core and the periphery of the ruling coalition. In the process, he left the different fragments of that coalition weak and divided, each having to fend for itself. The second moment in the breakdown of elite unity transpired when Leguía fell from power and his coalition disintegrated. Having destroyed the previous coalition, and having left nothing in its place, Leguía undermined elite unity as a whole.

The impact of the Oncenio on nation building, however, did not end here. As noted above, Leguía had risen to power in 1919 on a tide of populist, working-class support. This was reflected in Leguía's 1920 Constitution, which was modeled in part on Mexico's 1917 charter and promised to better workers' lives through cheap and hygienic housing, nutritious and affordable food, and even social insurance. This labor state, as Paulo Drinot terms it (see chapter 6), was a pillar of the Oncenio. It was intended to foster a disciplined (and implicitly nonindigenous) workforce, thus calming the labor militancy of 1918–19, and prevent the spread of radical ideologies. But the labor state was not just reactive; it was also forward-looking: "civilizing" Peru and providing abundant, productive human capital for a planned industrialization.[7] The labor state sought to guide labor away from radical or leftist ideas through arbitration that delivered meaningful concessions to labor at the cost of capital but also embedded labor in a form of citizenship that depended on state intervention in the name of social and economic development.

Even though the labor state engaged only a small number of workers in its limited programs, it discursively reinforced the exclusionary nature of lived citizenship that marginalized the majority (indigenous, Afro-descendant, Chinese-Peruvian) in a new and seemingly modern manner.[8] Indeed, the failure of Leguía's Patria Nueva to fulfill the Constitution of 1920's promised "social guarantees" to Peru's worker-citizens was even more notable when compared to the gains made by Mexico's workers, who claimed meaningful social rights through invocation of revolutionary citizenship.[9]

As the foregoing suggests, Leguía subsequently alienated his working-class support. The continued growth of laboring populations in the capitalist corridors, however, meant that it was impossible to turn back the clock. By the end of the Oncenio, the "masses" had become a permanent fixture in political life (see chapters 5 and 6). With the collapse of the Leguía regime (in 1930), Peru's dispersed and divided elite groups struggled in vain to find ways of aggregating around a joint project of rule. The country's laboring populations, however, managed to come together in more of a shared project of protest. The vehicles of their unity were political parties: the Alianza Popular Revolucionaria Americana (APRA, Popular American Revolutionary Alliance) and the Partido Comunista Peruano (PCP, Communist Party of Peru).[10] These acted as forces that could aggregate the country's dispersed nuclei of resistance, at a time when elite groups lacked any such aggregating mechanism.

For several years after the fall of Leguía, the absence of a shared project of elite rule combined with the rise of populist, working-class politics to produce civil-war-like conditions. A return to order came only when General Óscar Benavides (1933–39) assumed national leadership after the assassination of the previous military strongman, Colonel Luis Sánchez Cerro (1930–33). The tensions that Benavides stepped in to contain remained unresolved, and as a result, the Peruvian military was in power for much of the 1930–56 era. During the era's brief periods of civilian rule, the armed forces were always close by, keeping a careful eye on things.

As David Nugent explores in chapter 7, as long as it could count on the cooperation of powerful regional allies, Leguía's regime was able to compel the rural, indigenous population to provide unpaid labor service for public works. With the collapse of the Oncenio, the new regime formally abolished the labor draft but found itself without the labor it required to develop infrastructure. To make matters worse, the regime could no longer count on the collaboration of once-powerful regional elites, the *castas*, whose unity had been undermined by the fall of Leguía. Officials in Chachapoyas, facing the inability to either exact enough labor via a sub rosa corvée to build roads or to admit the state's failure, conjured into being imaginary foes who were said to be undermining government efforts to help the nation progress.

POSTREVOLUTIONARY MEXICO: REAGGREGATION AS CLASS INTEGRATION

As the foregoing suggests, by the early 1930s the forces of order and those of change in Peru had arrived at a kind of impasse, in which neither could prevail over the other.[11] Furthermore, these opposing forces found themselves in a stalemate that would continue unresolved for decades. Such was not the case, however, in Mexico. Although the extended period of repressive, authoritarian rule associated with the Porfiriato produced a highly polarized society, one in which oppressive conditions of lived citizenship were in blatant violation of liberal principles, the regime that emerged after the revolution sought to extend new forms of lived and formal citizenship to previously excluded groups like workers, peasants, and (to a degree) women. Indeed, the armed phase of the revolution created unprecedented opportunities for laboring populations to become key participants in, and to some degree help shape, broader projects of citizenship and nationhood being pursued by contending elites. The dominant faction—the antecedent of the PRI—could never completely abandon a notion of revolutionary citizenship even after Cárdenas left power in 1940. Mexico's working peoples enjoyed moments of empowerment but also suffered periods of repression.

The collapse of the Díaz regime in 1911 created a power vacuum that a range of contenders sought to fill. They found it extremely difficult, however, to occupy the position that Díaz had vacated. The first attempt to do so was made by Francisco Madero, who sought a return to the purported normalcy of the Porfiriato (without its corruption, cronyism, and electoral fraud). A short-lived counterrevolutionary episode under General Victoriano Huerta helped draw a range of more radical forces into the escalating conflict. The main contending forces that emerged out of this process were the Zapatistas, the Villistas, and the Constitutionalists. As these groups sought to prevail, they were compelled to involve large numbers of rural cultivators and other laboring populations as their soldiers and noncombatants providing vital logistical support. In the process, much of the national population was mobilized for the war effort.

As the foregoing suggest, several competing projects of formal citizenship and nationhood took shape at this time. One of these was liberal and reformist in nature and was associated with Madero. A second project was agrarian and associated with Zapata, focused on rural democracy and restoration of peasant land seized during the Porfiriato via collective grants and smallholder production. A third project was soldier-citizenship based and was associated mainly with Pancho Villa, whose followers were promised land via military colonies distributed individually. The winning faction in the armed phase of the revolution, Álvaro Obregón and his more radical wing of the Constitutionalists, forged a fourth project that included elements of the other three, as well as appeals to labor union membership as a basis for political incorporation. For the present purposes, what is interesting about these projects is that they had broad national (or nationwide) followings and constituencies rather than regional or corridor-based ones. Furthermore, they were involved in a nationwide conflict with one another about what citizenship and nationhood should consist of.

There was enough support for these competing citizenship and nationhood projects that none could prevail over their adversaries without broad, popular support. In order to keep popular groups engaged and committed, elites were compelled to offer them inducements of an unprecedented nature. They commonly consisted of land, which was often seized from adversarial elites. They included as well protection from forced labor drafts, support for demands of organized labor, and *municipio libre*, or "local self-rule." As a result, more radical forms of formal and active citizenship found their way into the official programs and the on-the-ground policies of otherwise not-so-progressive groups.

The armed phase of the revolution ended in 1920 with the deposition of Carranza by a fraction of Carranza's own Constitutionalist group (along with surviving Zapatistas and labor organizations) headed by President Álvaro Obregón (1921–24) and Plutarco Elías Calles (1924–28). Although this signaled that the revolution as a military process was officially "over," the new postrevolutionary regime was nonetheless faced with ongoing challenges to its position from a range of opposition forces. As reflected in the repeated coup attempts of the 1920s and the Cristero War (1926–29), a series of disaffected groups were determined to undo the efforts to build up a new, postrevolutionary coalition. This meant that, if they were to remain in power, Obregón and Calles needed to maintain the active, ongoing support of laboring populations. It also meant continuing to provide these groups with protections, guarantees, concessions, and entitlements that would keep them committed to postrevolutionary regimes.

Toward that end, during and after the armed phase of the revolution a number of governors turned their respective jurisdictions into "laboratories of revolution." All supported organized labor and anticlerical efforts, and ended debt peonage. Some carried out their own land reform. Many also expanded education, and one governor, Salvador Alvarado, even extended (to some degree) a range of opportunities to women to participate in public life. These regional experiments help us understand how the dispersionary tendencies that were unleashed by the Mexican Revolution were ultimately overcome as a result of a process of a highly distinctive process of aggregation.

Unlike the other cases that we have discussed, the aggregation that brought the revolution to a close was not exclusively a process of reconsolidating elite interests. Rather, ruling class interests re-formed during the revolutionary interregnum in a context in which many old elites, particularly large landowners, had been ruined or fled, and elites both new (revolutionary) and old (surviving Porfirian) were compelled to forge new alliances that were *cross-class* in nature. A number of the entitlements and guarantees that elites were forced to offer to subalterns found their way into the Constitution of 1917 and helped define what might be thought of as "revolutionary citizenship." What was important about these rights and protections, however, was that they were more than discursive. They were an indispensable part of the strategy by which elites built up a postrevolutionary coalition that allowed them to reconsolidate and maintain their position as elites.

The contrast with Peru could not be more extreme. At the end of the War of the Pacific (1883), the strategy pursued by Peruvian elites was the opposite of that followed by their Mexican counterparts. Compared to Mexico, where the old agrarian elite was ruined across much of the country, much less of the old elite was ruined or fled.[12] Peruvian elites reestablished control not by creating new openings for subaltern groups but by foreclosing possibilities that were present at the time. Elite groups in Peru went so far as to cut their ties with rural cultivating populations, whose support they had enlisted during the conflict, to ensure that laboring groups were forced back into their former, subordinate positions.

Indeed, the Peruvian elite went out of their way to make public examples of rural cultivators who resisted elite efforts to return to the status quo—subalterns who championed alternative citizenship projects or forms of nationhood, and who sought to establish new entitlements for subaltern groups. Somewhat later (circa 1930), when APRA and the Communist Party formed, the situation remained polarized between the forces for order and those for change. There were no laboratories of revolution to speak of in Peru. Nor were there powerful elites whose ability to consolidate their position in a national coalition depended on supporting more expansive citizenship projects for subaltern groups.

Even so, there were real limits to the degree to which the Mexican Revolution could be revolutionary. The so-called Sonoran presidents (Obregón and Calles) headed a broad coalition including not only key generals but also radical labor and agrarista leaders. Nevertheless, the Sonoran presidents had to reconcile with U.S. finance, in part to frustrate harsh demands from U.S. oil and landowning interests and in part to jumpstart the economy of the war-torn country. Coming to terms with U.S. financial capital limited the Sonoran presidents' ability to enforce the more radical provisions of the Constitution. For instance, they went slow on agrarian reform in most states and did not

attempt to seize foreign oil. Furthermore, after the revolution a number of leading generals became landowners and businessmen, and they had to be given free
rein to pursue their activities. Additionally, because the export zones (cotton,
henequen, oil) that had arisen during the Porfiriato represented such important
sources of revenue for the national treasury, they were considered too lucrative
to nationalize. Finally, the need to attract domestic capital frightened off by
the revolution led to the formation of a national bank in 1925, which reassured
and in some ways favored Mexico's traditional, elite investing class. In short,
while Mexican capitalism was in some sense revolutionary, due to its focus on
domestic accumulation and respect for social guarantees that emerged out of
the revolution, it was still capitalism.

In chapter 8, Ben Fallaw explores a regional attempt to combine revolutionary capitalism and citizenship during Calles's era. In the early 1930s, Yucatecan governor Bartolomé García Correa hoped to use producer and consumer
cooperatives to balance private and public interests and extend significant
new economic and social rights to white-collar "intellectual workers," small
farmers, bus drivers, street vendors, and some workers. García Correa's socialist party also fostered a new revolutionary sociability through participation in
the party's paramilitary and sporting clubs, as well as educational reforms. In
spite of its shortcomings—above all the structural limits imposed by the Great
Depression—García Correa created one of the strongest and enduring regional
affiliates of the ruling party.

When Lázaro Cárdenas broke with his erstwhile mentor Calles in late 1935
and early 1936, Calles and his allies like García Correa were accused of ignoring the plight of workers and peasants and enabling revolutionary millionaires
(politically connected businessmen and bureaucrats) to accumulate substantial
capital at the nation's expense. To oust Calles's loyalists and counter the lingering effects of the Depression, Cárdenas turned to more radical measures.
By the mid-1930s, the regime no longer faced the same range of enemies that
it had confronted in the decade after the revolution's armed phase. The PRI—
formed in 1928–29 (under a different name) to protect the ruling coalition and
revolutionary capitalism—was able to establish the beginnings of a corporate
structure of inclusion for working populations, rural and urban alike. As time
passed, regimes became less and less revolutionary, and more and more capitalis-
tic. In 1929 global economic collapse threatened to create such great social stress
that the regime feared the emergence of a political rival on either the left or
the right. However, because the ruling regime had been forced by the Mexican

Revolution to extend a series of unprecedented inducements and protections to laboring populations, it had the capacity to fend off challengers by extending more inducements and protections to its laboring populations during the presidency of Lázaro Cárdenas. It is to the details of this process that we now turn.

FORGING REVOLUTIONARY CITIZENSHIP IN MEXICO

The relatively rapid collapse of the Porfiriato in 1910–11 is usually explained by a convergence of factors: the aging dictator's inability to pick a successor who could keep the elite unified, drought and a global economic downturn, landlessness and rural poverty, and labor unrest. When Francisco Madero announced his opposition to Díaz's eighth reelection in 1909, the Porfirian regime delayed repressing his Anti-Reelectionist Party, allowing its spread. Madero's campaign was fundamentally moderate, seeking to restore economic prosperity and protect liberal citizenship rights (especially for the better-off) by ending rampant corruption, cronyism, and electoral fraud. More radical elements, however, also mobilized at this time in response to Madero's challenge to Díaz, above all agraristas and urban anarchists. When Díaz belatedly sought to repress Madero's campaign, Madero escaped to the United States and issued a call for revolt on November 20, 1910.

The revolution that erupted took a full decade to conclude. The conflict had many dimensions, but conflicting claims regarding the nature of citizenship and capitalism played a central role. One prominent set of claims was predominantly liberal in nature. The enormous gap between formal (i.e., liberal) and active citizenship provided a framework for claims-making on the part of multitudes of ordinary Mexicans—who invoked rights guaranteed them by the 1857 Constitution. Madero provided validation for such claims by calling for a redemption of those very rights.

Other groups, however, took up arms to establish alternative forms of citizenship that went beyond liberal conceptions and were based on what might be called social rights. Most important in this regard were rights to land, water, and forest. Land rights in particular acted as a rallying cry that brought together a wide range of groups of diverse social origins. These included members of peasant (and often indigenous) communities, especially in Morelos. They also included military colonists in locales such as Chihuahua who had lost their hard-won village autonomy as well as their land with the end of the Indian

Wars in the 1880s (and who formed the core of Pancho Villa's Division of the North).[13] Those who rallied around the demand for land also included the indigenous Yaquis, whose lands were seized on an extensive scale during the Porfiriato and who were attacked in a genocidal campaign from 1903 to 1907. The Yaquis were the best infantry in the army of Álvaro Obregón, the popular warlord of the northwest.

In central Mexico, rancheros and peasants whose grandfathers fought for the Liberals against Conservatives and the French Intervention inherited a "popular, folk liberal tradition" grounded in patriarchal male democracy and a strong military tradition.[14] Under the banner of Emiliano Zapata, they embraced a form of citizenship based on social rights in land and water that directly contradicted Porfirian agrarian capitalism. Indeed, Zapata's 1911 Plan de Ayala demanded the return of extensive areas of land stolen from peasants, even as it protected small property holders like Zapata. The Zapatistas of the central-southern states became a virtually unbeatable guerrilla fighting force within their home region.

The 1910 Revolution was far too complex to be reduced to a revolt against foreign investment or capitalism. Even so, the cumulative effects of the previous three decades—which had seen Mexico's productive resources concentrated in the hands of a small number of domestic elites and foreign investors, and the country's popular classes dispossessed and immiserated—profoundly shaped the revolution's origins, process, and eventual outcome. Initially, elites who had turned their back on Díaz were reassured by Madero's gradualist approach to land reform and his refusal to disband the Porfirian army. Madero's caution, however, spurred Zapata to revolt against him in 1911, which in turn convinced many large landowners and business interests of Madero's weakness. These elements of the old elite encouraged a counterrevolutionary coup by high-ranking generals, a plot drafted in U.S. ambassador Henry Lane Wilson's office. After chaotic fighting in downtown Mexico City, the brutal general Victoriano Huerta took power.

Huerta attempted to raise a huge military, restore the Porfirian social order (and its economic model), and roll back the political gains made by many popular groups during Madero's *apertura*. His efforts to do so, however, backfired. Indeed, Huerta sparked a second, even stronger series of revolts, above all in the northern states—the cradle of Madero's 1910–11 revolt. Trapped between Villa and other rebels in the north, and Zapata and other agraristas in central Mexico—and squeezed by U.S. president Woodrow Wilson's occupation of Veracruz—Huerta was forced out in mid-1914.

The victorious factions then sought to draft a new constitution. Delegates were chosen by warlords, a clear demonstration that political decision-making was a highly restricted affair and was also linked to military participation. It was male, martial, and personalistic. The convention split, however, triggering a war of the winners in the struggle against Huerta. Zapata and Villa's factions were left in control of the convention and sought to govern from Mexico City. Their rivals, the Constitutionalists, created a rival regime based temporarily in Veracruz.

After several months of intense conventional warfare, the Constitutionalists prevailed in late 1914 and early 1915, although some supporters of Villa and Zapata continued guerrilla warfare until 1920. The victory assured, Venustiano Carranza became president. Some see Carranza's victory as a triumph of capitalism over popular forces championing radical reform. It is true that Carranza returned much land to hacendados, and he kept henequen and oil exports flowing to supply vital war matériel for the United States. In 1915, however, the Constitutionalists adopted agrarian reform as part of an attempt to create a less unequal and less foreign-dominated capitalist economy. They also hoped to gain much-needed political support from agraristas. The Constitutionalists also found it necessary to form alliances with the urban working class and urban intellectuals, to whom they also made concessions—and in the process, found themselves pushed to the left.

The Villistas and especially the Zapatistas are seen as favoring agrarian reform while the Constitutionalists opposed it. However, Villa and Zapata kept most large estates intact for fear of wrecking the economy at least until the war's end. Both the Villistas and the Zapatistas had strong ranchero constituencies that defended private (if predominantly smallholder) property in land. In fact, the profound differences between the Constitutionalists and the Villista-Zapata coalition over the size and strength of the national government were just as important as the agrarian question when it came to which forms of capitalism and citizenship they favored.

Villistas and Zapatistas planned to weaken the central government in order to protect local democracy and thus defend the cherished ideal of egalitarian (if patriarchal) citizenship. The Constitutionalists, on the other hand, favored a strong central government that encouraged domestic capital accumulation, above all in industry and finance, and that defended marginalized groups like Indians, workers, and (less energetically) women. Faced with these choices, bankers, industrialists, and many large landowners viewed the Constitutionalists as the lesser of two evils.

If the Constitutionalists hoped to reform and "Mexicanize" (i.e., nationalize) capitalism through government policy, some Constitutionalist military governors used more radical means to achieve this goal. These "revolutionary proconsuls" used their extensive powers to convert their jurisdictions into "laboratories of the revolution," extending new rights and protections to many groups that had been repressed during the Porfiriato. The end of debt peonage, support for organized labor, and (halting) attempts to allow women more access to education and the workplace stand out as achievements.

By 1920 Obregón's wing of the Constitutionalists had ended ten years of civil conflict, in part by making peace with surviving Zapatistas and dispatching the more conservative president Carranza. In the process, this faction laid the foundation for a period of economic growth that was based on principles of economic nationalism and included a range of important social rights chartered by the 1917 Constitution. The revolutionary Magna Carta was something of a hybrid affair. It reaffirmed the commitment of the 1857 charter to the (liberal) rights of citizenship, including private property. But leftists who had joined the coalition inserted a range of important social rights, such as unionization and land reform. They also curbed private property rights, in two important ways. First, Article 27 of the Constitution of 1917 (re)nationalized subsoil wealth. Second, Article 28 gave the government extensive power to fight monopolies, set prices, and even set up parastatal companies in economic sectors designated as strategic. "Revolutionary" capitalism thus did more than promote economic nationalism, domestic accumulation, and social guarantees. Thus, the Constitution of 1917 allowed for a much larger public sector.

While the Constitution of 1917 did indeed include a range of important social rights, the conditions of lived citizenship with which laboring groups were confronted during the postrevolutionary period evolved together with Mexico's peculiar form of revolutionary capitalism. As the new political elite sought economic growth in the 1920–32 period, they pursued generally conciliatory policies toward capital. During the 1933–38 period associated with President Lázaro Cárdenas (1934–40), the political elite moved left in response to the Great Depression and growing popular demands. A rightward correction began in 1938 and accelerated during the 1940s, as the postrevolutionary state focused on industrialization in (quiet) partnership with foreign and domestic capital.

Even when postrevolutionary regimes sought to encourage domestic and foreign investment, however, they were compelled by expediency to respect the social rights of marginalized groups. During the 1920s, for example, the government was forced to rely on agrarian militias made up of recipients of land grants during military coups and the Cristero War—and rewarded militia members with land seized from conservative landlords. During the same period, radical governors mobilized workers, peasants, leftist intellectuals, and religious minorities—and at times women. Several carried out regional land reforms.

These popular gains were reflected in the 1928–29 formation of a national political party known today as the PRI. The PRI sought to create corporatist affiliates for workers, peasants, and a vaguely defined "popular sector" (the middle class, cooperatives, young people, and, to a lesser extent, women). Over time, the ruling party's corporatism would diminish mobilization from below, marginalize leftist ideologies, and stimulate bossism. It would also allow some favored popular groups—a kind of revolutionary "aristocracy of labor"—like industrial workers and bus drivers to claim not just patronage but also the benefits of an industrial welfare regime.

While the revolution helped give expression to a new project of formal citizenship, conditions of lived citizenship often deviated significantly from the revolutionary ideal. The archives are filled with pleas to powerful patrons for *garantías*, or rights, above all for personal security. Postrevolutionary governments did ultimately control chronic violence, at least in urban areas. This stability at the top, however, was achieved in part by tolerating and even instrumentally using endemic local-level violence, especially in rural areas.[15]

In chapter 9, Benjamin Smith discusses one very important contradiction between lived and formal revolutionary citizenship: the labor drafts enforced on indigenous Mexicans after the revolution well into the 1950s. As he shows, revolutionary indigenist rhetoric made it easier to ignore constitutional prohibitions against unpaid labor, as teachers and politicians invoked the need to uplift the Indian in justifying demands for uncompensated work to build roads and schools. Unlike the increasingly self-deluded government officials in Peru during the afterlife of the Conscripción Vial, Mexico's caciques and officials had both the local knowledge and the degree of political legitimacy needed to make demands stick when persuasion failed. Unpaid labor by mostly poor and indigenous citizens thus helped build a national road network decades after the Porifiran corvée had supposedly been ended by the revolution.

REVOLUTION AND CAPITALISM IN MEXICO

While the 1917 Constitution promised to reform capitalism through government action and by empowering workers and peasants, postrevolutionary regimes faced formidable limits to their power to do so. This was in part because, as time passed, the relationship between postrevolutionary governments and private capital became increasingly close if not symbiotic. Indeed, new political elites found ways to evade postrevolutionary limits on property rights, fiscal regulations, and agrarian reform. Generals exercised much power informally and extralegally in favor of capital, in no small part because over time, many became landowners and, in some cases, businessmen.

Landowners and businessmen for their part sought out revolutionary generals as silent partners to protect themselves from expropriation, rising labor costs, and unwanted taxation and regulation. In the political culture of the time, these new elites felt entitled to benefit from having risked their lives in the armed phase of the revolution and the often bloody postrevolutionary public sphere that followed. These entrepreneurs saw no conflict between public service and the accumulation of landed estates and businesses (including casinos) or receiving preferential loans from government-sponsored banks.

The need to restore Mexico's credit-worthiness was another important restraint on the postrevolutionary government's radical wing. To rebuild Mexico's busted banks, in 1925 Calles and his chief financial consigliere, Alberto J. Pani, created and helped fund the Banco de México (Banxico), in partnership with holdover Porfirian bankers. The involvement of government stakeholders reassured private bankers. The banks that thrived often owed their success to political ties—northern states' banks and larger banks did best. But just as with Banamex created by the Porfiriato, the concessions given to Banxico failed to increase competition among banks, discouraged lending to small- and medium-sized firms, and encouraged insider lending. Even so, the postrevolutionary government technocrats were able to arrange access to foreign credit to fund developmentalist goals without complete reliance on the old Porfirian bankers.[16]

International pressure also channeled the revolution in a more moderate direction at key moments. During the armed phase of the revolution, the United States wisely refused to intervene and occupy large tracts of Mexican territory for protracted periods of time, as some reactionary U.S. oil interests demanded. Such a foreign military intervention would likely have radicalized the revolution, as it did in the Russian and French Revolutions. Second, U.S. demand for minerals, henequen, and oil would have made the cost of national-izing these key productive resources prohibitively high.[17] Even so, U.S.-Mexico relations remained strained until the late 1920s. By that time, oil, a key bone of contention between the two countries after the Constitution of 1917 nation-alized subsoil rights, had become a symbol of national sovereignty for many Mexicans.

The Great Depression exacerbated economic problems stemming from the Cristero War (1926–29), which devastated the Bajío, Mexico's breadbasket, and the decline of oil revenues. Austerity, the government's remedy, only made matters worse. In early 1932, the government reversed course, beginning deficit spending that mitigated the worst of the depression. Unemployment, a credit crunch, and growing poverty helped empower the left wing of the regime, lead-ing the regime to tap Lázaro Cárdenas for the 1934–40 term.

Cárdenas accelerated land reform, backed labor unions, and challenged many powerful businessmen and hacendados and their political allies. The high-water mark of Cardenista radicalism was the nationalization of U.S. and British-Dutch oil companies in March 1938. Oil nationalization, however, diverted increasingly scarce federal funding, leaving less to promote the col-lective farming of cash crops like henequen and cotton. In the end, Cárdenas simply lacked the resources to support all the ejidos and schools he sought to create.[18] That said, Cárdenas's heterogeneous, improvised coalition managed to implement far-reaching, redistributionist policies that mitigated the worst of the depression and pushed the revolutionary regime in a more radical direc-tion before retreating from his most ambitious goals during the second half of his administration.[19]

Cárdenas's post-1938 moderation was also due to widespread conservative political and social resistance that compromised some elements of postrevolu-tionary policy. It forced Cárdenas to exclude small landholdings, *pequeña propie-dad*, from agrarian reforms demands. This exception proved to be surprisingly elastic and was stretched to spare even large holdings. Catholicism's defense of private property as a natural right, combined with Catholic resistance to Cárdenas's socialist education and alleged communistic tendencies, proved to be a formidable framework for resistance to Cárdenas's radical reforms. Pro-Cárdenas governors were forced to rely on regional power brokers with strong ties to Catholic organizations like parents' groups, which also checked the power of leftist Cardenistas and pushed the regime rightward.[20]

MEXICO AND PERU AT MIDCENTURY: DIVERGENCE AND (SOME) CONVERGENCE

The rightward tilt in federal policies evident in the last three years of Cárdenas's presidency became more pronounced after he left office in 1940. Agrarian reform was partially undone by a counteragrarian reform, as most ejidos were starved of state support and commercial agriculture was favored in lending and irrigation policies. Culturally, the right was reassured as well, as anticlericalism and any trace of admiration for Communism was purged from the education curriculum in the 1940s.

After 1940 Mexico's postrevolutionary regime continued to intervene in the economy, but instead of trying to create worker cooperatives and peasant ejidos it promoted import substitution industrialization. Mexico's entry into World War II and the boost in U.S. purchasing gave Mexican mining and especially agriculture much-needed stimulus. This watershed period—the 1940s—marks the start of three defining events of mid-twentieth-century Mexico: the (economic) miracle, the PRI's Golden Age, and a marked increase in "corruption" within the PRI.

Most accounts assume corruption was crucial in the PRI's *dictablanda*, as co-optation overshadowed but never completely supplemented violence. Was capitalism exceptionally corrupt during the PRI's Golden Age? Did it facilitate economic growth or siphon off profits from it? Unfortunately, the analytical value of the term *corruption* is at times overshadowed by its more judgmental, if not ethnocentric, dimensions. Indeed, the study of corruption presents major epistemological challenges.[21] While there are cases of outright expropriation, extortion, and embezzlement by politicians, their fortunes were more commonly made "in the protective shadow of the revolution"—through insider knowledge, public contracts, and favorable loans from national development banks.[22] Remarkably, one of the most prominent defenders of the postrevolutionary order, former treasury secretary Alberto J. Pani, rationalized the activities of "revolutionary capitalists" like himself as moral benefactors of the nation.[23]

The ideal revolutionary capitalists, however, seemed few and far between. More common were the politically connected speculators and traffickers in alcohol and governmental concessions—individuals who profited from revolutionary upheaval through political connections and predatory lending. One such person was U.S. immigrant William Jenkins of Puebla, who assembled a vast sugar-producing enterprise centered on the mill of Atencingo in the 1920s.

Jenkins paid peons poorly and relied on subornation, strong-arming, and the support of prominent political protectors to avoid taxation and regulation. That said, Jenkins created the most productive sugar estate in Latin America, based on large investments in technology, modern business practices, and economies of scale. Like the ideal (and perhaps imaginary) model revolutionary capitalist, Jenkins reinvested in sectors ranging from manufacturing to cinemas rather than exporting profits.[24]

Mexican industrialists benefited from the developmentalist policies of a series of postrevolutionary regimes. As described by Benjamin Smith in this volume, these included road construction, which helped complete the work begun by Porfirian railroads of knitting the vast nation together into a single domestic market. Import substitution industrialization, including subsidies, tariffs, and investments in infrastructure and human capital, offered Mexican manufacturers substantial advantages. Ironically, although businessmen bemoaned Cárdenas's leftism, Cárdenas created a stable environment for the accumulation of capitalism even during the peak of his radical reforms.[25]

Mexico's surge in industry in the 1940s was shepherded by developmentalist policies and entrepreneurs who claimed the mantle of revolutionary capitalist. Over the long run, however, Mexican industry failed to modernize technologically and also failed to engage in production for export. These faults were at least in part due to protectionism and to the failure of banks to support technological innovation.[26]

It could be argued that Mexico's model of development was ultimately more successful politically than economically. Specifically, postrevolutionary economic policy neutralized or co-opted potential opponents among Mexico's upper class, who might have spurred greater innovation. Starting in the 1920s, bankers proved willing to work with revolutionary governments, even during the radical Cardenista era. So did some progressive industrialists, who benefited from the stronger domestic market created by rising wages, as well as tariffs. By the early 1940s, industrial capital no longer had to turn to generals-turned-businessmen for protection. Instead, it could count on state-sponsored lobbying organizations, which helped overcome Mexican businessmen's suspicions of the intentions of the revolutionary government.[27]

By 1950 Mexico's postrevolutionary regimes had largely completed the process of aggregation of dispersed, corridor-based nodes of interconnected industrial, agrarian, and financial capitalism (although some, like the "Monterrey Group," retained a degree of autonomy). It could be argued that the revolution began by trying to tame capitalism, but forty years later capitalism had tamed the revolution. Agrarian reform had been slowed if not reversed, the integration of working people through corporatist organizations had diverted and dulled demands for redistribution, and economic nationalism had delivered market protections, subsidies, a healthier and better-educated workforce, and a larger domestic market.

By 1950 Peru's post-Oncenio regimes, in contrast, had been unable to aggregate the country's dispersed corridors of capitalism into a coherent, national coalition. Nor had Peru been able to find a place in such a coalition for the country's many regional powerholders, who were at a remove from the capitalist corridors. As a result, government regimes found themselves pushed and pulled in contradictory directions, by a range of centripetal and centrifugal forces. Further complicating efforts to form a national coalition was an additional fact: in stark contrast to what had transpired in Mexico, ruling elites in Peru were not compelled to make concessions to laboring groups that integrated them into the ruling coalition. To the contrary, in Peru elite interests were best served by denying such concessions to working populations. As a result, by 1930 relations between elites and subalterns had arrived at a tense impasse—one that was not to be resolved for decades. This was so much the case that it fell to the military to maintain order.

Over the next twenty years, Peru experienced repeated political upheavals, which successive central regimes sought to manage and ameliorate. Drinot's carefully crafted case study of the Ticapampa mines in chapter 6 demonstrates that the labor state that consolidated under Leguía survived his fall, as government agencies sought to increase their capacity to mediate between labor and capital (first during the short-lived administrations of Luis Sánchez Cerro [1931–33] and Óscar Benavides [1933–39], and later beyond). The labor state, understood as a set of legal and discursive possibilities, sought to shape relations between labor and capital and to give the midcentury regimes in Peru some measure of stability and legitimacy.

The democratic spring experienced in much of Latin America during World War II (most notably in Guatemala) reached Peru. In 1945 a weak but reform-minded president, José Bustamante y Rivero, legalized APRA, as part of a negotiated restoration of civilian rule. However, when APRA swept the congressional elections, the conservative opposition accused the party of refusing to respect constitutional norms. In addition to infuriating its opponents, APRA also made ever-deeper inroads in the military, to the horror of high-ranking generals. In 1948 militant Apristas—acting without Víctor Raúl Haya de la Torre's blessing—conspired with like-minded elements in the military to launch an ill-fated coup.[28] In response, General Manuel Odría and a handful of leading generals launched a countercoup, seized power on October 27, 1948, and unleashed a campaign of brutal repression against APRA. In a sense, Peru returned to the same historical situation as in the early 1930s, when the country was bitterly divided and neither APRA nor its antagonists, a coalition of generals and elites, was strong enough to definitively or permanently gain the upper hand.[29]

Mexico and Peru began the twentieth century on seemingly different historical trajectories. The Porfiriato had achieved international recognition for implementing cutting-edge liberal economic policies that subordinated the citizenship rights of the laboring majority to the demands of fiscal and political stability. The Porifian regime encouraged domestic capital accumulation and successfully courted investment from the Global North. The Aristocratic Republic of Peru pursued similar policies with less notable results. Only Mexico could boast of a truly integrated national coalition, heavy industry, or a rail network spanning most of the nation.

The Porifiriato collapsed spectacularly in Latin America's first social revolution, and a new regime could come to power only by making a series of concessions to its working peoples—what we term revolutionary citizenship. At its maximum expression under Cárdenas, revolutionary reforms included the nationalization of the foreign-owned petroleum industry and highly capitalized agrarian estates.

The contrast with Peru between 1920 and 1940 could not be greater: Leguía's regime deposed the Aristocratic Republic but then moved to demobilize popular forces and make a number of concessions to domestic and international capital. The Oncenio lasted only eleven years and was followed by what we would call a Peruvian stand-off: a conservative coalition that represented capital export sectors, established interests, and the Church held on to power only through continued repression and military rule.

In spite of these considerable differences, by the middle of the twentieth century, Mexico and Peru's trajectories seemed to be coming together, if in limited ways. As Ragas notes in chapter 4, after the collapse of Leguía the new regime was forced to begin the slow process of expanding suffrage, although illiterates were not granted the right to vote until 1979. Starting around 1938, the more progressive and inclusive postrevolutionary regime in Mexico began to undermine revolutionary citizenship in favor of capital accumulation, industrialization, and political stability. Peru's experiment with import substitution industrialization after World War II proved short-lived, but here too the Andean country seemed to be adopting economic policies and political practices embraced by Mexico decades earlier, albeit in a more moderate, cautious manner. Meanwhile the influence of the revolution on capitalism and citizenship in Mexico continued to wane during the 1940s. By midcentury, the paths of the two nations, which had diverged dramatically due to the impact of the Mexican Revolution and the Oncenio's rise and fall decades earlier, seemed to converge.

NOTES

We have found the following works to be especially useful in framing this section of the chapter: Manuel Burga and Alberto Flores Galindo, *Apogeo y crisis de la república aristocrática* (Lima: Rikchay Perú, 1979); Julio Cotler, *Clases, estado y nación en el Perú* (Lima: Instituto de Estudios Peruanos, 1978); Paulo Drinot, *The Allure of Labor: Workers, Race, and the Making of the Peruvian State* (Durham, N.C.: Duke University Press, 2011); Peter F. Klarén, *Modernization, Dislocation and Aprismo: Origins of the Peruvian Aprista Party, 1870–1932* (Austin: University of Texas Press, 1973); Daniel Masterson, *Militarism and Politics in Latin America: Peru from Sanchez Cerro to Sendero Luminoso* (Santa Barbara, Calif.: Praeger, 1991); Steve Stein, *Populism in Peru: The Emergence of the Masses and the Politics of Social Control* (Madison: University of Wisconsin Press, 1980); Denis Sulmont, *El movimiento obrero en el Perú, 1900–1956* (Lima: Pontífica Universidad Católica del Perú, Fondo Editorial, 1980); and Lewis Taylor, *Bandits and Politics in Peru: Landlord and Peasant Violence in Hualgayoc, 1900–30* (Cambridge: Centre of Latin American Studies, University of Cambridge, 1986).

1. Friedrich Katz, *The Secret War in Mexico: Europe, the United States and the Mexican Revolution* (Chicago: University of Chicago Press, 1981), 7–9.

2. Katz, *The Secret War in Mexico*, 35–39.

3. The coastal elite of the turn of the century bore a striking resemblance to the coastal elite of the guano age. Both were highly Europeanized and looked to the old-world centers of civilization (in particular, Paris) as their cultural point of reference. Both regarded the highland indigenous population as primitive and uncivilized.

4. The "Forty Families" is a term used in Peru to refer to the small coterie of inter-linked elite families who controlled much of the country's export-oriented wealth and most of its important positions of political power.

5. Leguía's supporters included junior army officers and elements of the military rank and file.

6. Leguía had actually planned to borrow a total of $250,000,000 (the equivalent of approximately $3.44 billion in 2016 dollars) but was removed from office before he could reach that goal. Leguía had no collateral to support these loans, other than a balanced budget and a record of economic growth during the Aristocratic Republic.

7. Drinot, *The Allure of Labor*, 53–56.

8. Drinot, *The Allure of Labor*, 232–34.

9. Drinot, *The Allure of Labor*, 112. In another parallel with revolutionary Mexico, Leguía also embraced indigenism, celebrating the Inka past and (for a while at least) supporting the work of the Comité Pro Derecho Indígena Tahuantinsuyu, which advocated education as well as ritual celebration of Peru's indigenous past. Fiona Wilson, "Leguía y la política indigenista," in *La Patria Nueva: Economía, sociedad y cultura en el Perú, 1919–1930*, ed. Paulo Drinot (Raleigh: Editorial A Contra Corriente, 2018), 150–53. As in the case of the outreach to workers, Leguía's promises to uplift indigenous Peruvians were largely unfulfilled yet served to distinguish his regime from the Civilista past and delineate an appealing if vague future of an industrial, modern Peru.

10. A number of scholars have observed that APRA was especially influential among elements of the working class that were organized into unions, and that the party's popularity was much less among informal groups. This important point applies with special force to Lima, the national capital.

11. Our discussion of the armed phase of the revolution and the postrevolutionary period (1920–40) is indebted to John Coatsworth, "Comment on 'The United States and the Mexican Peasantry,'" in *Rural Revolt in Mexico and U.S. Intervention*, ed. Daniel Nugent (San Diego: Center for U.S.-Mexican Studies, University of California, San Diego, 1988), 61–68; José Alfredo Gómez Estrada, *Lealtades divididas: Camarillas y poder en México, 1913–1932* (Mexico City: Instituto Mora, 2012); Nora Hamilton, *The Limits of State Autonomy* (Princeton, N.J.: Princeton University Press, 1982); Katz, *The Secret War in Mexico*; Alan Knight, *The Mexican Revolution*, 2 vols. (Lincoln: University of Nebraska Press, 1986); Alan Knight, "The Peculiarities of Mexican History: Mexico Compared to Latin America, 1821–1992," *Journal of Latin American Studies* 24, no. 1 (March 1992): 99–144; Mary Kay Vaughan, *Cultural Politics in Revolution: Teachers, Peasants and Schools in Mexico, 1930–1940* (Tucson: University of Arizona Press, 1997); Mark Wasserman, *Pesos and Politics: Business, Elites, Foreigners, and Government in Mexico, 1854–1940* (Stanford: Stanford University Press, 2015).

12. The exception would be the coastal estate sector. The 1880s and 1890s witnessed a wave of foreign takeovers, as domestic elites found themselves unable to compete with foreign capital.

13. Friedrich Katz, "The Agrarian Policies and Ideas of the Revolutionary Mexican Factions Led by Emiliano Zapata, Pancho Villa, and Venustiano Carranza," in *Reforming Mexico's Agrarian Reform*, ed. Laura Randall (Armonk, N.Y.: M. E. Sharpe, 1996), 21–24.

14. Knight, *The Mexican Revolution*, 1:309; Florencia Mallon, *Peasant and Nation: The Making of Postcolonial Mexico and Peru* (Berkeley: University of California Press, 1995), 224.

15. Alan Knight, "Habitus and Homicide: Political Culture in Revolutionary Mexico," in *Citizens of the Pyramid: Essays on Mexican Political Culture*, ed. Wil Pansters (Amsterdam: Thela, 1997), 107–29.

16. Noel Maurer, *The Power and the Money: The Mexican Financial System, 1876–1932* (Stanford: Stanford University Press, 2002); Susan Gauss, *Made in Mexico: Regions, Nation, and the State in the Rise of Mexican Industrialism, 1920s–1940s* (College Station: Pennsylvania State University Press, 2010).

17. Coatsworth, "Comment on 'The United States and the Mexican Peasantry,'" 64.

18. Ben Fallaw, *Cárdenas Compromised: The Failure of Reform in Postrevolutionary Yucatán* (Durham, N.C.: Duke University Press, 2001), 162–63.

19. Alan Knight, "Cardenismo: Juggernaut or Jalopy?," *Journal of Latin American Studies* 26, no. 1 (February 1994): 73–107.

20. Ben Fallaw, *Religion and State Formation in Postrevolutionary Mexico* (Durham, N.C.: Duke University Press, 2013).

21. See preface, note 5.

22. Francisco Naranjo, "Los millonarios de la Revolución: Exordio," *Diario de Yucatán*, July 27, 1948, 1, 6.

23. Arnaldo Córdova, *La ideología de la Revolución Mexicana: La formación del nuevo régimen* (Mexico City: Era, 1985), 367–68n123.

24. Andrew Paxman, *Jenkins of Mexico: How a Southern Farm Boy Became a Mexican Magnate* (Oxford: Oxford University Press, 2017).

25. Hamilton, *The Limits of State Autonomy*.

26. Stephen Haber, *Industry and Underdevelopment: The Industrialization of Mexico, 1890–1940* (Stanford: Stanford University Press, 1989).

27. Gauss, *Made in Mexico*.

28. Víctor Raúl Haya de la Torre was the founder and leader of APRA.

29. Masterson's book (*Militarism and Politics in Latin America*, 65–110) has been especially useful in understanding the Byzantine background to the failed 1948 uprising and subsequent coup.

5

SHIFTING STATE-LANDLORD-PEASANT RELATIONS IN THE DISTRICTS OF ASUNCIÓN AND COSPÁN (CAJAMARCA, PERU), 1920–1930

LEWIS TAYLOR

Perhaps the most important change that Peru has experienced over this century has been the transition from a closed oligarchic society to one of citizens, via a process that has not yet been concluded.

—SINESIO LÓPEZ, *CIUDADANOS REALES E IMAGINARIOS: CONCEPCIONES, DESARROLLO Y MAPAS DE LA CIUDADANÍA EN EL PERÚ*

STANDARD INTERPRETATIONS of Peru's "long nineteenth century" (to 1919) hold that independence from Spain ushered in decades of instability and decline that the wealth generated during the guano age (1845–1918) failed to arrest. It is posited that the integrated economy characteristic of the colonial era dissolved as the country split into various weak regional markets, leading to stagnation—a situation exacerbated by financial collapse during the 1870s, Chilean victory in the War of the Pacific (1879–82), and a damaging civil war (1883–85). Although during the Aristocratic Republic (1895–1919) efforts were made at economic modernization, these were mostly confined to the coast and centered on an expanding plantation economy (sugar, cotton, rice). Outside those areas benefiting from railway construction and directly linked to international markets (essentially the wool trade that linked Puno and Cusco with Arequipa in the south and mining in the central highlands), negligible socioeconomic change is said to have occurred in the sierra, where the domination of the great estate and a natural economy orientated toward the production of use values predominated.[1] In consequence, "the Andean reserve" supposedly became divorced from national economic and political life; its "social structures were incompatible with the generalization of a free contract economy," to an extent that the mass of the highland population remained "separated from disencumbered access to the market and the state."[2] Such a widely held perspective has led to claims that in the latter period of Peru's "adrift" nineteenth century, capitalism on the littoral coexisted alongside "precapitalism" in the sierra, where "the peasants retreated from the money economy and consequently the highlands separated from the coast."[3] At the political level it is argued that the Peruvian state remained largely absent in the interior. After a period of chaotic rule by military caudillos, a compromise settlement eventually emerged whereby an unholy alliance of Lima-based mercantile "oligarchs" and provincial *gamonales* (local strongmen / political bosses) of "feudal" persuasion governed the country, the latter being allowed considerable operational autonomy in their backyards in return for maintaining social control over the rural and urban poor. Taking their cue from José Carlos Mariátegui, the traditional accepted position holds that Peru lacked a progressive "national bourgeoisie" capable of promoting economic development or advancing social and political modernization, so to convert excluded subjects into citizens.[4]

According to mainstream historiography, this panorama modified during President Augusto Bernardino Leguía's Oncenio (1919–30), when a concerted effort was undertaken to address the country's socioeconomic fragmentation and assert tighter control throughout the national territory via (1) a more rigorous selection of departmental prefects whose loyalty lay primarily with the executive in Lima; (2) expanding the ranks of centrally contracted civil servants (898 in 1920, rising to 5,313 in 1931); and (3) the creation of a national police force, the Guardia Civil (in 1924).[5] Given the absence of a party, Leguía had to construct a clientele. To consolidate patron-client networks outside Lima, Leguía established regional parliaments: the Congreso Regional del Norte served as a ploy to promote centralization under a veneer of decentralization; prominent among its membership figured more progressive elements of the landlord class from across northern departments. Other integrative initiatives designed to promote "progress" included an ambitious road construction program utilizing corvée labor (Conscripción Vial), along with related infrastructural improvements (ports, railways, and large-scale irrigation schemes, notably on the northern coast). The education system also underwent reorganization and expansion. In addition to responding to middle-class aspirations for jobs, development, and "modernity," Leguía acted to counter an increasingly vociferous *indigenista* movement by establishing in 1920 the Indigenous Affairs Department in the Ministerio de Fomento (Ministry of Development), under the directorship (until his dismissal in 1923) of prominent socialist Hildebrando Castro Pozo and staffed by committed functionaries who traveled throughout the Andes sounding out grievances. Official recognition of peasant communities was written into the 1920 Constitution as part of a strategy to forge patron-client ties between the administration and rural populace as well as placate pro-Indian activists.

Leguía's objective vis-à-vis the sierra not only embraced capitalist modernization from above while controlling the peasantry. The president also sought to diminish gamonal autonomy. As a consequence of such policies and general social change underway since the turn of the century, upon Leguía's ousting in August 1930, subtle modifications had occurred in landowner-peasant-state relations. New sources of power, networks of authority, and ideological currents emerged that complicated government administration, hacendado suzerainty, and the maintenance of social control. This chapter seeks to explore these shifts through examining developments during the 1920s and 1930s in the districts of Asunción and Cospán, contiguous jurisdictions located in the department of Cajamarca in Peru's northern sierra. Before the extension of the road network and the advent of motor vehicles in the late 1920s, they lay approximately five to six hours by horseback from the town of Cajamarca, the departmental capital. In the conclusion, the perceived sociopolitical developments are examined vis-à-vis classic state theory (Max Weber).

HISTORICAL BACKGROUND, 1870–1919

In contrast to stereotypical accounts of Andean society during the second half of the nineteenth century through to the Aristocratic Republic, this highland area had not been divorced from the money economy or separated from the coast. Given its strategic position on the western cusp of the Andean range and proximity to east-west trade routes, all strata of the population participated consistently in local and regional commodity and labor markets.[6] A long muleteer tradition also pushed male inhabitants into considerable circular migration, with northern coastal valleys as well as neighboring highland provinces.[7]

Commercial activity and mobility were stimulated by the construction of the railway from the port of Pacasmayo up the Jequetepeque Valley to the small settlement of Chilete (completed in 1871), while road improvements deeper into the Andes to better link the railhead with the departmental capital were carried out during the 1890s. Although sizeable haciendas monopolized the soil, the area's agrarian social structure contained medium-scale properties and numerous peasant smallholdings—mostly independent freeholders but including a number of (as yet officially unrecognized) peasant communities.

While real, landlord power was far from absolute and did not go uncontested. Unsurprisingly, given the importance of muleteer employment, banditry and related types of rural crime flourished—subaltern scope for maneuver being facilitated by the local state's weak coercive capacity and the centrality of factional political conflict, which fractured elite unity and enabled the more astute among the disenfranchised to play off one group against the other. Enthusiastically pursued intersettlement rivalry fueled by a strong sense of *paisanaje*, especially between the small district capitals of Asunción and Cospán, comprised a further source of social disorder. Indeed, the denizens of the two districts frequently resisted attempts by the authorities to collect taxes, requisition their labor power for road work, or conscript them into the army. In no way did the inhabitants conform to Santiago Távara's portrayal of a submissive highland peasantry resigned to "perpetual servitude," lacking "the energy to demand justice against swindlers and given to passive indifference."[8]

Quite the contrary, prior to the War of the Pacific parishioners from Cospán had acquired a well-earned reputation for overt insubordination, spirited independence, and bellicosity—with habitants of the hamlet of Huatún being especially famed for brigandage and assassination. By the late 1870s, they were led by local warlord Anacleto Hoyos, whose fundo covered a small valley surrounded by high peaks that stood between Asunción and Cospán. Hoyos managed to build up a sizeable following among his many relatives as well as fugitives fleeing from the law elsewhere in Cajamarca and the coast: the caudillo provided his children and runaways with a plot of land to cultivate and protection in return for entering his band of armed dependents. As Huatún lay close to trade routes linking highland Cajamarca with sugar- and rice-producing valleys in the departments of La Libertad and Lambayeque, highway robbery was one of the Huatuneros' specialities. These tough mountain people were also accomplished rustlers. Livestock stolen from estates in the Andes would be driven down to the Chicama and Jequetepeque valleys, the animals destined for sale to dealers who traded with sugar and rice haciendas on the littoral. In return, their merchant accomplices supplied the Huatuneros with arms, ammunition, basic necessities, and even European goods imported through Pacasmayo. In addition to running an effective brigandage operation, Anacleto Hoyos had a history of involvement in factional politics, the fierceness of his *pistoleros*, and an ability to muster a substantial number of combatants, making the caudillo a formidable opponent—or a valuable ally.

Ample opportunity to engage in these activities arose with the outbreak of the War of the Pacific. On two occasions during November 1879, columns of conscripts assembled by the prefect of Cajamarca found themselves attacked by a large contingent of Huatuneros (including women) as they marched from the interior down to Pacasmayo prior to embarkation for Lima to help defend the capital. Each time, the (no doubt unwilling) troops were ambushed and stripped of their weapons and mounts before being threatened and scattered at rifle point. When a force organized by the authorities (including the governor of Asunción) to quell the rebels approached Huatún, it encountered around three hundred people set in defensive positions among the dense woodland that covered two mountainsides overlooking the *caserío* and had to suffer the indignity of being taunted with cries of "Viva Chile" and "Mueren los asuncioneros." Numbering only forty, the government assault force was repelled easily and had to withdraw, leaving the town of Asunción unprotected and its governor in fear of assassination.[9]

Thereafter events took an unexpected turn. When the Iglesias faction, dominant in the province of Cajamarca, entered into a peace agreement with the Chileans for the "salvation of Peru," the Huatuneros sided with Andrés Avelino Cáceres and regional caudillo José Mercedes Puga, who determined to continue fighting the invading forces. Between 1882 and 1885, they consequently participated actively in *montonera* columns loyal to Puga that operated throughout the northern sierra as well as engaged in various sweeps down to the coast—the pursuit of factional enemies, personal vendettas, and straightforward pillage being practiced with equal vigor. During these turbulent years the Iglesista authorities managed to retain a tenuous control over the small settlements designated as district capitals, while the countryside remained in the grip of the insurgents: in a typical incident reported by the governor of Asunción, at two o'clock on February 21, 1885, a group of "bandits" from Huatún attacked the town "amid cries of 'Viva Cáceres' and 'Viva Puga,' with the usual aim of robbery and looting. The dogged and enthusiastic detachment under my command offered fierce resistance throughout a combat that lasted until seven o'clock at night, when the aggressors withdrew."[10]

Upon the fall of Iglesias and the accession of Cáceres to the presidency (December 1885), montonera activity abated and a modicum of peace descended on the area. Livestock rustling and armed robbery nevertheless continued apace—it being necessary to earn a living by whatever means possible in a rural economy shattered by civil war. Reflecting on this situation, the district governor noted:

> I have disarmed Asunción, but this has not been possible in Huatún, where there are approximately two hundred armed individuals. Collecting weapons in this town without first disarming Huatún might provoke a barbaric night attack by the latter, because those evil people dream of the complete destruction of all that exists here.[11]

The Cacerista authorities even managed to install a lieutenant governor in Huatún and collect the head tax (*contribución personal*) for 1887—neither of which had occurred in more than a decade.[12] Commenting on the changed atmosphere, the governor also reported (undoubtedly with no small degree of exaggeration) that "no grave incident to perturb the citizens and authorities of this district took place during the fiesta of Asunción. All has been peace and tranquility, particularly between the people from Huatún and Asunción, who now appear to be brothers."[13] Over the ensuing years, however, repeated attempts to pacify the Huatuneros proved futile, the outcome being that standard outlaw activity was punctuated by regular incidents of greater magnitude, as in October 1890, when eighteen well-armed bandits from the caserío invaded the small town of Magdalena, sited on the main trade route from Cajamarca to the coast. Indicatively, the town's authorities could not muster a force capable of repelling the attackers, who withdrew at their leisure after sacking commercial establishments.[14]

The situation in Asunción and Cospán changed significantly in March 1895, when forces loyal to Nicolás de Piérola attacked Lima, deposed Cáceres, and proceeded to govern in alliance with the Partido Civil (Civilista Party). In Cajamarca this sea change in political fortunes propelled the Iglesista faction back into power and the Huatuneros into their saddles for political, not just thievish, motives. After a period of mounting tension, they participated in the Cacerista revolt led by Agustín Verástegui that careered through the southern provinces of Cajamarca and the neighboring department of La Libertad in 1898. The following year (November–December 1899) Anacleto Hoyos and his band overran the neighboring province of Contumazá before riding into the Chicama Valley. According to the subprefect of Contumazá, the insurgents were performing

> criminal extortions, for the sole objective of these gangs of montoneros is pillage and the committing of every kind of abuse. All the localities they enter are fleeced completely. As there is no force to repress them, it is clear that they will continue their attacks and this will go on interminably. For this reason, it is of the utmost urgency that a police force be stationed here.[15]

Hoyos and his men continued on the rampage along the coast until the end of December 1899, but when the hoped-for nationwide anti-Piérola rebellion failed to materialize, momentum evaporated and he turned back home into the Andes.

Conscious of the threat posed by the caudillo and his *clientela* (underlined in November 1899 by the kidnapping of the governor of Asunción), in January 1900, the Iglesista authorities mounted an expedition to crush him. A column of 170 troops directed by the subprefect of Contumazá headed into the mountains in search of Hoyos, while another detachment of soldiers marched on Huatún from Cajamarca, the objective being to encircle the rebels. Several skirmishes took place on January 16, before the Huatuneros melted away, escaping the trap prepared for them. Hoyos and his followers then moved around the *jalca* (high moorland), lifting livestock and robbing travelers. Additional arms and ammunition were purchased from traders based in Ascope (a small town in the Chicama Valley) to enable the outlaws to continue their criminal pursuits. Eventually the troops tired of chasing the elusive montoneros and withdrew, thus allowing even greater freedom for bandit activity.[16]

Despite official claims that Hoyos and his men had been defeated, they remained active through the end of the Aristocratic Republic in 1919, successfully outwitting a succession of poorly contrived, half-hearted attempts to impose the state's fiat. Outlaw status notwithstanding, Hoyos still felt able (indeed entitled) to participate in the 1905 election, although as reported by the governor of Cospán, his involvement did not pass without incident.

> Messrs. Alarcón and Saens are continually committing abuses in this district. The elections on 25 May passed off without problems. On Friday Alarcón and

Saens started firing shots and grossly insulting all the citizens who assembled to vote at the ballot table of Mr. Nata. Refusing to be provoked, the electors retired to their houses. On Saturday 27 May, the last day of the poll, the people from Siracat in the company of don Anacleto Hoyos, who was coming to vote in this district, were attacked some two blocks outside the town by Messrs. Alarcón and Saens, who shot at them with Peabody and Combles weapons belonging to the state. Because of this assault and exchange of shots, don Antonio Plasencia (nephew of don Anacleto Hoyos) and Eduardo Mendis were killed. Upon witnessing these assassinations, the voters responded in self-defense, inflicting three fatalities on the opposing side. On one of the victims, José Concepción Saens, a Comble with ten unused bullets was found, even though the combat had lasted for two hours.[17]

High levels of lawlessness continued to afflict Asunción and Cospán, facilitated by the vacuum created by the absence of effective state coercive power. In September 1907, the prefect instructed the subprefect of Cajamarca to arrest Hoyos and eight of his accomplices for committing "various homicides." Symptomatically, the order remained unenforced.[18] Seemingly responding to an ongoing chaotic situation, April 1914 witnessed the authorities in Lima promising the prefect of Cajamarca that they would install a police post in Cospán to "provide security to farmers in the district . . . who are frequent victims of the criminals and rustlers who circulate throughout the locality."[19] No effective action materialized, with the result that three years later the prefect of Cajamarca was once again complaining to the Ministry of the Interior in Lima that the town of Asunción remained in danger of being seized by bandits, for which reason he lodged a request for troops to be drafted in from the capital to pacify the district. Until such a force arrived, he ordered the governor to form an urban self-defense platoon in the hope it would proffer a modicum of security.[20] Yet again the prefect's plea met with a feeble response—the zone consequently remaining "tierra de nadie," as illustrated when Hoyos assassinated the lieutenant governor of the caserío of Catillambi in August 1918.[21] Tellingly, the crime went unpunished—an unsurprising outcome given that in December 1918 the police force for the whole department of Cajamarca amounted to a paltry six officers and fifty *guardias*.[22]

Taking the repetitiveness of these events into consideration, it is difficult to avoid the conclusion that during the Aristocratic Republic the Peruvian state in outlying provinces of Cajamarca remained pitifully weak in two key aspects:

consent and coercion. Even so, although political fragmentation remained substantial, micropolitical analysis reveals that it was not complete, for events and changes in fortune at the national level exercised an impact at the local level and determined the contours of village-based struggles. Having one's allies in power in Lima did not guarantee obedience or cooperation by middle- and lower-ranking factional supporters, however. A fundamental problem in this regard was that the state lacked legitimacy. The political system denied an overwhelming majority of the adult population meaningful participation; electoral manipulation allied to the parceling out of power and jobbery fed a widespread belief that politics comprised a mere instrument of ambition, thus diminishing popular estimation of all state institutions. Its grassroots representatives (district governors, lieutenant governors at the village level, mayors, justices of the peace, tax collectors, etc.), being appointed largely through personal connections, consequently failed to command respect, which in turn made it difficult for them to achieve compliance.

This state of affairs was highlighted in November 1907, when the provincial tax collector accompanied by two gendarmes attempted to conduct their duties in Cospán. They found themselves blockaded in a house and fired upon by an angry group of locals who vociferated: "Down with taxes! Let's kill these thieves!" The district governor felt powerless to intervene as the mob "were drunk, too numerous, and armed with rifles and revolvers." Upon attempting to flee the town, the exciseman and police were surrounded and overwhelmed, before being forced to prostrate themselves on the ground, whereupon they were relieved of their money and mounts. Fearing for his life, the governor managed to take advantage of the fracas to escape and seek refuge in Campodén, a neighboring hacienda.[23]

Where deference and obedience prevailed, in the first instance it flowed from an officeholder's strength of personality and status in the community (usually involving a willingness to use firearms) rather than legitimacy invested via their public position. Although individuals occasionally sought redress through the formal judicial system, this too was held in poor regard due to cost, corruption, and inefficiency; the private settling of accounts therefore proved more attractive to all social sectors. Hand in hand with the "oligarchic" state's failure to build an effective "machine bureaucracy" and acquire "ideological hegemony" went a pervasive caudillismo, which—paradoxically—lessened landlord power through providing subalterns with greater opportunity to pursue a relatively risk-free career in rural crime.[24] Prior to 1919 the state's anemic coercive capacity undermined not only hacendado but also its own authority. How, and to what extent, did this situation modify during Leguía's Oncenio? How did socio-economic and political developments over the 1920s alter state-peasant, state-landlord, and landlord-peasant relations in Asunción and its environs?

LEGUÍA'S STATE-BUILDING PROJECT, 1919–1930: IMPACTS ON BUREAUCRATS, LANDLORDS, AND LOCAL POPULATIONS

Toward the end of the Aristocratic Republic, a new player entered the local scene, one that would exercise a profound effect on landlord-state-peasant relations throughout the 1920s and beyond. By the end of World War I, the Empresa Agrícola Chicama (EACh) had emerged as the largest and most efficient sugar producer in Peru: consequent upon a purposeful strategy of engrossment, its landholdings covered some 11,500 hectares of fertile terrain in the Chicama Valley centered on the Casa Grande estate. Driven by an urgent need to supply the large labor force with foodstuffs, in 1916 Heinrich Emil Gildemeister arranged the purchase of the hacienda Huacraruco (ca. 15,000 hectares), shortly followed by the acquisition of Sunchubamba (ca. 43,000 hectares), to form the largest latifundio in the department of Cajamarca and an enterprise that dominated the districts of Asunción and Cospán. Almost immediately after attaining ownership, the company installed an administrative structure similar to that operating on the Casa Grande plantation and began to capitalize their Andean estates via a large-scale program of fencing, drainage, irrigation, and more rational pasture management. Pedigree cattle and sheep were imported from Europe and Patagonia.[25] Given these costly investments, the activities of Anacleto Hoyos and other brigands represented a threat in need of urgent address.

EACh employees based in the organization's Lima office consequently lobbied the Leguía administration to get a police post installed in Asunción, a request that was granted in August 1921, when a six-strong detachment under the command of José María Verjel was stationed in the settlement.[26] Significantly, Verjel had been hand-picked by the EACh owing to his prior effectiveness in suppressing banditry in the Chicama Valley; the sugar corporation also agreed to cover all the wages and running costs for the new police station. Once installed, Verjel, a ruthless and determined individual "con los pantalones bien puestos," proceeded to carry out his orders, leading to a succession of clashes with armed peasants loyal to Hoyos and other outlaws circulating the area. Although registering some successes, Verjel and his fellow guardias lacked sufficient firepower to tackle Hoyos and his followers, who at this juncture numbered a minimum of seventy experienced fighters.

Such an unsatisfactory situation led the company's representative in Cajamarca town, Alberto Behr, to put pressure on the prefect to act more energetically against Hoyos.[27] Another coordinated attempt to eradicate Hoyos and his band was subsequently launched in February 1923, when the Asunción police backed by thirty-one additional guardias drafted in from Cajamarca and a second column dispatched into the Andes from the Chicama Valley moved to encircle their prey. On penetrating Potrerillo, one of the residences of Hoyos, the troops were attacked by approximately forty gunmen, the confrontation continuing from 7:00 a.m. until 2:00 p.m., when the rebels retreated into the dense woodland that covered the *cerro* Peña Blanca. Fearing ambush, the police decided not to pursue their opponents, allowing them to escape. Instead, the police sacked and burned the homes of Hoyos and his *parentela* before making off with all the livestock they encountered. Shortly afterward, the government force repeated the operation in Tayal, another fundo owned by Hoyos.[28] Documents found during this undertaking purported to reveal plans to participate in an anti-Leguía insurrection and to assassinate *comisario* Verjel. The prefect's efforts proved unsuccessful, however, as its main objective—the capture of Hoyos and destruction of his band—remained unaccomplished. After an appropriate absence, the Huatuneros returned, rebuilt their homes, and continued committing crimes, one of the most high profile involving the murder of the governor of Cospán, Teodoro Alcalde, on December 29, 1925.

Although state actors failed in their objective, the EACh succeeded in attaining some advantage from the affair. The persecution and destruction of his assets made Hoyos and his associates act with added caution vis-à-vis property belonging to Huacraruco and Sunchubamba, which soon enabled an informal nonaggression pact to be struck behind the back of the prefect and other members of the departmental bureaucracy.[29] As this incident illustrates, during Leguía's tenure in office the state proved only partially capable of addressing effectively the problem of rural crime in the Andes. While rustling remained a thorn in the side of state authorities and managers administering the EACh's highland estates, another headache soon appeared: the development of a well-organized peasant movement, clearly antilandlord in orientation and strengthened as a result of backing from a vociferous urban support network. This represented a shift from a mainly covert and individual (rustling, crop lifting, and similar acts) to an overt collective response to class and official oppression, although the former regularly meshed with the latter.

Various socioeconomic and political trends help explain why smallholders living in San Juan de Yanac, San Juan de Cachilgón, La Rinconada, Ogoriz, and surrounding hamlets sited along the northern boundary of the hacienda Huacraruco entered into an intense period of mobilization from the mid-1920s. First, demographic increase leading to land fragmentation had been mincing the household economy since the turn of the century, forcing the cultivation of ever more marginal lands, which in turn reduced the area available to pasture livestock.[30] Many peasants sought a solution to subsistence difficulties through seasonal migration to the coast to engage in waged employment or striking a tenancy agreement in neighboring haciendas. At the very time when this proletarianization process was gathering momentum among peasant freeholders, Huacraruco and Sunchubamba began to curtail certain income- and food-generating avenues that local campesinos had customarily enjoyed. The modernization of livestock-rearing practices in these properties brought a considerable expansion in *demesne* pastureland, the spread of barbed wire, and the expulsion of tenants or their relocation to smaller, less fertile plots—changes with negative consequences for the *minifundista* household economy prevalent outside the hacienda boundary. Simultaneously, migration to coastal plantations propelled smallholders into contact with new political ideas (anarcho-syndicalism, socialism), forms of organization (trade unions), and the consciousness-raising experience of the bitter strikes that hit the sugar industry between 1912 and 1922—all of which reinforced an antistate outlook nurtured initially through participation in Anacleto Hoyos's band.

Their cause was assisted by social changes underway in urban Cajamarca, especially the departmental capital. Declining living standards due to war-induced inflation produced a certain radicalization among the town's artisans and laborers, leading to the formation of the Sociedad de Obreros (Workers' Association) in August 1922. Encouraged by indigenista currents active in Lima and radical rhetoric emanating from inside the Leguía government, during the previous year a Sociedad Pro-Defensa Obrera e Indígena (Society for the Protection of Workers and Indians) had been formed (February 1921), with the stated goal of "uniting all the laboring classes of Cajamarca." This body included among its honorary members progressive lawyers (such as Aníbal Zambrano and Felipe Alva), schoolteachers employed in the expanding public education system, and other urban professionals critical of Peru's antiquated political system and unjust social order. Antilandlord and pro-agrarian reform messages began to be disseminated through newspapers published in Cajamarca from 1923, particularly *El Perú*, a broadsheet that attracted an expanding readership as the indigenista movement grew in popularity throughout the 1920s.[31]

These trends produced a complex conjuncture that rendered problematic any straightforward "limpieza con sangre" response to peasant unrest. The standard interpretation of power relations in the Andes during the 1920s portrays an omnipresent *gamonalismo* able, with the willing compliance of provincial officials, to suppress rural dissent with impunity.[32] In reality, the prefect and subprefect based in Cajamarca town, as well as EACh administrators, had to act with circumspection in their dealings with campesinos settled in and around Huacraruco and Sunchubamba. With regard to officialdom, during Leguía's Oncenio the departmental prefecture was headed by an outsider appointed by the national government in Lima, who possessed no blood ties, business links, or, necessarily, loyalty to Cajamarca's landowning class. On occasions this could result in social marginalization.[33] His prime concern was to maintain order with a minimum degree of fuss, obey (or give the appearance of obeying) instructions sent from Lima, keep his job, and lead as peaceful a life as possible before being posted to another department—usually every eighteen months to two years. They formed the embryo of a new bureaucratic caste that was to expand in later decades. Usually being a Cajamarquino, the subprefect (the leading official at provincial level) found himself in a somewhat different position, one that brought more contradictory pressures. On the one hand, he had to acquiesce to orders originating from Lima and passed down the administrative hierarchy by the prefect. On the other hand, he became subject to approaches from family and long-standing friends (Cajamarca having only one middle-class secondary school for boys), both pro-landowner and locally educated radicalized professionals acting on behalf of subaltern groups.

The prefect's and subprefect's predicament was compounded by the regular flow of reformist-oriented pro-peasant memoranda that continued to land on their desks, even after 1923, when—according to mainstream historiography—Leguía's administration reputedly entered its "conservative" phase (communication between Lima and Cajamarca having been facilitated by the construction of a telegraph line in 1923). The president made his ambition to promote a more "democratic" rural society clear in an interview published to coincide with Peru's independence-day celebrations in July 1925. Pointedly, he chose to disseminate his views in the *West Coast Leader*, an English-language trade gazette targeted at Peru's business community.

> When I asked the landed aristocracy to sell lands to the Indian on easy terms, they refused. If they fixed a price it was excessive. One reason is that a certain wealthy class in this country fears to give the Indian opportunity for economic advancement lest he rise and become a power. I say let him rise! In consequence, I have expropriated large sections of land belonging to various old interests and have instigated irrigation projects on them. . . . In Peru, the line of least resistance to the financial and social oligarchy that ruled so long is the cultivation of a middle class through the exploitation of the land in relatively small holdings and at a price within popular reach.[34]

June 1926 also saw the *Registro Oficial de Cajamarca* print a central government decree in favor of "The Promotion of Small-Scale Agricultural Property," to be achieved through "the division of the extensive lands belonging to existing haciendas," which would be sold in plots no larger than ten hectares, the objective being to intensify cultivation on smaller units and thereby increase domestic food supply and lower prices.[35] In addition to well-ventilated calls for agrarian restructuring, during the previous year the Director General de Fomento in Lima wrote an internal memorandum to Cajamarca's prefect reminding him that "a central policy of the government of the President of the Republic is the rehabilitation of the Indian and his incorporation into the nation, to make him a contributor to progress and a more productive element of society"; the prefect (Enrique Zegarra) consequently had to clamp down on all forms of abuse against "los indígenas" and to impress upon his subordinates lower down the administrative chain that these orders had to be observed to the letter "bajo responsibilidad."[36] The prefect dutifully passed on these instructions to the subprefect, inscribing in the margin: "For information and the strictest implementation."

How was the EACh affected by this political environment and how did it lobby to promote its interests? As mentioned, by the 1920s, the Gildemeister family were majority shareholders in the most important agricultural enterprise in Peru and employees in the company's Lima office enjoyed open access to high-ranking functionaries working in the Ministry of the Interior and other departments, as well as having frequent lunchtime contact with congressmen at the Club Nacional and *tertulias* attended by Lima's tightly interconnected elite. Nevertheless, this degree of economic power and influence did not signify that garnering official support to mobilize the coercive branches of the state apparatus to solve boundary disputes and other issues was an uncomplicated affair, for Heinrich Emil and Hans (Juan) Gildemeister experienced important constraints in their dealings with the Leguía government.[37] Being an astute operator with a finely tuned political antenna, Hans was well aware that the EACh was widely regarded as a German concern (the sugar enterprise had experienced considerable commercial difficulties during the war, having been placed on the "black list" by the UK and U.S. administrations, blocking access to its main markets). The company's rapid expansion between 1900 and 1930 had also attracted envy and hostility across the social spectrum on national-ist grounds, so the bloody repression of seemingly powerless "descendants of the Incas" in the fervid political atmosphere of the 1920s could well provoke a national and regional scandal of a magnitude that would be damaging to the EACh's long-term business interests.[38]

Gildemeister therefore had solid grounds for attempting to avoid excessive force that might lead to bloodshed against those smallholders from Asunción and Cospán whom he regarded as illegal squatters. Instead he judiciously sought a legal solution to the conflict. This in turn complicated the company's position, because after 1920 not all the judges and lawyers in Cajamarca were impervious to the fashionable pro-Indian and anti-imperialist sentiment spreading through Peru's urban middle and working classes: the economically disadvantaged could gain the services of progressive lawyers for a minimal fee or no fee at all. Nor were high-echelon officials in the government bureaucracy immune from anti-gringo and anti-gamonal opinion, with the result that despite the annual Christmas gift of a case of whisky from the EACh to the prefect, energetic official action against peasant recalcitrance regularly failed to ensue after cordial conversations and "cast iron" promises made behind closed doors in Cajamarca's prefecture or over lunch at the town's only decent restaurant.

Similar attitudes and comportment could be found among Guardia Civil detachments sent to evict squatters from land claimed by Huacraruco: between 1925 and 1930 some officers acted more resolutely than others, but, much to the chagrin of the hacienda's German administrator, the police usu-ally carried out their mission in a half-hearted fashion. The outcome was a succession of partial evictions and arrests, followed almost immediately by the release of peasant leaders and reinvasion. On occasions, the campesinos gained the upper hand through surrounding the heavily outnumbered police, disarming them, and sending them packing back to Cajamarca with their tails between their legs.[39] As the boundary dispute dragged on, the prefect's position became progressively more intricate owing to (1) the participation of low-ranking members of the state's administrative structure (lieutenant governors) in the peasant movement; (2) the close relationship established between the campesinos and their legal representative, Wenceslao Arroyo, and prominent officials employed in the Sección de Asuntos Indígenas (Bureau of Indigenous Affairs) in Lima, resulting in a stream of dispatches demanding "amplias garantías" landing on his desk; and (3) the opening of schools in Asunción, Cospán, and surrounding districts (during 1925–27), staffed by teachers sympathetic to the peasant cause, which provided an additional link to support networks based in Cajamarca town.[40] This also increased the flow of information that could be published in a sympathetic local press and fed to national dailies. Faced with this labyrinthine political situation, in 1933 the EACh sought a compromise solution to the conflict, ceding land in return for a commonly agreed boundary and a more equitable division of waters from the San Juan river and its tributaries.

TENSIONS IN STATE-PEASANT-LANDLORD RELATIONS: LA CONSCRIPCIÓN VIAL

In addition to boundary disputes, brigandage, and livestock rustling, another issue that provoked three-way strains between the state, landowners, and the rural population concerned the disposition of labor. During the 1920s a key point of grievance centered on the Leguía administration's ambitious road-building and public works program, aimed at stimulating interprovincial commerce and expanding market opportunities. Under the Conscripción Vial law no. 4113, enacted on May 10, 1920, all adult males between eighteen and twenty-one and fifty and sixty years of age were obliged to work six days per annum on highway construction; those in the twenty-one- to fifty-year age bracket had to fulfil twelve days, or six per semester. Conscripted laborers were to be remunerated according to the rate appertaining within their province of residence, but with permission from the commissioner in charge of the scheme at the local level, individuals could exempt themselves through payment of a sum equivalent to the daily wage, so that funds were available to hire a replacement. In effect this exclusion clause signified that road construction quotas fell chiefly on peasant shoulders. Understandably, the rural poor resented this imposition and sought to evade compliance by whatever means possible, which on occasions necessitated the striking of tactical alliances in order to garner support from state and nonstate actors.

Indeed, given the proximity of Asunción and Cospán to the main artery linking the central and southern provinces of Cajamarca with the coast, dissent surrounding forced labor predated the enactment of law 4113. On January 23, 1919, highway engineer Dibarbú had informed the prefect about the "scarcity of men" presenting themselves for work, while in April 1919, his colleague (E. Banaillier) penned a report stating that despite having notified district governors that they should remit the largest possible number of hands—ideally three hundred per day—the populace was refusing to comply unless daily wages were increased to S/.1.20.[41] This represented an early example of many incidents that pitted country dwellers against the state as a consequence of Conscripción Vial exactions. Writing from Asunción in June 1919, Andrés Partilla, Rosario Gutierrez, and Fidel Muñoz complained to the prefect that the district's inhabitants were "suffering all classes of tyranny and threats against our well-being" at the hands of a police officer (*comisario rural*) who, they claimed, "was perpetuating in this district abuses against working people belonging to our class" through seeking to force them to toil for only fifty centavos, a wage on which "it was impossible to subsist."[42] Five months later, officials from the municipal council of Asunción protested in person to Cajamarca's subprefect that the chief engineer responsible for maintaining the road was

> threatening the populace with jail and the embargo of their belongings in order to compel them to work on the highway at a rate of eighty centavos per day, from six in the morning until six in the evening, without tents to rest in or any alimentation. This wage does not cover food costs, which are very high and forces them to take victuals from the mouths of their children. . . . Local haciendas pay sixty centavos but with rations; on the coast wages are S/.1.50 along with a daily ration of two pounds of rice and one pound of meat. The population do not think it just that the authorities, contravening individual rights, coerce people to work for eighty centavos without food, nor provide protection from the inclement weather during the rainy season. Furthermore, these actions prevent people from earning a higher remuneration elsewhere. The denizens of Asunción believe that as the road represents an important project that benefits the common good, they would be prepared to work for a daily wage of S/.1.20,

for a nine-hour shift without rations, but including the provision of tents in order to prevent illnesses.[43]

When this grievance was conveyed to the prefect, he requested additional information and an account of the behavior of the chief highway engineer, who replied that the mayor and district governor of Asunción had circulated a public decree "advising the populace to refuse to perform road work unless they were paid S/.1.20 per day. The local authorities have also proclaimed that any advanced wages received from labor contractors should not be returned if the cash had already been spent, because nobody possessed the right to demand repayment."[44]

By 1925 the nodal points of conflict remained. The governor of Asunción informed the prefect that during the first week of November only seventeen men had turned up, instead of the official quota of one hundred, while in the following week just fourteen attended. Resistance was widespread, he claimed, because the daily wage was only fifty centavos instead of the promised eighty centavos, adding that delays in payment had also spread disillusion and stiffened noncompliance among the locals, who threatened to migrate and offer their services to coastal sugar and rice haciendas if their demands were not satisfied.[45] For his part, the governor of Cospán had informed the prefect during the previous year that it was impossible to supply the number of hands levied on the district under his jurisdiction because the male workforce was absent, employed in neighboring haciendas. In any case dire poverty meant that the rural population would be unable to fulfil their legal obligations without receipt of a daily food ration to supplement cash wages.[46] Dispatches penned shortly afterward added that the "heinous crimes" committed by local brigands had "reduced the citizens to penury"; unless the population urgently received protection from "thieves and bandits," the current situation could not be altered.[47] Given that issues of dirt, hunger, and fear continued to be unaddressed, the authorities were unable to resolve the problem of intransigence among the lower orders through the twilight of Leguía's eleven-year presidency: confronted by widespread refusal, in September 1929, the governor of Cospán again requested the presence of a police detachment so that "absentees could be forced to fulfil their obligations" under law 4113, only to be informed by the prefect that he had no personnel available.[48] The following year the governor of Asunción likewise complained to his superiors about the difficulties he was experiencing in enforcing compliance with the law. He noted that "the infamous hamlets of Huatún and Catillambi are inhabited by rebellious people . . . dedicated to thievery and who do not obey anybody. They claim to have been 'soldiers' of Anacleto Hoyos (deceased) and are still intent on pursuing his evil ways. In these locations many are armed . . . every month there are complaints about rustling and other crimes."[49] The deeply ingrained spirit of independence, rebelliousness, and disregard for state authority shown by smallholders in these parishes during the War of the Pacific was still in evidence during Leguía's final months in office.

While poor country folk found themselves resorting to multiple "everyday" subterfuges as they sought to circumvent state exactions and manipulate an unjust system to their minimum disadvantage, another dimension of the ever-shifting triangular state-landlord-peasant relationship concerned the rural elite's response to state modernizing initiatives such as the Conscripción Vial. On this score there was no unified position. Certain prominent hacendados actively collaborated with the authorities, a stance that was especially discernible among the proprietors of large estates sited deep in the interior east of the Cajamarca Valley, who anticipated that improved transport links would facilitate access to all-important coastal markets.[50] For this reason, in May 1928, Carolina Puga, who was keen to expand commercial livestock operations on La Pauca, supplied 108 corvée laborers from her latifundio to work on the link to the coast, paying their wages as well as providing food rations and coca. In August 1928, the local press reported with approval that Manuel Cacho Sousa, proprietor of Polloc and a pioneer of modern dairy farming in the department, had drafted 100 men from his estate to enhance the Cajamarca-Celendín road, also covering wage costs and providing three meals a day. October 1928 found the owners of the haciendas Quilcate (Leopoldo Rodríguez) and Chala (César Miranda) contributing manpower and cash so that improvements could be made to the Cajamarca–Hualgayoc route.[51] During the same year, the landowner of Quindén (Flavio Castro) reportedly invested the considerable sum of £p.14,000.0.00 to better connect his estate to the railway at Chilete.[52]

Despite the government's drive to facilitate the circulation of agricultural commodities, not all landowners proved willing to collaborate with the state's schemes, including the Empresa Agrícola Chicama.[53] Having embarked on an ambitious modernization program in 1920, the owners of Huacraruco and Sunchubamba sought to mobilize all the labor power at their disposal and consequently viewed efforts to divert hacienda employees away from their own immediate needs with hostility. Article 5 of Conscripción Vial law 4113 that permitted exemption upon payment of the appropriate amount of money provided a relatively straightforward avenue for allowing hacienda laborers to escape being drafted. When in October 1924 the governor of Cospán notified the manager of the Sunchubamba estate to supply men for road work, Kurt Hagemann reminded him that cash had been supplied to enable replacements to be hired.[54]

A more intractable bone of contention concerned the habit of functionaries charged with road construction to detain laborers who had been contracted to Casa Grande and compel them to work. Anticipating difficulties on this score, in 1921 the EACh had donated £p.98.0.00 to the departmental highway construction fund, the quid pro quo being that laborers hired by the company would not be harried as they traveled down to the Chicama Valley cane fields. By 1925 this agreement had unraveled under twin pressures. First, El Niño–induced torrential storms in that year wreaked substantial damage to infrastructure and farmland throughout northern Peru, including landslides that swept away lengthy sections of the artery linking Cajamarca to the coast. Second, this natural disaster coincided with the appointment of a prefect who was an enthusiastic road builder and determined to reconstruct the highway in the shortest possible time. Faced with this scenario, Erwin Wolff in the Agencia Cajamarca informed Hans Gildemeister about the local political situation.

> Unfortunately, rumors in the local press concerning the prefect's dismissal have not materialized, which is a negative outcome for us because this man is obsessed with the construction of his road, despite the fact that it has been destroyed again. From the beginning of the year we have experienced constant difficulties concerning our peons during their journey to the coast. Men who have fulfilled the twelve days stipulated by law do not receive a receipt and become vulnerable to abuse as they are coerced by the military police to work. In other cases, six of which I have personal knowledge (although the labor recruiters state there are many more), the passes signed by the president of the highway construction commission are not recognized by the military police stationed along the road, who confiscate and destroy them. The police then compel the people, after stealing their ponchos and other belongings, to forced labor. Their journey to the coast to work for us is therefore delayed. I have constantly raised this matter with the prefect and subprefect, providing documentary evidence. . . . They greet me very amiably with insincere smiles and make vague promises like: "We will immediately stop these illegal abuses." . . . The prefect is obsessed with the project and hopes to enhance his reputation by it. . . . This is absurd and patently damages our interests.[55]

Wolff proceeded to suggest that company employees in Lima should lobby the central government for the suspension of road work. After making appropriate soundings, Carlos Semsch (who was temporarily managing Casa Grande while Hans Gildemeister was in Germany attending to a health problem and getting married) advised Wolff to

> try and get on well with the prefect. Given the current political situation I do not think that the government will transfer him because it needs experienced and trustworthy administrators. . . . A suspension of the law is unthinkable, but I have requested Lima to attempt this—or at least get work on the Magdalena road stopped for one year because of the extensive destruction caused by the latest flood here in the valley.[56]

As a change of prefect proved unlikely, the EACh sought to establish a better personal relationship with the incumbent in an attempt to resolve their difficulties. To help achieve this goal, Wolff provided the management hierarchy in Casa Grande with details of the prefect's personality traits and suggested some targeted gift giving as a means to secure a greater degree of cooperation.

> Prefect: he acts with propriety regarding the law, as well as in personal money matters. . . . Under no circumstances can we expect that our peons will be excused from road work. However, he is going to halt the previous abuses—committed by the same individuals—who demand more days labor than stipulated by law. This is the best we can hope for. I would therefore like to remind you about a request the prefect made to señor Szamos: that Casa Grande purchase a good mule for him. The prefect is a big man, was in the cavalry, and I believe he is a good horseman, which will be important to consider when selecting an animal.[57]

Gildemeister opined that to send a mule up from the coast was not appropriate because it would require a year to acclimatize to Andean conditions. It would consequently make more sense to purchase a suitable animal in the highlands or supply one from the hacienda Sunchubamba, a donation for which he "did not expect to be paid."[58] Once the mount had been delivered, Wolff reported that the prefect "only liked its size and body frame, but not its gait. In reply to my comment that mules from the mountains are sturdy with plenty of stamina, but do not offer a comfortable ride, he remarked that he had requested an animal from the coast; acclimatizing and training it would have been his responsibility."[59]

Although not fully pleased with his present, the prefect promised to clamp down on illegal behavior by the highway engineers and gendarmerie, but with the end of the rainy season Wolff reported that he had embarked upon road construction with "renewed fanaticism." In view of this development, it would be opportune, he suggested, for Hans Gildemeister to write directly to the prefect because "in contrast to local custom, the prefect is not corruptible. He is very receptive to personal compliments, however. I therefore think that an invitation to Casa Grande to show him the installations and work practices would be very much to his liking."[60] By October 1926, familiar problems had arisen anew. According to Hans Niemann, the recently appointed administrator of the Agencia Cajamarca, part of the reason was that while Wolff had built a modus operandi with the prefect, "my predecessor did not attempt to cement good relations with low-ranking functionaries in the prefecture or the police. These people always take especial delight in—insidiously—doing us harm."[61] In any event, the prefect was recalled to Lima in December 1926 and no replacement was immediately appointed. This led Niemann to inform his superiors that "the sub-prefect, who is presently in charge of the prefecture, wishes to collaborate with us. He has issued orders that we can dispatch our workers to the coast accompanied by our own foremen and *comisarios*," the latter being paid by the company.[62] Via this agreement the issue attained a solution to the satisfaction of the sugar corporation.

Indulging personal caprices also produced a cooperative attitude from the incoming prefect, as recorded in a memo sent by Niemann to Gildemeister shortly after the official's arrival in Cajamarca.

Prefect: last week this gentleman asked me to accompany him on his inspection of the Cajamarca-Chilete road, providing him with the necessary mount. I have done this. As you know, we rely heavily on his support and I was also interested to discover how many of our peons are being detained by the highway contractors. The prefect has issued strict orders to all labor gangers and highway engineers that our people should be allowed free passage. . . . On the journey the prefect rode a trotting horse [*caballo de trotar*] supplied from Sunchubamba. . . . He liked the horse so much he kept it. Every day he asks how much he owes for the animal. Perhaps we could give it as a present? I have said I could not name a price and needed to consult. He is also interested in the German shepherd dogs, but for the moment I think the horse will suffice.[63]

Apart from occasional presents bequeathed in order to facilitate the cultivation of personal relationships with individuals occupying strategic positions inside the state administration at the local level, the head of the Agencia Cajamarca was authorized an entertainment allowance. Thus in his February 1927 report, Niemann detailed expenditures of £p.3.6.00 incurred over the festive season while inviting members of the judiciary ("los señores de la corte"); an additional £p.1.7.50 was spent on hospitality involving the prefect and subprefect, along with £p.2.9.00 wining and dining the head highway engineer.

LEGUÍA'S LEGACY: THE STATE OF STATE-LANDLORD-PEASANT RELATIONS DURING THE 1920S INTO THE 1930S

How are we to understand these developments? What shifts had occurred in the complex interplay of state-landlord-peasant power relations in Asunción and Cospán during the 1920s? What was their impact into the following decade? Over Leguía's Oncenio certain sociopolitical processes can be observed, including the first moves away from classic militaristic caudillismo, as epitomized by the taming of Anacleto Hoyos, and an end to the montonero rebellions endemic in the late nineteenth century. This went hand in hand with the appearance of a more clearly ideological, class-framed mode of political discourse and competition—which I discuss in more detail below. There had indeed been a concomitant strengthening of the state's presence in the countryside, indicated by higher school attendance (even including schools in some local haciendas); significant improvements and extension in the communications network (allowing the spread of road transport in the Andean hinterland); and the opening of police posts in hitherto unattended district capitals, in addition to guardias stationed for long spells in the hacienda Huacraruco. A greater propensity to utilize the official judicial system—by rich and poor alike—can also be perceived, providing further testimony to the state's growing influence over decision-making calculations on the part of individuals across the social spectrum (in Weberian terms, a trend away from "charismatic" in the direction of "rational-legal" authority). Alongside moves toward the creation of a more centralized, cohesive, and effective state apparatus and a decline in old-style caudillismo, landlord independence also diminished—a reflection of the state's "relative autonomy," with Leguía cast in Bonaparte's role of the "hero" intent on employing his power to accelerate economic modernization while restricting the elite's political freedom of action.[64]

Even so, it would be wrong to overemphasize the growth of state power in Asunción and surrounding districts over these years. Popular resistance to official edicts—from at least the 1870s a feature of local life—proved effective, as evinced by persistent collective opposition to Conscripción Vial obligations and tax collection. Another indication of the limits of state building under Leguía in both its coercive and "hegemony"/consent dimensions is the continuance of banditry, especially livestock rustling.[65] The extreme Andean topography clearly hindered the attainment of secure control over territory. Although (at least in official eyes and from a legalistic perspective) the state might have been invested with a monopoly of "legitimate" violence, it did not enjoy exclusivity in this regard: political assassinations continued during the 1920s and armed assaults on low-ranking administrative appointees and political opponents occurred at regular intervals, actions viewed with approval among elements of the local population. By 1930 the state still exercised incomplete "power" in Asunción and Cospán, understood as a situation whereby officials possessed the capacity to impose their will over the populace "despite resistance." Equally, the state exerted a limited degree of "domination," defined as a state of affairs where a functionary within an "established order" can impart instructions to subordinates and nonstate actors and expect them to be obeyed because their authority is viewed as legitimate.[66] Rational-legal forms of domination were on the rise but by 1930 remained weakly embedded within the population at large, especially in the countryside. Such an outlook was comprehensible: for the majority rural population the "Peruvian state idea" conjured up negative connotations (conscription, taxation, forced labor); the beneficial dimensions of state activity (access to health care, protection from arbitrary violence, etc.) were absent; and the public education provision in rural parishes comprised a recent phenomenon.[67]

Trends underway within the peasant household economy also worked to steel grassroots noncooperation when confronted with official attempts at appropriating labor power. Smallholders enduring a subsistence crisis could ill-afford the "luxury" of engagement in off-farm work below a certain level of remuneration, whether in cash or a combination of cash and rations. Subaltern agency was not only enhanced as a consequence of continued anemic state coercive capacity. A willingness to migrate in conjunction with the availability of employment opportunities in coastal agriculture empowered the rural poor with extra maneuverability in their efforts to circumvent government impositions. The opportunity to vote with their feet functioned as a safety valve, introducing an element of flexibility into state-peasant linkages, which helps explain why no explosive incident resulting in multiple loss of life occurred in Cajamarca due to the Conscripción Vial, as elsewhere in the Andes.[68]

If the state continued to exhibit a profound legitimacy and "power" deficit in 1930, it also demonstrated a significant degree of internal incoherence, in sharp contrast to Weber's "ideal type" depiction of a "machine bureaucracy" operating "rational" decision-making procedures in a disinterested fashion with clear command structures allowing the seamless flow of accurate information and instructions up and down the administrative chain. Instead of unity, multiple fractures occurred within the state apparatus that undermined efficacious governance. Being centrally appointed from a pool of civil servants loyal to the regime and an "outsider" possessing no familial or personal ties at the departmental level, the prefect could be expected to dutifully convey executive policy to other official institutions and his immediate subordinates and request its implementation. Communication with Lima had also been improved through the completion of a telegraph line to Cajamarca in 1923. Nevertheless, the prefect's ability for decisive intervention was hampered by financial constraints that restricted the number of functionaries who could be hired. As well as quantity, the quality of provincial-level administrative personnel acted to diminish competence and encourage bureaucratic inertia—the relatively small size of the urban middle class reduced the pool of available talent. Considerable fragmentation between different branches of the state apparatus also acted to undermine effective action. Having their own institutional interests, priorities, and concerns, the judiciary and police regularly "complied" with prefectural instructions in an irresolute fashion. To complicate matters, as many judges, court officials, and police possessed local roots, they came under contradictory social pressures from family and friends; they may also have been less committed to Leguía's political project, or even hostile to the regime. Whatever the motive, such tergiversation restricted the prefect's ability to implement initiatives emanating from Lima. Indeed, difficulties in this regard (and a development that rendered the prefect's position especially precarious) took on a more intimidating dimension during the early 1930s. This flowed from attempts by the Alianza Popular Revolucionaria Americana (APRA, American Popular Revolutionary Alliance) to infiltrate the state's repressive organs, which engendered a succession of barrack revolts in Cajamarca city and outlying provinces (in 1932, 1933, and 1935) involving army and police personnel. Their opéra bouffe complexion notwithstanding, such actions threatened the political status quo as well as the physical safety of high-ranking appointees.

Similar limitations vis-à-vis the wielding of purposeful authority arose within the political arm of the state. The subprefect of Cajamarca's office was housed in the prefecture, which made this official subject to closer day-to-day control. On the contrary, distance from the watchful eye of the prefect afforded district governors and village-level lieutenant governors a greater degree of autonomy and opportunity to engage in what may be described as "obstructive ambiguity." Ample room for maneuver at the base of the state structure not only complicated the decision-making process and hindered decisive implementation. Flexibility in the enforcement of commands originating from the apex of government proved welcome to low-ranking appointees because a lack of protection placed them in physical danger: their immediate constituency could not be ignored given continued endemic lawlessness, the widespread distribution of firearms, and their residence amid a population accustomed to employing their weapons.[69] In addition to legitimate self-preservation concerns, grassroots officials frequently felt greater loyalty to their local community when charged with overseeing unpopular policies initiated by a faraway government based in Lima or the departmental capital. This situation became evident in relation to Leguía's road construction program. District-grade officials and municipal authorities felt obliged to inform their superiors of grassroots discontent regarding wage levels and working conditions—complaints with which they often sympathized—resulting in recourse to feigned compliance or the voicing of pretexts to circumvent executive decrees.

What changes occurred in the position of the most important landlord in Asunción and neighboring districts during the Oncenio? Despite its weighty economic position as the largest agricultural enterprise in Peru in terms of income generation and employment, the absence of a "machine bureaucracy" greatly complicated the EACh's dealings with state institutions and individual public sector employees in Cajamarca. On the one hand, government financial constraints and low salaries provided opportunity for the Gildemeister brothers to attain influence through targeted gift giving in cash or desired items, but not all functionaries possessed itching palms. On the other hand, although key policies like the Conscripción Vial were prioritized throughout Leguía's Oncenio and legal obligations might be clearly defined in law, the degree of energetic implementation fluctuated according to who happened to be in post. Such inconsistencies meant that company employees had to try to establish an advantageous modus operandi after each change of personnel involving upper- and middle-ranking civil servants at the local level in order to attempt to secure uniform application of the state's own legislation. To complicate matters for the sugar corporation—because of envy, anti-gringo nationalist sentiment, or (usually concealed) sympathy with peasant and rural proletarian struggles—office holders within the political and repressive branches of the state apparatus could acquiesce to lobbying by company representatives in face-to-face conversations, only to engage in obfuscation when it came to enactment. Flummery aside, operational autonomy signified that the personal whims of particular bureaucrats and police officers exercised an influence on behavior and outcomes disproportionate to Weber's "ideal type" model. Such a disconnect between clearly defined official policy and actual execution became an even greater problem for the EACh during the 1930s, when support for APRA surged throughout Cajamarca, causing the state to encounter increasing difficulties in appointing staff who were not Aprista members or sympathizers.

Socioeconomic and political changes underway during the 1920s and early 1930s also acted to recalibrate the rural population's relations with landowners and government departments. The state's "relative autonomy" during the Oncenio gave country people in Asunción and Cospán additional space to organize while simultaneously complicating matters for hacendados through rendering simple repression problematic. In addition to a tempering of state hostility enabling wider "opportunity" for collective action (aided by open and covert support from appointees at the base of the state apparatus), the growth of reformist political movements enabled rural activists to assemble valuable urban linkages that added strength to their struggles.[70] The indigenista press printed articles in support of peasant protests and denounced what it viewed as landowner aggression. Importantly, sympathetic lawyers who were well connected with officials in the Indigenous Affairs Department in Lima and enjoyed everyday contact with judges and clerks employed in Cajamarca's court opened new avenues for otherwise excluded country dwellers to access sites of bureaucratic influence at the center and the legal system at the departmental level.

As Marx noted in "The Eighteenth Brumaire," state power cannot be suspended in midair indefinitely.[71] Leguía was ousted in a coup in August 1930 led by Luis Sánchez Cerro. After the assassination of Sánchez Cerro (April 1933), the "oligarchic" Óscar Benavides assumed the presidency (1933–39) and the Peruvian state became more landlord "friendly" and repressive. A contraction of "relative autonomy" did not throw grassroots rural mobilization in Asunción and Cospán into retreat, however. Indeed, during the 1930s, local campesinos proved able to continue engaging in acts of *asedio externo* (external encroachment) against the hacienda Huacraruco and to successfully resist landowner efforts to bring them to heel. One development occurring at this juncture that worked in favor of supposedly powerless peasants in a seemingly adverse political environment was the rise of "modern" politics—albeit with pronounced traditional caudillo leadership styles. As noted, in Asunción and surrounding districts this signified Aprismo, which swept the area between 1930 and 1935. Despite the widespread repression that followed failed APRA insurrections in Trujillo and Cajamarca during the early 1930s, the party's continued (largely clandestine) growth allowed campesinos to consolidate dense departmental and regional networks of support.[72] By the late 1930s, this led to the organization of peasant unions, tellingly with the assistance of local schoolteachers (overwhelmingly Aprista), lawyers based in Cajamarca town, and the occasional turbulent priest. During Leguía's Oncenio, the old order had begun to disintegrate, a development that (as mentioned) would eventually result in the expropriation of the Huacraruco and Sunchubamba latifundios under General Velasco's land reform. As Sinesio López noted, the rural population had embarked along the bumpy road from "Indians" to "citizens," a journey that has not been concluded.

NOTES

I use the following abbreviations in the notes: Archivo del Fuero Agrario / Correspondencia Empresa Agrícola Chicama Limitada (AFA/EACh); Archivo Regional de Cajamarca / Corte Superior de Justicia / Causa Criminales (ARC/CSJ/CC); Archivo Regional de Cajamarca / Fondo Documental de la Prefectura / Goberación de Asunción (ARC/FDP/GoA); Archivo Regional de Cajamarca / Fondo Documental de la Prefectura / Gobernación de Magdalena (ARC/FDP/GoM); Archivo Regional de Cajamarca / Fondo Documental de la Prefectura / Prefectura (ARC/FDP/P); Archivo Regional de Cajamarca / Fondo Documental de la Prefectura / Particulares (ARC/FDP/Pa); Archivo Regional de Cajamarca / Fondo Documental de la Prefectura / Subprefectura de Cajamarca (ARC/FDP/SpC); Archivo Regional de Cajamarca / Fondo Documental de la Prefectura / Subprefectura de Contumazá (ARC/FDP/SpCo); Archivo Regional de Cajamarca / Fondo Documental de la Prefectura / Varios (ARC/FDP/V); Archivo Regional de Cajamarca / Ministerio de Agricultura (ARC/MA).

1.   See, for example, Nelson Manrique, "Desarrollo del mercado interior y cambios en la demarcación regional en los Andes centrales del Perú (1820–1930)," in *Estados y naciones en los Andes: Hacia una historia comparativa; Bolivia, Colombia, Ecuador,*

Perú, 2 vols., ed. Jean-Paul Deler and Yves Saint-Geours (Lima: Instituto de Estudios Peruanos, 1986), 1:248.

2. Jean Piel, "Las articulaciones de la reserva andina al Estado y al mercado desde 1820 hasta 1950," in *Estados y naciones en los Andes: Hacia una historia comparativa; Bolivia, Colombia, Ecuador, Perú*, 2 vols., ed. Jean-Paul Deler and Yves Saint-Geours (Lima: Instituto de Estudios Peruanos, 1986), 1:329, 331. All translations are mine unless otherwise indicated.

3. Julio Cotler, *Clases, estado y nación en el Perú* (Lima: Instituto de Estudios Peruanos, 1978), 145, 149.

4. Ernesto Yepes, *Economía y política: La modernización en el Perú del siglo XX; Illusión y realidad* (Lima: Mosca Azul, 1992).

5. Peter Flindell Klarén, *Peru: Society and Nationhood in the Andes* (New York: Oxford University Press, 2000), 241–51.

6. In September 1878, the governor of Asunción recorded that at the district's annual fair (August 15) some 50,000 soles of business had taken place. Approximately eight hundred head of cattle, eight hundred pigs, and four thousand sheep were traded, most being exported to the coast. Similar ferias were held in Cospán. While these weeklong fairs comprised high points in the local calendar, trade in agricultural produce formed an everyday occurrence. ARC/FDP/GoA, September 20, 1878.

7. In June 1862, the governor of Asunción informed the prefect in the town of Cajamarca that "all the mules in this and neighboring districts have left for the coast, are occupied elsewhere in the province or in local haciendas. . . . The mules from San Jorge [an adjacent *caserío*—hamlet] have been contracted by Messrs. Burga and Gonzales, who left for Trujillo two weeks ago. All the muleteers from Cospán are away working." ARC/FDP/GoA, June 27, 1862.

8. Santiago Távara, *Emancipación del indio decretada el 5 de julio de 1854 por el libertador Ramón Castilla* (Lima: Printed by J. M. Monterola, 1856), quoted in Efraín Kristal, *The Andes Viewed from the City: Literary and Political Discourse on the Indian in Peru, 1848–1930* (New York: Peter Lang, 1987), 37–40.

9. ARC/FDP/GoA, November 7, 1879, November 17, 1879, November 21, 1879.

10. ARC/FDP/GoA, February 22, 1885.

11. ARC/FDP/GoA, January 20, 1886.

12. ARC/FDP/GoA, November 27, 1887.

13. ARC/FDP/GoA, August 18, 1887.

14. ARC/FDP/GoA, October 20, 1890; ARC/FDP/GoM, October 15, 1890; ARC/FDP/P, October 16, 1890.

15. ARC/FDP/SpCo, November 26, 1899, December 26, 1899.

16. ARC/FDP/SpCo, January 11, 1900, January 13, 1900, January 17, 1900, January 23, 1900, January 29, 1900, February 15, 1900, February 27, 1900, February 28, 1900.

17. ARC/FDP/SpC, May 29, 1905.

18. ARC/FDP/P, September 19, 1907.

19. ARC/FDP/P, April 7, 1914.

20. ARC/FDP/P, November 16, 1917.

21. ARC/FDP/SpC, August 27, 1918.

22. ARC/FDP/SpC, March 31, 1905, January 2, 1919.

23. ARC/FDP/SpC, November 17, 1907.

24. See Max Weber, *Economy and Society*, 2 vols. (Berkeley: University of Califor-
    nia Press, 1978); Antonio Gramsci, *Selections from the Prison Notebooks of Antonio
    Gramsci*, trans. and ed. Quintin Hoare and Geoffrey Nowell-Smith (New York:
    International Publishers, 1971).

25. For additional details, see Lewis Taylor, "Desarrollo económico y relaciones socia-
    les en las haciendas Huacraruco y Sunchubamba, 1920–1939," in *Estructuras agrarias
    y cambios sociales en Cajamarca, siglos XIX–XX* (Cajamarca: Asociación Obispo
    Martínez Compañón, 1994), 193–292.

26. During the 1920s, the EACh's Lima office was staffed by a small number of
    employees who enjoyed the complete confidence of the Gildemeister family. One
    such individual was Carlos Semsch, an Austrian who played a prominent role in
    the administration of Casa Grande during the 1910s and early 1920s before being
    transferred to Lima in 1922. Hugo Cohen comprised a second key player. The son of
    a family that migrated from Germany to Peru in the 1860s, he became the Empre-
    sa's accountant and financial adviser. An able lobbyist, he also exercised influence
    through membership of important committees within the Sociedad Nacional
    Agraria, the representative body of Peru's agrarian elite, especially the owners of
    coastal enterprises producing export commodities such as sugar and cotton.

27. The EACh maintained an office in the town, called the Agencia Cajamarca, staffed
    by a small number of employees headed by a German administrator. Its prime
    responsibility was to organize the contracting of laborers via the *enganche* system
    (in which labor recruiters in highland Cajamarca provided cash advances to local
    campesinos, who then journeyed down to coastal plantations to work off their debt
    at the prevailing daily rate) to supply field hands to Casa Grande, as well as the
    purchase of livestock and food products to feed the sugar plantation's work force.
    The administrator was tasked with developing cordial ties with key players in the
    local bureaucracy (the prefecture, judiciary, and municipality) in order to promote
    the company's interests.

28. ARC/FDP/P, February 25, 1923. Details have also been taken from the "Report on
    military actions against Anacleto Hoyos," written in German by Werner Pottgiesser
    to the General Administration in Casa Grande, AFA/EACh, February 20, 1923.

29. Alberto Behr, the head employee in the Agencia Cajamarca, informed Hans Gild-
    emeister in Casa Grande that on September 14, 1923, he rode out of Cajamarca
    town to a secret rendezvous with Hoyos

    > accompanied by his nephew Amilcar Saenz. Different guides took us by an
    > indirect route via the Callancas estate and from there to Huatún, where we
    > met in the open. Between Callancas and Huatún we encountered more than
    > 50 armed individuals. Hoyos came with his children and other relatives, eleven

strong and all well armed. We spent approximately an hour listening to him complain about everything that Verjel and the police robbed in Huatún. I said that the expedition had been ordered by the government. . . . The Company had nothing against him—if he leaves us in peace, we will do nothing to prejudice him. Hoyos stated he wanted to be a good "friend" of Casa Grande, especially the Gildemeister family and he wished to live in peace. . . . As they did not capture Hoyos during lieutenant Iparraguirre's operation—and I doubt they ever will—it will be advantageous to be on good terms. . . . If a political revolt erupts in the near future, some party is going to need Hoyos and we should be concerned that he might inflict damage on the haciendas. . . . If we want to be on good terms with Hoyos, it would be beneficial to give him a present—maybe a horse, a breeding bull or some good heifers.

Hans Gildemeister sagaciously replied that Hoyos should be mollified while kept at arm's length. It would be difficult to overcome "our long-standing enmity, but if we act judiciously it should be possible to avoid conflict with Hoyos without conceding too much. . . . I hope we can manage to maintain a superficial friendship with this man." Alberto Behr to Hans Gildemeister, AFA/EACh, September 19, 1923; Hans Gildemeister to Alberto Behr, AFA/EACh, November 21, 1923. This correspondence was conducted in German to enhance confidentiality.

30. In 1912, for example, the district of Asunción officially registered 304 births and 27 deaths; Cospán 101 baptisms and 12 deaths. ARC/FDP/SpC, July 9, 1913.

31. Additional information of these developments is provided in Lewis Taylor, "The Origins of APRA in Cajamarca, 1928–1935," *Bulletin of Latin American Research* 19, no. 4 (2000): 437–59.

32. Julio Cotler, for example, argued that the fall in agricultural prices after 1921 "affected adversely the precapitalist [i.e., Andean] reserve, causing landowners to engage in ever greater oppression of the peasantry in order to maintain income levels gained from the commercialization of foodstuffs acquired through extra-economic coercion [*por medios neo-coloniales*]." On the political front, Leguía's "pseudo-populist policies of the early years altered, as he oppressed peasant movements, granted amnesty to officials who perpetuated these massacres and, during his last years in office, passed a law that allowed landowners without proper titles, or no titles whatsoever, to obtain them. In this fashion, the expropriation of peasant land was legalized by new *latifundistas* incorporated within Leguía's clientele." Cotler, *Clases, estado y nación en el Perú*, 195, 199.

33. In February 1925, Erwin Wolff informed Hans Gildemeister regarding "the prefect's isolated position"; he had "only one friend among the educated people here," the lawyer Aníbal Zambrano. Erwin Wolff to Hans Gildemeister, February 12, 1925, AFA/EACh. Wolff had replaced Alberto Behr as head of the Agencia Cajamarca in December 1924.

34. Augusto Leguía, interview by Isaac F. Marcosson, *West Coast Leader* 14, no. 702 (July 28, 1925).

35. "El fomento de la pequeña propiedad agrícola," *Registro Oficial de Cajamarca* 60, no. 21 (June 5, 1926). The stated aim was to establish a government department charged with purchasing land with access to irrigation that could be redistributed to agriculturalists, who would be provided with free technical advice. This entity was to be supplied with an initial capital fund of £p.1,000.0.00 (*libras peruanas*—Peruvian pounds).

36. ARC/FDP/P, April 20, 1925.

37. Heinrich Emil (1880–1965) headed the management of Casa Grande until 1921, when his younger brother Hans (1896–1957)—usually known as Juan—assumed overall control after he returned from fighting in World War I. By unfortunate coincidence, Hans happened to be studying at an agricultural college in Germany when war broke out and got caught up in the conflict. For the first two years after his return to Peru, he was taught how to run the plantation by Carlos Semsch.

38. Enmity toward the EACh heightened after the Gildemeisters acquired the Roma sugar plantation at a knock-down price in January 1927. Roma's owner, Víctor Larco Herrera, actively participated in the postwar "dance of the millions." Having made significant investments in the plantation, he proved unable to meet his obligations and was forced to declare bankruptcy once the international sugar price fell after 1921. Larco, who had stood as vice president on Leguía's electoral slate in 1919, was widely viewed as a paternalistic patron, in contrast to the more disciplined "Protestant ethic" approach to management exhibited by Juan Gildemeister, perceptions that were popularized in the local press.

39. One such incident occurred on November 4, 1928, when farm manager Hermann Dobbertin and other employees of Huacraruco attempted to conduct a rodeo on the disputed land with the intention of charging smallholders ten centavos per day for the embargoed livestock. They were accompanied by five policemen stationed in Asunción as well as the district governor. As the group approached the casa hacienda with the impounded livestock, they were overpowered by a throng of smallholders from surrounding communities (including the local lieutenant governor) before being relieved of their weapons and mounts. Dobbertin managed to flee, but the police had to be rescued by another detachment of gendarmes. "Delito de extorción ilícita por Hermann Dobbertin y otros empleados de la hacienda Huacraruco contra Flavio Saenz y otros comuneros de San Juan," 1928, ARC/MA, leg. 212.

40. Indicatively, in May 1930 the prefect informed the subprefect of Cajamarca that he had been ordered by the Director de Fomento in Lima to provide all "constitutional guarantees" to the peasants of San Juan de Yanac and not allow the seizure of their land, livestock, and other possessions. ARC/FDP/P, May 21, 1930.

41. R. Dibarbú to the prefect, ARC/FDP/V, January 23, 1919; E. Banaillier to the prefect, ARC/FDP/V, April 26, 1919.

42. Andrés Partilla, Rosario Gutierrez, and Fidel Muñoz to the prefect, ARC/FDP/V, June 26, 1919.

43. Communication from the subprefect to the prefect of Cajamarca, ARC/FDP/P, November 21, 1919. The following day an editorial appeared in *El Ferrocarril*

denouncing the failure to pay "los pobres indígenas" (the suffering/hapless Indians) who were laboring on the coastal road. Support was voiced for their grievances. *El Ferrocarril*, November 22, 1919.

44. ARC/FDP/P, December 4, 1919. Two days earlier Dibarbú had written directly to the prefect also stating that the governor of Asunción had instructed the populace to refuse to work for less than S/.1.20 per day. ARC/FDP/V, December 2, 1919.

45. Governor of Asunción to the prefect, November 3, 1925, November 10, 1925, ARC/FDP/SpC. Months before the governor had advised his superiors that as the prevailing daily wage in the district stood at eighty centavos, laborers engaged on the Conscripción Vial should consequently receive that sum. ARC/FDP/SpC, May 12, 1924.

46. ARC/FDP/P, October 18, 1924.

47. ARC/FDP/P, October 31, 1924, November 1, 1924.

48. ARC/FDP/P, September 10, 1929.

49. ARC/FDP/P, June 28, 1930.

50. Efforts by members of the local agrarian and mercantile elite to open up the coast road to motor vehicles predated the enactment of Leguía's legislation. In 1916 Carolina Puga (owner of the hacienda La Pauca) and Hilbeck Kuntze (proprietor of Cajamarca's leading general store) were providing cash and manpower to improve the road to the railway. See Editorial, *El Ferrocarril*, July 1, 1916.

51. These initiatives were published in the local press. See "Ayer ingresaron 108 viales de la hacienda La Pauca," *El Perú*, May 28, 1927; see also editorials of August 27, 1927, and October 1, 1928. By 1929 some 127 motor vehicles were circulating in Cajamarca. Editorial, *El Perú*, December 10, 1929.

52. Details originally reported in the magazine *Ciudad y Campo*, October–December 1928, and reprinted in *El Perú*, November 11, 1943.

53. The common interpretation of relations between the coastal planter "oligarchy" and the Leguía administration stresses animosity, especially during the "reformist" first phase, 1919–23. Michael Gonzales, for example, states that "the Aspíllagas and other planters viewed Leguía as an enemy and felt threatened by his regime." Michael J. Gonzales, *Plantation Agriculture and Social Control in Northern Peru, 1875–1933* (Austin: University of Texas Press, 1985), 173. Bill Albert in his monograph on the sugar industry notes: "Leguía's victory and the policies that he subsequently pursued caused considerable unease among sugar hacendados. This was particularly true in the case of the Pardos and Aspíllagas, Leguía's direct political opponents who faced harassment at the hands of the new government." Bill Albert, *An Essay on the Peruvian Sugar Industry, 1880–1920* (Norwich: University of East Anglia, 1976). A review of internal correspondence does not reveal a level of hostility to the regime consistent with the aforementioned interpretation. The company obviously meddled in politics, but the Gildemeister family was not identified clearly with the Partido Civil elite and remained to some degree "outsiders." Indeed, although the company opposed government calls for reform of rural social structures, it sought to establish cordial relations with the state and was not seen as a potential or actual threat to the president.

54. ARC/FDP/SpC, November 1, 1924. In previous months Hagemann successfully parried the governor's requests by claiming that the hacienda peons were busy with their harvests (permissible grounds under the law) or were absent working cane fields in the Chicama Valley. ARC/FDP/SpC, July 22, 1924, August 13, 1924.

55. Erwin Wolff to Hans Gildemeister, AFA/EACh, May 12, 1925.

56. Carlos Semsch to Erwin Wolff, AFA/EACh, May 27, 1925. The previous month Hans Gildemeister had counseled a similar approach to dealings with the prefect: "You need to be on good terms, but do not indulge him. You should attempt to dissuade him from continuing with constructing the road." Hans Gildemeister to Erwin Wolff, AFA/EACh, April 27, 1925.

57. Erwin Wolff to Hans Gildemeister, AFA/EACh, February 21, 1926. By no means were all officials so honest. When in October 1923 the previous prefect approached the Agencia Cajamarca for money, he was handed £p.30.0.00 out of petty cash. Eventually displeased with the regularity of such approaches, Gildemeister sent Behr the following instructions: "We need to limit payments provided as favors. When someone approaches you soliciting money, you can state that you cannot consent without prior authorization from Casa Grande. Before approval has been granted the majority of people will have forgotten their request." Alberto Behr to Hans Gildemeister, October 8, 1923, AFA/EACh; Hans Gildemeister to Alberto Behr, November 21, 1924, AFA/EACh.

58. Hans Gildemeister to Erwin Wolff, March 1, 1926, AFA/EACh.

59. Erwin Wolff to Hans Gildemeister, April 18, 1926, AFA/EACh.

60. Erwin Wolff to Hans Gildemeister, April 26, 1926, AFA/EACh. It is not known if this visit materialized.

61. Hans Niemann to Hans Gildemeister, AFA/EACh, October 4, 1926, AFA/EACh. Wolff received notice that he would be removed from his position due to poor health (malaria) on August 26, 1926. He was replaced by Niemann in September 1926.

62. Hans Niemann to Hans Gildemeister, March 5, 1927, AFA/EACh.

63. AFA/EACh, June 4, 1927.

64. Mark Cowling and James Martin, eds., *Marx's "Eighteenth Brumaire": (Post)Modern Interpretations* (London: Pluto Press, 2002); Nicos Poulantzas, *Political Power and Social Classes* (New York: Verso, 1975).

65. See Perry Anderson, "The Antinomies of Antonio Gramsci," *New Left Review* 100 (November–December 1976): 5–81.

66. On "power" and "domination," see Max Weber, *Economy and Society*, 2 vols. (Berkeley: University of California Press, 1978), 1:53. For a wide-ranging discussion on the issue of state legitimacy, see David Beetham, *The Legitimation of Power* (Atlantic Highlands, N.J.: Humanities Press, 1991).

67. It is argued that nation-states need to earn "the right to rule" through the delivery of essential services and—crucially—the provision of physical security to citizens. Bruce Gilley, *The Right to Rule: How States Win and Lose Legitimacy* (New York: Columbia University Press, 2009).

68. For an account of a conflict in the village of Lachaqui (province of Canta, department of Lima) that resulted in the police shooting three peasants and arresting sixteen villagers who claimed they had fulfilled their work quota, see Mario Meza Bazán, "Estado, modernización y la Ley de Conscripción Vial en el Perú," *Revista Andina* 49 (2009): 165–86.

69. Old habits die hard! In February 2015, Marcos Cruzado, a leader from the Sunchubamba annex of the José Carlos Mariátegui cooperative (Huacraruco and Sunchubamba were expropriated under Juan Velasco's agrarian reform), was shot dead at close range in Cospán. His assassination was reputedly motivated by the murder three years previously of a denizen of the community of Shirac, where smallholders blamed cooperative members for his death and swore revenge. As well as long-standing hacienda-peasant community land disputes, internal conflicts also resulted in bloodshed. On May 29, 2018, José Abanto was gunned down in the Huacraruco annex, it being alleged that the administrator hired pistoleros to eliminate a rival who was challenging his control over land and position of authority within the cooperative. Ana Cabrejos, "Investigan asesinato en la hacienda Huacraruco," *La República*, May 29, 2018. This incident brought to eight the number of homicides due to such altercations committed in Huacraruco, Sunchubamba, and environs during recent years. Personal communication from the public prosecutor for Cajamarca, Dr. Luis Lingán, June 10, 2018.

70. See Sydney Tarrow, *Power in Movement: Social Movements and Contentious Politics* (Cambridge: Cambridge University Press, 1998).

71. See Karl Marx, *The Eighteenth Brumaire of Louis Bonaparte* (1852; repr., New York: International Publishers, 1994).

72. Villagers from Asunción and Cospán participated in the failed July 1932 Trujillo revolt against the Sánchez Cerro regime, those who escaped being shot in the ruins of the Chan Chan pre-Inca archaeological site while fleeing back to their smallholdings in the highlands. ARC/FDP/V, n.d. (1932). This document, based on information supplied by an anonymous informant, names three individuals who allegedly joined in the assassination of captured Guardia Civil officers in the city.

6

LABOR CONFLICT, ARBITRATION, AND THE LABOR STATE IN HIGHLAND PERU

PAULO DRINOT

THIS CHAPTER explores labor conflict at the Anglo-French Ticapampa Silver Mining Company mines located at an altitude of approximately four thousand meters above sea level in Ancash, Peru, surrounded by some of the highest mountains in the Western Hemisphere. Established in the first decade of the twentieth century, by the 1920s the Anglo-French Ticapampa Company was the most important producer of silver in Peru. Its famous "casa de gerencia" (management house) was the place where, according to some versions of the story, the famous cocktail "pisco sour" was invented. Yet relatively little is known about the company or its operations in Ancash. Most studies of the history of mining and labor relations in mines in Peru have, for good reasons, focused on the central highlands, and particularly on the Cerro de Pasco Copper Corporation, which was by far the most important mining concern in Peru in the first half of the twentieth century.[1] However, the existence of rich, if patchy, documentation on labor disputes in Ticapampa in the 1920s and 1930s provides a unique opportunity to examine close-up the ways in which the regime of labor relations, and more specifically the management of labor conflict, in the mining industry evolved in the first half of the twentieth century beyond Cerro de Pasco. In particular, the study of Ticapampa sheds light on the operation of labor justice in even the most distant places where labor and capital came into conflict.[2]

As I have shown elsewhere, in the first few decades of the twentieth century, and particularly in the 1920s and 1930s, Peruvian modernizing elites viewed the resolution of the labor question as a matter of civilization while workers came to be seen as a valuable resource to be protected and improved through the actions of the state.[3] In a country perceived by its elites as held back on the march to progress by its primarily indigenous and rural population, workers, understood as nonindigenous and associated with modern industry, were imagined as a key actor in a broader project of industrialization as a means to progress. Labor policy, in the shape of labor laws and state agencies aimed at addressing the labor question, was motivated not only, as has tended to be argued, by a desire to contain labor militancy and undermine the appeal of emerging left-wing political ideologies and parties. It also reflected the belief of modernizing elites that workers could be agents of progress and that social action by the state could protect and improve workers in their immediate (the workplace) and mediate (the worker communities) environments. Miners occupied a particularly central role in this racialized understanding of the potential of industry to bring about a new era of progress based on a modern workforce. As a privileged environment where Indians came into contact with modern industry, mines, like haciendas, were understood to be spaces where the indigenous, thanks to the paternalistic practices of their employers but also of the state, could be redeemed by undergoing a cultural and even racial transformation from Indians into workers.[4]

Though in some ways liminal spaces between the indigenous and nonindigenous spheres, mines belonged to the sphere of labor and therefore of progress. Although the workers in the mines may have been phenotypically or even culturally "Indian," they were considered workers and as such were subject to labor legislation and to the system of labor justice. As I have shown elsewhere, labor and indigeneity were two incommensurable spheres of constitutional and legal action. As miners, and therefore as workers, the men and women who worked in mines across the country became subject to a series of labor laws introduced from the first decade of the twentieth century onward, some specific to miners, but most, such as the 1911 work accident law, extensive to all who were considered workers. Likewise, they were entitled, indeed in some ways required, to form unions, in order to participate, from the late 1910s onward, in the system of collective bargaining and labor arbitration that came into force, and was enshrined, in articles 48 and 49 of the 1920 Constitution. Finally, miners fell under the purview of the Sección del Trabajo of the Ministerio de Fomento (Labor Bureau of the Ministry of Development), established in 1919, which had the power to recognize labor unions and oversee collective bargaining. The laws, agencies, and ideas constituted what I call the labor state, a state coproduced by workers through how they accommodated, resisted, and ultimately transformed the way it addressed the labor question.

Regardless of their phenotype or indigenous background, workers at the Ticapampa mine thought of themselves as workers. They made use of traditional instruments of labor struggle such as the strike but also the newly created labor rights and collective bargaining legislation to bring employers to the negotiating table and seek better wages and working conditions. In forming a union, the Ticapampa workers inserted themselves into a tradition of organizing that tied them to a history of labor that transcended the Peruvian context and globalized their own struggle against capital. In bringing their grievances to the attention of state agencies charged with implementing labor arbitration, the men and women who labored in the mines and in the mill of Ticapampa summoned the Peruvian state to their mining camp. Through labor arbitration, the miners invoked the labor legislation that they knew existed to protect them from exploitative employers such as the Anglo-French Ticapampa Company and at the same time mobilized a discourse that reflected the idea that as workers they were agents of progress. As we will see, they may not always have succeeded in securing better wages or working conditions, but the fact that workers drew on such laws, state agencies, and discourses points to how the coproduction of the labor state by workers and state agents could take place even at four thousand meters above sea level.

THE ANGLO-FRENCH TICAPAMPA SILVER MINING COMPANY

Although set up as early as 1892, and reorganized as a company in 1903, the Anglo-French Ticapampa Silver Mining Company took over a mining operation in Ticapampa that began as early as the 1860s, developed by a Pole named Sokolosky and a French national called Henry Thierry.[5] In this sense, the Anglo-French Ticapampa investment was part of a broader trend of foreign capital penetration in mining in Peru, which, as Rosemary Thorp and Geoff Bertram noted some years ago, radically changed the pattern of ownership of the mining sector from the beginning of the twentieth century until the 1920s. Of course, the most important and most visible company in this process of "denationalization of mining" was the Cerro de Pasco Corporation in the central highlands.

However, in Ticapampa too, this process was at play.[6] Although not on the same scale as in the central highlands, mining's impact on the local economy in Ancash was significant. In 1905, there were some 315 mining concessions in Ancash, which made it the second-largest mining department after Junín, where Cerro de Pasco was located, which boasted as many as 1,892 concessions.[7] Ancash employed the second-largest number of miners, some 2,100 "mineros" and 470 "metalurgistas" (Junín's equivalent figures were 4,200 and 600).[8] Yet the department was largely characterized by small mineral producers who employed a reduced workforce and worked the silver seams "intermittently," producing on average no more than ten tons per year. This type of production was highly price sensitive. When silver prices fell, production fell accordingly.[9] Indeed, of twenty-nine mines identified in Ancash in mining statistics for 1906, only half were in operation.[10]

As in the central highlands, though again at a much smaller scale, the penetration of foreign capital led to investment in and modernization of the mining activities, thus likely heightening the differences between foreign owned and run mines such as Ticapampa, which were highly capitalized and endowed with the latest technology, and smaller, artisanal miners that were unable to access such sources of capital and technology (and which, available evidence suggests, came to rely on larger concerns such as Ticapampa to process their ore). Although located at close to four thousand meters above sea level, Ticapampa acquired an industrial character and was at the forefront of a major technological transformation in silver mining in Peru.[11] By the 1910s, the mining camp boasted the "most powerful" lixiviation plant in the country and a smelter. Harry Franck, a U.S. writer and "adventurer" who traveled through much of Peru in the 1910s, described Ticapampa as the "headquarters of a French mining company, the several tall chimneys of which were belching their black smoke into the brilliant sky, their ugliness offset by the first suggestion of industry in Peru."[12] According to one source, in 1936, Ticapampa employed 385 workers (*operarios*) and 4 white-collar workers (*empleados*). Average pay for an eight-hour work day was 1.45 soles, the highest rate in the *departamento*, though significantly lower than at Cerro de Pasco, where workers were paid between 2.10 and 3.28 soles, and lower also than at another important silver mine, Caylloma in Arequipa, where workers received 2.00 soles.[13]

One of the Anglo-French Ticapampa Company managers, Jacques Veigle, who was based at the mine between 1916 and 1919, provided a description of the place in a talk given at the Société de Géographie de Genève in 1945.[14]

According to his account, Veigle reached the mining camp of Ticapampa after riding on horseback up the Peruvian coastal desert from Lima and turning into a mountainous region, "with deep gorges crossed by disturbing bridges." After passing a summit at 4,700 meters above sea level, he reached the valley where the mining camp is located, between the "White" and "Black" cordilleras that cross the department of Ancash, "bigger than Switzerland." Veigle described Ticapampa itself as having "a harsh and violent landscape, with a climate characterized by sudden changes of temperature, where the altitude accelerates the pulsations of the heart and forces one to work more slowly." In keeping with this representation of the landscape as alien and threatening, Veigle described the local population in the dominant racialized register of the time as primitive and backward: "As for the natives, they are Cholos. They live from sheep farming, wear ponchos and felt or straw hats. Their dwellings are rudimentary; infant mortality is very high." Whether Ticapampa drew its workforce from the local population is unclear but likely, at least for the less highly skilled tasks. Higher-skilled workers, employed in the lixiviation process, for example, may have been drawn from further afield.[15]

Despite the perception of an inauspicious environment and a suboptimal local population, the investment made by the French company appears to have paid off, at least initially. In 1908 and then 1917, the building of deep shafts enabled access to a rich seam of silver, known as Collaracra, which according to one report was 1 meter thick and produced 2.5 kilograms of silver per ton mined. In 1917 the mine produced 18,500 kilograms of silver.[16] According to J. Fred Rippy, the company "paid its first dividend in 1905 and an average of nearly 16 percent annually down through the year 1919 on a nominal capital ranging from £100,000 to £140,000." However, he goes on to add that the company made "no further payment to its owners between 1920 and 1950!"[17] The profitability of the company did not go unnoticed by Peruvian observers: "The prosperity of this company can be judged by the last dividends distributed to its shareholders, which have been 20% in 1910, 20% in 1911, 25% in 1912, and 20% in 1913."[18] The reasons the company stopped paying dividends after 1920 are unclear. The company reports suggest that it continued to invest in its mining operations in the 1920s.[19] In 1918 the *Boletín del Cuerpo de Ingenieros de Minas* singled out the Anglo-French Ticapampa Company as one of only two mining companies that continued to focus primarily on mining silver (the other was the Sociedad Explotadora de Caylloma, based in Arequipa). Ticapampa had made the most of high prices for silver, producing net gains of more than 1.5 million French francs and a dividend of 27 percent. This favorable situation had allowed the company to put aside significant reserves of half a million Francs in order to cover the cost of building a railway to the coast.[20]

Though the mining operations appear to have been generally successful, their location presented real challenges. The U.S. traveler Annie Peck was certainly impressed by the region: "The mineral riches may rival the Klondike as the scenic splendor surpasses that of Chamonix."[21] But, located one hundred kilometers from the coast, the Anglo-French Ticapampa Company depended on mule and llama trains to transport the mineral to the port of Huarmey, where in 1905 the company had been authorized to build a wharf.[22] As Veigle explained, llamas could only carry 45 kilograms and travel 20 kilometers per day.[23] In effect, anything weighing more than 130 kilograms (the weight a mule can bear) could not be carried up to or down from the mine. In its report of 1918, the company noted that the creation of a means of communication with the coast was "essential to the development of our mining region, whose wealth is growing day by day." In its estimation, a railroad would be too expensive and not necessary, since the mineral is high value and has a low volume and weight. Instead a road would suffice. The report proposed the use of tractors (which the European war had demonstrated were powerful and adaptable), which could provide a regular service between the mine and the coast.[24] By 1920 the company had undertaken the building of a road to the port of Huarmey, and had made some progress, with up to forty kilometers of road accessible to trucks.[25]

Another challenge faced by the company was labor. The region had one of the highest population densities in the country. Annie Peck noted that "along the [valley] are the considerable towns of Caráz, Yungay, Carhuaz, and Huaráz, capital of the Department, each with populations of several thousand, besides the people at haciendas and at mining centers on either hand. This is one of the richest and most thickly settled portions of Peru."[26] However, the large number of mines and haciendas in the region meant that labor was scarce and obtaining labor to work in the Ticapampa mine was expensive and difficult: "In the Sierra the workers are so scarce that the miners snatch them from each other and, to keep them, the owners of the plantations, sugar mills, etc. need to make great advances in wages."[27] Company reports from 1907 similarly point to the fact that retaining labor was not straightforward: "The availability of workers has suffered a bit due to the creation of a new company in our mining area. Thanks to the facilities we are seeking to provide to the workers for their food and housing, the number of defections has decreased, and the current contingent is sufficient to meet our needs."[28] The following year, the report noted that "the workers we hired were sufficient for our needs except in the planting season."[29] As this suggests, workers could be easily enticed to join another company—it was necessary to provide incentives in the shape of good food and accommodation to retain them. Regular advertisements in local newspapers such as *El Departamento de Ancash* and *Huascarán* suggest that labor recruitment was something the company had to pursue actively: "Workers needed for its mines and offices."[30]

At the same time, these company reports suggest, the workers employed by the company were not fully proletarianized. During the harvest and planting seasons, mine labor became scarce.[31] This was a general problem for the mining industry in much of Peru until the 1920s, as a 1917 report on mining conditions confirmed: "The number of workers occupied by the mining industry in Peru varies considerably, especially in the regions of the highlands, where the main mines are located, because most of them have small crops in nearby valleys and at harvest and planting time they leave the mines, sometimes producing major labor crises."[32] And yet, as we will see below, though some mine workers (more likely the less highly skilled) at Ticapampa may have retained some connection to agricultural activities, which during lean times such as the Great Depression served as a safety cushion (as Florencia Mallon has argued for the central highlands), the disputes that they engaged in were motivated by grievances that reflected their condition as mine workers, not as semiproletarianized peasants.[33] Moreover, the discourses that they employed, in both marking out their identity as workers and in invoking the social legislation and the regime of labor relations that was intended to protect them from capitalist exploitation, firmly inserted them into the sphere of labor.

THE 1918–1920 LABOR UNREST

In December 1918, the Spanish flu hit the mining camp at Ticapampa. Its effect was devastating, as it was around the world, where it resulted in a death toll of between 50 and 100 million.[34] In January 1919, *El Departamento de Ancash* reported that the pandemic was causing numerous deaths in Ticapampa "because it is not possible to effectively treat the sick due to a lack of doctors and medicines." The dead were being removed from the mines on the back of mules, while the company had been forced to shut down operations. Some five hundred workers were infected, the newspaper estimated.[35] The situation was catastrophic: "The population [of the mines] is totally alarmed, without medicine, lacking in all kinds of resources."[36] According to the company, 60 percent of factory workers (*ouvriers d'usine*) and 40 percent of miners were killed, a death toll confirmed by Dr. Amadeo Robles, who had gone out to the mines to help the ill but had fallen ill himself.[37] Production fell to zero in January and February and only restarted in March.[38] Jacques Veigle, who was working at Ticapampa at the time, confirms these figures. According to his account, he was himself "seriously ill" and lived through "tragic days."[39] These death rates were catastrophic and much higher than elsewhere in Peru, indeed than in nearby Huaraz, where mortality was estimated by Dr. Robles at 1 or 2 percent.[40] Based on available evidence, it appears that up to two hundred workers died as a consequence of the pandemic at Ticapampa.

The impact of the pandemic on the mining camp was devastating and possibly worsened by the actions of the company. When the company shut down its operations, the "bodega" or company store shut down. Workers had nowhere to purchase goods, thus considerably worsening the situation caused by the pandemic. As two workers noted in a letter published in *El Departamento de Ancash*: "It is truly horrifying to see lying in the street the corpses of our comrades who, lacking food and people to take care of them, left [their homes] in desperate search [for help] and there and then fell dead." The workers asked that the company provide basic foodstuffs to help them survive.[41] However, the effect of the flu pandemic was not only demographic. It coincided with a new phase in labor relations.[42] As the company report of 1919 noted, "our decimated worker populations also take part in the labor trouble that the Bolshevik wind has sown in all corners of the world. Some clues make us fear possible strikes that would further reduce our production."[43] As this suggests, in Ticapampa too, the wave of labor unrest that swept much of the world in the wake of the Russian Revolution and the end of World War I left its mark. As happened elsewhere in Peru in 1918–19, workers at Ticapampa turned to the strike as a means to extract higher wages and better working conditions. This occurred in, and contributed to, a context where national elites viewed the introduction of social legislation as a necessary and modernizing development. Such sentiments, however, often came into conflict with the interests of employers who resisted new labor legislation and attempted to roll back what they perceived to be state interference in labor-capital relations.[44]

The labor unrest of 1918–20 at Ticapampa can be gleaned from reports in the local press and from Ministerio del Interior documents held at the Archivo

General de la Nación. *El Departamento de Ancash* reported in March 1918 that a strike had broken out at Ticapampa, one of a number of "regular strikes." The article reflected a dominant narrative that explained worker militancy in Peru in this period: if workers struck, it was because of the influence of outside agitators. The strikes, it noted, "are a consequence of the incitements of well-known elements, who use all means to influence the workers of that company and push them to make all kinds of demands." The response to the strike was swift. Twenty-five gendarmes and the subprefect were dispatched from Huaraz to restore order in the mine.[45] However, the reports in the local press also reflected a second narrative: it was the responsibility of the authorities to ensure that the rights of workers and of capitalists were respected. Workers' demands were justified in light of the steep increase in prices that the end of World War I had brought about and the fact that their wages had not changed. The press applauded the actions of the subprefect in bringing the strike to a successful end: the company had agreed to increase wages by 20 percent; it would allow workers to use the company bodega; it would pay workers fortnightly (rather than monthly); and it would ensure that a doctor be available at all times, while considering establishing a hospital in the mining camp.[46]

The trouble was far from over, however. The apparent solution to the unrest was celebrated by the company in a letter sent by the company's general manager, Pedro Fontenay, to the prefect. In the letter, Fontenay thanked the prefect for his "effective intervention in the satisfactory and fair solution of the strike of our workers" but also, indirectly, for the detachment of eight soldiers that were seconded to the mining camp under the command of alférez (second lieutenant) Félix Davelouis.[47] A little over a month later, however, unrest had returned to the mine. Following what they viewed as the unfair dismissal of a worker, the Collaracra miners cut the electricity and telephone cables and let off sticks of dynamite, a form of protest that appears to have been used regularly in Ticapampa. At the same time, the workers in the mill demanded the dismissal of an employee, apparently disliked because he worked in the bodega (perhaps it was believed that he treated workers unfairly or that he was seen as a stooge of the company). The response, again, was to dispatch twenty soldiers to the mine. This appears to have convinced the workers to return to work. Again, the incident was framed in the narrative of the influence of outside agitators. The workers' demands, according to *El Departamento de Ancash*, "are merely the consequence of the intrigues and maneuvers of people who for some time now have tried to get others to do their bidding and push workers, who are simply trying to earn their daily bread, to reprehensible and dangerous extremes." The rights of workers could, the newspaper concluded, be taken to extremes "that are borderline insane."[48]

This was the context in which the workers of Ticapampa set up a union, the Sociedad de Auxilios Mutuos de Obreros y Artesanos de Ticapampa (Ticapampa Mutual Aid Society of Workers and Artisans). The union was created in late October 1918 and as such was part of a much larger wave of unionization that took place in Peru at this time.[49] The creation of the union or, strictly speaking, mutual aid society appears to have had some support from the company, at least initially. Federico Testolini, a company "ingeniero" who gave a standard as a present to the union, and Amadeo Robles, described as a company doctor, were present at the union's inauguration, a lavish affair that included champagne, a band of musicians, a priest brought from Recuay, and a corrida in the Ticapampa bullring. The speeches given by the president and treasurer of the union, Fortunato Montalvo and Alfredo Laguna, respectively, as well as by Daniel Villaizán, described as the "worker delegate," in effect the legal representative of the workers charged with interceding with the company, who the following year became mayor of Huaraz, point to the ideas that underpinned the creation of the union. They illustrate the extent to which miners at Ticapampa viewed themselves as workers, not semiproletarianized peasants. They inserted themselves in a narrative of worker struggle, organization, and identity that connected them to the history of labor in Europe and the United States as well as to the worker populations of the urban centers and the export industries on the Peruvian coast and elsewhere in the highlands. In so doing, they also located themselves firmly within the sphere of labor as defined by the labor legislation of the Peruvian state.[50]

Montalvo's speech began with what he called a "short account of proletarian life," which, in fact, was an erudite attempt to frame the labor struggles in Ticapampa in a global as well as long-run historical context. His overview started with Jean-Jacques Rousseau, the establishment of society, and class struggle, jumped back to Plato and Aristotle and Greek and Roman slavery, turned to the feudal institutions of the Middle Ages and the freedom offered to slaves in the afterlife by religion, and moved forward to the nineteenth century to the abolition of slavery and Abraham Lincoln proclaiming all men are created equal. The abolition of slavery had not ended oppression, Montalvo contended. The waged were now victims of a new and cruel tyrant: capital. Karl Marx had been the first to understand this, he noted. Montalvo's speech then moved through the 1848 revolutions, the workers' international, and the Communist Manifesto of Marx and Engels. He then turned to the rise of socialism and the idea, which he associated with Élisée Réclus, that armed struggle could not succeed when faced with "unconscious masses." He then turned to the process whereby socialists sought to return to politics and control parliaments in order to legislate in favor of the proletariat, a process that he associated with Alexandre Millerand in France and Woodrow Wilson in the United States. Faced with a railway strike, Wilson had declared that the state had to intervene in conflicts between capital and labor and side with workers "to prevent them becoming victims of the capitalist tyranny." The passing of the eight-hour-day law, Montalvo concluded, had put an end to a process that had begun with the Haymarket martyrs of Chicago.

Montalvo then turned to the Peruvian context. In so doing, he used a rhetorical device that suggests he was familiar with the writings of the famous Peruvian libertarian writer Manuel González Prada: "The Peruvian social problem is not in Lima, or Callao, or in any other city; it is here, in the real Peru which is not Lima; it is in the haciendas and the mines, where the hacendados and the mine owners become rich thanks to the sweat and even blood of the unfortunate."[51] Montalvo went on to criticize social legislation, focusing on what he called the trifling accident law, and criticized the fact that each time that workers had demanded their rights from the authorities, "the state has used military force to drown in blood all demands," while pointing to recent cases such as Chicama, Llaucán, Vitarte, Huacho, and Lobitos.[52] The situation at Ticapampa was, he argued, a unique exception, one in which the company bosses, the "educated worker" (obrero culto), and the political authorities had found a peaceful and just solution. But elsewhere, the situation was dire. In particular he pointed to the situation of the "indigenous race," which, he suggested, was now in a worse state than during the Ramón Castilla government in the mid-nineteenth century, when forced labor obligations had been banned. Now, however, the indigenous population had to contend with other forms of exploitation: "debt peonage [enganches], low wages, unpaid and coerced labor, etc." As this suggests, Montalvo viewed Indian exploitation as a grave matter but as separate (if connected) to the struggles of workers. This confirms further the idea that Ticapampa workers, regardless of their phenotype or background, imagined themselves as part of the sphere of labor, not indigeneity.

Montalvo finished his speech by applauding the creation of the union, whose function he presented primarily as consisting of assisting its members who fell ill or died, functions typical of mutual aid societies. This was also the message that Alfredo Laguna, the union's treasurer, tried to put across in his shorter speech. But Laguna also emphasized that the union represented unity and solidarity among the workforce, which would bring about the end of capitalist exploitation and the beginning of a new era, "and that, simply because our forces have united into a single one to guarantee our interests and to give us the indispensable mutual assistance that we must give to each other, in case of future contingencies." Finally, Daniel Villaizán, who declared himself to be a "worker of the mind and action," gave a somewhat patronizing speech, in which he praised the workers for having obtained a "deserved victory" in the strike, the company for having given way to the workers' demands, and the government for, in essence, not having used violence to repress the strike. He thanked the workers for having made him their "delegate," a role that he promised to fulfill "as an advanced sentinel who will guarantee the firmness and stability of the pact under whose protection, restrained and respectful toward your bosses, as always, you [returned] to the daily work, like tireless bees of the hive of progress."

It is unclear why the company gave its blessing to the union. Perhaps it thought that it would be a docile mutual aid society and nothing else. The rhetoric mobilized by Montalvo and Laguna should have disabused them of this belief. Only a few months later, trouble returned to the mine, and it was focused on the union. On April 2, 1919, *El Departamento de Ancash* reported on an altercation that had rocked the Sociedad de Auxilios Mutuos during a meeting at its "local." The problem began, according to the newspaper, when a faction headed by Fortunato Montalvo tried to replace Daniel Villaizán as worker delegate to the company with three other delegates, respectively Aurelio Valenzuela, Gustavo Pohl (someone we shall return to), and Víctor Thierry. This attempt to oust Villaizán was resisted by another faction, which appears to have succeeded in imposing its will, electing Agripino González to the presidency of the union. The conflict between these two factions turned violent. A fight broke out and a worker named Daniel Camones let off dynamite sticks, according to the press reports. In turn, this provoked the intervention of the police, led by the *teniente gobernador* of Ticapampa, Josué Espinoza, leading to the arrest of Camones and a confrontation, which resulted in several dead and injured. The situation escalated when Espinoza, accused by the workers of having started the trouble, was himself arrested by a Capitán Rodríguez. Espinoza then escaped. A large detachment of police officers was sent subsequently from Huaraz to investigate and arrest the troublemakers.

These acts of violence were presented in *El Departamento de Ancash* in a familiar narrative. Although the newspaper recognized in an early article that "undoubtedly, there is no such a state of harmony and equity in Ticapampa that would make the relations between the capital and the worker workable," it blamed the violence on a small group intent on undermining the general workforce, which, by contrast, was focused on work and not politics: "The majority of workers do not want a strike or disorder, . . . they want to work normally." The trouble, the newspaper insisted, had been motivated "by the disruptive attitude of some workers who are influenced by people who pretend to be defenders of the working class but whose motives are different and even contrary to the welfare of workers and employees of Ticapampa." Put differently, the newspaper blamed the violence on Montalvo and Camones and a small group of workers allied to them. By contrast, the authorities, and particularly the teniente gobernador, Josué Espinoza, were blameless. This was a narrative that the new "directive" of the union was clearly keen to make its own, as demonstrated by the decision to name Gonzalo Salazar, the editor of *El Departamento de Ancash*, as its "worker delegate." In the 1940s, Salazar went on to become a member of parliament for Ancash (as "diputado") and appears to have played an important role in local politics in the region for much of the 1930s and 1940s. He was, evidence suggests, an important member of the local Ancash elite and, as editor of the main local newspaper, had significant power at the local level.

What motivated Salazar to take such a direct interest in the situation at Ticapampa? To judge from reports in his newspaper, he viewed Ticapampa as a source of progress and modernity in the region. As a local elite, he may well have felt that it was in his interest, and those of his class, to protect the company's interests. He was clearly alarmed by what he saw as the dangerous militancy of the Ticapampa workers and may have feared that it could spread to other workers in the region, some of whom had also begun to set up unions.[53] The violence at Ticapampa gave Salazar, and his newspaper, an opportunity to further recast the interests of the workers as distinct from what he termed "materialist socialism": economic progress, he contended, would be achieved through a just and harmonious social regulation of labor and capital. Moreover, labor was to be organized "in accordance with the new human conditions to adapt them not to a materialist socialism in bankruptcy but rather to an effective system based on solidarity [*solidarismo*]."[54] An editorial, written a month after the conflict, returned to these notions. It started by establishing the illegitimacy of labor militancy at Ticapampa: "For some time now the mining company of

Ticapampa has been the victim of serious disturbances caused by false worker movements, which not only impact on the operations of the company, but also criminally besmirch the workers by making them appear insubordinate and lacking morality."[55] The editorial went on to stress that it would always side with workers against the exploitation of unscrupulous capitalists, but what was happening at Ticapampa was merely the work of outside agitators who pushed workers to "inconceivable extremes."

This was a narrative that again was reprised by the workers who had taken over the union, as reflected by a letter sent to *El Departamento de Ancash* by Agripino González and Daniel Cáceres, who argued that "for some time now, strange elements to the true [*sic*] working classes of the Company have been inciting a small minority to commit subversive acts that do not respond to any need but to external interests that damage our dignity as workers."[56] They claimed that Montalvo and a small group of workers had attacked them and burned their houses, an accusation that was corroborated by another item in the newspaper, a letter signed by Rocardo Rivero, an *intendente* or police officer, who claimed that Montalvo, whom he described as "one of the leaders of the rebels [revoltosos]," was responsible for a number of "criminal acts," including destroying the telephone line, removing railway sleepers over an extension of three hundred meters, and looting the properties of Luis González, Agripino González, Carlo Magno Montoro, and Víctor Moreno. His report suggested that the workers had tried to elect a new union leadership, presumably to replace Agripino González, and that they had been encouraged to do this by Gustavo Pohl. He added that the company manager had refused to recognize the union and its new leadership. He concluded that "this movement is provoked by some individuals who try to take advantage of the divergences between the workers and the Company, divergences that are very harmful to the Mining Company."[57]

Almost exactly a year later, another strike broke out at Ticapampa. It is possible to examine this strike from a closer vantage point thanks to documents that have survived in the Ministerio del Interior documentation and consist of correspondence from the prefect of Ancash, Manuel Pablo Villanueva, who attempted to resolve the dispute through arbitration. The strike quickly turned violent following the arrival in Recuay of Prefect Villanueva, who, it would seem, had decided to sort out the dispute on his own. On March 12, the prefect held a meeting with the striking workers in the Club de Tiro premises but refused to allow the workers' lawyer, Gustavo Pohl, to participate in the talks, forcing him out of the building. This appears to have exacerbated feelings and the two hundred or so workers who had gathered outside the locale reacted angrily, firing bullets in the air and blowing up dynamite sticks. A few days later, on March 14, a group of workers attacked the barracks in Recuay, "with all types of weapons and dynamite sticks," to free several workers who were being held prisoner in the barracks, including Manuel Camones and Emilio Huerta, described in one report as not being workers "but rather well-known agitators . . . some of the principal instigators of the revolt and challenge to the authorities."[58] The "combat" lasted from 12:30 a.m. to 5:00 a.m., but the attackers were repelled. The following day, according to officer Juan Faverón's report, as he was taking the prisoners to Huaraz, he was attacked outside Recuay by "several groups of strikers, who as soon as they saw my troops, started shooting violently with carbines, rifles and revolvers, while others appeared over the hills and also fired their weapons and used slingshots to fire dynamite sticks and stones of all sizes."[59]

It is difficult to establish the credibility of these reports. The prefect's own report, sent to the Director de Gobierno, portrayed the events at Ticapampa and Recuay as "seditious acts" and reproduced the idea that workers were motivated not by genuine grievances but rather by political objectives: "The labor agitation of Ticapampa was not caused by the real and resounding needs of the workers, but owed to censurable incitements of people alien to the union, who pursued political ends."[60] Some reports point to collusion between former local authorities, such as "ex gobernador Román Bojorquez" and "ex-Alcalde Josué Espinoza," and the striking workers, though this is surprising given the past history between these authorities and the workers. One report suggests that during the protests the workers "shouted slogans and among others I heard 'Death to the Prefect who has been bribed! Long live the strike! Let's start the looting! Long live Pardo! Death to Leguía! Long live our leader Doctor Pohl!"[61] These reports, ultimately, attempted to portray the workers' actions as being orchestrated by local elites who had lost their positions following the change of national government (President Augusto B. Leguía, who ruled until 1930, deposed José Pardo in 1919). Whether there was some degree of collaboration between these elites and the workers is unclear, but what we can conclude is that this framing of the situation suited the broader attempt to present workers' demands as illegitimate. The workers, through their representative Gustavo Pohl, presented a very different story: the recently installed gobernador of Recuay, a certain Aguero, viewed as responsible, with the prefect, for the recent unrest and violence, was an "employee of the Mining Company of Ticapampa."[62]

In this context, an arbitration tribunal apparently constituted exclusively by Prefecto Villanueva ruled on the dispute on March 22. The ruling gave both miners and mill operators a 20 percent wage increase, more than the 12 percent offered by the company but significantly less than the 50 percent demanded by the workers. The company also agreed not to raise prices in the bodega during a whole year, to provide a doctor in the mining camp who would offer his services for free to workers and their families, to introduce filters to reduce pollution from the mill's chimneys, and to make improvements to the workers' dwellings.[63] However, the wording of the ruling pointed to the rationale that guided the prefect in bringing a solution to the dispute. Workers' wages, he insisted, had risen continuously since 1913. The hours of work had fallen, and workers were paid overtime. The prices of goods sold in the company store were cheaper than in Recuay, while workers' wages in Ticapampa were higher than those paid in other mines and haciendas in the region and workers already received health and pension benefits as well as accident insurance. At the same time, the company's profits, the prefect noted, were limited by the lower mineral yield; the company had invested "important sums" in the region, including in the road from Huarmey to the mine. Finally, the workers had told the prefect that they appreciated the "goodwill of the Company to improve the situation of its workers." It followed that the strikes were not a product of conditions at the mines but "of the pernicious action of strange elements, who pursue egoistic ends, which harms the interests of the workers and leads to a frequent alteration of the public order."[64]

The prefect clearly viewed or at least sought to present the company as a benevolent employer that had the workers' well-being in mind. Some company employees, such as the "ingeniero" Federico Testolini, who awarded the workers' union its standard, may have shared such sentiments. But the company managers did not. The 1921 report produced by the company for its shareholders painted a grim picture: the war years had made it impossible to acquire spare parts for the mill and the railways, and much-needed repairs had not been undertaken. Moreover, the mineral yield had been far below expectations. In addition, exchange rate fluctuations had led to a sharp depreciation in the French franc, which meant that the assigned budget of 2,500,000 francs was no longer worth 100,000 Peruvian pounds but only 33,000 Peruvian pounds. The situation was compounded by what the company described as "problems with the workforce." Decimated by the pandemic, the company had had little choice but to reconstitute it "with undocile and uppity people." This explained the growing tensions with the workforce, which had resulted in a suspension of production in the final three months of 1920. In order to "discipline the workers," the company not only stopped operations in the mine; it fired all its workforce.[65] This decision was explained to the chargé d'affaires at the French legation by one of the company heads as owing to "the complete anarchy of the workers, whose continuous strikes and even armed violence make it indispensable to stop the work for at least a prudential time to allow us to completely separate the dangerous elements."[66] The company decision to fire its entire workforce paid off, at least as far as it was concerned. The workforce, it claimed, "chastened by a long stoppage, has returned more disciplined and less demanding."[67] Reports from later years suggest that the labor trouble the company had experienced in the years 1918–20 subsided significantly.[68]

A range of factors shaped labor unrest in Ticapampa in 1918–20. The company viewed the flu pandemic as being the source of much of the disruption. In replacing the decimated workforce, it recruited workers who were less docile, if not openly rebellious. Its decision to shut down operations entirely and hire a new workforce reflected this understanding. Certainly, as we have seen, the establishment of the union and the speeches at its inauguration point to the presence of workers with what we could call working-class consciousness but also a knowledge and understanding of labor legislation and the framework of state–labor relations that had begun to be put in place since the early twentieth century. The tensions within the union suggest that not all miners at Ticapampa welcomed such developments, though we cannot know for sure if the new ideas arrived with the new workers. In any case, strikes were hardly new at Ticapampa; they dated back to at least 1913. The intervention of local elites such as the owner of *El Departamento de Ancash*, who projected onto the unrest his own ideas about the role of capital in developing the region and the threat of militant labor in undermining such development, gave the Ticapampa disputes a broader significance for the region as a whole. Finally, the clearly biased actions of political authorities such as Prefect Manuel Pablo Villanueva, charged with resolving the unrest in the spirit of the new legislation governing labor arbitration, points to the evident problems of implementing such initiatives in a place like Ticapampa.

THE 1938 DISPUTE

On April 19, 1938, Amadeo Torre, Roberto Huerta, and Agustín Esquivel submitted an eleven-point *pliego de reclamos* (list of grievances) on behalf of the workforce to the Anglo-French Ticapampa Company.[69] The demands included significant wage increases, in most cases of 100 percent in the salaries of eight different categories of workers; strict observance of the holiday law; the suppression of "*premios*" (bonuses), which led some workers to put in twelve-hour shifts; the banning of registering workers as "new" when they had been with the company for years; compensation for workers who had suffered accidents and were disabled; payment of holiday and Sunday work as established by law; the provision of protective equipment for workers; the suppression of monopolies (a reference to the company store, no doubt); provision of medicines and first aid kits in the mines for injured and ill miners; guarantees for the worker delegates; and finally, that the worker delegates be allowed to take their grievances to the authorities if these demands were not met. The list of grievances included one additional demand, which appears to have been added later: the *bodeguero*, or company storekeeper, Atanasio Pachecho, who "among other abuses has injured the workers Leoncio Maguiña, doña Julia Espinoza and others," was to be fired. As should be evident, these demands were quite similar to the ones that had motivated strikes in the 1918–20 period discussed above. Little, it would seem, had changed.

However, in fact, quite a lot had changed. For one thing, the union established in 1919 had disappeared. When or why is unclear. But the worker delegates who signed the pliego de reclamos did so as, respectively, presidente, tesorero (treasurer), and secretario of a "Strike Committee," not of the Sociedad de Auxilios Mutuos de Obreros y Artesanos de Ticapampa. But a lot more besides had changed. In contrast to the 1918–20 period, the 1938 pliego de reclamos set in motion a process of labor conciliation and arbitration that was very different from the arbitration process that Prefect Villanueva had established in 1920 to solve that year's strike. Only three days later, on April 22, 1938, a conciliation tribunal was convened in Huaraz, at the prefecture. Torre, Huerta, and Esquivel attended, in representation of the workers, along with their lawyer, Dr. César Castro.[70] The company manager attended together with the company lawyer. Also present were the "agente fiscal," Pedro M. Cáceres; a procurator, who presided over the tribunal; and the temporary ("accidental") prefect, Daniel Orjeda. The twelve grievances were discussed at the meeting. Since no agreement was reached, an arbitration tribunal was established. The workers designated Gustavo A. Pohl, who, as we saw, had acted on behalf of the workers in the past, as their *arbitro*.[71] The company designated Alejandro Boza as theirs. The judiciary designated Julio R. Barrón, a "juez de primera instancia," as the president of the tribunal and the representative of the state.[72]

The tribunal met a little over a month later, on May 25, 1938. In the month leading up to the first meeting of the tribunal, correspondence between the worker delegates and the president of the arbitration tribunal points not only to the workers' clear understanding of labor legislation but also to their ability to deploy a language that evoked a framework of state–labor relations that legitimized their demands. The workers complained that they had been fired and that the company was flouting labor legislation: "Improper abuses are being committed in a country that has laws that regulate the relationship between capital and work." They claimed that the company was refusing to pay compensation (equivalent to fifteen days' wages per year worked), as required by law, to workers who were no longer able to work because they were no longer able to perform backbreaking labor in the mines. The company claimed that compensation was only to be paid to workers who were fired and not those who left work voluntarily. Moreover, the mine manager had decreed that workers who did not return to work by April 27 would only be reinstated as new workers, thus voiding their legitimate right to accrued compensation in case of dismissal.[73]

The company lawyer, Juan Clímaco Hurtado, seemingly chosen to represent its interests in the arbitration process, similarly framed his rejection of the workers' demands by referencing labor law. The strike, he argued, was illegal. The three workers acting on behalf of the workforce, he claimed, did not have the workforce's support. More generally, he suggested that the workers' demands were unwarranted. Workers had already received wage increases and, in effect, benefited from the fact that the goods sold in the company store were cheaper than in the local markets: "They benefit from at least 20 centavos per day."[74] He insisted, by contrast, that the company implemented rigorously the holiday legislation as well as the accident law and the Sunday rest law. He refuted all the other demands: there was no monopoly on goods provision, and workers could purchase goods somewhere other than the company store if they wished to; adequate medical supplies and first aid were provided in the mining camps; protective equipment was provided and a new ventilation pump had been ordered from the United States. Moreover, Clímaco stressed, the company was in no position to raise wages: it faced significant losses as a consequence of the low mineral content of the extracted ore and because of low international prices for silver, lead, and copper.

Through its representative, the company also attempted to bar the workers' arbitro, Gustavo Pohl, from serving in the arbitration tribunal. Clímaco claimed that Pohl not only had acted as a legal representative (*delegado*) of the workers in past disputes but had been in fact behind the strike in 1920. In 1928, moreover, Clímaco claimed, Pohl had led a campaign against the company "for supposed harms caused by the smoke produced by the Company mill." He argued further that Pohl "has not been recognized as a lawyer by this court and this prevents him from practicing law." Though Pohl appears to have claimed that this failure to ratify his status was a consequence of the Luis Manuel Sánchez Cerro revolution of 1930, Clímaco argued that Pohl had sided with Sánchez Cerro. His failure to obtain ratification had been confirmed by the Supreme Court, he insisted. Finally, Clímaco referred to Pohl's "violent spirit" and "well-known short temper," concluding that "he does not possess the qualities of serenity, culture and sufficiency that are indispensable to practice law."[75] Judge Barrón, however, ignored these attempts to have Pohl removed as arbitro, a first defeat for the company. In later correspondence, Clímaco returned time and again to this topic, going as far as to claim that Pohl was acting on behalf of the workers and that the letters they wrote to the tribunal were written on Pohl's typewriter and by him.

A telegram published in *El Comercio*, Peru's leading newspaper, signed by Amadeo Torre, Roberto Huerta, and Agustín Esquivel on July 2, 1938, and sent to the Director de Trabajo framed the dispute in a manner that contrasted the pursuit of legitimate and harmonious labor relations enabled by a proactive and progressive state and the rogue behavior of a foreign company. This dispute, the workers argued, "is the first time that the grievances of the workers of Ticapampa have been processed in strict accordance with the laws." The grievances had unveiled "systematic disregard of labor legislation and the elementary principles of the labor contract" by the company. Indeed, "the foreign company Ticapampa has always drowned the workers' demands by using violence and intrigue and it has tried to do so again without success." The arbitration of the dispute marked a "new era of guarantees and progress for the working class of Ancash, which now feels protected, comforted." The workers thanked President Óscar Benavides and promised to work hard to bring prosperity to the company and to the nation.[76] The local press reprised the narrative of an exploitative foreign company. *El Departamento*, once a firm supporter of the company, as we saw, now criticized the Ticapampa managers not only for failing to resolve a dispute that was "clearly legitimate" by accepting the workers' demands. It also pointed to much more damaging revelations that the company had failed to declare taxable exports of half a million soles.[77]

The ruling, a majority ruling though not a unanimous one, of the arbitration tribunal, issued on July 19, was favorable to the workers. It established, first, that the workers' wages were too low to meet the basic needs of a worker's family, and that the increase in wages that the workers were demanding was consistent with wages that the company had paid in the past. Second, it noted that the company's argument that it had suffered a steep drop in revenue in 1937 because of the fall in prices of metals was irrelevant. The company had done very well in earlier years and could continue to do very well in the future. A fall in revenue in one year was not a reason to adjust wages. Third, it ruled that the company had acted illegally, taking reprisals against workers on strike by firing them. Fourth, it confirmed that the signatures on the pliego had not been shown to be false. Finally, the tribunal ruled against Clímaco's attempt to bar Gustavo Pohl from acting as arbitro. The tribunal ordered the company to increase the wages of the eight different categories of workers (though the amounts awarded were lower than those the workers had originally requested) and to reinstate the workers who had been fired, including Amadeo Torre, Roberto Huerta, Agustín Esquivel, and twenty-eight others.[78] The sentence was accompanied by two further documents, one signed by Pohl and the other by the arbitro representing the company (not the original arbitro, who failed to show up on the day of the ruling, but another by the name of Morán).

The document signed by Pohl was an addendum to the ruling, which looked at the same issues in more detail but also reframed the arguments of the ruling in a language that evoked the idea of state-mediated labor relations as essential to national progress. The low wages the company currently paid, Pohl argued, reflected "an exploitative, oppressive system, that breaches the Peruvian laws that protect workers and the respectable principles of the defense of human capital, such as the eight hour working day, the fixed salary, the strict prohibition of the work of minors in the mine." These wages represented "starvation wages, wages of malnutrition, that seriously affect the conservation of human capital." These meagre earnings could only cover about 50 percent of a miner's family food needs. The company's position, Pohl insisted, was at odds with both social ideas and the national interest:

Such a system, moreover, used by a foreign Company, is cruel and at odds with the social conscience of our times, both of our people [de la nacionalidad] and of the State or Government, and it runs counter to the interests of the Nation; As the Ministro de Hacienda, don Benjamín Roca, noted in his radio broadcast of April 6, there is a supreme need to ensure the economic well-being of the proletariat as a means to achieve social and political peace and in so doing guarantee the interests even of foreign companies; this is an incontrovertible argument.[79]

In this conception, wages to be paid to workers reflected a broader social notion of human well-being and the national interest. Fair wages were a means to personal and national improvement as well as social and political peace.

By contrast, Clímaco's rejection of the ruling, while claiming that the presence of Pohl invalidated the ruling altogether, mobilized a very different conception of labor–capital relations: "As happens with the labor question, the rise in wages demanded by them is intimately linked to the profits of the company and the social and economic reality of workers." The wages the workers received were sufficient for them to meet their needs, he insisted, adding that workers could obtain basic goods at the company store at affordable prices. In addition, he stressed, the company was facing a difficult economic situation: "The company has experienced a fall in profits because the price of metals has dropped." It would not be fair, he concluded, "regardless of whether the workers' demands are justified," to force the company to raise wages in this situation.[80] In later correspondence with the president of the arbitration tribunal, Clímaco reiterated these points.[81] He added, moreover, that the ruling fixed wages for certain categories of workers such as the *barreteros* (miners who use a pick or drill to remove the ore), but this made no sense since some workers had a greater aptitude for work than others and the "natural differentiation in workers' personal aptitudes" were being ignored. In this conception, it was the company's prerogative to fix wages according to criteria that reflected on the one hand its financial situation and on the other its own assessment of the value of a particular worker's labor.

The tension between these opposite conceptions of what wages ultimately represented is further illustrated by the demands put forward by Amadeo Torre, Roberto Huerta, and Agustín Esquivel, the three worker representatives who had initiated the dispute and who the company now refused to reinstate. In two letters sent on the same day, July 23, to the president of the arbitration tribunal, the three workers framed their arguments in terms of justice and equity while appealing to a sense of economic nationalism. The company was getting rich thanks to high metal prices while workers' wages had not risen in nine years: "This process reveals a tremendous injustice, a nameless cruelty on behalf of the aforementioned Company and an inhuman exploitation of a foreign company, toward a group of unfortunate Peruvian workers, which must be addressed in some way, albeit belatedly, and we trust that the well-known spirit of justice of the current Government will lead to a reparation." The company, they added, had used false accounting to cheat the government of tax revenue and systematically flouted labor legislation. It exploited the workers "in the most inhuman way, making us work like animals, paying us salaries that cannot meet our most urgent needs, and they have taken this brutal exploitation to the extreme of making us work on Sundays, holidays, overtime and all night, while only paying us the ordinary wage, *thus breaking the laws that protect workers*, and obtaining an illicit enrichment at the cost of the hunger and the very life of Peruvian workers." The workers urged the government to intervene and to ensure that "the laws of our country are respected and applied."[82]

The company, meanwhile, tried to overturn the ruling by turning to state authorities higher up the chain while restating its conception of what determined workers' wages. On July 25, 1938, Clímaco wrote to the Director de Trabajo. He repeated the accusation that Pohl was unqualified to serve on the tribunal and that he had an agenda against the company. At the same time, he repeated the argument that the company could not raise wages because it faced a difficult financial situation because of the price of metals and that the wages were sufficient to meet the workers' needs.[83] Meanwhile, Carlos A. Lozano, the Lima-based lawyer of the company, wrote to the minister of public health, labor, and social foresight. In his letter, in effect a thinly veiled threat, he noted that in light of the tribunal's ruling and the current price of silver, the company had no choice but to halt production, resulting in the unemployment of four hundred workers and the shutdown of other mines in the region that depended on Ticapampa for the processing of their mineral. He stressed that "it was the Ministry's role to resolve this conflict, that the workers had always been content with the wages they received, and that the conflict had arisen because there were people who wanted to harm the Company."[84] A second letter, dated July 28, repeated these same arguments and incorporated those that Clímaco had made to the Director de Trabajo.

The available evidence does not provide a clear picture of how the conflict was resolved, or if it was resolved. On September 19, 1938, the Director del Trabajo wrote to the prefect of Huaraz to reiterate an earlier telegram in which he indicated that the dismissal of the workers Torre, Huerta, and Esquivel was an "unacceptable reprisal" and that they were to be reinstated immediately. If the company failed to do so, the prefect was to "take the necessary measures."[85] This suggests that the state attempted to implement the ruling in spite of company opposition, but whether the prefect followed through with the order or what measures he had at his disposal is unclear. Regardless of the actual outcome, what the documentation of the arbitration tribunal reveals is that beyond the question of wages, what was at play in the Ticapampa dispute were differing conceptions of labor relations. The company viewed increased wages and better working conditions as something that it could determine on the basis of its financial health. By its estimation, workers were already receiving good wages and enjoyed good working conditions. By contrast, in making their demands, the workers mobilized an idea of social rights as the basis of their own well-being and the well-being of the nation. This was an idea that could be mobilized by appealing to both a sense of nationalism (and in the process denouncing the unpatriotic behavior of a foreign company) and also a sense of a just social order mediated by a state that guarded the interests of labor.

CONCLUSION

In this chapter, I have tried to show that the regime of labor relations that was established in the early twentieth century in Peru found its way—indeed, was summoned—to the Ticapampa mines. Here too, among the high peaks of the Cordillera Negra and the Cordillera Blanca, workers mobilized the labor state to mediate their relations with capital. The miners at Ticapampa constituted themselves as workers—they established a union like many other workers across the country did in the late 1910s. They made their own, and forcefully articulated, a global discourse about labor struggle and the exploitation of capital that circulated increasingly widely in the wake of the Russian Revolution. But they also made demands for better wages and better working and living conditions by invoking the labor legislation that successive governments had begun to put in place from the 1900s onward and the spirit of social justice and national progress that such legislation was intended to reflect and enable. In so doing, they inserted themselves fully into the sphere of labor, making themselves both objects of intervention by the labor state and, in turn, agents of an industrial progress that was to transform the country. To be sure, not all workers welcomed such developments, tensions abounded among the workforce, and the union was short-lived. But this was true elsewhere in Peru too.

The managers of the Anglo-French Ticapampa Company, and local elites such as the owner of *El Departamento de Ancash*, like employers and local and national elites elsewhere in the country, viewed these developments with alarm. They mobilized a counterdiscourse that framed worker grievances as illegitimate and the work of outside troublemakers and hotheads. For them, even when they paid lip service to the progressive nature of labor legislation or acceded to labor arbitration, improvements in wages and working conditions were not a matter of labor law or even social justice. They were matters for the company to determine in accordance with its own priorities. As this suggests, as elsewhere in Peru, labor conflict at Ticapampa reflected a broader conflict over the scope of action of the labor state and of its capacity to enforce labor laws and, more specifically, compel both workers and employers to submit to arbitration. In the 1920s, this capacity was constrained by the fact that local authorities charged with overseeing the functioning of the labor state, like Prefect Villanueva, were not always invested in the project of the labor state. In the 1930s, the capacity was greater, though resistance, from both employers and, it must be said, workers, was not always overcome. But regardless of the outcome of particular disputes, as the case of Ticapampa shows, the labor state, as both a series of laws, legal processes, and state agencies and an idea about the role of labor in the progress of the nation, profoundly shaped relations between labor and capital in early twentieth-century Peru, even at four thousand meters above sea level.

NOTES

I use the following abbreviations in the notes: Archivo General de la Nación (AGN), Ministerio de Fomento (MF), Ministerio del Interior (MI), Ministerio de Relaciones Exteriores (RREE). All translations are mine unless otherwise indicated. I am grateful to Angela Vergara, Peter Winn, and Julio Pinto as well as to audiences at conferences held in Belfast, Buenos Aires, La Paz, and Lima for comments on earlier versions of this chapter. Elías Amaya Nuñez provided excellent research assistance.

1. On Cerro de Pasco, see, among others, Alberto Flores Galindo, *Los mineros de la Cerro de Pasco: 1900–1930* (Lima: Pontificia Universidad Católica del Perú, 1974); Dirk Kruijt and Menno Vellinga, *Labor Relations and Multinational Corporations: The Cerro de Pasco Corporation in Peru (1902–1974)* (Assen: Van Gorcum, 1979); Florencia E. Mallon, *The Defense of Community in Peru's Central Highlands: Peasant Struggle and Capitalist Transition, 1860–1940* (Princeton, N.J.: Princeton University Press, 1983); Nelson Manrique, *Mercado interno y región: La sierra central, 1820–1930* (Lima: Centro de Estudios y Promoción del Desarrollo, 1987); and Federico M. Helfgott, "Transformations in Labor, Land and Community: Mining and Society in Pasco, Peru, 20th Century to the Present" (PhD diss., City University of New York, 2013).

2. See Leon Fink and Juan Manuel Palacio, *Labor Justice in the Americas* (Urbana: University of Illinois Press, 2017).

3. Paulo Drinot, *The Allure of Labor: Workers, Race and the Making of the Peruvian State* (Durham, N.C.: Duke University Press, 2011).

4. On paternalism in the Mexican and Chilean mining industries, see, in particular, William French, *A Peaceful and Working People: Manners, Morals, and Class Formation in Northern Mexico* (Albuquerque: University of New Mexico Press, 2008); Thomas Klubock, *Contested Communities: Class, Gender, and Politics in Chile's El Teniente Copper Mine, 1904–1951* (Durham, N.C.: Duke University Press, 1998); and Eugenio Garcés Feliú and Angela Vergara, "El Salvador: A Modern Company Town in the Chilean Andes," in *Company Towns in the Americas: Landscape, Power, and Working-Class Communities*, ed. Oliver J. Dinius and Angela Vergara (Athens: University of Georgia Press, 2011), 178–97.

5. No archives of the Anglo-French Ticapampa Company, a freestanding company, survive. I have only been able to locate yearly financial reports produced in Paris by the company for its top management. These reports are available in the Bibliothèque Nationale de France. These reports, which were in turn based on reports received from company managers in Lima, unfortunately contain limited information on the mines' workforce. In fact, they contain relatively little information about the operation of the mines and are, perhaps naturally, much more focused on financial matters, including the financial situation of the company from year to year and issues such as dividends. The earliest report dates from 1907 and the last report from 1933, though some years are missing. Despite the English name, and despite the fact the company had its headquarters in London at 56 Cannon Street, it was "actually constituted by French capital and managed by French directors," based at 13 Rue Auber in Paris. See *Bulletin périodique de la presse sudaméricaine*, April 3, 1920. On freestanding companies, see Mira Wilkins and Harm Schroter, eds., *The Free-Standing Company in the World Economy, 1830–1996* (Oxford: Oxford University Press, 1998).

6. See Rosemary Thorp and Geoffrey Bertram, *Peru, 1890–1977: Growth and Policy in an Open Economy* (New York: Columbia University Press, 1978), 370.

7. Admittedly not all concessions were in production. According to one report, "most mining concessions are acquired not to exploit them, but to avoid dangerous neighbors or for the purpose of speculation." See M. A. Denegri, *Estadística minera del Perú en 1905* (Lima: Imprenta la Industria, 1906), 42–44.

8. Germán Klinge, *Estadística minera del Perú en 1906* (Lima: Imprenta la Industria, 1907), 39.

9. Carlos P. Jimenez, *Estadística minera del Perú en 1907* (Lima: Litografía y Tipografía Carlos Fabbri, 1908), 52–53. See also Carlos P. Jimenez, *Estadística minera del Perú en 1913* (Lima: Imprenta Americana, 1915), 40.

10. Klinge, *Estadística minera del Perú en 1906*, 32–33.

11. See Carlos Contreras, *El aprendizaje del capitalismo: Estudios de historia económica y social del Perú republicano* (Lima: Instituto de Estudios Peruanos, 2004), 114–46. On silver mining in nineteenth-century Peru, see José R. Deustua, *The Bewitchment of Silver: The Social Economy of Mining in Nineteenth-Century Peru* (Athens: Ohio University Press, 2000).

12. Harry A. Franck, *Vagabonding Down the Andes* (Garden City, N.Y.: Garden City Publishing, 1917), 304.

13. Oscar Alayza T., "La industria minera en el Perú, 1936," *Boletín del Cuerpo de Ingenieros de Minas del Perú*, no. 119 (1937): 212–27.

14. "Un voyage au Pérou, il y a 25 ans," *Le Globe: Revue genevoise de géographie* 84, no. 1 (1945): 13–14.

15. The company advertised jobs in the local Ancash press. See several numbers of both *El Departamento de Ancash* and *El Huascarán*, 1918–20.

16. *Bulletin périodique de la presse sudaméricaine*, April 3, 1920.

17. J. Fred Rippy, *British Investments in Latin America, 1822–1949: A Case Study in the Operations of Private Enterprise in Retarded Regions* (Minneapolis: University of Minnesota Press, 1959), 131. Annie Peck, writing in the 1920s, confirmed this general view: "An Anglo-French Company with mines near Huarmey has made large dividends." Annie S. Peck, *Industrial and Commercial South America* (New York: Thomas Y. Crowell, 1927), 198.

18. Carlos P. Jimenez, *Estadística minera del Perú en 1914* (Lima: Imprenta Americana, 1916), 70.

19. See, for example, Anglo-French Ticapampa Silver Mining Company, *Assemblée générale ordinaire du 7 juillet 1922: Rapports du conseil d'administration et du commissaire des comptes* (Paris: Imprimerie Chaix, 1922).

20. The company continued its operations until 1967, when the mines were sold to a new company, Compañía Minera Alianza, owned by the Picasso and Brescia families, who invested further in the mines, broadening production from silver to lead and zinc.

21. Peck, *Industrial and Commercial South America*, 165.

22. Anglo-French Ticapampa Silver Mining Company, *Assemblée générale ordinaire du 24 mai 1907: Rapports du conseil d'administration et du commissaire des comptes* (Paris: Imprimerie Chaix, 1907).

23. "Un voyage au Pérou, il y a 25 ans," 13–14.

24. Anglo-French Ticapampa Silver Mining Company, *Assemblée générale ordinaire du 3 mai 1918: Rapports du conseil d'administration et du commissaire des comptes* (Paris: Imprimerie Chaix, 1918), 7.

25. *Bulletin périodique de la presse sudaméricaine*, April 3, 1920.

26. Peck, *Industrial and Commercial South America*, 165.

27. "Memoria sobre la escursion de vacaciones en 1885 a los asientos minerales de 'Recuay & Huallanca' presentada por los alumnos Emilio G. Villa & Julio F. Galvez," Universidad Nacional de Ingeniería, Archivo. This was of course a general lament from those concerned with the Peruvian mining industry. According to a report published in 1905 in the *Boletín del Cuerpo de Ingenieros de Minas*, "the working population occupied in the mines is not stable in Peru because Indians go to the mines in search of work, to complement their income at certain times, but not to devote themselves exclusively to mining, because their natural indolence, their small agriculture plots [*sic*], and their small flocks, allow them to live more or less miserably, without having to work for others, for fixed hours, for generally low wages." *BCIM*, no. 41 (1905): 27.

28. Anglo-French Ticapampa Silver Mining Company, *Assemblée générale ordinaire du 24 mai 1907*, 5.

29. Anglo-French Ticapampa Silver Mining Company, *Assemblée générale ordinaire du 3 juin 1908: Rapports du conseil d'administration et du commissaire des comptes* (Paris: Imprimerie Chaix, 1908), 5.

30. *El Departamento de Ancash*, January 14, 1918.

31. For a detailed study of this process in the central highlands, see Heraclio Bonilla, *El minero en los Andes* (Lima: Instituto de Estudios Peruanos, 1974).

32. Carlos P. Jimenez, *Estadística minera del Perú en 1915* (Lima: Imprenta Americana, 1917), 136. See also Mallon, *The Defense of Community in Peru's Central Highlands*; and Manrique, *Mercado interno y región*, among others.

33. See Mallon, *The Defense of Community in Peru's Central Highlands*.

34. On the 1918–19 influenza pandemic, see David Killingray and Howard Phillips, eds., *The Spanish Influenza Pandemic of 1918–1919: New Perspectives* (London: Routledge, 2003); and Maria-Isabel Porras Gallo and Ryan A. Davis, eds., *The Spanish Influenza Pandemic of 1918–1919: Perspectives from the Iberian Peninsula and the Americas* (Rochester: University of Rochester Press, 2014).

35. *El Departamento de Ancash*, January 8, 1919.

36. *El Departamento de Ancash*, January 10, 1919.

37. *El Departamento de Ancash*, January 14, 1919.

38. Anglo-French Ticapampa Silver Mining Company, *Assemblée générale ordinaire du 21 juin 1919: Rapports du conseil d'administration et du commissaire des comptes* (Paris: Imprimerie Chaix, 1919), 12.

39. "Un voyage au Pérou, il y a 25 ans," 13–14.

40. On the impact of the Spanish flu in Peru, see G. Chowell et al., "The 1918–1920 Influenza Pandemic in Peru," *Vaccine* 29 (Suppl. 2) (2011): B21–26.

41. *El Departamento de Ancash*, January 14, 1919.

42. In fact, according to *El Departamento de Ancash*, labor conflict in Ticapampa dated back to 1913, the year when a wave of strikes, at least one per year, began. See *El Departamento de Ancash*, April 2, 1919.

43. Anglo-French Ticapampa Silver Mining Company, *Assemblée générale ordinaire du 21 juin 1919*, 12.

44. See Drinot, *The Allure of Labor*, particularly chapters 2 and 3.

45. *El Departamento de Ancash*, March 13, 1918, March 15, 1918.

46. *El Departamento de Ancash*, March 20, 1918.

47. *El Departamento de Ancash*, March 25, 1918.

48. *El Departamento de Ancash*, May 4, 1918.

49. See Drinot, *The Allure of Labor*, chapter 2.

50. The speeches were published in installments in *El Huascarán*, a newspaper largely sympathetic with the Ticapampa workers, between October 28 and November 7, 1918.

51. This statement echoes González Prada's famous aphorism, from his speech at Lima's Politeama theater: "The groups of criollos and foreigners that inhabit the

strip of land located between the Pacific and the Andes do not form the real Peru; the nation is formed by the multitude of Indians scattered in the eastern range of the Cordillera." Manuel González Prada, *Pensamiento y librepensamiento* (Caracas: Biblioteca Ayacucho, 2004), 24.

52.   Only a few years earlier, a report on the state of mining in Peru recognized the limited implementation of the accident law: "The 'Law of Workplace Accidents' is beginning to be applied but given its recent decree and certain complications in the legal procedures it establishes, it is not widely applied yet, but this will happen when the workers become familiar with it and come to understand the benefits it brings them and they will then be able to demand the rights granted to them." Jimenez, *Estadística minera del Perú en 1913*, 102.

53.   In Huaraz, for example, a Sociedad de Auxilios Mutuos de Artesanos de Huaras [*sic*] was shut down in March 1918. See *El Departamento de Ancash*, February 2, 1918, March 12, 1918. *El Huascarán* reported regularly on meetings of other unions, including shoemakers and typographers.

54.   *El Departamento de Ancash*, April 7, 1919.

55.   *El Departamento de Ancash*, May 5, 1919.

56.   *El Departamento de Ancash*, May 5, 1919.

57.   *El Departamento de Ancash*, May 9, 1919.

58.   Juan Faverón to Prefecto, March 15, 1920, AGN/MI/211/Ancash.

59.   Juan Faverón to Prefecto, March 15, 1920, AGN/MI/211/Ancash.

60.   Prefecto to Director de Gobierno, March 23, 1920, AGN/MI/211/Ancash.

61.   Alferez Manuel Rojas to Subprefecto de la Provincia del Cercado, March 15, 1920, AGN/MI/211/Ancash.

62.   See letter from Gustavo Pohl to Pedro Rojas Loayza, Senator for Ancash, March 22, 1920, AGN/MI/211/Ancash.

63.   The reason for this strike may well be found in the solution to the strike that took place at the end of 1919. The company then had promised essentially the same things. See *El Huascarán*, November 25, 1919.

64.   "Fallo arbitral," March 22, 1920, AGN/MI/211/Ancash.

65.   Anglo-French Ticapampa Silver Mining Company, *Assemblée générale ordinaire du 29 août 1921: Rapports du conseil d'administration et du commissaire des comptes* (Paris: Imprimerie Chaix, 1921), 6.

66.   Letter from Ministro de Relaciones Exteriores to Ministro de Gobierno, January 4, 1921, AGN/MI/221/RREE.

67.   Anglo-French Ticapampa Silver Mining Company, *Assemblée générale ordinaire du 29 août 1921*, 13.

68.   The 1922 report pointed to a much-improved situation, resulting in new investments. As in the previous year, the report noted: "Following the temporary shutdown of the work, the workforce came back more docile and less demanding." Anglo-French Ticapampa Silver Mining Company, *Assemblée générale ordinaire du 7 juillet 1922*, 4. Reports from 1923 onward make no reference to labor, though they continue to inform on further investments in production.

69. "Pliego de reclamos que los obreros de las minas de The Anglo French Ticapampa Silver Mining Co. Ltd., presentan a la gerencia de la negociación en esta forma," AGN/MF/15:30.

70. Tribunal de conciliación, April 22, 1938, AGN/MF/15:30.

71. We know little about Pohl, other than that he was a lawyer and, it would seem, became mayor of Huaraz between 1925 and 1927. In the 1940s, he appears to have worked at a small mine called Recuperada. What motivated him to serve as the legal representative of the Ticapampa workers for at least twenty years is unknown.

72. Amadeo Torre, Roberto Huerta, and Agustín Esquivel to Prefect, April 27, 1938; Juan Clímaco Hurtado to Presidente Corte Superior, April 28, 1938; Corte Superior to Julio R. Barrón, April 29, 1938, all in AGN/MF/15:30.

73. See letters from workers to president of arbitration tribunal, April 30 and May 2, 1938, AGN/MF/15:30.

74. Juan Clímaco Hurtado to Presidente del Tribunal Arbitral, May 3, 1938, AGN/MF/15:30.

75. Juan Clímaco Hurtado to Presidente del Tribunal Arbitral, May 3, 1938, AGN/MF/15:30.

76. *El Comercio*, July 2, 1938, included in AGN/MF/15:30.

77. *El Departamento*, July 7, 1938, included in AGN/MF/15:30. Clímaco claimed that Pohl had leaked this information to the press. See Juan Clímaco to Presidente del Tribunal Arbitral, July 18, 1938, AGN/MF/15:30.

78. "Sentencia pronunciada por el tribunal arbitral," July 19, 1938, AGN/MF/15:30.

79. Pohl went further, arguing that the company was defrauding the national treasury.

80. "Voto del suscrito arbitro por la Empresa Ticapampa," July 19, 1938, AGN/MF/15:30.

81. See Clímaco Hurtado to Presidente Tribunal Arbitral, July 22, 1938, AGN/MF/15:30.

82. Two letters from Amadeo Torre, Roberto Huerta, and Agustín Esquivel to Presidente del Tribunal Arbitral, July 23, 1938, AGN/MF/15:30, emphasis added.

83. Juan Clímaco Hurtado to Director de Trabajo, July 25, 1938, AGN/MF/15:30.

84. Carlos A. Lozano to Ministro de Salud Pública, Trabajo y Previsión Social, July 21, 1938, AGN/MF/15:30.

85. Director de Trabajo to Prefecto Huaraz, September 19, 1938, AGN/MF/15:30.

7

NOTES ON THE "AFTERLIFE"

Forced Labor, Modernization, and Political Paranoia in
Twentieth-Century Peru

DAVID NUGENT

*I have endeavored to break the great chain of forces that has enslaved us to the
past . . . so that Peru can escape from the rut of its own misfortunes and strike
out valiantly on the road toward the future.*
—PRESIDENT AUGUSTO BERNARDINO LEGUÍA, MAY 24, 1929

IN THE middle decades of the twentieth century (1920–50), government
regimes sought to impose a series of forced labor programs on the rural
societies of the Peruvian Andes. These initiatives were designed to involve
the entire adult male population in projects regarded as crucial to the nation's
future because they were intended to help effect a break with its past. First initiated in the 1920s, during the Oncenio of Augusto Bernardino Leguía, these
programs were intended to modernize the country's vast mountainous interior,
which was regarded as backward and feudal, and a major obstacle to Peru's
ability to progress.

In the present chapter, I examine how these government initiatives affected
state and class formation. Focusing on the Chachapoyas region, I compare two
periods in the history of conscription activities and political processes. The
first dates to the 1920s, the era of Leguía's infamous Conscripción Vial. This
was a law stipulating that all adult males were required to work six to twelve
days per year on the construction of highways, bridges, and so forth.[1] Leguía's
forced labor law precipitated conscription on a massive scale. It also generated
widespread resistance. In the Chachapoyas region, however, labor mobilization
during the Oncenio was an entirely orderly and unproblematic affair. Indeed,

corvée activities strengthened governing groups and solidified the position of the ruling elite.

The second period I examine explores the "afterlife" of the Conscripción Vial—the corvée programs that continued after Leguía's forced labor law was abolished, in 1930. These programs have been the focus of limited scholarly attention but were of major importance in Chachapoyas. Efforts to organize corvée labor continued to be crucial to the dynamics of state and class formation in the 1930s–1940s but because these efforts failed rather than succeeded.

After 1930 government officials found it increasingly difficult to compel the population to provide labor for modernization projects. Indeed, attempts to mobilize a workforce during the 1930s and 1940s proved to be profoundly disruptive to existing social and political relationships. The overall effect of conscription was neither to strengthen the power of governing groups nor to solidify the position of elites. Rather, efforts to conscript the rural populace provoked extensive disorder and conflict and ultimately precipitated a crisis of rule. Within just decades, government officials had concluded that dark and dangerous forces were interfering with conscription. These forces were extremely difficult to control because they acted surreptitiously, behind a mask of support for modernization.

The history of labor conscription in Chachapoyas challenges conventional views of the state—especially those that view it as an institution and find inspiration in the writings of Max Weber. According to these formulations, the state is distinguished from other political forms in enjoying a monopoly on claims to legitimate violence within a given territory.[2] Developments in Chachapoyas contradict this view. There was in fact an inverse relationship between the degree to which the state exercised a monopoly on coercive violence and its ability to conscript labor. *Contra* Weber, in Chachapoyas the state was at its most potent and its most coercive when it had virtually no armed force at its disposal—during the Oncenio. Prior to 1930 it was not the state but elite-led, multiclass political coalitions (called "*castas*") that controlled armed force in this region.

Institutional understandings of the state regard political forms like castas as competing with the state to monopolize force—as producing "weak" states.[3] In Chachapoyas, however, the coercive ability of the state was contingent not upon the elimination of nonstate political forms but on their preservation. After 1930, the castas of Chachapoyas broke down and central government officials could no longer look to them to support central projects and plans. As officials lost the help of their regional allies, they found themselves unable to govern the region.

After 1930 the region's elite-led castas—the very kind of coercion-wielding political form that was regarded as such a major obstacle to central control—disintegrated. They also lost control over the use of violence and the ability to ignore the dictates of the central government. Revealingly, it was from this moment onward—when the central government had finally established a monopoly on the use of legitimate force—that state officials lost the ability to coerce or compel and found it increasingly difficult to recruit the workforce needed for modernization.

The history of labor conscription in Chachapoyas raises broader questions about what the state is and does. It would appear that the state is not an institution that establishes a monopoly on the use of legitimate force by eliminating competing organizations.[4] Indeed, the case at hand suggests just the opposite. The more government officials eliminated competing, violence-wielding political forms the less able they were to govern the region.[5]

The history of efforts to organize corvée labor in Chachapoyas presents a series of paradoxes that prompt a rethinking of the state. These paradoxes turn in part on the difficulty of knowing what the state is. They turn as well, however, on the difficulty of knowing where the state is, who is in charge of it, and what gives it power and potency. They turn as well on an issue that is rarely raised: what visible signs indicate the presence or absence of the state?

Government officials did indeed find themselves unable to mobilize a workforce after 1930. Their inability to do so had two additional effects that have important implications for reassessing what the state is. First, officials' inability to conscript labor made them question whether their regime was a state. They had at their disposal a police force, a judiciary, and a state bureaucracy; performed political rituals on a regular basis; and made generalized use of state symbolism. However, the fact that the conventional trappings of rule were present but the ability to coerce or compel was absent made the familiar organs of state seem like an empty shell. It also convinced the government that the existence of a police force, a judiciary, and so on could not be assumed to indicate the presence of a real state. Officials were bewildered by the inability of their regime to "be like a state" and produced an elaborate explanation to account for this apparent anomaly. They attributed the dissipation of their own power and potency to the concentration of power and potency in a competing polity.

Although there was very little evidence to support such a view, government officials concluded that the integrity of their regime's state institutions had been deeply compromised by the activities of political subversives. The latter, it was believed, had surreptitiously filled the ranks of the police, the judiciary, the state bureaucracy, and so forth—a vantage point from which they had been able to undermine normal state activities. Although these subversives were posing as public servants, they were only feigning loyalty to the central government, and were biding their time, waiting for the appropriate moment to strike. As a result, while the ruling regime took on the appearance of a real state, officials concluded, appearances were not to be trusted. The state was indeed an empty shell, with little if anything of substance within.

The second effect that was produced by officials' struggles with conscription is related to the first. The deterioration of the state's capacity to mobilize a workforce convinced government officials that something powerful and malevolent was interfering with their efforts. Only something state-like, they concluded, would have been capable of disrupting the power of a state. Government officials' inability to coerce or compel despite the presence of all the trappings of rule convinced them that their efforts to govern were being undermined by a subterranean counterstate.

This underground polity had been organized by the Alianza Popular Revolucionaria Americana (APRA, American Popular Revolutionary Alliance), a radical political sect that had committed itself to the violent overthrow of the existing order. The members of the Aprista counterstate were deep fanatics, officials believed, and would stop at nothing to achieve their subversive ends. This counterstate, officials surmised, was buried somewhere deeply underground and could not be seen with the naked eye. It represented a grave threat to the ruling regime.

Government officials had only the most limited and circumstantial of evidence to support their view that this underground state existed. Even so, officials assumed that only a polity that partook of all the powers of stateness associated with conventional regimes would be capable of thwarting their own designs. Indeed, officials believed they saw glimpses of underground stateness everywhere. They regarded these as conclusive proof that the subversives had elaborated a subterranean polity that was filled with power and potency. They attributed to that polity all the capacities that their own state so obviously lacked.

These developments raise questions about what the state is, where it is, who is in charge of it, what gives it power and potency, and what may be taken as evidence of its presence. What would conventionally be understood as a "real" state—one that confronted not a single violence-wielding competitor and had all the trappings of rule visible to everyone—was regarded as artificial and empty. What would conventionally be regarded as an imaginary state—which could not be seen and was not able to display any conventional state trappings— was regarded as malevolent, potent, and real.

In the following sections of this chapter, I review the history of labor conscription and state formation in the Chachapoyas region. This history begins in the 1920s, the period of the Conscripción Vial. It continues into the 1930s and 1940s, during the afterlife of the Conscripción Vial. The story ends in 1949–50, when the government experiences a crisis of rule, and officials respond with encryption and paranoia.

FEUDALISM BEGETS MODERNIZATION: THE ONCENIO IN CHACHAPOYAS

When the Leguía regime began to implement its modernization schemes in Chachapoyas, it encountered a regional society that was organized according to the very kinds of "feudal" principles the government sought to do away with. Chachapoyas was divided into highly unequal social strata.[6] A handful of aristocratic families made up the "noble," landed elite. They saw it as their inherited right to rule the region free from interference, whether from central government officials or other elite families. The elite of Chachapoyas regarded the region's Indios and mestizos as having no legitimate role in public life and minimized all social interaction with them. All such interactions involved public deference and subservience from the subaltern.

The landed class, however, was far from unified. Rather, the elite was divided into factions, each of which maintained an extensive clientele of mestizos and Indian peasants. These elite-led, multiclass political coalitions—each of which numbered in the hundreds—engaged in violent competition for control of regional affairs. Referred to as castas, they were named for the pair of closely allied aristocratic families that made up their core.

Chachapoyas was on the margins of the country's export economy. Neither its products nor its labor force participated in the booming commercial activities of Peru's political economy. Because of the poverty of agrarian pursuits, castas fought viciously to control the rent taking associated with political office.[7] Prior to 1920, this competition came to a head at five-year intervals— during elections. Out-of-power castas chose electoral periods to challenge the coalition in power because the ruling casta could not rely on support from its national patron.

Elections were settled by means of violent street battles involving large numbers of people. The coalition that prevailed controlled the voting booths and was able to "count" the votes.[8] Success at the polls allowed the victorious casta to monopolize posts in the government bureaucracy, which made it possible to brutalize members of opposing coalitions with impunity. Indeed, deposed coalition leaders found it necessary to retreat into their fortified hacienda homes, where their armed retainers would defend them from assault. From this vantage point, deposed leaders would continue to coordinate the affairs of their coalition.

Having been denied access to official political posts, deposed casta leaders would organize a parallel political network that adopted the same form as (and was largely indistinguishable from) the legal state apparatus.[9] It was essential for them to do so. Only in this way could out-of-power leaders protect the interests of their coalition or mitigate ruling casta efforts to extort labor from their clients. Furthermore, by maintaining their own state structure, opposing casta leaders were prepared to do what out-of-power castas always sought to do—replace the ruling casta on a moment's notice. Indeed, castas could remain in power for only five years (occasionally ten) before being deposed by the opposition.[10] Because they reigned for such short periods, no casta could do permanent damage to its competitors. Rather, all castas went from victim to victimizer and then back again on a recurrent basis.

The Oncenio interrupted the normal process of casta succession, in which castas replaced one another according to a regular cycle. It allowed one coalition (the Pizarro-Rubio) to remain in control of regional affairs for an unprecedented twenty-one years—four times longer than most castas had ruled until that time. Drawing upon its exceptional longevity, the Pizarro-Rubio were able to do what previous ruling coalitions had been unable to do. They were able to inflict permanent damage on their adversaries—the Burga-Hurtado.

During their extended period of rule, the Pizarro-Rubio were able to establish a regional political order of the most repressive kind imaginable. As their tenure wore on, they succeeded in weakening the Burga-Hurtado progressively by visiting upon them an entire range of abuses. Clients of the opposing casta found themselves the target of assault, rape, murder, arson, and castration, to name but a few. Furthermore, because the Pizarro-Rubio controlled the courts and the judiciary, members of the ruling coalition were able to carry out these aggressions with complete impunity. An article from *Amazonas*, a progressive

newspaper published in the latter half of the 1920s, captures the nature of political life under the Pizarro-Rubio very effectively.

The Department of Amazonas Has Been Converted into a True Fief: Twenty Years of Prostration and Servilism

In the oriente of Peru there is a department that, despite the amazing fertility
of its soil, the variety of its products, the spiritual richness of its children, and
its infinite yearning for progress, writhes in backwardness and abandonment
due to the negligence of its political representatives.

We refer to the department of Amazonas, that since its creation in 1832 up
to the present is nothing but a fief, a hacienda of useless and hateful castas,
who believe that they have the right to rule and to exploit [people] iniquitously
and scandalously . . . [who] have struggled ceaselessly over the right to exercise
power, to lord over their spoils . . . to benefit themselves alone, increasing their
substantial fortunes.

1909 [was] a sad hour for the department [because] one of its sons, Doctor
Miguel A. Rojas, taking advantage of a high political position that he . . . occupied [he was minister of government during Leguía's first term in office] . . .
cast out the ill-fated Burga-Hurtado casta, and . . . sent to [Chachapoyas] a . . .
political authority [Prefect Pázara] who permitted women to be jailed, men to
be flagellated, and the most intimate sanctuary of human dignity to be sullied,
all with the goal of enthroning the Pizarro-Rubio [casta].

Thus . . . ascended this casta, which [since then] has monopolized everything in its favor, that allows no act of rebellion, nor even of independence, that
divides what are virtually lifelong public positions that are loaded with "extras"
among those of its circle . . . that has taught servilism as if in a school and has
introduced abjection and what amounts to a thinly masked form of slavery
among the men, who in order to gain a livelihood, [to gain] bread for their
children . . . must necessarily beg for a job after having had to submerge their
dignity in humiliation.[11]

During their extended period of rule, the Pizarro-Rubio succeeded in consolidating a regional political order the likes of which the region had never
seen—one that was unusually repressive and "backward." Having done so, they
went on to visit upon the Burga-Hurtado a campaign of violence and persecution that was unprecedented in intensity and ruthlessness. The effects of

this campaign were apparent by 1924, the first presidential elections following Leguía's ascent to power in 1919. Ordinarily, the Burga-Hurtado—as the main opposing casta—would have used the elections of that year to mount a major armed challenge to the Pizarro-Rubio (as the Burga-Hurtado had in all previous elections). By this point in time, however, the Burga-Hurtado had been out of power for a decade and a half and during that entire time had been subjected to relentless persecution by the Pizarro-Rubio.

These trying conditions had taken a very heavy toll on the outcast coalition. By 1924 the parallel state structure that the Burga-Hurtado had previously employed to promote and defend their casta was a thing of the past. The hundreds of rural cultivators who had formerly looked to the Burga-Hurtado for protection and patronage had been abandoned by their patrons and had been left to fend for themselves. By the end of the 1920s, the Burga-Hurtado casta had ceased to exist.

WEAK STATE, STRONG CASTA: LABOR CONSCRIPTION DURING THE ONCENIO

As the Burga-Hurtado casta steadily disintegrated during the 1920s, the Pizarro-Rubio were able to establish a social order that violated all the progressive, forward-looking principles the central government sought to advance. It was in this context of uncontested regional dominance that the ruling casta began to implement Leguía's modernization schemes.

The most important of these schemes was the Grand Chachapoyas-Pimentel Highway.[12] The project was authorized by the 1920 Ley de Caminos. Work on the highway project began in September 1926 and continued until August 1930—when the Oncenio came to a crashing halt. Funds for the Highway came from the Ministerio de Fomento (the Ministry of Development) and were given to provincial highway committees, which were composed of the mayor, judge, and military chief. They looked to the juntas of the districts to mobilize a workforce. These latter juntas were made up of the district governor, mayor, and justice of the peace. Prior to conscripting laborers, each district junta would compile a detailed list of all individuals who were obliged to provide labor services. The junta would then mobilize the large workforce required for the project.

What was remarkable about efforts to organize forced labor during the 1920s was how utterly unremarkable they were. It was as if the dynamics of conscription during the Oncenio were an inversion of those of the afterlife. What accounts for these differences? First, the *juntas de conscripción* facilitated corvée during the 1920s. It would be a mistake to regard these juntas as representing the central government, for they were made to obey the dictates of the Pizarro-Rubio. *Contra* Weberian understandings of strong and weak states, however, it was this very "weakness" that made them effective at conscription.

Because the Pizarro-Rubio had become such a dominant force, they were able to appoint their clients to all positions in the bureaucracy. The members of each district junta de conscripción thus had a single set of concerns and were able to work together toward the same goal (conscription). This made for a degree of coordination and integration that was unprecedented for the region as a whole. It also helped establish a region-wide structure of surveillance that was very difficult to evade.

Labor conscription during the Oncenio was also characterized by a high degree of regularity and legibility. Regarding regularity, after compiling detailed lists of all conscripts, the district juntas would issue three successive calls for labor (for different age categories). In consultation with the prefect, the provincial juntas devised a staggered work schedule for all districts. This helped ensure that there were no delays or interruptions. Regarding legibility, the lists of conscripts were posted in highly visible, public locations, well in advance of work duty. This made it possible for everyone involved to plan their activities ahead of time.

The regularity and legibility of conscription had important implications regarding the relationship between power, knowledge, and publicity. The ruling casta was so confident in its ability to monitor and control people's movements through space that it adopted procedures that became impossible during the afterlife. Indeed, the Pizarro-Rubio warned people publicly in advance about official plans to force them to work against their will. The Pizarro-Rubio were utterly unconcerned about a possibility that would become a virtual certainty after 1930—that many who were advised about government conscription plans would do everything in their power to evade this enormously disruptive intrusion into their lives. The Pizarro-Rubio were certain that there was no possibility of escape from their system of surveillance. Nor were these elites mistaken. A third distinctive feature of labor conscription during the Oncenio was that it was very effective. The officials who were responsible for organizing corvée succeeded in assembling an unusually large number of workers week after week, month after month, with little resistance or evasion. In other words, what made labor conscription so effective during the 1920s was the "strength" of the Pizarro-Rubio casta.

MODERNIZATION BEGETS DISORDER: THE AFTERLIFE OF THE LEY DE CAMINOS

As we have seen, by the end of the 1920s the Pizarro-Rubio had done away entirely with the other elite coalitions. It was therefore not a casta that rose up to challenge the Pizarro-Rubio. Rather, in a process that reflected similar shifts in power relations in the national capital, a coalition of popular groups drove the Pizarro-Rubio into hiding and became the dominant political force in the region.[13] Thereafter, these popular forces went on something of a witch hunt, systematically hounding and persecuting everyone associated with the Oncenio.[14]

Among the most important effects of the Oncenio in Chachapoyas was that it destroyed the pre-Oncenio elite power structure of competing castas without leaving anything in its place. As a result, 1930 was something of a watershed for the nobility of the region. From this time forward, the aristocratic families went into a period of steep decline. With the collapse of the casta structure, the elite found their powers greatly reduced. The extended networks of allied families that had worked collaboratively to coerce and compel splintered, leaving each individual family alone and isolated. Political office continued to be the most effective means of gaining access to wealth, and each aristocratic family continued to fight fiercely over political office. But their strategies for doing so were in stark contrast with those of the casta period. During the afterlife, no single elite family could control more than a few political positions. As a result, families that had formerly belonged to warring castas came to occupy influential positions in the government at the same time.

Rather than ending competition between these families, however, this change shifted the terrain on which they did battle. From this point onward, it was the *inner workings* of government rather than the state apparatus as a whole that became the ground on which individual elite families waged war—making the terrain of government into something of a war of all against all. During the post-casta period, however, aristocratic families did not employ armed bands of followers and open street battles, as they had in the past. Instead, violence went underground and was masked behind a concern for the common good.

To wage war across the new bureaucratic field of battle, elite families employed two main strategies. First, each family sought to show that it could fulfill all the obligations associated with the position(s) it did control. Second, each family sought to prevent the others from fulfilling their official obligations. Because the successful completion of most official tasks required the cooperation of several functionaries, it was simple for functionaries to interfere with the effectiveness of others, even as they pretended to do the opposite.

Elite families went beyond simple obstruction in order to discredit their adversaries; they also employed discursive means of attack. Having created conditions in which it was virtually impossible for their foes to carry out their duties, elite families would then use government discourse to accuse their enemies of failing to carry out their duties (due to corruption, incompetence, etc.)—problems for which the accuser was in no small part responsible. Accusations of this kind began to circulate through government offices in increasingly large numbers. As they did so, a wholly new dynamic took shape among the various offices of government. Functionaries who once would have cooperated to carry out official extortion went to great lengths to interfere with one another. The effect was to produce extensive disorder in the operation of the state.

The fragmentation of casta coalitions, and the involution and competition that came to characterize bureaucratic relations, undermined the regularity and legibility of conscription. This was true despite the fact that many of the same branches of government and positions in the bureaucracy were involved in corvée. District functionaries—the governor, mayor, and justice of the peace—were still responsible for mobilizing labor for modernization.[15] Each of these functionaries, however, sought to interfere as extensively as possible with the activities of the others. So did their superiors in the provincial capital—the subprefect, mayor, and judge; each sought to show that he could fulfill his conscription obligations while his adversaries could not. Provincial officials sought to prevent their counterparts from conscripting labor. They were also unlikely to assist district functionaries with conscription problems in their districts, or to help find missing conscripts when they fled to other districts. In sum, the new competitive circumstances of the afterlife undermined the close cooperation that had formerly obtained between members of the state apparatus. Because government officials were no longer members of a single, overarching casta, they found it impossible to work together in a coordinated fashion. Instead, each sought to interfere with the activities of his counterparts.

This new state of affairs undermined the structure of surveillance that had been crucial in enabling conscription during the Oncenio. In the absence of this structure, the laboring population found that evasion was much easier than it had been. After 1930 district officials found it increasingly difficult to compile the kinds of detailed lists of conscripts that had acted as the basis of corvée during the Oncenio. Indeed, most abandoned any attempt to do so. Without a region-wide structure of surveillance to locate missing workers, names were of no help.

Instead of searching for the specific individuals in each district who were expected to provide labor, government officials took a different approach. They sought to locate the total number of workers from each district or province that were required for any given task. The "unit of conscription" thus shifted from the individual to the administrative unit (district or province)—to population in the aggregate.

In this context, the regularity and legibility that had formerly characterized corvée disappeared. Now that evasion was possible, and now that it was no longer feasible to search for particular individuals, the relation between power, knowledge, and publicity underwent a transformation. It no longer made sense to post lists of conscripts well in advance of the time these individuals were to work. Instead, knowing that the population would flee the moment they were forewarned, officials did everything they could to ensure that information about corvée remained secret.[16]

Some continuities with the past remained. Laboring populations were told the total number of days they were expected to work. And provincial officials continued to devise schedules that detailed which districts would be expected to work, when, and how many men they were to provide. But this information was kept secret, for fear that people would go into hiding. Even so, details would leak out, provoking many men to flee.[17] Not even a visit from the police—which became typical during the afterlife but had *never* been necessary during the 1920s—could produce the desired number of conscripts. There was a constant shortage of workers. This meant that high-ranking government officials had to deviate from their own (secret) schedules and were compelled to go back to the same districts over and over again, way ahead of schedule.

If there had been not a single case of evasion, however, there still would have been labor shortages of the most severe kind. This was because scarcity was being generated by other factors. As noted above, with the collapse of the casta structure, it was no longer the case that officials in all branches of government were members of the same coalition. Nor was it the case that they all worked together to pursue the common interests of their casta. Rather, functionaries in different branches of government were independent of one another. They were at pains to show that they could fulfill the obligations of their position, and that their adversaries in other branches could not. The competitive logic that obtained between these different branches of government, and between different positions in the state apparatus, articulated with the modernization plans of the central government to produce ongoing, artificial shortages of labor.

As the afterlife wore on, the government had increasingly ambitious plans to modernize the highlands and sought to implement a wide range of modernization projects. Some of these—for example, the construction of an extensive network of roads, bridges, and airfields to facilitate movement through the national space—were a continuation of projects begun in the 1920s, under Leguía. Others were carried out in the modernizing spirit of the Oncenio. These projects all relied on the conscripted labor of the peasantry. As the number and scale of these projects suggests, implicit in central plans to modernize the highlands was the assumption that the government would be able to draw upon a vast field of untapped peasant labor. This field did not exist in fact but in the imaginations of central planners. Once they had imagined this field of labor into being, however, government officials went on to insist that it was there—despite overwhelming evidence to the contrary.

They did so for a simple reason. To ensure that they had access to the sources of wealth that made an elite lifestyle possible, each official was under great pressure to show that he could carry out all his duties and that his adversaries could not. Since these duties increasingly revolved around providing laborers for modernization projects, all functionaries were determined to produce every worker they had been called upon to provide, down to the last man. As a result, the war of all against all that broke out within the terrain of government was of a particular kind. It was fought over the control of an (only partially existing) rural labor supply.

I next show how this distorted vision of rural labor abundance combined with the realities of competition between government functionaries to disorder the state. I do so by focusing on the projects of the post-Oncenio era that called for the largest numbers of conscripts: military conscription and highway construction. As we will see, these two initiatives alone called upon government officials to produce a pool of conscripts that was *twice* the size of the actual population.

STRONG STATE, NO CASTA:
CORVÉE DURING THE AFTERLIFE

Changes in military conscription provide a useful point of departure for understanding how central planners imagined into being a labor force that did not exist. During the Oncenio, the ruling casta had ensured that conscription focused on highway construction and that few men were drafted into the army. After 1930, however, when the casta structure collapsed, there was no elite coalition in place that could interfere with the army's efforts to conscript. The absence of powerful, coercion-wielding competitors should have established a state monopoly on legitimate force. This in turn should have facilitated military conscription. Instead, however, it contributed to the extensive disorder that characterized government activity during the afterlife and ultimately helped precipitate a crisis of rule.

In an effort to expand the armed forces, military planners in Lima established a quota for the provinces of the Chachapoyas region. Each was to provide the army with 2,125 men. Comparing the number of men the army insisted on being available with the number actually available is startling, for there were fewer than 2,125 in all but one of these four provinces.[18] In other words, were they to have been implemented, the plans of this one branch of government alone would have removed from the countryside virtually the entire adult male population. Indeed, it would have left a labor deficit across virtually the entire region.

But the government's hunger for labor did not end here. Other projects threatened to deepen the deficit of labor beyond that created by the military. A case in point is the Chachapoyas-Cajamarca Highway (formerly, the Grand Chachapoyas-Pimentel Highway). During the Oncenio, the ruling casta had coordinated all corvée activities and had balanced the forced labor needs of this project with those of other initiatives. After 1930, however, there was no such coalition on hand that could take on this coordinating role. At the same time, those who were entrusted with the highway project were determined to move ahead with construction as quickly as possible. Indeed, much was at stake in their ability to demonstrate that they could do so. Just as was true of the armed forces, the Oficina de Caminos (Office of Highways) was free to project its labor needs and to plan its activities without interference or involvement from a powerful, coercion-wielding organization like a casta. The Office of Highways was equally free to plan its activities without interference from other branches of government, such as the military. The growing independence and autonomy of this office, however, did not facilitate its efforts to draft labor but undermined them. In the process, the Office of Highways further contributed to the war of all against all that was being fought out within the apparatus of state—a war that produced extensive disorder and ultimately helped generate a crisis of rule.

The Chachapoyas–Cajamarca highway was a mammoth project. It lasted for three decades and at times called for 1,000 men to be at work. One of those times was in 1940, when there were 1,113 households in the districts where the Office of Highways sought its 1,000 conscripts.[19] This meant that each household was expected to surrender virtually its entire adult male work force (for twenty days every three months). This very onerous labor tax represented a great hardship for all households involved. These same households were also subject to the conscription demands of the military, and the plans of the army *also* threatened to deprive rural society of its entire adult male workforce. Between these two offices alone, the government sought a labor force roughly twice the size of the actual population and produced a huge deficit of imaginary labor. These were only two of many modernization projects, each with its own labor demands.

The forces acting to create an artificial scarcity of labor were not limited to the projects of central planners. Local government was equally implicated, for it had long relied on peasant labor to maintain the physical infrastructure (roads, bridges, churches, chapels, etc.) and the bureaucratic infrastructure (especially delivery of government correspondence). The demands of local government thus further inflated official labor needs and swelled the ranks of the imaginary workforce.

The sum total of all government demands for labor was huge. Because much of this labor force was invented in state offices, attempts to find it in the countryside were bound to fail. But that did not prevent high-ranking officials from insisting that their subordinates produce this labor. I next explore how these conditions of induced labor scarcity further disordered the state, with a focus on those individuals who had to procure labor that did not exist and implement projects that could not be implemented.

The prefect conveyed to his subordinates demands from the various government offices for labor. Because rural functionaries had to comply with these demands, this meant magically converting a limited number of real cultivators into the ever-expanding number of laborers imagined in state discourse. Making this especially difficult was the fact that the same personnel were expected to perform this conjuring trick for all the offices of government—local and national alike. As a result, the functionaries in question felt the weight of all official demands pressing down on them and were faced with a constant and ongoing deficit of (imaginary!) labor.

Because these personnel were under intense pressure to produce what did not exist, they found themselves having to offer their superiors explanations of their inability to carry out their orders. Some of their explanations spoke to the actual problems they confronted. But most were some combination of elision, fabrication, and outright lie—because there were certain basic truths about the government's activities that could not be uttered in political discourse. These revolved around the fundamentally coercive nature of the state's entire modernization effort.

Peru had gained its independence in the 1820s as the result of protracted struggle against colonial Spain. What was true of the other republics that emerged during the "age of revolution" was true of Peru. At the very core of the country's self-definition, from its very birth as a polity, were the "liberal" rights and protections. These rights were explicitly designed to protect individuals from the arbitrary use of state power—from the very kinds of programs that the Peruvian government was implementing on such an extensive scale! To acknowledge in political discourse that the state's entire modernization scheme was in direct violation of these principles—that its programs had to be imposed on the peasantry at the point of a gun—would be to acknowledge a contradiction at the very center of national life. As a result, there was a conspicuous silence about the fact that the state's extensive efforts to modernize the highlands were based on the widespread and systematic use of force. Instead, these programs were described as if they were consensual—as if they were in perfect harmony with the principles of popular rule.

The attempt to implement programs that could not be implemented and the inability to acknowledge why the programs were bound to fail played a major role in disordering the state. These conditions compelled functionaries to generate highly distorted accounts of their problems. They were forced to remain silent about the true causes of their difficulties and to invoke problems that were only tangentially related to the dilemmas they faced. Because they could only draw the attention of their superiors to these tangential concerns, the state was forever chasing phantoms.

Government functionaries invoked three (phantom) problems that were said to be undermining their attempts to procure labor: (1) greedy and unscrupulous state functionaries, who were said to be abusing their positions of public trust for private gain; (2) the Indian peasantry, which was said to be incapable of understanding its obligation to contribute to important national causes; and (3) APRA, whose fanatics were said to be encouraging the peasantry to ignore their obligations as citizens.

One of the (phantom) problems that government functionaries invoked to explain their own inability to procure labor was the behavior of other state functionaries. Unprincipled government personnel were said to be diverting labor away from its intended, legitimate public purposes and to be using that labor for illicit, private ends. Furthermore, these self-serving government workers were said to be using coercion to force peasant cultivators against their will, and thus were violating the peasants' constitutional rights. Claims such as these asserted that within the very body of the state were individuals who had a powerful, corrupting influence. These unscrupulous, greedy public servants were said to be undermining the state's entire modernization effort—by violating the rights of its citizens and interfering with projects designed to advance the common good.

In a context in which functionaries were under intense pressure to deliver large quantities of labor that did not exist, accusations of this kind began to pour into the offices of high-ranking officials. Officials responded to this troubling state of affairs by employing novel forms of legislation, surveillance, and punishment to cleanse the state of those who sought to corrupt it. Government officials passed an entire series of decrees that criminalized interference with government efforts to recruit labor. On the one hand, the decrees imposed fines, jail sentences, and the threat of dismissal on anyone in the bureaucracy who disrupted labor conscription. On the other hand, all public servants were encouraged to report any and all cases of corruption that they observed on the part of other government officials.

There was a problem, however, with this effort to protect the integrity of the state by distinguishing between legitimate and illegitimate forms of labor recruitment (coercive and non), and between honorable and untrustworthy government functionaries. All government projects were based on the coercion of the rural population. Furthermore, everyone in the bureaucracy was continually and unavoidably interfering with the efforts of other functionaries to conscript labor by legal, legitimate means, even as they went about legal efforts of their own. As we have seen, because government officials had imagined into being a vast field of peasant labor, there was far less labor available than the government asserted. As a result, each time virtually any government functionary complied with the legal labor demands of one office, he was necessarily compelled to neglect the equally legal demands of other offices.

In other words, high-ranking officials responded to the disorder they themselves had provoked with their massive program of forced labor by displacing responsibility for that disorder onto the shoulders of "unscrupulous functionaries"—whose behavior officials then sought to police. The reason that there was a continual labor shortage, however, had nothing to do with the criminal inclinations of individual public servants. Rather, the shortage of labor was a function of the fact that the government insisted on coercing the rural populace in numbers far greater than the actual population size.

While focusing on the greed of individuals appeared to address a real problem, as noted above, it actually created a false one. It also masked the circumstances that made it inevitable that all functionaries would be compelled to "betray the public trust" on an ongoing basis. Government policy nonetheless singled out "unscrupulous functionaries" as an issue of major concern—as being one of several forces that threatened to undermine the entire modernization effort. As a result, the government became deeply invested in attempts to monitor and control the behavior of deviant individuals, to whom officials attributed extraordinary powers. In reality, however, these individuals were a phantom concern and had little to do with the problems the government faced.

This attempt to find individuals who could be held accountable for structural problems produced something of a war of all against all within the bureaucracy (where elite factions were already doing battle). Governors, for example, took to accusing their district-level counterparts (mayors and justices) of obstructing their recruitment efforts, and vice versa. The police—who traveled to the rural districts to "escort" conscripted peasants to their work sites—accused district functionaries of interfering with their efforts, and vice versa. The heads of the Army Conscription Office, the Office of Highways, and other offices accused both the police and rural functionaries—and one another.

In other words, officials at all levels of the bureaucracy came to regard each other as sources of danger. Knowing that everyone was under pressure to show that they were not culpable for failing to produce the labor called for by official plans, government personnel sought to cast blame elsewhere.[20] But it was not only unscrupulous functionaries to whom they attributed their difficulties. Government officials invoked two other (phantom) problems that were also said to be undermining their efforts to procure labor: the Indian peasantry and APRA.

Because of limitations of space, I will focus on APRA. But before discussing the government's responses to the "Party of the People," as APRA liked to call itself, I provide a bit of background on the conditions out of which the party emerged. The disorder that characterized the period under consideration was not limited to that provoked by the massive program of forced labor initiated by the central government. Even more disruptive were the sweeping changes in the national social structure that accompanied the expansion of Peru's international export economy in the opening decades of the twentieth century. Export zones providing primary goods for the world market grew rapidly during this period, but the working classes that labored in these enclaves grew more rapidly still. There was a veritable explosion of laboring groups, who formed themselves into parties and became a powerful political presence. In so doing, they mounted the first serious challenge to the position of the export elite.

Contributing further to the general disorder of the era was the rapid influx of foreign capital. Once Peru repaid its enormous outstanding debt to British creditors in the late nineteenth century, foreign capital began to pour into the country at an unprecedented rate. In the process, existing patterns of production and exchange were extensively disrupted while new possibilities for accumulation emerged. As this occurred, social groups from across the spectrum struggled with one another to control what they could of the old patterns and to seize what they could of the new possibilities. It was a chaotic, insecure, and violent period.

It was in this context of widespread dislocation, insecurity, and immiseration that APRA was formed. The Party of the People was established in 1930, in the depths of the Depression. APRA called for a form of Latin American social-ism based on the nationalization of land and industry, the formation of worker cooperatives, and the expansion of entitlements for excluded social categories. Virtually overnight, it seemed, APRA succeeded in attracting a huge following, especially among working- and middle-class groups. Among the most notable aspects of the party was that it formed a hierarchical organization made up of cells and committees that spanned the country. This created the impression that the party was everywhere.

During its early years, APRA was involved in a series of violent civil-military uprisings and coup attempts in which it allied with elements in the police and the armed forces. This led to extensive government repression, which forced APRA underground and also crippled the party—or so it appeared. But every so often, the authorities would stumble upon evidence that suggested that things were not entirely as they seemed—at least on the surface. I next provide an example of one such disturbing discovery.

EXPOSING SUBVERSION

In the early morning hours of July 4, 1936, a Chachapoyas policeman who was making his rounds saw a young boy banging on the door of Nicolás Muñoz—one of the town's most respected carpenters. Muñoz opened the door and admitted the youth. Within seconds the policeman saw another man—who had been hiding in a concealed spot nearby—rush across the street to enter Muñoz's home. The policeman's suspicions having been aroused, he crossed the street from where he had been hiding and appeared in the doorway. He found Muñoz yelling at the boy and holding a file of papers, which he attempted to conceal when he saw the policeman. The file contained the "Manifesto of the Amazonas Action Committee, Aprista Party of Peru"—propaganda of the outlawed Party of the People.

The two men and the underage boy (who was fourteen) were detained. In the investigation that followed, the police took detailed statements from the detainees, all of whom denied having ever had any contact with APRA. The testimonies of the two men in particular bordered on the absurd, but they did implicate other individuals, who the police also detained and cross-examined. These individuals came from all walks of life: they included teachers, public employees, merchants, itinerant peddlers, artisans—over a half dozen in all—including the parents of the young boy messenger.

At the end of the investigation, the authorities had collected enough information to piece together an alarming, if partial, view of APRA's activities—one that suggested the existence of a vast network of underground subversion. It appeared that the Apristas were extensively involved in communicating with each other in secret. To allay the suspicions of the authorities, one strategy that the party employed was to use underage youth, like the one who had been detained. Boys such as he could wander about the streets at night without drawing the attention of government officials.

The testimony gathered by the police, however, also showed that the Apristas were availing themselves of other methods to maintain an underground system of communication. The individuals who had been detained had used a local cantina for the same purpose. Cantinas were virtually the only place where numbers of men could gather without drawing the attention of the authorities. The testimony of the detainees revealed that they had originally used this cantina to pass the Manifesto between them—and that other men had been involved as well (these men were also detained and interviewed).

Perhaps the most alarming piece of evidence the police collected, however, was a notebook that they seized from Nicolás Muñoz. The authorities were especially concerned about the notebook because they could not read it. This is because it was written in code. Two sets of coded entries were of special concern. The first was a long list of names—or rather, pseudonyms. Opposite each was an amount of money. The police interpreted this to be a list of party members, along with a record of the money each had tithed. The list was quite long and on this basis alone was of major concern. But even more alarming was the fact that the list did not reveal the actual identities of the Apristas. As a result, the authorities could only imagine who did and did not belong to the party. But the list was alarming for other reasons as well. On the one hand, it suggested that the Apristas were sufficiently fanatical that they voluntarily offered large sums of money to support the party. On the other hand, the list suggested that the Apristas had developed a secret language, all their own, that only they could understand.

The notebook also contained a second list—one that classified the many rural villages of the region according to the nature of their support for the Party of the People.[21] Because the list was written in code, however, it raised more questions than it answered. In particular, the authorities remained in the dark about two key questions: which villages were sympathetic to the party and which were not (thus hinting at a geography of subversion), and how APRA used the information it had gathered.

We are now in a position to return to the issue of imaginary labor, which was raised earlier. The messages from district functionaries in which they explained their inability to procure labor suggested one way that the Apristas were using the information about the political sympathies of different villages. It was not at all unusual for district-level functionaries to claim that APRA was systematically interfering with their efforts to recruit labor. But the communiqués did not stop here. Functionaries often linked APRA as one phantom cause with a second one—the essential nature of the Indian peasantry. Consider, for example, the following communiqué, sent to the prefect by a district governor who was seeking to conscript labor for the Chachapoyas highway.

Sr. Interim Prefect of the Department.

I have before me your oficio #1_ of May 1_th of this year in which you advise me that the Sr. Engineer . . . informs you that the braceros from this district who are called upon to work on the Chachapoyas . . . highway have yet to appear. . . . I have tried, Sr. Prefect, to comply with [this] order . . . but find that the leaders of the Aprista political party in this District interfere with my efforts. They have called the population together to declare that they should not be forced to work against their will. The innocent and simple Indians [of La Jalca] now defy my authority. . . . I request that you send the . . . police to this district as soon as possible to help reestablish public order.[22]

In light of messages like these, government officials came to regard APRA as a dangerous evil. Having discovered that some Apristas had used the labor of their underage children to deliver secret messages in the dead of night, it was difficult to avoid speculating how many other Apristas might be doing the same. Once the authorities learned that some Apristas had used their neighborhood cantina as a meeting place to spread seditious literature, they wondered how many other cantinas were being used in the same way. After tracing the party's influence (by means of the testimony the police collected) into local schools, reading clubs, musical groups, sports teams, the government bureaucracy, and so on (which I did not have time to review), the authorities questioned how much farther still APRA's networks extended. Having found (again, in the testimony collected by the police) that some Apristas were traveling to the countryside on a regular basis to work with the peasantry, the authorities could only reach the conclusion that there were many more party members doing the same— especially in light of communiqués like the one presented here.

In the aftermath of the police investigation just mentioned, the authorities came to fear that there was a great deal going on that they could not see. In an attempt to shed light on the situation, the prefect called for an entire range of new security measures to be established, in town and country alike. In a series of communiqués, the prefect called upon everyone to collaborate in a region-wide effort to control APRA, which he characterized as a grave threat to the region.

Government officials responded to the disorder of the era as a whole by displacing responsibility for it onto the shoulders of APRA. But the reason that there was such widespread dissatisfaction with the existing state of affairs had little to do with the party per se. Although the Apristas helped channel and organize this discontent, its origins lay elsewhere. Nonetheless, the government invested enormously in attempts to monitor and control APRA—to which the government attributed truly extraordinary powers of subversion. In reality, however, the party was a phantom issue—a concern that was only tangentially related to the problems the government faced.

CONCLUSION

Conventional views of the state regard it as an institution that exercises a monopoly on the use of legitimate force within a given territory. According to these views, state formation depends on the ability of central powers to eliminate violence-wielding competitors, who interfere with the monopoly on force the state seeks to establish. The evidence presented in this chapter suggests that this position is flawed. Indeed, it points in the opposite direction. The ability of the central government to impose its will in remote sections of the national space was contingent not upon the elimination of violence-wielding competitors but on their preservation. Indeed, when these nonstate actors were no longer present—when conditions resembled what would conventionally be understood as a state monopoly on the use of force—government officials found themselves incapable of governing the region. As we have seen, the absence of coercion-wielding castas after 1930 meant that conditions became increasingly chaotic, culminating in a crisis of rule.

The dynamics of state formation during the afterlife were integral to the production of that crisis. State formation during the 1930s and 1940s was riddled with contradictions. It was based on fantasy rather than rationality, introduced disorder rather than order, and revealed that there was no institutional nexus that monopolized the use of legitimate force. Nonetheless, there was a kind of coherence to the state. In closing, I would like to explore what that coherence might mean for contemporary debates about the state.

The coherence of the Peruvian state was based on "displacement." This term refers to the process by which public officials systematically misconstrued the nature of the problems they themselves sought to address, as well as the solutions that they proposed to deal with these problems. Officials did not adopt this strategy as the result of collective discussion or debate. Nor did they decide as a group the terms they would employ in the process of displacement. Nonetheless, displacement was an activity in which virtually all government personnel participated. Furthermore, virtually all used the same terms to misrepresent the problems they were compelled to address. Indeed, displacement was integral to all the explanations that district functionaries offered to their superiors. As a result, high-ranking state officials were forever seeking to correct problems with their failed modernization schemes by addressing issues that had little to do with the actual source of their problems, for the latter could not be named as such.

The state gained coherence as government officials identified a series of displaced problems upon which to focus official energies. This coherence was more than discursive. But it was not based on a monopoly on the use of force. Nor did it generate order, discipline, or rule-governed behavior within the bureaucracy. On the contrary, the coherence of the state depended on the creation of a series of imagined entities—vast fields of peasant labor, unscrupulous government functionaries, childlike Indians, and subversive Apristas—and on unsuccessful attempts to manage and control these imagined entities.

More than twenty years ago, the late William Roseberry made a signal contribution to understanding politics with his now famous article, "Hegemony and the Language of Contention." In that article, Roseberry argues that hegemony is not about consensus but disagreement—that hegemonic processes construct "a common material and meaningful framework for living through, talking about, and acting upon social orders characterized by domination."[23] To this I would add a small caveat. Shifting the focus slightly from hegemony to state formation, I would say that state formation establishes a shared material and discursive framework for systematically misrepresenting disorder as order—for masking key processes and focusing official efforts at surveillance and control on a series of imaginary concerns.

NOTES

1.   For an introduction to debates about the significance of the Conscripción Vial, see Paulo Drinot, *The Allure of Labor: Workers, Race, and the Making of the Peruvian State* (Durham, N.C.: Duke University Press, 2011); Florencia Mallon, *The Defense of Community in Peru's Central Highlands: Peasant Struggle and Capitalist Transition, 1860–1940* (Princeton, N.J.: Princeton University Press, 1983); and Nelson Pereyra Chávez, "Los campesinos y la Conscripción Vial: Aproximaciones al estudio de las relaciones estado-indígenas y las relaciones de mercado en Ayacucho (1919–1930)," in *Estado y mercado en la historia del Perú*, ed. Carlos Contreras and Manuel Glave (Lima: Pontifica Universidad Católica del Perú, 2012), 334–50.

2.   Max Weber, *From Max Weber: Essays in Sociology*, ed. Hans Gerth and Charles Wright Mills (New York: Oxford University Press, 1958), 78.

3.   Joel S. Migdal, *Strong Societies and Weak States: State-Society Relations and State Capabilities in the Third World* (Princeton, N.J.: Princeton University Press, 1988).

4.   Miguel Angel Centeno, "Blood and Debt: War and Taxation in Nineteenth-Century Latin America," *American Journal of Sociology* 102, no. 6 (1997): 1565–1605; Fernando López-Alves, *State Formation and Democracy in Latin America, 1810–1900* (Durham, N.C.: Duke University Press, 2000); Charles Tilly, "War Making and State Making as Organized Crime," in *Bringing the State Back In*, ed. Peter B. Evans, Dietrich Rueschemeyer, and Theda Skocpol (Cambridge: Cambridge University Press, 1985), 169–91.

5.   For a parallel case that shows the importance of violence-wielding, nonstate organizations in enabling state formation, see Ben Fallaw and Terry Rugeley, eds., *Forced Marches: Soldiers and Military Caciques in Modern Mexico* (Tucson: University of Arizona Press, 2012).

6.   For a more detailed discussion of the processes outlined in the following section, see David Nugent, *Modernity at the Edge of Empire: State, Individual, and Nation in the Northern Peruvian Andes, 1885–1935* (Stanford: Stanford University Press, 1997).

7.   Nugent, *Modernity at the Edge of Empire*, 58–103.

8.   Jorge Basadre, *Elecciones y centralismo en el Perú* (Lima: Centro de Investigación de la Universidad del Pacífico, 1980), 76–80.

9.   David Nugent, "State and Shadow State in Turn-of-the-Century Peru: Illegal Political Networks and the Problem of State Boundaries," in *States and Illegal Practices*, ed. Josiah Heyman (London: Berg, 1999), 63–98.

10.   Nugent, *Modernity at the Edge of Empire*, 58–103.

11.   Ricardo Feijóo Reina, "The Department of Amazonas Has Been Converted into a True Fief: Twenty Years of Prostration and Servilism," *Amazonas* 4, no. 19 (May 1929). All translations are mine unless otherwise indicated.

12.   This highway was given a range of different names during the construction process. For reasons of simplicity, I have selected one.

13.   Paulo Drinot, "Peru, 1884–1930: A Beggar Sitting on a Bench of Gold?," in *An Economic History of Twentieth-Century Latin America*, vol. 1, *The Export Age: The Latin American Economies in the Late Nineteenth and Early Twentieth Centuries*, ed. Enrique Cardenas, José Antonio Ocampo, and Rosemary Thorp (Basingstoke: Palgrave Macmillan, 2000), 152–87; Steven Jay Hirsch, "The Anarcho-Syndicalist Roots of a Multi-Class Alliance: Organized Labor and the Peruvian Aprista Party, 1900–1933" (PhD diss., George Washington University, 1997); Steve Stein, *Populism in Peru: The Emergence of the Masses and the Politics of Social Control* (Madison: University of Wisconsin Press, 1980); Nugent, *Modernity at the Edge of Empire*, 104–41.

14.   A similar witch hunt occurred across the country.

15.   The juntas de conscripción vial, which were associated with the hated regime of Augusto Leguía, were disbanded after the Oncenio.

16.   For exceptions to this pattern, see David Nugent, *The Encrypted State: Delusion and Displacement in the Northern Peruvian Andes* (Stanford: Stanford University Press, 2019), 193–215.

17.   Changing one's residence in order to evade official labor conscription is a very old pattern in the Andes, dating to the colonial period. Ann M. Wightman, *Indigenous Migration ad Social Change: The Forasteros of Cuzco, 1570–1720* (Durham, N.C.: Duke University Press, 1990).

18.   The figure of 2,125 men per province assumes that men pressed into military service were gone for an average of five years, a figure that is based on extensive discussion with informants. In 1940, there were 2,110 men in the province of Chachapoyas, 1,441 in Bongará, 1,415 in Mendoza, and 4,980 in Luya. Ministerio de Hacienda y Comercio [Peru], *Censo nacional de población de 1940*, vol. 9 (Lima: Dirección Nacional de Estadística, República del Perú, 1942), 5–12.

19.   See Ministerio de Hacienda y Comercio [Peru], *Censo nacional de población de 1940*, 5–12.

20.   The fact that government functionaries throughout the bureaucracy felt compelled to conceal so much made it extremely difficult for them to work together toward any common goal.

21.   The existence of this list suggested that APRA had subjected the entire region to a unified party gaze and utilized the intelligence thus obtained to pursue party goals.

22.   Gobernación del Distrito de La Jalca al Sr. Prefecto Interino del Departamento, June 15, 1932, Oficios de los Gobernadores, 1932, Archivo Subprefectural de Chachapoyas, Peru.

23.   William Roseberry, "Hegemony and the Language of Contention," in *Everyday Forms of State Formation: Revolution and the Negotiation of Rule in Modern Mexico*, ed. Gilbert M. Joseph and Daniel Nugent (Durham, N.C.: Duke University Press, 1994), 361.

8

INTELLECTUAL WORKERS, SOCIALIST SHOPKEEPERS, AND REVOLUTIONARY MILLIONAIRES

The Political Economy of Postrevolutionary Yucatán,
1924–1935

BEN FALLAW

THIS CHAPTER examines Mexico's postrevolutionary regime in the southeastern state of Yucatán during the formative period between the armed phase of the Mexican Revolution and President Lázaro Cárdenas's radical reforms. It analyzes one of the regional pillars of the national postrevolutionary state, the Partido Socialista del Sureste (PSS, Socialist Party of the Southeast) under Bartolomé García Correa. During this time, he held a series of high offices (senator 1926–29, governor 1930–33, senator 1934–40), and cofounded the direct antecedent of the Partido Revolucionario Institucional (PRI, Institutional Revolutionary Party), the Partido Nacional Revolucionario (PNR, National Revolutionary Party) in 1928. García Correa believed that cooperativism would create a model Yucatán: industrialized, modern, urban, egalitarian, and democratic. Many Yucatecan socialists shared his faith.[1] Although a host of postrevolutionary leaders across the country rhetorically championed a generic revolutionary capitalism as benefiting all Mexicans, the Yucatecan socialist variant was among the most ambitious.[2]

I will focus on how bartolista socialism, meaning the PSS under García Correa, sought to use funding from the export of henequen (a plant fiber that was a valuable global commodity from the 1880s to 1950s) to underwrite a Yucatecan brand of revolutionary capitalism. Instead of land reform breaking up the privately owned haciendas, bartolista socialism sought to create a mixed economy with an expanded state sector to support consumer and producer cooperatives favoring (initially, at least) mainly the middle sectors of Yucatecan society. Over time, even the poorest, most rural Yucatecans would have enjoyed socioeconomic benefits of revolutionary citizenship, defined as the rights and guarantees extended to working people by the Constitution of 1917, through participation in cooperatives. However, in the short run cooperatives principally aided "intellectual workers" (white-collar workers) and small proprietors (and those who aspired to become small proprietors). Moreover, politically connected bureaucrats, businessmen, and landowners—the so-called revolutionary millionaires—often enjoyed remarkable profits through collaborating with the revolutionary government's cooperatives. That said, many of the shortcomings of the bartolista brand of revolutionary capitalism were due mainly to structural forces beyond García Correa's control, above all the Great Depression.

My perspective on García Correa's bartolista socialism goes against the historiographical grain. Historians long dismissed the bartolista era as a peninsular Thermidor, in Gilbert Joseph's words "an empty interval, a time when the region slumbered—or drifted back into old repressive patterns."[3] Indeed, critics compared García Correa unfavorably to the previous leaders of Yucatecan socialism, Constitutionalist military-governor Salvador Alvarado (1915–18) and radical governor Felipe Carrillo Puerto (1922–23). Alvarado founded the PSS, creating a strong, centralized structure with affiliated *ligas de resistencia* in every workplace, neighborhood, and village. This corporatist structure allowed the PSS to monopolize elections. Alvarado fundamentally altered Yucatán's political economy of henequen by setting up a public-private corporation that monopolized exports and associated services and infrastructure. I will refer to it by the name it assumed in 1925, Henequeneros de Yucatán. Henequeneros' revenue underwrote Alvarado's "revolutionary laboratory" of massively increased schooling, bureaucratic expansion, and the extension of state services, as well as PSS-run cooperatives. Carrillo Puerto intensified popular mobilization via an ambitious agrarian reform that affected nonhenequen land and even threatened to affect henequen haciendas. Leftist supporters of Cárdenas and conservative foes of García Correa used terms much stronger and negative than Thermidor to describe García Correa's brand of socialism. Their black legend of *bartolismo* emphasizes corruption, authoritarianism, and political violence, especially the deaths of around forty peasants in Opichén on April 15, 1933, and the closure of the *Diario de Yucatán* newspaper from October 1931 to March 1933.[4]

Using archival evidence, the press, ethnographies, and underutilized micro-histories, this chapter suggests a more nuanced picture of the bartolista era. Rather than betraying Alvarado and Carrillo Puerto's legacy, García Correa in fact continued important elements of Yucatán's revolutionary tradition while rejecting agrarian reform in the henequen zone. García Correa rebuilt the political power of the PSS, which had been in decline since 1924, by reaching out to sectors of the middle and working classes through cooperativism—a project begun by Alvarado. In another echo of Alvarado's reforms, García Correa defended Henequeneros' control over key aspects of the economy, including finance and infrastructure—the "commanding heights" of the regional economy. Although not considered here, bartolista institutions and practices reached deep into rural Yucatecan society and economy through the use of Maya language and cultural forms—a clear echo of Carrillo Puerto's indigenism.

In the next section, I will provide a brief overview of the macro- and microlevels of the political economy of henequen, including the groups who benefited most from the bartolista brand of revolutionary capitalism. I will then analyze how bartolista cooperatives incorporated and disciplined sections of the middle class. Finally, I have some concluding remarks about García Correa's contested legacy.

Before moving on, however, two terms merit definition: state formation and political economy. By *state formation*, I mean not only Daniel Nugent and Gilbert Joseph's notion of a "repertoire of activities and cultural forms" but also a process in which the state seeks, in William Roseberry's words, to "organize both bourgeoisie and proletariat, both through its own structure and the structure of the parties that contend for power."[5] I am interested in the cultural mission of the schools of the PSS and the forms revolutionary sociability fostered via paramilitary and sporting clubs, as well as how the unions, ligas de resistencia, parastatal companies, and cooperatives of the PSS regimented and disciplined society. The bartolista project served as a model that other regional political machines and the PNR-PRI itself sought to imitate but could never duplicate.[6]

Economic forces and factors have generally been overlooked in studies of postrevolutionary state formation over the past two decades or so.[7] To right the balance, I draw on the concept of political economy to capture the interaction of government, society, and economic forces. I adopt William Roseberry's definition of political economy as stretching from the global to the local, and taking into account both agency and structure, including "larger historical, political, and economic movements" such as coercive labor systems, colonialism, postcolonial state making, and global commodity markets.[8]

BARTOLONOMICS: GARCÍA CORREA'S REVOLUTIONARY CAPITALISM

García Correa's economic project was by no means a purely personal effort. He had a team of economic advisors, including Enrique Manero, who had deep expertise in taxation as well as the henequen industry; successful businessman and financier Alberto Montes Molina; and numerous hacendados and businessmen associated with the PSS since the day of Alvarado and Carrillo Puerto, the so-called socialist hacendados.[9] But García Correa was himself a successful businessman trained as an accountant. His portfolio grew during his political career, although reports of a vast fortune were greatly exaggerated. Bartolomé García Correa grew up in Umán, southwest of Mérida, in the heart of the henequen zone. He helped run his parents' general store, selling corn (and reportedly alcohol) on neighboring haciendas, where he became intimately familiar with the operation of henequen estates.[10]

As I explore below, during his early political career from 1915 to 1928, he had consistently advocated cooperativism, above all for other small merchants like himself, as a crucial part of revolutionary capitalism. I have termed García Correa and other, similar small-scale, often mestizo, upwardly mobile merchants (and those who aspired to join their ranks) "socialist shopkeepers" because they sought to use the Mexican Revolution and Yucatán's PSS to displace Porfirian elites atop the regional economy and political system without radically redistributing wealth through (for example) land reform in the henequen zone. They sought to use cooperativism as a key part of this strategy: banding together, combined with state government support, would allow cooperative members to access credit, control competition, and gain other advantages to equalize chances against larger competitors who often hailed from Mérida's elite families. From the bartolista leaders' perspective, cooperativism would make the economy more egalitarian, without replacing capitalism with a more radical alternative. Alliances with elite actors (both national politicians and elements of the old regional oligarchy), the history and political practices of the PSS, the desire for upward social mobility of key constituencies in Yucatecan society, and his own background all shaped García Correa's support for cooperativism.

From its inception, socialist cooperativism depended on the political economy of henequen. Only revenue from Henequeneros could fund the tremendous investments required to set up and subsidize cooperatives. The centrality of the monocrop for bartolista socialism is underscored by comparing profit streams derived from henequen exports before and after the revolution. During the Porfiriato, approximately three hundred large haciendas were owned by a relatively small number of interrelated families. Labor costs were low due to brutal debt servitude and an extremely exacting labor system that operated with an almost industrial precision. Capital investments in narrow-gauge rail and steam-driven defibration machinery greatly increased profitability, although large mortgages often forced the bankruptcy of haciendas during busts in the global fiber market. When prices boomed, however, the plantocracy enjoyed windfall profits, allowing them to share the opulent existence of the U.S. and European great bourgeoisie in the Gilded Age. We can image a vast river of henequen wealth going to the hacendados, with intermittent streams running to creditors (some Yucatecan) and European and U.S. industries exporting capital goods; a small creek of fiscal revenue to the Porfirian state; and a minor brook of profits to local suppliers of corn, alcohol, and goods like leather tackle. Little trickled down to the individual peons.

The revolution considerably changed henequen's revenue streams. Hacendados still enjoyed a diminished yet considerable revenue flow. The trickle to workers increased a bit, at least until the Great Depression. The government of Yucatán and (after 1926) the nation taxed henequen exports and imposed a variety of fees, which amounted to a considerable diversion of wealth from the hacendados to the state. Henequeneros' fiscal revenue helped greatly expand officialdom in the state and Mérida government. Intellectuals escaped their historical reliance on the large landowners for patronage, as they could now write or work for government or party.[11]

A closer look at the labor and land policies reveals what the revolution did—and did not—change about the political economy of henequen and the distribution of wealth in Yucatán. In spite of Alvarado's reforms—above all the monopolization of exports by Henequeneros and the abolition of debt peonage—haciendas' land and processing machinery remained in the hands of the same families. Alvarado resisted partitioning haciendas and "reconstructed" much of the hacienda labor regime to protect tax revenue to fund his other goals and because he believed indigenous people to be incapable of exercising revolutionary citizenship at least for the foreseeable future.[12] As a result,

Alvarado's revolutionary state preserved much of the old Porfirian racialized social hierarchy on haciendas, prevented peon out-migration and effective collective bargaining, and bolstered hacendado and overseer authority. Work in the henequen fields remained low-paid, low-skill, "Indian" work. Alvarado's labor legislation—the template for subsequent legislation—denied henequen laborers the revolutionary Constitution of 1917's guarantees of minimum wage and severance pay.[13]

Besides the need to ensure a steady flow of fiscal revenue from henequen exports to fund the state government, other political reasons and complex economic factors prevented socialist regimes in Yucatán from implementing a land reform to break up the henequen haciendas. Presidents Venustiano Carranza, Álvaro Obregón, and Plutarco Elías Calles; the United States; and the hacendados themselves exerted formidable political pressure to thwart agrarian reform in the henequen zone. Moreover, several socialist policy makers and politicians questioned its feasibility. Defenders of the hacienda argued that it was the most economically rational way of producing henequen, pointing to economies of scale that alternative producers (smaller haciendas, *parcelarios* who farmed a small plot of henequen, peasant or peon cooperatives) lacked. The large hacienda alone could buy and maintain the expensive defibrating train (really a small factory employing skilled technicians) and manage the optimal balance of fields in production, planting, and rest.[14] Transforming henequen haciendas into cooperatively farmed ejidos, they argued, would have required landowners, the state, and peasants and peons themselves to pay a high transition cost for years, or have the state or federal government assume financial responsibility for them.[15]

When García Correa began his rise to regional power, he inherited an entrenched socialist regime that depended on the mixed (public-private) political economy of henequen. The haciendas remained in the hands of the oligarchy but were taxed, regulated, and governed by a PSS regime that was determined both to preserve and to exploit it. As president of the PSS in the late 1920s, García Correa proved quite astute at diverting henequen revenue away from the hacendados and toward favored groups, mostly politically connected, middle-class entrepreneurs and officials. He made the most of a 1926 legal reform that made fiber production a public interest "under the vigilance and safeguarding of the government" implemented after four years of economic and political upheaval that had undermined the henequen economy.[16] This was a clear example of revolutionary capitalism: the state stepped in to mediate between labor and capital in order to revive a vital but troubled part of Mexico's economy by improving the quality and quantity of output. By doing so, the legislation assured federal support for Henequeneros, but it also allowed García Correa to expand and extend practices first developed under Salvador Alvarado's revolutionary governorship (1915–17), practices that gave state agents the power to intervene in the daily operations of the henequen hacienda. Under the 1926 legislation, Henequeneros now could count on new state bureaucratic agencies (Departamento de Estadística y Clasificación de Henequén [Department of Statistics and Classification of Henequen]; and the Bolsa de Trabajo [Labor Exchange]) and García Correa's PSS to organize and discipline some sixty thousand peons and *eventuales* (day laborers residing in nearby villages and towns) who worked in the henequen fields. García Correa personally oversaw labor relations on henequen haciendas. He supervised bureaucrats, dealt with local socialist politicians and caciques, and personally heard appeals from hacendados.[17]

The extension of PSS and state authority into the hacienda did not favor the peons and day laborers for the most part, although Henequeneros now set aside a portion of tax revenue for a workers' fund. On the local level, those who did best were a host of groups mainly from the middle class linked to the bartolista socialist regime. For instance, petty merchants who replaced the old Porfirian operators of the company store on haciendas—above all the concessionaires of alcohol sales—enjoyed something of a captive market. Specialists in supplying and overseeing hacienda labor also did well. A surprising number of these men moved from jobs as hacienda administrators to positions in the state labor bureaucracy and even elected office. Caciques of villages and towns organized labor gangs of eventuales to work on nearby estates and often skimmed part of their wages. This rent seeking relied on the continued existence of both the privately owned hacienda and state authority over it; the socialist shopkeepers and labor bosses enjoyed modest profits under the bartolista brand of revolutionary capitalism, while the peons and peasants had little to show for it.[18]

This stream of wealth was dwarfed by a veritable raging river of revenue from Henequeneros running to technocrats and financiers working for and with Henequeneros, the so-called Socialist Hacendados, as well as politically connected members of the old business elite. Critics of Henequeneros charged that so-called coyotes were trafficking illegally in production quotas allocated by the parastatal. Like other revolutionary millionaires cataloged by journalist Francisco Naranjo, they made their fortunes "in the shadow of the revolution." Rather than outright appropriation, their "inexplicable enrichment" could be traced to legal or semilegal transactions in gray areas of business with the state or parastatal agencies like Henequeneros.[19]

The very nature of Henequeneros' structure created many shady areas. Shortly after its reestablishment in 1926, Henequeneros began sponsoring a valorization scheme to drive up fiber prices. This was yet another aspect of revolutionary capitalism: the national bank (Banco de México, or Banxico) advanced credit to a vital economic sector to regain lost global market shares and avoid giving North American buyers the privileged position they enjoyed in the global fiber market before the revolution. With its new line of credit, Henequeneros bought up and warehoused henequen production to attempt to drive down global fiber supply and to pay hacendados advances (*anticipos*) to keep their fields in production. Interest due to Banxico was deducted from anticipos, meaning hacendados had no choice but to give up a share of their profits to pay for debts contracted by the parastatal. Moreover, Henequeneros deducted mandatory fees from hacendados' export earnings to cover insurance, transportation, warehousing, and a host of other services that Henequeneros monopolized. In 1933 Gustavo Molina Font, who would cofound the right-of-center opposition Partido Acción Nacional (PAN, National Action Party) seven years later, charged that Henequeneros' mandatory deductions were inflated by corruption, and thus cheated hacendados out of 2.1 centavos of the 14.1 centavos per kilogram of fiber, amounting to as much as 2 million pesos.[20]

Political opponents alleged that as governor García Correa used Henequeneros (as well as the state-run railroads, and other parastatal companies) to benefit privileged allies using opaque stock swaps; tax forgiveness and exemptions; loans; subsidies; and rental, sale, and purchase agreements.[21] For example, García Correa and his associates bought out the Compañía de Transporte del Golfo (Gulf Transportation Company), set up by then governor Álvaro Torre Díaz (1926–30) and industrialist and banker Arturo Ponce Cámara, and thus acquired lucrative contracts from Henequeneros to ship henequen at allegedly inflated prices.[22] Critics of the PSS charged that the so-called revolutionary millionaires used Henequeneros and the valorization scheme to profit personally.

In truth, from 1915 to 1935, Henequeneros did redirect a considerable part of the export revenue of Yucatán's monocrop economy to the state government's coffers and provided rent-seeking politicians and businessmen considerable profits as well (although the actual amount might well have been exaggerated by foes of the PSS). As governor, García Correa had much more ambitious plans to use fiber export revenues to profoundly transform Yucatán by turning the

PSS into a vast confederation of producer and consumer cooperatives. If successful, the bartolista cooperatives would have absorbed much of the political, economic, and social life of Yucatán. They would have been especially aiding an expanded middle class that would have enjoyed extensive social benefits as well as greater profits and opportunities for ownership. In other words, bartolista socialism promised an advanced form of revolutionary citizenship via participation in PSS cooperatives.

THE ORIGINS OF COOPERATIVISM IN YUCATECAN SOCIALISM, 1915–1930

García Correa and his key collaborators planned to make cooperativism the future axis of the PSS years before he was sworn in as governor in February 1930. Indeed, cooperativism had a long, socialist pedigree in Yucatán. Some of the urban labor organizations that predated the PSS probably advocated cooperativism. Alvarado helped key PSS affiliates (or ligas) like railroad workers to set up consumer cooperatives, carpenters to set up a producer's cooperative, and cooks and waiters to acquire a collectively run restaurant.[23]

García Correa had a history of personal involvement in a string of state-sponsored cooperative organizations. Before joining the PSS, he had cofounded a Unión Obrera Mutualista (Workers' Mutualist Union) in his hometown of Umán, which organized a consumer cooperative that later collapsed amid charges of profiteering in 1914.[24] By late 1918, García Correa was involved in a PSS committee in Mérida set up by Alvarado's Compañía Peninsular de Consumo (CPC, Consumer Company of the Peninsula), which used revenue from Henequeneros to import staple goods from the United States at wholesale for distribution. In early 1919, García Correa was president of the Board of Directors of the Unión Cooperativa del Centro de Detallistas de Yucatán (UCCDY, Center for Small Store Owners of Yucatán's Cooperative Union). This form of revolutionary capitalism promised benefits to consumers—especially the poor at the mercy of the rising price of imports—but it also benefited socialist shopkeepers who ran the UCCDY like himself. He even traveled to the United States in May 1919 on behalf of the Alvarado administration to arrange for direct bulk purchases to be shared by 108 shareholding small merchants, who would then distribute basic goods to consumer cooperatives for subsidized sale at low prices to PSS members. As a state congressman, he passed legislation to cut taxes on small, privately run stores. At the same time he supported raising taxes on large businesses and industries as well as large landowners. Even at this early stage in his political career, he saw no contradiction between advancing socialism and helping small shopkeepers, whether as cooperativists or petty capitalists.[25]

Although most PSS consumer cooperatives collapsed in 1919–20 due to persecution of the CPC by a reactionary army commander in the so-called Zamarippazo, García Correa's support for cooperativism showed no sign of waning.[26] However, he had to overcome its troubled legacy: many local consumer cooperatives failed due to mismanagement and suspicions of corruption. For instance, in June 1919, Tizimín's consumer cooperative collapsed after 200 pesos disappeared; investigations revealed that the manager was "an honorable person but with little knowledge in questions of numbers."[27]

Nevertheless, socialist advocates of cooperativism like García Correa continued to advance it as a means of radically transforming Yucatecan society. In 1921 the Second Party Congress of the PSS presided over by Carrillo Puerto endorsed cooperativism in an anarchist form (exchange among producers replacing the market) as a pillar of Yucatecan socialism. García Correa was vice president of the Congress and likely supported reviving the consumer cooperativism that he participated in via the UCCDY.[28] Although Carrillo Puerto's gubernatorial administration ended prematurely in the *delahuertista* coup months before his death on January 3, 1924, Carrillo Puerto was planning to convert abandoned haciendas into cattle, corn, and sugar-farming peasant cooperatives.[29]

García Correa served as PSS president under Governors José María Iturralde (May 1924–January 1926) and Torre Díaz (February 1926–January 1930). He probably encouraged Iturralde's ill-fated attempt to revive the Compañía Peninsular de Consumo and the old Union of Storekeepers (now renamed the Alianza de Abastecedores [Alliance of Wholesalers]). Iturralde also instituted a longer-lasting butchers' cooperative and a producer cooperative to run the two biggest sugar plantations, although García Correa's participation in these ventures (or other cooperatives) is unknown.[30] Under Governor Álvaro Torre Díaz (1926–29), García Correa sought to revive the small shopkeepers–consumer cooperative to import wholesale goods, as well as setting up rural producer cooperatives, including one to spread the cultivation of castor oil plants. García Correa petitioned President Calles to tap the Henequeneros' workers' fund to set them up. This foray into rural producer cooperatives, combined with vocational schooling (*escuela granja*, or farm school), would answer

President Calles's call to use cooperativism to mold and discipline workers, peasants, and indigenous groups.[31] García Correa rationalized the diversion of the Henequeneros' workers' fund (originally intended to provide a dividend for peons and peasants) on the grounds that indigenous field hands would simply waste whatever they received on alcohol.[32] Like Alvarado before him, García Correa believed indigenous working people in henequen fields were incapable of exercising revolutionary citizenship without the prolonged tutelage of the revolutionary government—in this case via cooperatives.

Garcia Correa's appeals to Calles resonated with the Sonoran president's notion of revolutionary capitalism. As president (1924–28), Calles stressed cooperatives to make the government a "rector" of Mexico's capitalist economy, typical of the developmentalism of revolutionary capitalism.[33] As president and then as Jefe Máximo (1929–35), Calles advanced legislation to foster cooperatives for workers, consumers, and small producers. Calles also linked citizenship to cooperativism, emphasizing the economic and social benefits and downplaying political rights in the classical liberal context. For him, membership in cooperatives would help meet social needs without stifling individualism or entrepreneurialism. Cooperatives would forge, in other words, what Beatriz Urías Horcasitas calls the Callista "new man," a hybrid with the best characteristics of both the working and middle classes, possessing a collectivist, nationalist mentality that still respected private property.[34] Because the federal government provided credit, expertise, and guidance to cooperatives, their co-owner/members would be linked to the single national party-state, the PNR, although this goal of cooperativism remained largely unrealized.[35] The PSS in 1932 complained that hundreds of requests to the federal government to form cooperatives were gathering dust in Mexico City.[36] When it came to peasant cooperatives founded on collective land grants, or ejidos, Calles believed they would serve to provide "discipline, organization, and a sense of responsibility among the [ejidatario]."[37] For Calles, like García Correa, cooperatives would instill a form of revolutionary citizenship that did not bestow rights in the classical liberal sense but gave workers, peasants, and the petty bourgeoisie a chance to participate in decision-making within cooperatives and receive social benefits (special schools, medical care).

While cooperativism was implemented slowly and unevenly in most of Mexico, in the nearby southeastern state of Tabasco a remarkable, large-scale experiment in cooperativism took place under strongman Tomás Garrido Canabal. Tabasco's cooperative republic would serve as a model for García Correa (and a number of other prominent founders of the PNR-PRI). Inspired by Alvarado's revolutionary regime (he briefly served as interim governor of Yucatán), Garrido Canabal made cooperativism the structural foundation for the most radical regional laboratory of the Callista era. Indeed, Calles, like Lázaro Cárdenas and Francisco Múgica, celebrated Garridista Tabasco as a proving ground for doctrines and institutions they hoped to spread across Mexico—at least until Cárdenas's break with Calles in 1935. While revisionist historians long derided Garrido's cooperativism as reactionary for rejecting agrarian reform, historian Stan Ridgeway argues that it was in fact a pragmatic form of developmentalism that reconciled populist and statist impulses. Cooperatives of peasant banana cultivators with Garrido Canabal's backing leaned on Standard Fruit Company to pay higher prices for their produce. Garrido Canabal's regime also raised taxes on the U.S.-based multinational and used the fiscal revenue to fund an impressive number of schools, public health campaigns, and infrastructure.[38] Ideologically, the Tabascan model of cooperativism as revolutionary capitalism mirrored ideas expressed by Calles: assimilation and uplift of indigenous peoples and taming capitalism—particularly foreign capital—while encouraging individual initiative.[39]

Between 1926 and 1929, García Correa's plans to create a Tabasco-style federation of consumer and producer cooperatives depended on Governor Álvaro Torre Díaz's backing. The moderate governor sought to circumscribe the power of the PSS to placate Mérida's business community and prevent partisan or social violence. Torre Díaz did support cooperativism, likely motivated by a combination of developmentalism and the need to disperse patronage to key constituents. He kept Iturralde's surviving cooperatives intact and set up new ones for charcoal and firewood, as well as light industries and grain mills. The governor also licensed large cooperatives to import corn from Chiapas and beef from Tabasco.[40] However, Torre Díaz did not back García Correa's attempt to rebuild the large networks of consumer and producer cooperatives of Alvarado and Carrillo Puerto.

Producer cooperatives formed or sustained in Mérida during the Torre Díaz administration under García Correa's presidency of the PSS were closely affiliated with specific socialist ligas, like those for the butchers ("Álvaro Peña"), passenger bus drivers (Unión de Camioneros and Alianza de Camioneros), street vendors or *baratilleros* ("Andrés Ortega"), and coal and firewood vendors (Liga de Expendedores de Carbón y Leña "Bartolomé García Correa").[41] They were economically independent because they did not require direct subsidies or extensive funding from the state for the most part, but they were profitable because of tax exemptions, monopoly status, and favorable regulatory treatment. The socialist state government also ensured several had excellent schools and sporting facilities, not to mention access to the massive new headquarters of the PSS, the Casa del Pueblo.[42] Members of these favored cooperatives enjoyed many benefits, ranging from insurance to medical care. In return, they were expected to support the PSS. The bylaws of the baratilleros' liga required 50 percent of its membership to turn out for PSS rallies.[43] As PSS president and then governor, García Correa nominated many leaders of these cooperatives for the Mérida city council and state congress.

Although Torre Díaz confined PSS cooperatives to Mérida, he backed García Correa's gubernatorial ambitions for the 1930–33 term. By 1928 one of García Correa's key advisors, Edmundo Bolio Ontiveros, was already drafting plans to be unveiled at a new socialist party congress to tap the workers' fund of Henequeneros (among other sources) in order to create hundreds of new PSS-run cooperatives across the state to revive the party and transform Yucatán's economy.[44]

GARCÍA CORREA'S GUBERNATORIAL ADMINISTRATION: SOCIALISM AS COOPERATIVISM, 1930–1933

While García Correa's gubernatorial campaign was overwhelmingly successful, the Great Depression struck before he took office, greatly complicating his anticipated cooperativist project. Henequen exports plummeted, dragging state revenue down as well. To halt the free fall, García Correa sought an emergency line of credit from Banxico to fund a valorization scheme, but it failed to reverse the plunge in fiber prices.[45] Seeking to turn the crisis into an opportunity, leading bartolistas touted cooperativism as the solution to the Great Depression by "establishing economic equilibrium, [and] securing and increasing social wealth."[46] They argued that cooperativism would help pull Yucatán's economy out of its tailspin by pointing to the international trend toward cooperativism. At a time of rampant price deflation, producer and service-provider cooperatives would prevent ruinous overcompetition by setting prices and wages at levels considered fair. Cooperatives' dividends would also be used to provide social insurance during tough times, relieving the overstressed government of this obligation.[47] That said, the Depression and Banxico's demands that the state and Henequeneros impose harsh austerity measures meant that relatively little financial support would be forthcoming for cooperatives from state and federal government sources or Henequeneros. This posed a very serious problem for García Correa, and it profoundly limited the number of cooperatives that could be created.

Although the bartolista socialist regime never realized most of its plans for transforming the PSS into a confederation (or conglomeration) of cooperatives sketched at its Third (May 1–7, 1930), Fourth (May 1–4, 1931), and Fifth (May 1–6, 1932) Party Congresses, examining them closely reveals their staggering cost and other problems that were never overcome.[48] Setting up hundreds of cooperatives would have required tax exemptions, marketing help, and subsidies and credit to acquire everything from agricultural tools and cattle to factories—a huge outlay. Moreover, setting up hundreds of producer and consumer cooperatives would have posed a daunting organizational challenge. A confederation of cooperatives to serve as a coordinating agency, a special PSS Technical Commission, and relevant state agencies would need to find, train, and pay hundreds of professional managers and accountants to provide centralized management.[49]

The keystone of the entire project was the Almacén General (Central Warehouse). Aspects of it were clearly modeled upon Alvarado's Compañía Peninsular de Consumo and the *detallistas* (shopkeepers) cooperative (1918–19) that García Correa once led. The Almacén General would have imported manufactured goods like hardware and staples to sell to consumer cooperatives at wholesale prices. Moreover, García Correa planned for the Almacén General to coordinate exchanges among hundreds of producer and consumer cooperatives in a kind of barter system that in theory promised to deliver lower prices to consumers and higher prices to Yucatecan producers by eliminating the middle man and inefficiencies. To lower transportation costs, it would even have taken over the state-run railroads (and likely port facilities, to boot). A share of the dividends of the cooperatives would have helped fund an advanced social welfare program.[50] Had it come to fruition, the PSS would have been converted into a vast, diversified network of cooperatives stretching from Mérida to the smallest pueblo. Revolutionary citizenship would have been inseparable from participation in cooperativism.

Although the dream of a coordinated, top-down economy seemed to challenge some basic aspects of capitalism, these utopian plans remained on the drawing board. Most of socialist cooperativism in Yucatán easily fit in the rather broad category of revolutionary capitalism—an attempt to make a capitalist economy more equitable, less vulnerable to foreign influence, and more compatible with the social changes fostered by the revolution. The extent to which it would change or challenge capitalism—how "revolutionary" it was—divided socialist leaders. García Correa and key ideologue Edmundo Bolio Ontiveros believed cooperativism would tame—not replace—the market by providing "guidance and balance" between labor and capital.[51] In fact, on García Correa's first May Day as governor in 1930, the party magazine *Tierra* announced, "Socialism needs capitalism to exist."[52] Bartolista socialism generally followed the line of cooperativism as complementary to capitalism, an approach that mirrored Calles's and echoed Alvarado's. That said, there was the occasional rhetorical radicalism: Miguel Cantón, a Yucatecan socialist leader (and briefly interim governor) who collaborated with Garrido Canabal in Tabasco, called cooperativism "anticapitalist."[53] Perhaps the creation of a vast confederation of cooperatives centered on the Almacén General would have eventually absorbed the rest of the economy; or else Cantón was referring back to Carrillo Puerto's often-antagonistic attitude toward capitalism. Legally, members of bartolista cooperatives were defined as both workers and capitalists, which left little doubt that capitalism in some form would remain.[54]

Downplaying anticapitalism rhetoric dovetailed with another fundamental characteristic of cooperativism: incorporating so-called intellectual workers along with (manual) workers and peasants into the popular base of the PSS. Under Carrillo Puerto, peasants and workers were the primary beneficiaries of socialist reforms, although sectors of the petty and even gran bourgeoisie enjoyed substantial advantages under his regime. Bartolista socialism sought to mobilize and incorporate government employees, clerks, and other white-collar workers generally considered middle class as opposed to proletarian by appealing to them as intellectual workers. The elastic term *intellectual worker* could even stretch to include teachers and other government employees. For instance, Luis Cáceres Baqueiro, president of both the Baratilleros' cooperative and liga, was not even a vendor or small merchant. In fact he was the principal of the Baratilleros trade school.[55]

The "Carlos Marx" liga of the PSS based in northwest Mérida played a central role in bringing intellectual workers into the party. The Marx liga described its three hundred members as "workers of all classes both manual and cerebral."[56] But it was these cerebral workers—often teachers, lawyers, or homeopathic doctors employed by the PSS or the state or municipal government—that provided most of its leadership and delivered social services to laborers and the poor. In an article titled "Socialism and the Middle Class," Marx liga president Luis Escalante posited that the intellectual worker was "the longest suffering and the most anguished" member of society "without class and neither worker nor privileged."[57]

Yucatecan socialism's growing concern with the oppressed salarymen mirrored national trends. In 1923 then presidential candidate Calles argued that "in the class struggle in the modern world, there is a third class that should play a great role: the middle class. Always repressed, the middle class has been put down and exploited by those above, without achieving a sufficient degree of understanding by those below." Calles called for the middle class to "come to occupy its rightful place, balancing the other two classes for the benefit of the Republic."[58] The strategy of the PSS to identify its own project with Calles likely reinforced outreach to intellectual workers.

During 1928–29, the formative period for García Correa's political project, the PSS press often privileged groups in the middle of Yucatecan society as recipients of state attention. The January 1928 *Tierra* article "Ideas Make the Revolution" rejected hunger as the revolution's cause and noted that the party's new recruits are not "the poorest salaried men."[59] The Liga Carlos Marx's newspaper, *El Clamor del Obrero*, helped flesh out bartolista socialism's "new ideas" to "link the interests of civilization with the popular cause" and create an egalitarian society without either rich or poor.[60] This new society would be created not through the radical revolution that Carrillo Puerto advocated but through evolutionary measures.[61] García Correa and his collaborators advocated cooperativism as the most important tool of guided, peaceful change, one especially attuned to the needs of those neither patrician nor plebian.

Given the party's history and Calles's policies, it is not surprising that bartolista cooperativism sought to appeal to groups in the middle class like government employees or detallistas. Moreover, cooperatives had an especially strong appeal to those who hoped to join the middle class, such as street vendors looking to expand sales, drivers who wanted to co-own their own passenger bus, and peasants looking to become owners of their own small plot or a head or two of cattle. Bartolista socialism and cooperativism appealed most to those in the unskilled and historically unorganized sectors. Not coincidentally, these were the same groups that the Confederación Regional Obrera Mexicana (CROM, Mexican Regional Labor Confederation), the most important national labor organization backed by Presidents Obregón and Calles, organized in Mexico City. What did those groups have in common? Often workers in these sectors desperately needed state intervention to regulate chaotic markets and organize small, dispersed workplaces.[62] The cooperatives of the PSS seemed to offer what they needed. Just as with the CROM (and the Confederación de

Trabajadores de México [CTM, Confederation of Mexican Workers] that came after it under Cárdenas), the bartolista PSS never had much luck organizing "old labor," skilled groups like railroad workers, electricians, and stevedores with more radical political traditions. These workers needed no help to unionize and regulate workplaces. Moreover, in the case of railroad and dock workers, their rising wages drove up the price of henequen and weakened its global competitiveness against other fibers, causing a string of socialist administrations dating from Carrillo Puerto to ban strikes in these sectors.[63]

While bartolista cooperativism was mainly urban, at least initially, in the countryside it did make inroads. Rural cooperativists were usually *parcelarios* (small farmers of a plot of henequen) and even small- and medium-sized hacendados. In the all-important henequen sector, producers' cooperatives seemed to be an extension of the Liga de Medianos y Pequeños Productores de Henequén (LMPPH, League of Medium and Small Producers of Henequen), founded by the PSS in 1925.[64]

Crucially, there was no discussion of agrarian reform to transform henequen haciendas into collectively worked cooperatives because cooperativism's scientific, rational management would reverse the decline of the henequen industry and encourage the emergence of a new class of rural, market-oriented parcelarios organized in cooperatives. This rendered any discussion of agrarian reform in the henequen zone moot. For the most part, rural socialist cooperatives offered revolutionary citizenship to its members, but relatively few of the rural poor were included, at least in the short run. In some ways, then, rural cooperativism seemed to be a wager on the strong.

If exclusion of most of the poor was one of the contradictions of this form of revolutionary citizenship, then tension between democratic governance and centralized organization of cooperativism was another. In the 1931 and 1932 party congresses, bartolista leaders emphasized that cooperativism was inherently democratic and egalitarian.[65] Indeed, the Socialist Civil Law of Cooperatives (October 11, 1932) guaranteed that dividends would be paid not according to capital invested but by labor contributed, and would provide social benefits like medical care and good schools to all members.[66] Yet the planned cooperatives were to be supervised and managed by a new, technocratic elite, whose authority rested on their expertise and was firmly backed by the state government. Moreover, cooperatives would be grouped into a vast, centrally organized confederation of cooperatives. This contradicted the grassroots democratic tradition both fostered by Carrillo Puerto and encouraged by many advocates of cooperativism. The PSS explained that only this kind of top-down direction could yield "the most productive economic evolution that Progress and Science have ever produced."[67] Some members of the PSS feared this kind of vertical arrangement would prevent participation because poorer members did not have spare time to devote to attending meetings of federated cooperatives, especially those in the state capital. Alfonso Pérez Berzunza questioned how there could be a conference of cooperatives without many members of such cooperatives present—as he put it, the conference would be "lentil soup without lentils."[68]

The PSS never reconciled the conflict between member participation and scientific management in cooperativism. In fact, bartolista cooperativism did allow for a degree of political participation—with two caveats. First, elected representatives of cooperatives in state congress and Mérida's city council hailed from middle ranks of the PSS and the leadership of unions-cum-cooperatives. Second, those most empowered were those urban, economically independent cooperatives founded in the 1920s. Those fledgling, often underfunded, mostly rural cooperatives set up in the 1930s seemed to have little influence with the party.

Funding for cooperatives reflected this dichotomy between the fortunate few—generally older and urban with more legal advantages like de facto monopolies and state-provided social services—and the struggling, rural, and younger majority. Structural factors beyond García Correa's control help explain these unequal outcomes to an extent. At the start of his administration, García Correa hoped to use Henequeneros revenue to fund agricultural, industrial, and popular banks that would have helped all cooperatives. However, in exchange for a massive extension of credit from Banxico during the 1930–32 period, García Correa had to implement harsh austerity measures that precluded much credit. Even attempts to redirect the workers' fund of Henequeneros to create more consumer and producer cooperatives—a dream for years—likely was precluded by Banxico. Attempts to tax ejidos (there were dozens farming corn and a few henequen) were bitterly resisted by old socialist leaders associated with the rural areas.[69] Nonetheless, it does seem that the urban cooperatives of the PSS in the 1920s did benefit from loans made on extremely generous terms by the Banco Refaccionario de Yucatán (Development Bank of Yucatán).[70]

CONCLUSION: THE LEGACY OF SOCIALIST COOPERATIVISM

Between 1915 and 1935, Yucatecan socialism sought to use cooperatives as a key means of transforming the prerevolutionary political economy of henequen as well as extending revolutionary citizenship to previously excluded or marginalized social sectors, although in practice, middle-class (and would be middle-class) party members benefited most. The category of "intellectual worker" helped justify this outcome. Henequeneros (and its antecedents) helped redirect the profits of the monocrop fiber export to support a progressive government that redistributed wealth from the regional oligarchy to the rest of society, although revolutionary millionaires' rent seeking undermined its success. Cooperativism was one of the favored—and potentially effective—means of doing that. García Correa, like his more celebrated socialist predecessors Alvarado and Carrillo Puerto, relied on cooperativism to transform regional society but found that powerful outside structural forces limited change. Moreover, the contradictions and inequalities inherent in it were never fully resolved.

That said, Henequeneros and small-scale cooperatives did play a crucial role in state formation. In Roseberry's terms, they both helped bring together factions of the bourgeoisie and—to a lesser extent—working classes into a coherent coalition that provided a reliable political, social, and cultural foundation for the postrevolutionary regime in the southeast. At the same time, the revolutionary millionaires (including some scions of the Porfirian oligarchy) accumulated significant capital by participating in a host of economic activities that were part of Henequeneros and cooperativism.

This helps explain why bartolista socialism and its cooperative project have been so vociferously criticized by both the conservative regional oligarchy and supporters of President Lázaro Cárdenas (1934–40). To consolidate their own power in Yucatán, Cardenistas attacked partisans of the president's former patron-turned-nemesis Plutarco Elías Calles, like García Correa, as immorally profiting from politics. In late 1935, a high-ranking federal education official critical of bartolista socialism complained that Henequeneros functioned as a trust, which fused "the Public Local power and the Economy of the State" and so controlled the henequen economy, "almost the only way of life" in Yucatán.[71]

Yet even after Cardenismo displaced the bartolista cooperative leaders and politicians, weakened the PSS, and carved out more than one hundred henequen-producing ejidos from henequen haciendas, PSS cooperatives and their leaders proved remarkably resilient. Although bartolista cooperativism was discredited for alleged corruption and *caciquismo* (petty bossism), under Cárdenas the bus drivers' cooperatives survived virtually untouched, and a number of cooperatives reconstituted themselves under new names and new legal and political structures. Luis Cáceres Baqueiro, baratillero leader, was charged with corruption in 1934 but was soon back in power, with the cooperative-liga now renamed a union. The postrevolutionary regime in Yucatán (and likely elsewhere as well) was simply too dependent politically on cooperatives to abolish them. While some might see caciquismo or governmental incompetence behind the survival of cooperative leaders and organizations, one could also argue that they enjoyed a degree of genuine popular support from their members. In any event, as late as the 1950s, cooperatives were a backbone of the ruling party in Yucatán, and the bus drivers' power endured even longer.[72]

Cooperativism did fundamentally weaken the postrevolutionary regime in some important ways as well. The extension of revolutionary citizenship through cooperativism at times reproduced rather than challenged social inequalities, by favoring urban over rural people and nonindigenous over indigenous Yucatecans. The rural poor gained relatively little compared to those who could be considered middle class. For instance, in intervening in favor of streetcar workers in July 1927, PSS president García Correa argued that the socialist government should help Mérida workers ahead of the rural poor because peasants could count on an abundant corn harvest but urban labor lacked food security.[73]

The persistence of cooperatives long after the end of bartolista socialism should not be attributed solely to politicians and some sectors of the middle and working classes. While the regional oligarchy at times criticized revolutionary politicians for "coyotaje" and other corrupt practices in the operation of Henequeneros and cooperatives, these forms of revolutionary capitalism depended on the active collaboration of many businessmen. Moreover, there is considerable evidence that regional oligarchs preferred state intervention to pure laissez faire economics with a minimal state. Before the revolution, two leading oligarchic families, the Escalante and Peón, leveraged the state government to set up Compañía Consolidada de los Ferrocarriles, Muelles y Almacenes de Yucatán (Consolidated Company of Railroads, Docks and Warehouses of Yucatán), including a massive new Almacén General, to control almost all infrastructure in the state—a remarkably similar strategy to Henequeneros and García Correa's Almacén General.[74] In 1911 the state government gave Olegario Molina and his allies and kin a monopoly on importing grains to Yucatán and livestock to Mérida.[75] In fact, while at times hacendados demanded a restoration of the free market in henequen, many preferred to collaborate with Henequeneros to their own economic advantage rather than dismantle it.[76]

Had a more favorable global political economy of henequen existed in the early 1930s, and had the PSS enjoyed more time to resolve the tension between grassroots demands for democratic governance and centralized organization to maximize efficiency, cooperativism might have given even poor, rural Yucatecans a chance to enjoy the benefits of revolutionary citizenship enjoyed by the "nobility" of cooperativists like the bus drivers and baratilleros. While it lacked the radical if not utopian promise of Cárdenas's agrarian reform in the henequen zone, it also lacked its colossal problems of mismanagement and economic losses that plagued the ejidos of the henequen zone. Like García Correa himself, bartolista cooperativism played a crucial role in the consolidation of a lasting postrevolutionary order but remains largely overshadowed by the hero cults of Alvarado, Carrillo Puerto, and Cárdenas.

NOTES

1. PSS intellectuals defined socialism in a variety of ways, ranging from the ideas of Henry George to those of Karl Marx. Edmundo Bolio Ontiveros, consigliere to a series of Yucatecan socialist governors from 1915 to 1933, defined socialism as "liberty, culture, and civilization." Others stressed ending the worst features of capitalism, or capitalism entirely. Edmundo Bolio Ontiveros, *Pluma obrera: Cuestiones sociales* (Mexico City: n.p., 1918), 25.

2. Other roughly contemporary examples of revolutionary capitalism include Garrido Canabal's model of cooperativism in Tabasco, and the model cotton-growing zone centered on Ciudad Anáhuac in Nuevo Leon. On the former, see Stan Ridgeway, "Monoculture, Monopoly, and the Mexican Revolution," *Mexican Studies / Estudios Mexicanos* 17, no. 1 (Winter 2001): 143–69. On the latter, see Casey Walsh, *Building the Borderlands: A Transnational History of Irrigated Cotton Along the Mexico-Texas Borderland* (College Station: Texas A&M University Press, 2008), 57–64. Cooperatives organized by the most important labor federation between 1918 and 1933, the Confederación Regional Obrera Mexicana (CROM, Mexican Regional Labor Confederation), as well as Pacific and Gulf Coast worker cooperatives, remain largely understudied.

3. Gilbert Joseph, *Rediscovering the Past at Mexico's Periphery: Essays on the History of Modern Yucatán* (Tuscaloosa: University of Alabama Press, 1986), 123–24.

4. Leftist supporters of Cárdenas of the mid-1930s and Marxian revisionist historians of the 1970s and 1980s depicted García Correa as a corrupt, sultan-like figure who opposed land reform and squashed organized labor to protect the upper class. Vicente Lombardo Toledano, *El llanto del sureste*, 2nd ed. (Mexico City: Centro de Estudios Históricos del Movimiento Obrero Mexicano, 1977). The contemporary Yucatecan and national independent press cast García Correa as a tropical despot, often using racially tinged and classist terms. See Carlos R. Menéndez, *En pos de la*

justicia: La clausura forzosa del "Diario de Yucatán" (Mérida: Compañía Tipográfica de Yucatán, 1932).

5. Gilbert Joseph and Daniel Nugent, "Popular Culture and State Formation in Revolutionary Mexico," in *Everyday Forms of State Formation: Revolution and the Negotiation of Rule in Modern Mexico* (Durham, N.C.: Duke University Press, 1994), 14; William Roseberry, *Anthropologies and Histories: Essays in Culture, History, and Political Economy* (New Brunswick, N.J.: Rutgers University Press, 1989), 226. Unlike the Venezuela case analyzed by Roseberry, in postrevolutionary Mexico only one national party governed, and it relied on regional affiliates like the PSS to organize factions of both the bourgeoisie and the proletariat until the mid-1930s.

6. Diane Davis is one of the few scholars to analyze the postrevolutionary regime attempts to cultivate middle-class support through cooperativism and other initiatives aimed at remedying capitalism's shortcomings. See Diane Davis, "Uncommon Democracy in Mexico: Middle Classes and the Military in the Consolidation of One-Party Rule, 1936–1946," in *The Social Construction of Democracy, 1870–1990*, ed. George Reid Andrews and Herrick Chapman (New York: New York University Press, 1995), 161–89; and Diane Davis, *Discipline and Development: Middle Classes and Prosperity in East Asia and Latin America* (New York: Cambridge University Press, 2004), 274–75, 290–311. On the role of socialist parties in southeastern Mexico in developing organization forms and political practices later adopted by the national ruling party, see Sarah Osten, *The Mexican Revolution's Wake: The Making of a Political System, 1920–29* (New York: Cambridge University Press, 2018).

7. On the perils of overlooking economic factors in postrevolutionary Mexican history, see Emilia Viotti da Costa, "New Publics, New Politics, New Histories: From Economic Reductionism to Cultural Reductionism—In Search of Dialectics," in *Reclaiming the Political in Latin American History*, ed. Gilbert Joseph (Durham, N.C.: Duke University Press, 2001), 17–31.

8. William Roseberry, "Political Economy," *Annual Review of Anthropology* 17 (1988): 169–70.

9. Ben Fallaw, "Bartolocallismo: Calles, García Correa, y los Henequeneros de Yucatán," *Boletín del Archivo Plutarco Elías Calles* 27 (April 1998): 1–32; Ben Fallaw, "Los fundamentos económicos del bartolismo: García Correa, los hacendados yucatecos y la industria del henequén, 1930–1933," *Unicornio* 7, no. 338 (October 19, 1997): 3–9.

10. Biographical information in this paragraph and throughout the chapter is drawn from Ben Fallaw, "Bartolomé García Correa and the Politics of Maya Identity in Postrevolutionary Yucatán, 1915–1935," *Ethnohistory* 55, no. 4 (Fall 2008): 553–78.

11. Alvaro Gamboa Ricalde, *Yucatán desde 1910*, 3 vols. (Veracruz: Imprente Standard, 1943), 1:31.

12. Paul Eiss, "Redemption's Archive: Remembering the Future in a Revolutionary Past," *Comparative Studies in Society and History* 44, no 1 (January 2002): 106–36, esp. 127.

13. Paul Eiss, "A Measure of Liberty: The Politics of Labor in Revolutionary Yucatán, 1915–1918," in *Peripheral Visions: Politics, Society, and the Challenges of Modernity*

in Yucatán, ed. Edward Terry, Ben Fallaw, Gilbert Joseph, and Edward Moseley (Tuscaloosa: University of Alabama Press, 2010), 54–55, 62, 67–70.

14.   Bartolomé García Correa to Plutarco Elías Calles, September 25, 1930, Fideicomiso Archivos Plutarco Elías Calles y Fernando Torreblanco (hereafter FAPECYFT), APEC (Archivo Plutarco Elías Calles), expediente (hereafter exp.) 67, "Garcia Correa, Bartolomé," legajo (hereafter leg.) 2; Enrique Manero, *Hacia una económica henequenera racionalmente dirigida* (Mérida: Oriente, 1935).

15.   On the cost, complication, and chaos incurred by attempts to transform most henequen haciendas into collective ejidos supported by the federal government, see Ben Fallaw, *Cárdenas Compromised: The Failure of Reform in Postrevolutionary Yucatán* (Durham, N.C.: Duke University Press, 2001).

16.   Jaime Orosa Díaz, *Legislación Henequenera en Yucatán*, 4 vols. (Mérida: Universidad Autónoma de Yucatán, 1962), 4:130–31.

17.   Alberto García Cantón, *Memorias de un ex-hacendado henequenero*, 3rd. ed. (Mérida: Shared Pen, 2012), 99–101.

18.   I borrow my definition of *rents* from anthropologist Christopher Cramer: "income derived from non-market interventions: e.g., governmental intervention to transfer use rights between beneficiaries or to create or maintain monopoly market structure." Christopher Cramer, *Violence in Developing Countries: War, Memory, Progress* (Bloomington: Indiana University Press, 2007), 174n.

19.   Francisco Naranjo, "Los millonarios de la revolución: Exordio," *Diario de Yucatán*, July 27, 1948, 1, 6.

20.   Molina insisted that Henequeneros should charge only 2.417 centavos per kilogram. Comité "Pro-Henequen," *Ante la ruina del henequen: Documentos relativos a las labores efectuadas en defensa de la industria henequera por un grupo de productores* (Mérida: Compañía Tipográfica Yucateca, 1933), 53–55. In 1933 Henequeneros exported some 97,465,500 kilograms of henequen, meaning the contested deductions could have amounted to some 2,046,775 pesos, plus another 1,235,440.58 pesos in state taxes and 487,327.50 in federal taxes. Because advances were based on the quality of henequen, the amount was probably somewhat lower. Siegfried Askinasy, *El problema agrario de Yucatán*, 2nd ed. (Mexico City: Ediciones Botas, 1936), 103.

21.   Foes alleged García Correa siphoned off funds from Henequeneros in the guise of donations to hurricane victims in Tampico and the ill-fated monument to Felipe Carrillo Puerto. *El Yucatanista*, October 28, 1933. As was the case with most of these charges, diversion of funds did not necessarily amount to theft of the funds.

22.   *La Lucha*, October 4, 1930.

23.   *Diario Oficial*, October 2, 1918, November 18, 1918; David Arthur Franz, "Bullets and Bolshevists: A History of the Mexican Revolution and Reform in Yucatán, 1910–1924" (PhD diss., University of New Mexico, 1973), 143–44.

24.   Edmundo Bolio Ontiveros, ed., *El Partido Socialista del Sureste y el futuro gobierno del Prof. Bartolomé García Correa* (Mérida: Pluma y Lapiz, 1930), 69–70; Albert Nardelli, *Un hombre representativo: Bartolomé García Correa, sus ideas y su acción en pro de los anhelos populares de Yucatán* (Mérida: Basso, 1928), 17; S. Cetina Moreno

to governor, January 21, 1917, Archivo General de Estado de Yucatán (hereafter AGEY), Poder Ejecutivo (hereafter PE), caja 565.

25. *Diario Oficial*, December 2, 1918, January 16, 1919, February 8, 1919; *La Revista de Yucatán*, January 13, 1919, February 3, 1919, June 17, 1919; *La Voz de la Revolución*, May 27, 1919, June 18, 1919.

26. Franz, "Bullets and Bolsheviks," 194; *Diario Oficial*, August 18, 1919.

27. *La Revista de Yucatán*, June 21, 1919.

28. Partido Socialista del Sureste, *Segundo Congreso Obrero de Izamal*, 2nd ed. (Mexico City: Centro de Estudios Históricos del Movimiento Obrero Mexicano, 1977), 55–61.

29. Franz, "Bullets and Bolsheviks," 194; Enrique Montalvo Ortega, *Yucatán: Sociedad, economía, política y cultura* (Mexico City: Universidad Nacional Autónoma de México, 1997) 67; Orosa Díaz, *Legislación Henequenera en Yucatán*, 4:59–62, 63–64; *Diario Oficial*, August 18, 1919.

30. *Diario Oficial*, January 21, 1918, December 2, 1918, and January 4, 1926; Rafael Bustillos Méndez, *El gran Kanxoc: José María Iturralde Traconis* (Mexico City: Fuentes Impresores, 1987), 69; Bonifacio Frías Conor, *Divorcios célebres y amores fugaces. Historia auténtica de un famoso abogado especialista en divorcios* (Mexico City: Botas, 1939), 282.

31. Carlos Macías, ed., *Plutarco Elías Calles: Pensamiento político y social* (Mexico City: Fondo de Cultura Económica, 1988), 307–9, 323–25.

32. García Correa to Calles, February 26, 1926 FAPECYFT, exp. 67, "Garcia Correa, Bartolomé," leg. 1/5; *La Lucha*, March 6, 1926; *Diario de Yucatán*, June 26, 1926; *El Clamor del Obrero*, April 10, 1929.

33. Macías, *Plutarco Elías Calles*, 307–9, 323–25.

34. Beatriz Urías Horcasitas, "Retórica, ficción y espejismo: Tres imágenes de un México bolchevique (1920–1940)," *Relaciones: Estudios de Historia y Sociedad* 26, no. 101 (2005): 263, 269.

35. Jürgen Buchenau, *Plutarco Elías Calles and the Mexican Revolution* (Lanham, Md.: Rowman and Littlefield, 2007), 111–12; Ricardo Zeveda, *Calles, el presidente* (Mexico City: Editorial Nuestro Tiempo, 1983), 116–17.

36. Partido Socialista del Sureste, *Memoria del Quinto Congreso Obrero del Partido Socialista del Sureste, inspirado en las tendencias cooperativistas: Se celebró en la ciudad de Progreso los días del 10 al 6 del mayo de 1932* (Mérida: n.p., 1932), 16.

37. Lorenzo Meyer, *Historia de la Revolución Mexicana, periodo 1928–1934: Los inicios de la institucionalización; La política del maximato* (Mexico City: El Colegio de México, 1978), 87–88.

38. Ridgeway, "Monoculture, Monopoly, and the Mexican Revolution"; Stan Ridgeway, "The Cooperative Republic of Tomas Garrido Canabal: Developmentalism and the Mexican Revolution" (PhD diss., University of North Carolina at Chapel Hill, 1996).

39. Fernando Tudela et al., *La modernización forzada del trópico: El caso de Tabasco* (Mexico City: Colegio de México, 1989), 66.

40. Baltazar Naranjo Morales, *El doctor Torre Díaz y su actuación* ([Mexico City?]: n.p., [1928?]); anonymous federal employee to Luis Morones, February 26, 1928, Archivo General de la Nación (hereafter AGN), Presidentes Obregón y Calles 307-y-2.

41. Ligas were political components of the PSS with certain social functions (representing members in labor disputes, for instance); they were not legally entitled to perform the functions of a cooperative. The distinction between ligas and cooperatives was often blurred in practice, however.

42. On the social benefits of PSS members, see Álvaro Torre Díaz, *Cuatro años en el gobierno de Yucatan, 1926–1930* (Mérida: Compañía Tipográfica Yucateca, 1930) 67, 76–81. See also party publications like *El Proletario*, June 15, 1929, and *El Clamor del Obrero*, March 20 1929.

43. On the baratilleros, see *Reglamento Interior de la Liga de Baratilleros "Andrés Ortega" y Seción de Veladoras adscritas al Gran Partido Socialista del Sureste*, 2nd ed. (Mérida: n.p., 1929), 11. On the bus drivers, see Manuel Cirerol Sansores, *Historia del transporte de pasajeros en Mérida* (Mérida: Talleres Gráficos del Sudeste, 1960); *Reglamento Interior de la Liga Protectora de Chauffeurs del Estado adscrita al Gran Partido Socialista del Sureste* (Mérida: n.p., 1925); and Carlos Loret de Mola, *Confesiones de un gobernador* (Mexico City: Grijalbo, 1978), 199–200.

44. Edmundo Bolio to Bartolomé García Correa, April 9, 1928, AGEY PE, caja 853, exp. Sección Gobierno p. 1.

45. Fallaw, "Los fundamentos económicos del bartolismo," 5.

46. Partido Socialista del Sureste, *Convocatoria para el Tercer Congreso Obrero del Partido Socialista del Sureste que se efectuará en esta ciudad del 10. al 6 de mayo de 1930* (Mérida: Gráficos "Basso," 1930), 4–5.

47. John Lear, *Workers, Neighbors, and Citizens: The Revolution in Mexico City* (Lincoln: University of Nebraska Press, 2001), 107.

48. See Partido Socialista del Sureste, *Memorias del Cuarto Congreso del Partido Socialista del Sureste: Primero del carácter agrícola-ganadero celebrado en Mérida los días del 10 al 4 de mayo de 1931* (Mérida: Gobierno del estado, 1931); Partido Socialista del Sureste, *Memoria del Quinto Congreso*.

49. Bartolomé García Correa, "Informe [de 1932] de García Correa," FAPECYFT, APEC, exp. 67, "Garcia Correa, Bartolomé," leg. 3/5 and 4/5, p. 19; Partido Socialista del Sureste, *Código del Partido Socialista del Sureste estudiado y decretado por el Tercer Congreso Obrero, reunidos del 10 al 7 mayo de 1930* (Mérida: Pluma y Lápiz, 1930), 19–20.

50. Nardelli, *Un hombre representativo*, 19, 49; Antonio Mediz Bolio and José Castillo Torre, *La agonía de Yucatán: Exposición de la actual situación política, social y económica del estado* (Mexico City: Partido Socialista del Sureste, 1932), 22.

51. Nardelli, *Un hombre representativo*, 36; Bolio Ontiveros, *El Partido Socialista del Sureste*, 34–35.

52. Luis G. Sepulvada, "El capital y el socialismo," *Tierra*, May 8, 1930. See also *Tierra*, February 9, 1928; and *Clamor del Obrero*, August 10, 1929.

53. Miguel Cantón, *En tiempos de conquista: Veinte años de acción socialista* (Mérida: Editora "Mayab" S.A., n.d.), 81–87.

54. Ley de Sociedades Cooperativas Civiles para el Estado de Yucatán, October 11, 1932, Article 25, reprinted in Partido Socialista del Sureste, *Memoria del Quinto Congreso*, 236.

55. *Clamor del Obrero*, January 17, 1929, May 10, 1929; *Diario del Sureste*, January 17, 1933.

56. *Clamor del Obrero*, December 13, 1928. See also *Clamor del Obrero*, March 31, 1929. The first use of the term *intellectual worker* in Yucatán to my knowledge occurs in the formation of the Liga de Trabajadores Intelectuales (League of Intellectual Workers) of the PSS on June 29, 1925. Its mission was "to seek the union of workers with intellectuals." Its first leadership was apparently all intellectual and no manual laborers. AGEY PE, caja 804, exp. Sección Gobierno.

57. *Clamor del Obrero*, September 29, 1928. See also Miguel Arceo Pérez, *Informe del Presidente de la Liga "Carlos Marx" relativo a su actuación en el año social de 1929* (Mérida: El Porvenir, 1929).

58. Jürgen Buchenau, "Plutarco Elías Calles and Revolutionary-Era Populism in Mexico," in *Populism in Twentieth Century Mexico: The Presidencies of Lázaro Cárdenas and Luis Echeverría*, ed. Amelia Kiddle and María Muñoz (Tucson: University of Arizona Press, 2010), 46–47.

59. "Los ideas hacen la Revolución," *Tierra*, January 16, 1928.

60. Nardelli, *Un hombre representativo*, 19, 49.

61. Partido Socialista del Sureste, *Convocatoria para el Tercer Congreso*, 9–10.

62. Lear, *Workers, Neighbors, and Citizens*, 347–350; Alicia Hernández Chávez, *Historia de la Revolución Mexicana, período 1934–1940: La mecánica cardenista* (Mexico City: Colegio de México, 1979), 130–31.

63. Daniela Spenser, "Workers Against Socialism? Reassessing the Role of Urban Labor in Yucatecan Revolutionary Politics," in *Land, Labor and Capital in Modern Yucatán: Essays in Regional History and Political Economy*, ed. Gilbert Joseph and Jeffrey Brannon (Tuscaloosa: University of Alabama Press, 1991), 220–42.

64. Efraim Palma Castro, *La cuestión henequenera: Ecos de un debate periodístico* (Mérida: Oriente, 1933), 7–8.

65. Partido Socialista del Sureste, *Convocatoria para el Tercer Congreso*, 4–5; Bartolomé García Correa, "Informe [de 1932] de García Correa," FAPECYFT, APEC exp. 67, "Garcia Correa, Bartolomé," leg. 3/5 and 4/5.

66. Partido Socialista del Sureste, *Memoria del Quinto Congreso*, 234.

67. Partido Socialista del Sureste, *Convocatoria para el Tercer Congreso*, 4.

68. Partido Socialista del Sureste, *Memoria del Quinto Congreso*, 125, 164.

69. Partido Socialista del Sureste, *Memoria del Quinto Congreso*, 188, 192–98.

70. Mediz Bolio and Castillo Torre, *La agonía de Yucatán*, 42.

71. Séptimo Pérez Palacios, Informe, November 12, 1935, Archivo Histórico de la Secretaría de Educación Pública, Dirección de Educación Federal de Yucatán, caja 1395, exp. Asuntos administrativos.

72.   Frank Ralph Brandenburg, "Mexico: An Experiment in One-Party Democracy" (PhD diss., University of Pennsylvania, 1956), 260; Loret de Mola, *Confesiones de un gobernador*, 199–200.

73.   *Diario de Yucatán*, July 5, 1927, cited in Timothy Henderson, "Unraveling Revolution: Yucatán, 1924–1930" (master's thesis, University of Texas, 1988), 154n1. The relationship between gender inequality and cooperativism requires further investigation. With García Correa's support, Elía María Aban organized a cooperative in 1930–31 to manufacture and sell hammocks and other goods. In an interview, she said that women should enjoy suffrage only by participating in production and no longer being economically subordinated—without abandoning their domestic responsibilities as mothers. *Diario del Sureste*, December 10, 1931.

74.   Gabriel Ferrer de Mendiolea, "Historia de las comunicaciones," in *Enciclopedia Yucatanense*, vol. 3 (Mexico City: Gobierno de Yucatán, 1977), 563–64.

75.   José Luis Domínguez, "Situación política en el partido de Sotuta (1911–16)," in *Yucatán: Peonaje y liberación*, ed. Blanca Gonzalez R. et al. (Mérida: Fondo Nacional para Actividades Sociales, 1981), 202nn24–25.

76.   Fallaw, "Los fundamentos económicos del bartolismo," 3–5.

9

COMMUNAL WORK, FORCED LABOR, AND ROAD BUILDING IN MEXICO, 1920–1958

BENJAMIN T. SMITH

I N 1940 a group of villagers from the Oaxaca town of Zapotitlán Lagunas wrote to the president to protest that the local authorities were forcing them to build a new road for free. Every day, local policemen stormed into their houses, pulled them out of bed, and marched them to the site of the new route. Here, they were forced at gunpoint to work for twelve hours without food, rest, or remuneration. They had never agreed to the project and as "proletarians" they deserved at least the minimum salary for such labor. In reply, the local mayor claimed that these villagers formed a small minority. They were longtime refuseniks, who had repeatedly disobeyed the authorities and simply wanted to "interrupt works of public utility" and "hamper a village that wants to progress." As the mayor explained, "Tomorrow Zapotitlán will be a town of great improvements, an airfield, a road, and other improvements . . . from which we will obtain happiness." Most had accepted his claims and "offered their labor with good will."[1]

In the years following the Mexican Revolution, the Mexican state attempted to rebuild the country. The program involved political debates between federal forces and regional powerbrokers, socioeconomic ventures including land distribution and union support designed to diminish inequality, and cultural efforts aimed at integrating Mexico's socially and ethnically diffuse population into the nation. But the scheme also involved the construction of major infrastructure projects, airfields, schools, civil buildings, and most importantly roads. To date, few historians have examined this process, preferring to view the practice of state formation as a set of relatively pacific cultural negotiations between government-backed emissaries and the mass of urban and rural Mexicans.[2] Yet, as a handful of historians have started to argue, postrevolutionary state formation comprised not only cultural but also material processes.[3] These reconfigured national, regional, and local economies; realigned political and economic elites; and reestablished social hierarchies. They also regularly involved the deployment of violence by soldiers, local police forces, and off-the-books hitmen.[4] Often, this violence had overtly political aims and was designed to impose unpopular authorities, disband troublesome voters, or extinguish small-scale insurrections. But, as in the case of Zapotitlán Lagunas, federal and local governments also used coercion of the poorest, most vulnerable, and often indigenous members of society in order to fulfil what they deemed as economic necessities. The modern, interconnected, economically stable Mexico that emerged in the 1940s and 1950s was as much the product of forced labor as intricate cultural interactions.

In the immediate postrevolutionary period, bureaucrats and intellectuals often debated the line between consensual communal work (also called *faena*, *fagina*, *tequio*, and *cuatequitl*) and coerced labor. According to the revolutionary Constitution of 1917, the former was admissible while the latter was banned. As a result, supporters of the practice, like the Zapotitlán Lagunas mayor, often stressed that villagers offered their services voluntarily. Thus, in the early 1920s, the Sierra de Puebla's military commander reported that the local communities built the required roads with such "overwhelming enthusiasm," the national government only needed to supply "technical advice and equipment." Even equipment was not really needed: "there is already much in the Sierra," and workers were happy to use their own picks and shovels.[5] A handful of visiting anthropologists were similarly enthused. For Robert Redfield, who lived in the Morelos village of Tepoztlán during the late 1920s, cuatequitl (another term for communal labor) was a pre-Hispanic tradition that carried with it a common moral obligation and "was not lightly denied."[6] For Guillermo Bonfil Batalla, villagers undertook collective work "with a fiesta spirit, an atmosphere of social sharing between the members of a lineage, a barrio or an entire community." It "reinforce[d] solidarity" and had "social, symbolic and entertainment functions as well as purely economic ones."[7]

But many Mexicans, like the refuseniks of Zapotitlán Lagunas, were less enthusiastic. Instead they emphasized the coerced nature of much of the labor, which they held to run contrary to the emancipatory promises of the revolution. In 1941, for example, the head of Oaxaca's Departamento Autonómo de Asuntos Indígenas (Department of Indigenous Affairs) called communal work "a regime of slavery," in which "peasants are forced to lend their services against their will and without remuneration as messengers, shepherds, and beasts of burdens to authorities and private companies. . . . They deny it is slavery and instead call it '*tequio*' [the name for communal labor in Oaxaca]."[8] Urban intellectuals, who made brief trips out to the countryside, were also horrified. One broadsheet journalist called the communal labor of Guerrero's Costa Chica "a slavery like that of the colony."[9] And a handful of anthropologists such as Oscar Lewis, who lived in Tepoztlán two decades later than Redfield, were similarly unenthused. Lewis viewed cuatequitl as the colonial bastardization of a pre-Hispanic practice, "a coercive rather than a voluntary institution," which predominantly fell on the poor as they had "little political influence and a greater fear of the authorities." In fact, villagers so resented the custom that children taunted each other with the refrain, "Unless you do this, I will give you cuatequitl."[10]

As the Zapotitlán Lagunas situation suggests, at the local level, the imposition of communal labor had even more disruptive effects. Intellectual debate was one thing; being forced from one's bed at gunpoint and obliged to build a road for free was another. As we shall see, the line between communal and forced labor exposed the paradoxes of postrevolutionary state formation in three distinct ways. First, it showed the disjunction between the state's modernization projects and its inability to collect sufficient taxes to fund these plans.[11] As even its supporters argued, communal labor allowed Mexican elites to build roads, irrigation canals, and schools on the cheap. Second, it revealed the gap between the government's aspirations for political control and Mexican villages' tradition of political autonomy, which had, in part, motivated many to join the revolution.[12] In theory, all participants were meant to consent to communal labor. But what did this mean in practice? Did people agree through participatory democracy, at a public meeting and with a show of hands? Or did they have to obey by the rules of representative democracy and obey the commands of an elected town mayor or a faraway governor?[13] And what if people refused? Did the authorities have the right to force labor on the incompliant? Finally, it also exposed the conflict between the revolutionary regime's promises of economic redistribution and its maintenance of a capitalist economy. Labor projects were held to offer "communal benefits," but were these benefits distributed evenly throughout communities? Many believed they were not. Protestors complained that roads, in particular, struck at the redistributive aims of the revolution. In fact, they exacerbated economic inequality by offering those with large agricultural properties access to expanded markets and those with capital the opportunity to monopolize transport routes.

As communal labor exposed these fiscal, political, and redistributive contradictions, it generated ample opposition. Villagers not only wrote complaints; they took to the streets to protest their inconformity, voted out or ejected exacting local authorities, adopted go-slow policies, and, most often, refused to work. Throughout Mexico, authorities sought diverse solutions. Many simply used force, employing local police, judicial authorities, and nearby military detachments to force reluctant villagers to work. But others attempted more negotiated resolutions. Some reinserted participatory democracy into the system of representative government, establishing irregular village meetings where mass voting would decide on communal labor projects. Others tried economic concessions, persuading villagers to build roads in exchange for offers of jobs or land. Others still retreated, rerouting roads and irrigation channels around population centers that refused to offer their labor.

In order to examine the effects of the postrevolutionary state's employment of communal labor, I have divided this chapter into four sections. In the first, I offer a historical overview of the uses and abuses of communal labor up to the revolution. In the second, I use a handful of academic studies and more than one hundred complaints about the exploitation of communal work sent to Mexico's presidents from villages throughout the republic. These not only map out the chronology, geography, and local dynamics of exploitation but also reveal how the continuation of communal labor accentuated the paradoxes mentioned above. Third, I focus on struggles over the construction of roads, which accounted for the vast majority of peasant complaints. And finally, I look at ways in which the authorities used both force and negotiation in order to impose these labor regimes.

A BRIEF HISTORY OF COMMUNAL LABOR

Throughout the twentieth century, defenders of communal labor regularly pointed to the custom's pre-Hispanic roots.[14] But the ambit and aim of communal labor changed dramatically over time. And, if postrevolutionary tensions over the practice were particularly virulent, they were nothing new. For centuries, the use and abuse of communal labor had exposed anxieties over political control, social hierarchy, and race. During the nineteenth century, the practice became particularly politicized. Postindependence villages redefined communal labor to include former nobles and refocused work on immediate needs. Midcentury liberals redefined the practice yet again, banning personal services, extending labor to include nonindigenous groups, and curtailing its use to fulfill church tasks. And Porfirian elites, especially in the heavily indigenous states of Chiapas and Yucatán, co-opted the custom to provide labor for the expansion of capitalist, export agriculture.

Villagers had used communal labor to perform certain tasks since pre-Hispanic times. Nahua, Mixtec, Zapotec, and Maya communities had banded together to harvest crops, build irrigation canals, carve out and clear paths, clean ceremonial centers, and do piecemeal artisanal work for their lords for centuries.[15] A strong moral code enforced these labors. For one of Spanish chronicler Bernardino Sahagun's informers, "the good man" was "a worker, a sage, a willing worker—one who works willingly." The "bad man" was "uncooperative, irresponsible, impetuous, he works without consideration." And, at least according to post-Conquest sources, such collective work was undertaken voluntarily: "In the old days they performed their communal labor in their own towns. . . . They did their work together and with much merriment, for they are people who do little work alone, but together they accomplish something."[16]

The Spanish Conquest not only changed the social hierarchy but also shifted the process and aims of collective labor. Spaniards now harnessed communal toil to their own *repartimiento* system, a rotating scheme of draft labor designed to balance out the declining indigenous work force. Spanish-legitimated governors rather than the traditional ruling houses now decided on who would work. Peasants now worked under Hispanic employers or foremen. And the tasks were more "Hispanic in nature."[17] They included the construction and cleaning of Catholic temples, and the production of goods and materials to be sold on the market in Spanish cities.

In Mexico, repartimiento declined. But local elites continued to use communal labor. Elites in the main towns or *cabeceras* ordered men and women from small subject villages or *sujetos* to perform multiple tasks, including the collection of charcoal, the cleaning of central squares, and even the cooking of meals.[18] Like their pre-Hispanic forebears, indigenous nobles or caciques demanded that commoners provide both general and personal services. In the Oaxaca village of Cuyotepeji, in 1783 peasants claimed that the cacique requested not only thirty bushels of maize, beans, and chili but also "two Indian servants for his house and a woman to grind the corn."[19] Such duties were broadly accepted. They formed part of a moral economy. Governors and caciques were entrusted with protecting villages, securing outside aid, and administering justice fairly.[20] They also formed part of the indigenous village cargo system; each male community member was expected to perform such tasks in order to climb the village's political hierarchy.[21]

But increasingly such duties could also cause tensions. Many peasants resented more Hispanicized nobles using communal labor in order to profit off expanding markets for consumer goods. In the 1770s, villagers repeatedly complained about the female noble or *cacica* of Ihualtepec (Oaxaca), who demanded four Indians to work as textile workers and domestic servants in her house each week. Villagers were also forced to travel on their own dime "to distant lands" to sell her merchandise. In contrast, declining noble families begrudged doing communal labor at all.[22] Juan López of the Oaxaca Sierra village of Santa María Yabichui complained that by forcing him to fetch fodder for the priest's horse, villagers "wanted to treat me as a commoner, usurping the privileges acquired by my forefathers."[23]

After independence, communal labor transformed. As politicians banned hereditary distinctions, the personal services demanded by caciques disappeared. At the same time, remaining communal duties became more democratic. Former nobles were drafted into villages' work forces.[24] And communal labor focused on small-scale, communitarian tasks, including harvesting crops, cleaning the streets, clearing irrigation channels, and building and maintaining local churches and chapels. In fact, in many regions, religious works seem to have comprised the bulk of the major tasks.[25] For example, between 1821 and 1867 around a third of the northern Oaxaca district of Huajuapan's villages built churches. At the same time, they constructed thirteen sturdy houses for priests. These were all built through communal labor.[26] In 1845 the authorities of Miltepec (Oaxaca) started to construct a church around their miraculous image of a crucified Christ. The work not only "concentrated the desires of diverse classes"; some even came to work on their free days. And by appeasing the village saint, the work had brought "further benefits," reducing small-scale crime and increasing attendance at Mass.[27]

The ascendance of Mexico's liberals during the 1850s shifted communal labor yet again. Like their revolutionary descendants, many liberals viewed the practice as a colonial hangover. Article 12 of the 1857 Constitution explicitly prohibited the imposition of personal services on citizens without fair compensation and consent. Specific prohibitions varied from region to region. But many states were relatively strict, especially on the matter of the church's use of communal labor. The 1861 Puebla constitution outlawed all public officials from demanding services without remuneration and abolished the village office of *topil* or bailiff, the person normally responsible for handing out communal tasks. Traditional communal jobs like messengers, sacristans, and bell ringers were banned. But some services were still allowed, including community policing, the clearing of paths, and those services "required for common benefit and security." This clause permitted the use of communal labor for the construction and maintenance of roads, schools, and public buildings. Finally, in Puebla at least, nonindigenous villagers were commanded to perform these communal tasks. At first these reforms were extremely popular. Less pious villagers could now take exacting priests to court. In 1862 Puebla's civil court forbade the priest of Xalacapan from demanding that villagers construct him a new corral. And populist caciques, like Juan Francisco Lucas, employed the new measures to drum up support in indigenous villages by shanghaiing snooty mestizo elites to work on roads, bridges, and schools.[28]

But during the Porfiriato, the more exploitative use of communal labor returned. Porfirio Díaz's cash-strapped unelected regional chiefs, the *jefes políticos*, led the way. They viewed the custom as a cheap means to rebuild post–civil war Mexico. In the 1870s, Manuel Arriaga, the chief of Zacapoaxtla (Puebla), refused to listen to complaints about the constitutional abolition of the practice. Instead he reimposed communal labor as a means to construct roads, town halls, and schools.[29] The practice often bled into prohibited personal services. In Caxhuacan (Puebla), the mayor ordered villagers to build a new main square. To do so, villagers were forced to demolish the houses of two mestizo residents and erect replacements in their stead.[30] In Yucatán, jefes políticos also redirected the custom, using their "vast discretionary power over lives" to deploy peasants to build roads, clean plazas, and dredge the waters of rivers.[31] And in regions of expanding export crops like coffee, timber, and rubber, jefes políticos used communal labor to provide workers for unpaid agricultural work. In San Bartolomé (Chiapas), political authorities threatened villagers with conscription, confiscated their tools so they could not work on their own projects, and forced them to work unpaid for two weeks at nearby fincas.[32] In Zimatlán (Oaxaca), Zapotec villagers were forced to work one day for free at the hacienda of San Nicolás.[33] This refocusing of communal labor toward capitalist agriculture reimposed the practice's racial implications. By the end of the nineteenth century, mestizo elites used the custom of communal labor to exploit indigenous groups.

COMMUNAL LABOR IN POSTREVOLUTIONARY MEXICO

During the revolution, indigenous peasants took advantage of the breakdown of political control to slough off communal labor. In the Sierra Norte de Puebla, liberated villagers even stopped clearing water channels and nearby paths.[34] And in 1917 revolutionaries restated the old 1857 regulations regarding the practice. Article 5 prohibited personal services "without just retribution and full consent." The only exceptions were jury service, conscription, electoral office, and council work. Despite these rules, in postrevolutionary Mexico, much communal labor continued to be forced. Between 1934 and 1958, villagers sent more than one hundred letters and telegrams, which complained to successive Mexican presidents about local authorities continuing to use the practice without consent or remuneration.

These were the tip of the iceberg. Many indigenous Mexicans were unable to speak Spanish, let alone compose a letter of grievance. And many complaints never reached higher than the municipal authorities, the local deputy, or the state governor. My own work in Oaxaca indicates that the forcible imposition of communal labor for certain projects was prevalent and widely begrudged. And oral testimonies back this up. Frans Schryer found that in Hidalgo, Nahua peasants "bitterly resented [the] obligatory labor as well as the onerous duty of serving as messengers or couriers, even if they had done so once or twice in their life."[35] Florencio Cruz Cruz, a Zapotec peasant from the Sierra Juárez, remembered how three days of backbreaking labor on the Villa Alta–Oaxaca City road persuaded him to leave his village and flee to the comparative sanctuary of the local teacher training college.[36]

Despite the evidence's limitations, at the most basic level, these complaints suggest the geography of communal labor: the coercion of communal labor still fell most heavily on the country's indigenous population. Of the complaints, 68 percent came from the six southern states of Chiapas, Guerrero, Oaxaca, Puebla, Tabasco, and Veracruz (figure 1). These states all contained high proportions of indigenous groups. In 1940 Chiapas, Puebla, and Oaxaca alone contained more than half the country's monolingual indigenous adults. Other specific regions,

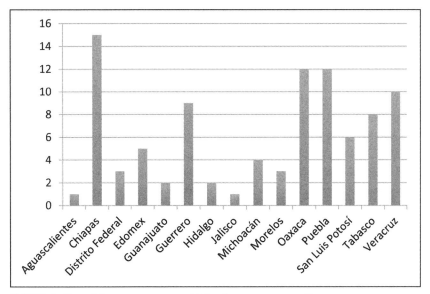

FIGURE 1. Complaints over communal labor by state, 1934–1958

which produced ample complaints, also comprised large indigenous groups. During the 1940s, Huasteca communities in the San Luis Potosí sierra made six complaints, which varied from the imposition of policing duties to forced labor on landowners' estates. A handful of explicit references back this up. In 1938 Marín Santiago of Tzicuilan (Puebla) complained that local authorities forced "exploited Indians" to work on bridge construction without pay.[37] A year later, Marcelino Santos protested that the "Indians and villagers" of El Bosque (Chiapas) were forced to work from 4:00 a.m. to dusk on the construction of a new road. Some were paid a risible amount, but most received nothing. "Threats, insults, and bad treatment" were frequent. And if villagers refused, local policemen hauled them from their beds and forced them to work.[38]

But not all complaints over communal labor came from remote, indigenous regions. In fact, a handful of urban authorities also tried to impose the practice on unwilling citizens. In 1941 Tomás Valencia from the Mexico City barrio of Tlalpan complained that the capital's authorities had forced poor locals to work on diverse construction projects for free.[39] Three years later, the men and women of San Miguel Ajusco, a village just outside Tlalpan, made a similar complaint, arguing that Mexico City representatives had tried to coerce them to work on the new water system running into the capital.[40]

These complaints also suggest the chronology of coerced communal labor (figure 2). During the presidencies of Lázaro Cárdenas and Manuel Avila Camacho, 70 percent of the complaints were made. Cárdenas's presidency, in particular, has often been viewed as the high point of the state's redistributive policies. But, like that of his successor, his term also combined a state-led drive for infrastructure construction with low tax income. And many authorities viewed unpaid communal labor as the sole means to get jobs done. These presidencies also experienced ongoing tensions over church-state relations. As we shall see, a handful of complaints exposed rural divisions between those who saw communal labor as a means to fulfill religious obligations and those who saw the practice as a way to provide secular schools, playing fields, and teachers' houses. During Miguel Alemán's tenure, complaints declined. There is some logic to this. Alemán often stressed that the country had reached the "constructive phase" of the revolution, and per capita spending on infrastructure did increase dramatically during the period.[41] But this also may be a statistical anomaly. There are no complaints from 1947 to 1950, which suggests gaps in the archival record rather than an effective program to wipe out the practice.[42] Complaints during Adolfo Ruiz Cortines's presidency were also relatively low. As I shall suggest, by this period national, state, and local governments had instituted means to dampen popular resentment over coerced communal labor.

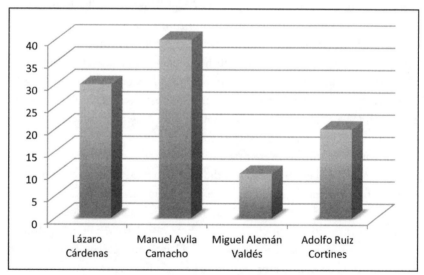

FIGURE 2. Complaints against communal labor by president, 1934–1958

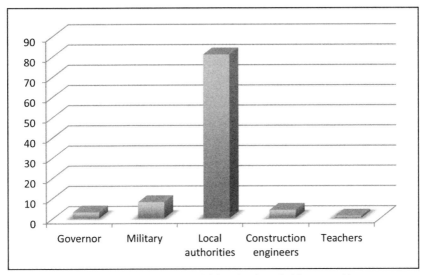

FIGURE 3. Complaints against communal labor, by those held responsible, 1934–1958

The complaints also indicate those responsible for imposing unpopular communal labor (figure 3). In 80 percent of cases, protestors blamed municipal governments explicitly. In theory, all adult males (and after 1947 all adult females as well) were allowed to take part in municipal votes. This was classic, representative democracy. These elections were designed to offer authorities a popular remit to impose communal labor as they saw fit. Election implied popular consent. But often, legal regulations over elections were not strictly applied. Governors, deputies, and caciques regularly imposed their own candidates, by scamming or by ignoring the popular vote.[43] And even when villagers elected the authorities by a fair majority, certain socioeconomic, ethnic, or geographically separate minorities resisted municipal control. Here, participatory democracy and traditions of horizontal decision-making clashed against the vertical expectations of representative government. Small minorities simply refused to do the work agreed upon by village majorities.

But not all complaints focused on municipal governments. Other state authorities also imposed coerced communal work. In eight cases, local military leaders shanghaied locals to build roads or construct barracks. As Thomas Rath argues, during the postrevolutionary period, the Mexican military effectively acted as a rural police force; 20 percent of municipalities contained small military detachments.[44] These were isolated, underfunded, and under little local support. They were often also led by military commanders, who sought to use their position to secure private incomes. As a result, they regularly used armed force to compel rural villagers to complete works either on behalf of the government or for their own benefit. In 1943 the villagers of Zacacuautla (Hidalgo) complained that the military chief of the unit based in Honey (Puebla) forced locals to collect fodder for his horses and do unpaid work on the Mexico City–Tuxpan road. To ensure compliance, he set up a machine gun by the side of the road and ordered his men to shoot anyone who left. Discontent spread and at one meeting, a local man, Abraham Vargas, stood up to complain. Although he was "one-eyed and one-armed," the chief—Fortino Ortiz—took out his pistol and shot him dead. His soldiers then opened fire, killing three peasants and injuring another five.[45] In 1944 the commander of Ciudad Ixtepec (Oaxaca) was similarly exacting. He not only claimed Germany was going to win the war but also forced villagers to hang a soldier for drinking, rob railway runners, and "work like slaves on the Salina Cruz road." He demanded that each worker cart 150 wheelbarrows of dirt to the construction each day.[46]

Finally, the complaints reveal the types of communal labor that postrevolutionary Mexicans opposed. As the historical overview suggests, communal labor could apply to a wide range of activities. At the most acceptable end were small-scale traditional efforts with immediate, visible, economic benefits. In rural Mexico, neighbors continued to practice communal harvests and the clearing of local irrigation canals and paths. As Oscar Lewis witnessed, they did so without complaint.[47] But other practices were more controversial. In a handful of cases, villagers complained about lending their free labor to staff the local police. In 1945, for example, locals from San Martín Coyoc (Puebla) complained that the municipal president forced them to spend their nights on police patrols without remuneration. The president had written up the old custom as a municipal duty, but as the villagers pointed out, it was still unconstitutional.[48] Rural villagers also occasionally complained about erecting new municipal buildings. In 1941 villagers from Tzicuilan protested that the municipal president of Cuetzalan (Puebla) forced them to work every Monday "like beasts of burden" on the construction of the town hall. If they refused, municipal police arrived, knocked down their doors, dragged them to prison, and imposed a peso fine.[49]

During the first two decades after the revolution, controversies over the use of communal labor also exposed divisions over church–state relations.[50] In more Catholic towns, municipal authorities regularly teamed up with priests and lay church leaders to demand villagers voluntarily commit labor to projects that benefited the church. These were traditions going back centuries. But now anticlerical locals, encouraged by the state's opposition to the church, complained about fulfilling these works. In 1937 the villagers of Tlapexco (Morelos) complained that the mayor and the local priest both demanded that they build a road to the sanctuary of Zacualpilla. The road was designed to increase traffic to the annual fiesta. But, as the protestors, argued, it was not "of public utility" but simply increased the coffers of the church and a handful of rich merchants.[51] Four years later, the peasants of Pinotepa Nacional on the Oaxaca Coast complained that the municipal authorities, the landowners, and the local priest continued to appoint pliant indigenous men as "*mandones*," who were charged with forcing other indigenous locals to rebuild, repair, and clean the town's churches.[52]

In other regions, authorities employed communal labor to build schools. During the 1930s, when many Catholics still held the state policy of socialist education to be impious and even atheist, this could also cause conflict.[53] In 1936 the villagers of Churumuco (Michoacán) complained that the municipal president and the local teacher demanded that they construct the local school. They argued that this was unnecessary; they already had a small, Catholic establishment.[54] In 1937 the villagers of Techimal (Hidalgo) made a similar complaint. They claimed to appreciate that the authorities had established an indigenous boarding school in the village, but they complained that authorities and teachers were forcing them to build the school themselves. They were working ten to twelve hours and paid only twenty-five to thirty centavos a day.[55]

But protests over providing police services and building town halls, schools, and temples comprised only 10 percent of complaints. As I have suggested, these records represented only a small minority of actual conflicts. In remote, indigenous regions, in-depth research reveals that caciques in particular used the imposition of communal labor to dominate or punish certain groups. In Hidalgo, Juvencio Nochebuena used the collective labor of Nahua communities to work on his own fields and farms. (His sons, somewhat naïvely, thought Indians liked him so much they came "to work for him for free.")[56] In the Huasteca region, Gonzalo Santos did the same.[57] And in Oaxaca's Región Mixe, Luis Rodríguez also demanded municipal presidents provide indigenous workers for free labor at his beck and call. In a series of letters to the municipal president of Tlahuitoltepec (Oaxaca), he demanded what he termed "mozos" or servants to deliver messages; clean roads, squares, and public buildings; build schools; tend to his own coffee plantations; carry coffee; and even form musical bands and basketball teams.[58] In fact, in 1938 more than half the population of the Mixe village of Mazatlán ran away to live in the mountains and escape Rodríguez's demands. They complained that his local representative had used the cacique's gunmen to force all the community to carry concrete from the distant town of Matias Romero to build the local school.[59]

These examples are difficult to track down. In some regions, they were clearly relatively common. But evidence remains locked away in dusty municipal archives or in the memories of the victims. And, in general, outside remote indigenous areas, communal labor toward these ends was broadly agreed upon, or divvied up, in a manner that excluded groups that refused to work. National or state ministries of education often dealt directly with conflicts over school construction, and, during the 1930s, villages that refused to build educational establishments simply did not get schools.[60]

ROADS AND COMMUNAL LABOR

The vast majority (90 percent) of complaints over the coercion of communal labor concerned the construction of roads. During the postrevolutionary period, successive governments, whatever their political leanings, united over their support for road construction. As early as 1918, President Venustiano Carranza announced that "highways deserve special attention. . . . It is absolutely necessary that the country has a complete road network."[61] During the 1930s, left-wing president Lázaro Cárdenas agreed, arguing that roads allowed newly liberated *ejidatarios* to sell their crops on the cash market.[62] And a decade later, so did right-wing president Miguel Alemán. During the 1940s, officials claimed that roads would allow large commercial farmers and industrialists to sell their goods in the country's rapidly expanding cities or even abroad.[63] Such concerted efforts generated impressive results.

Bare statistics, however, fail to reveal the mechanics of road building at the local level. Financing road construction was a combined effort. The federal government offered considerable cash. In fact, in 1949 money for transportation and communications reached a peak of 30.7 percent of the national budget.[64] But such support was not enough. State and local governments were also expected to chip in. But during the postrevolutionary period, local tax revenues struggled to keep up. Land distribution and regulations protecting ejidatarios from overtaxing cut into property taxes. The centralization of industrial and commercial taxes reduced levies still further. And tax evasion and antitax protests kept revenues low. Between 1910 and 1949, federal taxes increased sevenfold, state taxes only threefold, and municipal taxes by barely 50 percent. By the 1960s, federal income dwarfed state and municipal incomes. Under Adolfo López Mateos, municipalities received just 3 percent of total contributions.[65]

Low fiscal revenues shaped local approaches to road building. And especially in rural, indigenous areas, authorities used free communal labor to save cash. These generated considerable disagreements. Most conflicts hinged on the matter of consent. Rural refuseniks repeatedly argued that they had never agreed to do the work. In politically divided regions, struggles were particularly intense. For example, during the 1920s, Sierra cacique Gabriel Barrios Cabrera and the town of Zacapoaxtla (Puebla) were in constant dispute. When Barrios Cabrera tried to persuade locals to use communal labor on the Zaragoza–Tecolutla road project, villagers flatly refused. And when he sent in gunmen to enforce the policy, villagers complained that they had never consented to the project and asked the government to end "the exploitation experienced by our people since the time of the conquest."[66]

During the 1950s, in the Morelos village of Tetela, conflicts were also frequent. Here, the village was divided into two political groups. One wanted to construct a local market, the other a bridge and road. When the pro-road group tried to force one hundred men to perform communal labor on the project, the pro-market group rebelled. Three died in the resulting shootout.[67] In the northern Oaxaca district of Huajuapan, conflicts over road building also overlaid political divisions. From the 1940s onward, villages or individuals that voted for the opposition party, the Partido Acción Nacional (PAN, National Action Party), repeatedly complained that they were targeted for communal work on road-building projects.[68] In 1950 the pro-PAN locals of Tequixtepec even claimed that the district military commander had forced them to work on the Tehuacán–Huajuapan road but had also deliberately deviated the route so as to avoid benefiting their village.[69]

Conflicts over consent also intersected with divisions between municipal head towns or cabeceras and small, subject villages called *rancherías* or *agencias*. These not only pitted influential powerbrokers against small, politically weak hamlets but also often cut across racial divisions. Most municipal authorities were mestizo while in the south especially agencias were more likely to be predominantly indigenous. In 1935 José P. Avila of Barrio del Carmen (Oaxaca) complained that the municipal authorities of Silacayoapan (Oaxaca) were forcing all the agencia's men to work on the road rather than harvest their crops.[70] A year later, the villagers of the small ranchería of Arena (Oaxaca) protested that the municipal authorities of Lalana (Oaxaca) had imposed a mestizo outsider as the ranchería's municipal representative. He was now coercing locals to build the Lalana–Choapan road.[71] In Yalálag (Oaxaca) during the 1930s, anthropologist Julio de la Fuente observed that villagers looked on communal labor with "repugnance and hostility . . . when it was not ordered by the pueblo authorities but by outsiders." Conflicts peaked in 1935 when the cabecera demanded that the villagers help construct the Villa Alta–Oaxaca City road. De la Fuente claimed that in Villa Alta (Oaxaca), the locals derided the Yalálag workers and called them the "slaves of Villa Alta."[72]

If some conflicts centered on matters of consent, others focused on the route's economic benefit. During the postrevolutionary period, left-wing politicians often extolled the equalizing potential of roads. In 1928 Veracruz governor Adalberto Tejeda argued that roads "dissolved monopolies and capitalist exploitation and gave back to the community more than they paid in taxes to construct them."[73] In some cases, this may have been the case. But, in general, it was not. And constructing a road from a municipal center to a market hub failed to distribute payback uniformly. Rich locals often provided the buses and trucks, which poor locals had to pay for; they also put traditional mule drivers out of business.[74] As markets expanded, large landowners, not small subsistence farmers, made the greatest gains. And faraway villages profited less than those close to the new road. Many Mexicans were well aware of these potential inequalities. They made quick, basic calculations and decided that offering their labor to build a road rather than using it to harvest more crops or focus on other economic activities was simply not worth it.

For example, in 1945 the villagers of La Victoria (Veracruz) complained that the municipal government was forcing them to work on the road to the petrol hub of Poza Rica for free. They acknowledged that the road would open up new sources of jobs, but long-term prospects would not satisfy short-term needs: "We do not believe it is just that we have to submit to inquisitorial work without any remuneration that will help our families that are in a precarious situation."[75] In 1953 Pedro Martínez protested that for five years, the municipal authorities of Zumpahuacan (State of Mexico) had forced the villagers of Aguacingo to work on the Tenancingo–Zumpahuacan road. If they refused to work, they were threatened with death. Yet for Aguacingo residents, the highway was unusable. They lived on the other side of the valley, a full day's walk from the start of the road.[76] Three years later, the villagers of Sánchez Magallanes (Tabasco) complained that the municipal authorities were forcing them to repair and clean the nearby road to Cuauhtemotzín. As they explained, villagers never used the road; they were subsistence farmers. Instead, most traffic consisted of Pemex oil trucks.[77] In the same year, the villagers of Xamatipan (Veracruz) made a similar complaint. Municipal authorities had ordered them to spend their faenas building a road from the cabecera to a nearby market town. As they explained, for them, the road was useless. Rains had washed away the bridges between their own village and the cabecera. They could not get to the road, even if they wanted to. Rebuilding the bridges was a more profitable use of their labor.[78]

As wage labor increased, the loss of potential cash income also shaped peasants' attitudes toward this type of communal work. Living on the edge meant many instinctively understood marginal rates of return. In 1955 the ejidatarios of San José Providencia (Puebla) grumbled that the local authorities were forcing them to offer free labor to build the municipal road. If they refused, they were thrown in jail and fined. As they explained, they were "poor, very poor." Working every day, they barely managed to feed their dependents. Unpaid labor, days in prison, and fines made life financially impossible.[79] Two years later Ascención Granada and fifteen other villagers from San José Iturbide (Guanajuato) made a similar complaint. They protested that the municipal president had ordered them to help build the road from their agencia to the municipality. They admitted that the route had long-term advantages, but three days of unpaid communal labor lost workers nine pesos per week. They simply could not afford to sustain their families.[80]

FORCE AND NEGOTIATION

Opposition to the use of communal labor for road building was extremely widespread, and local authorities sought a wide array of solutions. The most frequent was brute force. A handful of town chiefs allied with nearby military commanders to dragoon workers. In 1942 the mayor of La Unión (Guerrero) helped local soldiers track down suspected bandits. In return, the commander arrested vagrants and loiterers and put them to work cleaning and repairing the local roads.[81] But most used state or municipal police. These could preempt labor needs by periodically arresting villagers and forcing them to work. In 1949 in Teloloapan (Guerrero), every Sunday the police jailed fifteen people, who would work off their crime by toiling on the local pipeline for the next five days.[82] They could break into houses, turf people out of bed, and frog-march them to the roads like they did in Zapotitlán Lagunas and El Bosque in 1939 or Tzicuilan and Acatlán (Puebla) in 1942.[83] They could provide armed guards for reluctant workers. In 1946 more than three hundred San Luis Potosí ejidatarios complained that the municipal president of Coxcatlán (Puebla) not only shook them down for cash but also forced them to work for free on cross-country roads and on his own maize and sugar cane fields. When a handful protested, nearby police shot five dead.[84]

They could also lock refuseniks in jail. In 1941 police in Tecomatlán (Puebla) arrested three men for allegedly refusing to do communal work. At least two claimed they were sick.[85] As one villager from Pachivia (Guerrero) remembered, "The school, the town hall, the church, the electricity . . . if you don't cooperate you'll go to jail, if you don't cooperate for the school, for the church, you'll go to jail, and with a good thrashing."[86] Finally, they could impose fines. These varied from place to place. In Tzicuilan in 1942, the fine was one peso; in Zitacuaro (Michoacán) in 1958, it was five pesos; and in Coxcatlán in 1946, it was a punitive twenty-five pesos.[87]

Occasionally unwilling workers tried to bypass municipal police forces and bring in state arbiters. But this seldom worked. In 1957 in San José Iturbide, they requested the state prosecutor intervene in the dispute about communal labor. Instead, the governor sent the judicial police. After signing what they thought was their statement of complaint, the head of the judicial police revealed that the forced laborers had actually signed a promise to work: "Now you've really fucked yourselves and there's no way out, you'll have to work for Don Moises [the municipal president] and if you don't, we'll send you to Granaditas [a colloquial term for jail] and there we will hang you." Having sorted out the matter, the police chief went off to drink with the mayor.[88]

But not all local authorities used force. Officials also sought negotiated settlements. Some sought to ameliorate the economic losses of free laborers. If possible, they started to pay road-building villagers. Often they used food, alcohol, and cigarettes. The head of the work draft in El Potrero (Guerrero) always managed to find willing workers. "I did not forget," he claimed, "to bring picnics, and mescal, cigarettes, the people carried all [the telegraph poles] for me."[89] Oscar Lewis observed that one feature of collective labor in Tepoztlán was "the free use of drink": "It would seem that the Tepoztecans need the stimulus of drink to enable them to work together successfully."[90]

Others used the offer of free road-building equipment. During the 1920s, the governor of Veracruz offered peasants of Las Vigas the picks and shovels needed to build the nearby road.[91]

But some also started to pay the cash. In 1944 the government of Chiapas claimed that it had ordered villages working on the Pichucalco road to "pay workers retribution according to the law."[92] As municipal finances were so low, this often involved moving around government money. In Hidalgo, the state government gave municipalities a share in the tobacco tax to pay for peasant labor. In Oaxaca, the authorities of Ralu'a repeatedly sought government funds. In 1950 the village's road lobby visited Oaxaca City on at least twenty occasions. But in 1953, their efforts bore fruit. They received 525,000 pesos from the Papaloapan Dam Commission to pay village workers and finish the proposed road. If government cash was low, they collected donations in an ad hoc fashion. In Ralu'a they complemented government funds with donations from the region's rich merchants.[93] In Amatlán (Veracruz) they collected fifty centavos from each car that used the bumpy dirt-track road. The money eventually paid for the paving of the route.[94]

Other authorities tried to overcome the political objections to communal labor. State governments repeatedly ordered mayors to convince rather than force their villagers to work for free. In 1949 the governor of Oaxaca, Eduardo Vasconcelos, urged municipal authorities in Choapam (Oaxaca) to avoid conflicts by "persuad[ing] villagers of the significance of these works."[95] And municipal chiefs often pleaded that they had used persuasion to get people to work. In 1940 the mayor of Zapotitlán Lagunas argued that he had never coerced locals to toil but rather used "legal convincing," "calling attention to the importance of this particular matter." As a result, most villagers, inspired by his dreams of a modern future, "offered their labor with good will."[96]

But often persuasion was not enough. Some villages introduced ad hoc strategies of participatory democracy to gain citizens' full consent. These often trumped the legal framework of representative government. In San José de Gracia (Michoacán), municipal presidents rarely imposed communal work. If they did, they risked the sack. Locals dubbed one particularly enthusiastic president Uruchurtu after the modernizing Mexico City chief and threw him out after six months. Smart presidents relied instead on irregular "public assemblies" to test the village mood. These were convoked by the local priest, held on the patio of a local school, involved ample debate, and decided on the object of communal work through a show of hands. In 1967 locals decided to back the construction of a drinkable water system and a new secondary school. The municipal president then set about organizing the labor draft.[97]

During the 1950s, Ruiz Cortines attempted to impose a new institution that could fulfill this role. Municipal governments were asked to set up Boards of Material Improvements. These were private-public institutions, designed to take decision-making out of the hands of local mayors and raise money for village developments. Some were complete disasters. They became "party political organizations" or were hijacked by local entrepreneurs. Outside the fishing port of Ensenada (Baja California Norte), rich peasants used matching government funds to build a tavern, with the result that "drunkards hung around the bar molesting passing women and bringing scandal to the village."[98] But others were more successful. Savvy local leaders would use the boards to measure public opinion, choose popular projects, and gain official backing. In San Luis Potosí, during Salvador Nava's brief stint as mayor, he established boards in every barrio. Citizens worked together to pave roads and introduce electricity lines and drainage pipes.[99] Furthermore, the Partido Revolucionario Institucional (PRI, Institutional Revolutionary Party) incentivized good governance. Aspirant politicians who had run boards successfully and without disruption were put at the head of the list of potential PRI candidates. By the 1960s, 15 percent of Mexican mayors had previous experience on these infrastructure organizations.[100]

CONCLUSION

During the postrevolutionary era, communal labor, like land reform and education, was a highly controversial issue. State funds were low; demands for infrastructure projects were high. In many rural areas, especially in the south, local governments imposed communal labor by force. Violence, imprisonment, fines, and threats shaped Mexico's network of roads, in particular. Many villagers looked back on the era of the labor draft with considerable resentment. At the time, such strategies also generated conflict. Many villagers complained that they had not consented to provide such labor. Others complained that the projects provided little economic benefit. But, gradually, forced use of free labor seems to have declined. Funding for cash pay sometimes trickled down. In other regions, state or local governments attempted to use persuasion to gain locals' consent. In fact, by the 1960s, shifting demographic patterns had changed the meaning of communal labor yet again. As rural Mexicans moved en masse into the expanding cities, they reconfigured the practice. In the urban squatter communities of midcentury Mexico, ad hoc urban committees used the rural tradition to provide paved roads, electricity lines, drainage, and schools.[101]

NOTES

I would like to thank Elizabeth O'Brien for acting as my research assistant for this chapter. I would also like to thank Ben Fallaw and Paul Gillingham for their insights on this chapter.

1. Mateo Moran to President Cárdenas, March 28, 1939; Cipriano Valencia to President Cárdenas, January 4, 1940, both in Archivo General de la Nación (hereafter AGN), Presidente Lázaro Cárdenas del Rio (hereafter LCR), 540/68. All translations are mine unless otherwise indicated.

2. Gilbert Joseph and Daniel Nugent, eds., *Everyday Forms of State Formation: Revolution and the Negotiation of Rule in Modern Mexico* (Durham, N.C.: Duke University Press, 1994); Mary Kay Vaughan, *Cultural Politics in Revolution: Teachers, Peasants, and Schools in Mexico, 1930–1940* (Tucson: University of Arizona Press, 1997); Mary Kay Vaughan and Stephen Lewis, eds., *The Eagle and the Virgin: Nation and Cultural Revolution in Mexico, 1920–1940* (Durham, N.C.: Duke University Press, 2006).

3. Luis Aboites Aguilar, *Excepciones y privilegios: Modernización tributaria y centralización en México, 1922–1972* (Mexico City: Colegio de México, 2003); María Antonia Martínez, *El despegue constructivo de la Revolución: Sociedad y política en el alemanismo* (Mexico City: Porrúa, 2004); Wendy Waters, "Re-mapping the Nation: Road-building as State Formation in Post-revolutionary Mexico, 1925–1940" (PhD diss., University of Arizona, 1999); Michael Bess, *Routes of Compromise: Building Roads and Shaping the Nation in Mexico, 1917–1952* (Lincoln: University of Nebraska Press, 2017).

4. Alan Knight and Wil Pansters, eds., *Caciquismo in Twentieth-Century Mexico* (London: Institute for the Study of the Americas, 2006); Wil Pansters, ed., *Violence, Coercion, and State-Making in Twentieth-Century Mexico: The Other Half of the Centaur* (Stanford: Stanford University Press, 2012); Thomas Rath, *Myths of Demilitarization in Postrevolutionary Mexico, 1920–1960* (Chapel Hill: University of North Carolina Press, 2013); Ben Fallaw and Terry Rugeley, eds., *Forced Marches: Soldiers and Military Caciques in Modern Mexico* (Tucson: University of Arizona Press, 2012).

5. Keith Brewster, "Caciquismo in Post-revolutionary Mexico: The Case of Gabriel Barrios Cabrera in the Sierra Norte de Puebla" (PhD. diss., University of Warwick, 1995), 186.

6. Robert Redfield, *Tepoztlán: A Mexican Village; A Study of Folk Life* (Chicago: University of Chicago Press, 1930), 126–27, 146.

7. Guillermo Bonfil Batalla, *Mexico Profundo: Reclaiming a Civilization* (Austin: University of Texas Press, 1996), 31.

8. *Oaxaca Nuevo*, November 19, 1941.

9. Paul Gillingham, "Force and Consent in Mexican Provincial Politics: Guerrero and Veracruz, 1945–1953" (PhD diss., Oxford University, 2005).

10. Oscar Lewis, *Life in a Mexican Village: Tepoztlán Restudied* (Urbana: University of Illinois Press, 1951), 108–11, 141, 237.

11. Aboites Aguilar, *Excepciones y privilegios*, 206–16.

12. Alan Knight, *The Mexican Revolution*, 2 vols. (Lincoln: University of Nebraska Press, 1986), 1:78–170.

13. The question of what constituted el pueblo is dealt with by Paul Eiss, *In the Name of El Pueblo: Place, Community, and the Politics of History in Yucatán* (Durham, N.C.: Duke University Press, 2010); Paulina Ochoa Espejo, *The Time of Popular Sovereignty: Process and the Democratic State* (University Park: Penn State University Press, 2011).

14. Redfield, *Tepoztlán*, 126; M. Laura Velasco Ortiz, *Mixtec Transnational Identity* (Tucson: University of Arizona Press, 2005), 33.

15. James Lockhart, *The Nahuas After the Conquest: A Social and Cultural History of the Indians of Central Mexico, Sixteenth Through Eighteenth Centuries* (Stanford: Stanford University Press, 1992), 142–49; Pedro Carrasco, "La economía del México prehispánico," in *Economía política e ideologia en el México prehispánico*, ed. Pedro Carrasco and Johana Broda (Mexico City: Nueva Imagen, 1978), 13–77; Robert Redfield and Alfonso Villa Rojas, *Chan Kom: A Maya Village* (Chicago: University of Chicago Press, 1962), 77–80; Teresa Rojas Rabiela, *La organización del trabajo para las obras públicas: El coatequitl y las cuadrillas de trabajadores* (Mexico City: Instituto Nacional de Antropología e Historia, 1977).

16. David Carballo, "Labor Collectives and Group Cooperation in Pre-Hispanic Central Mexico," in *Cooperation and Collective Action: Archaeological Perspectives*, ed. David M. Carballo (Boulder: University Press of Colorado, 2013), 255.

17. Lockhart, *The Nahuas*, 431.

18. Arij Ouweneel, "From 'Tlahtocayotl' to 'Gobernadoryotl': A Critical Examination of Indigenous Rule in 18th-Century Central Mexico," *American Ethnologist* 22, no. 4 (1995): 768–69.

19. Juan Carlos Peralta Hernández, *Cuyotepeji: Desde la época de las aldeas; Reseña histórica* (Oaxaca: Consejo Nacional para Cultura y las Artes, 2006), 18.

20. Kevin Gosner, *Soldiers of the Virgin: The Moral Economy of a Colonial Maya Rebellion* (Tucson: University of Arizona Press, 1992), 9–10.

21. Peter Guardino, "Community Service, Liberal Law, and Local Custom in Indigenous Villages, Oaxaca 1750–1850," in *Honor, Status, and Law in Modern Latin America*, ed. Sueann Caulfield, Sarah C. Chambers, and Lara Putnam (Durham, N.C.: Duke University Press, 2005), 50–66, 52.

22. Tierras, vol. 494, AGN, exp. 5, fs. 155.

23. Guardino, "Community Service," 53.

24. Guardino, "Community Service," 59.

25. The increase in religious tasks may have been connected to increasing lay responsibilities for religious duties. William Taylor, *Shrines and Miraculous Images: Religious Life in Mexico Before the Reforma* (Albuquerque: University of New Mexico Press, 2010), 139–64.

26. Manuel Martínez Gracida, *Cuadros sinópticos de los pueblos, haciendas y ranchos del estado libre y soberano de Oaxaca* (Oaxaca: Imprenta del Estado de Oaxaca, 1883), 27–44.

27. Francisco Iglesias, March 26, 1845, Archivo General del Estado de Oaxaca (hereafter AGEO), Gobierno de Distritos, Siglo XIX, Huajuapan, 10.5.

28. Guy P. C. Thomson, *Patriotism, Politics, and Popular Liberalism in Nineteenth-Century Mexico: Juan Francisco Lucas and the Puebla Sierra*, with David LaFrance (Wilmington, Del.: Scholarly Resources, 1999), 10–12.

29. Ariadna Acevedo-Rodrigo, "Paying for Progress: Politics, Ethnicity and Schools in a Mexican Sierra, 1875–1930" (PhD diss., University of Warwick, 2004), 78.

30. Acevedo-Rodrigo, "Paying for Progress," 138.

31. Terry Rugeley, *Rebellion Now and Forever: Mayas, Hispanics, and Caste War Violence in Yucatan, 1800–1880* (Stanford: Stanford University Press, 2009), 308–9.

32. Sarah Washbrook, *Producing Modernity in Mexico: Labour, Race and the State in Chiapas, 1876–1914* (Oxford: Oxford University Press, 2012), 171–207.

33. *Periódico Oficial de Oaxaca*, November 24, 1928, 477.

34. Brewster, "Caciquismo in Post-revolutionary Mexico," 109.

35. Frans Schryer, *Ethnicity and Class Conflict in Rural Mexico* (Princeton, N.J.: Princeton University Press, 1990), 141.

36. Florencio Cruz Cruz, "Surgimiento de la escuela rural en la Sierra Juárez," in *Los maestros y la cultura nacional*, vol. 4, *Sureste* (Mexico City: Dirección General de Culturas Populares, Secretaría de Educación Pública, 1987), 155–86.

37. Marín Santiago to President Cárdenas, September 26, 1938, AGN, LCR, 52.1/674.

38. Marcelino Santos to President Cárdenas, December 15, 1939, AGN, LCR, 52.1/674.

39. Tomás Valencia to President Avila Camacho, February 21, 1941, AGN, Presidente Manuel Avila Camacho (hereafter MAC), 542.1/168.

40. Melquiades Olivar to President Avila Camacho, February 8, 1944, AGN, MAC, 541.1/1019.

41. James Wilkie, *The Mexican Revolution: Federal Expenditure and Social Change Since 1910*, 2nd ed. (Berkeley: University of California Press, 1970), 143.

42. It is possible that new electoral rules, which introduced internal PRI primaries, might have reduced tensions over communal labor. But the complete absence of complaints suggests that this is due to a hole in the archival material. Paul Gillingham, "'We Don't Have Arms, but We Do Have Balls': Fraud, Violence, and Popular Agency in Elections," in *Dictablanda: Politics, Work, and Culture in Mexico, 1938–1968*, ed. Paul Gillingham and Benjamin T. Smith (Durham, N.C.: Duke University Press, 2014), 149–71.

43. Richard R. Fagen and William S. Tuohy, "Aspects of the Mexican Political System," *Studies in Comparative International Development* 7, no. 3 (1972): 209; Wayne

Cornelius, *Mexican Politics in Transition: The Breakdown of a One-Party-Dominant Regime* (San Diego: Center for U.S.-Mexican Studies, 1996), 30.

44. Rath, *Myths of Demilitarization*, 134.

45. Carlos Bazan to President Avila Camacho, June 17, 1943, AGN, MAC, 542.1/871.

46. Carlos Castro M. and Antonio Ruiz to President Avila Camacho, January 13, 1944, AGN, MAC, 556.4/85.

47. Lewis, *Life in a Mexican Village*, 108.

48. Anon. letter, October 4, 1945, AGN, MAC, 542.1/1272.

49. Martín Pedro to President Avila Camacho, August 23, 1941, AGN, MAC, 542.1/380.

50. For an introduction to church-state relations during the period, see Matthew Butler, "Introduction: A Revolution in Spirit? Mexico, 1910–1940," in *Faith and Impiety in Revolutionary Mexico*, ed. Matthew Butler (London: Palgrave Macmillan, 2007), 1–20.

51. Rodolfo González to President Cárdenas, March 2, 1937, AGN, LCR, 515.1/263.

52. Juan Velasco to President Avila Camacho, February 22, 1941, AGN, MAC, 542.1/120.

53. For state anticlericalism, see Ben Fallaw, "Varieties of Mexican Revolutionary Anticlericalism: Radicalism, Iconoclasm, and Otherwise, 1914–1935," *The Americas* 65, no. 4 (2009): 481–509.

54. Ceferino Mateo to President Cárdenas, December 29, 1936, AGN, LCR, 543.3/611.

55. Pedro Manuel to President Cárdenas, February 17, 1937, AGN, LCR, 534.5/545.

56. Schryer, *Ethnicity and Class Conflict*, 141.

57. "Miles de campesinos huyen de la miseria," *Heraldo de San Luis*, May 10, 1961.

58. Luis Rodríguez to Municipal President of Tlahuitoltepec, September 22, 1952, Archivo Municipal de Tlahuitoltepec, caja 1, 1900–1950, Administracion, Correspondencia.

59. Felipe Luciano to Secretario General de Gobierno, November 30, 1938, AGEO, Gobernación 1937.

60. In the extremely Catholic region of Huajuapan, local authorities simply gave up building unattended state schools. Moises de la Peña, *Problemas sociales y económicos de las mixtecas* (Mexico City: Instituto Nacional Indigenista, 1950), 142–43.

61. Bess, *Routes of Compromise*, 1.

62. Bess, *Routes of Compromise*, 144.

63. Bess, *Routes of Compromise*, 91–93.

64. Wilkie, *The Mexican Revolution*, 143.

65. Benjamin T. Smith, "Building a State on the Cheap: Taxation, Social Movements, and Politics," in *Dictalanda: Politics, Work, and Culture in Mexico, 1938–1968*, ed. Paul Gillingham and Benjamin T. Smith (Durham, N.C.: Duke University Press, 2014), 255–76.

66. Brewster, "Caciquismo in Post-revolutionary Mexico," 186–94.

67. Patricia Arias and Lucía Bazán, *Demandas y conflicto: El poder político en un pueblo de Morelos* (Mexico City: Centro de Investigaciones Superiores del Instituto Nacional de Antropología e Historia, 1979), 62–63.

68. Luis de Guadalupe Martínez, *La lucha electoral del PAN en Oaxaca*, vol. 1, *1939–1971* (Mexico City: n.p., 2002), 145.

69. Luis Vasquez to Secretario Particular del Gobernador, June 9, 1956, Archivo del Municipio de Tequixtepec, Gobernación.

70. José P. Avila to President Cárdenas, February 23, 1935, AGN, LCR, 540/68.

71. Gerardo Perez to President Cárdenas, June 4, 1936, AGN, MAC, 542.1/1842.

72. Julio de la Fuente, *Yalálag, una villa zapoteca serrana* (Mexico City: Museo Nacional de Antropología, 1949), 226.

73. Waters, "Re-mapping the Nation," 82.

74. Waters, "Re-mapping the Nation," 93.

75. Antonio Resendiz to Secretario Particular, June 19, 1945, AGN, MAC, 515.1/2.

76. Pedro Martinez to President Ruiz Cortines, December 2, 1953, AGN, Presidente Adolfo Ruíz Cortines (hereafter ARC), 515.1/274.

77. Reyes Barahona to President Ruiz Cortines, June 23, 1956, AGN, ARC, 542.1/1190.

78. Antonio Morales to President Ruiz Cortines, February 22, 1956, AGN, ARC, 515/1/625.

79. Ejidatarios of San Jose Provindencia to President Ruiz Cortines, September 5, 1955, AGN, ARC, 542.1/985.

80. Vecinos of El Capuín to President Ruiz Cortines, July 30, 1957, AGN, ARC, 542.1/1352.

81. Pablo Rosas to President Avila Camacho, March 12, 1942, AGN, MAC, 542.1/423.

82. Gillingham, "Force and Consent," 56.

83. Marcelino Santos to President Cárdenas, December 15, 1939, AGN, LCR, 515.1/591; Juan Miguel to President Avila Camacho, July 8, 1942, AGN, MAC, 609/457; Eustorgio Cecillio to President Avila Camacho, March 5, 1942, AGN, MAC, 542.1/515.

84. Liga Central de Comité Agrarias to President Avila Camacho, June 26, 1946, AGN, MAC, 542.1/989.

85. Eustorgio Cecillio to President Avila Camacho, March 5, 1942, AGN, MAC, 542.1/515.

86. Gillingham, "Force and Consent," 272.

87. Juan Miguel to President Avila Camacho, July 8, 1942, AGN, MAC, 609/457; Pablo Bernal to President Ruiz Cortines, February 14, 1958, AGN, ARC, 703.4/1336; Liga Central de Comité Agrarias to President Avila Camacho, June 26, 1946, AGN, MAC, 542.1/989.

88. Vecinos of El Capuín to President Ruiz Cortines, July 30, 1957, AGN, ARC, 542.1/1352.

89. Gillingham, "Force and Consent," 272.

90. Lewis, *Life in a Mexican Village*, 141.

91. Waters, "Re-mapping the Nation."

92. Jose Castañon to President Avila Camacho, February 11, 1944, AGN, MAC, 515.1/261.

93. Lane Ryo Hirabayashi, *Cultural Capital: Mountain Zapotec Migrant Associations in Mexico City* (Tucson: University of Arizona Press, 1993), 55–56.

94. Waters, "Re-mapping the Nation."

95. *El Chapulín*, March 30, 1949.

96. Cipriano Valencia to President Cárdenas, January 4, 1940, AGN, LCR, 540/68.

97. Luis González y González, *San José de Gracia: Mexican Village in Transition* (Austin: University of Texas Press, 1982), 201.

98. Richard Fagen and William S. Tuohy, *Politics and Privilege in a Mexican City* (Stanford: Stanford University Press, 1972), 77; Antonio Ugalde, *Power and Conflict in a Mexican Community: A Study of Political Integration* (Albuquerque: University of New Mexico Press, 1970), 121–22.

99. "San Luis en el camino de la Revolución," n.d., AGN, Adolfo López Mateos (ALM), 702/113.

100. Benjamin T. Smith, "Who Governed? Grassroots Politics in Mexico Under the Partido Revolucionario Institucional, 1958–1970," *Past and Present* 225, no. 1 (November 2014): 255.

101. Alejandro Massolo, "Las políticas del barrio," *Revista Mexicana de Sociología* 56, no. 4 (1994): 165–84; Adrian Guillermo Aguilar, "Community Participation in Mexico City: A Case Study," *Bulletin of Latin American Research* 7, no. 1 (1988): 33–46.

BIBLIOGRAPHY

Aboites Aguilar, Luis. *Excepciones y privilegios: Modernización tributaria y centralización en México, 1922–1972*. Mexico City: Colegio de México, 2003.

Abrams, Philip. "Notes on the Difficulty of Studying the State." *Journal of Historical Sociology* 1, no. 1 (March 1988): 58–89.

Acevedo-Rodrigo, Ariadna. "Paying for Progress: Politics, Ethnicity and Schools in a Mexican Sierra, 1875–1930." PhD diss., University of Warwick, 2004.

Agamben, Giorgio. *State of Exception*. Chicago: University of Chicago Press, 2005.

Aguilar, Adrian Guillermo. "Community Participation in Mexico City: A Case Study." *Bulletin of Latin American Research* 7, no. 1 (1988): 33–46.

Alayza T., Oscar. "La industria minera en el Perú, 1936." *Boletín del Cuerpo de Ingenieros de Minas del Perú*, no. 119 (1937): 212–27.

Albert, Bill. *An Essay on the Peruvian Sugar Industry, 1880–1920*. Norwich: University of East Anglia, 1976.

Alfageme, Augusta, et al. *De la moneda de plata al papel moneda, Perú: 1879–1930*. Lima: Banco Central de Reserva del Perú, Agencia para el Dasarrollo Internacional, 1992.

Aljovín de Losada, Cristóbal, and Sinesio López, eds. *Historia de las elecciones en el Perú: Estudios sobre el gobierno representativo*. Lima: Instituto de Estudios Peruanos, 2005.

Anderson, Benedict. *Imagined Communities: Reflections on the Origin and Spread of Nationalism*. New York: Verso, 1983.

Anderson, Perry. "The Antinomies of Antonio Gramsci." *New Left Review* 100 (1976): 5–81.

Anderson, Perry. *The H-Word: The Peripeteia of Hegemony*. New York: Verso, 2017.

Anglo-French Ticapampa Silver Mining Company. *Assemblée générale ordinaire du 24 mai 1907: Rapports du conseil d'administration et du commissaire des comptes.* Paris: Imprimerie Chaix, 1907.

Anglo-French Ticapampa Silver Mining Company. *Assemblée générale ordinaire du 3 juin 1908: Rapports du conseil d'administration et du commissaire des comptes.* Paris: Imprimerie Chaix, 1908.

Anglo-French Ticapampa Silver Mining Company. *Assemblée générale ordinaire du 3 mai 1918: Rapports du conseil d'administration et du commissaire des comptes.* Paris: Imprimerie Chaix, 1918.

Anglo-French Ticapampa Silver Mining Company. *Assemblée générale ordinaire du 21 juin 1919: Rapports du conseil d'administration et du commissaire des comptes.* Paris: Imprimerie Chaix, 1919.

Anglo-French Ticapampa Silver Mining Company. *Assemblée générale ordinaire du 29 août 1921: Rapports du conseil d'administration et du commissaire des comptes.* Paris: Imprimerie Chaix, 1921.

Anglo-French Ticapampa Silver Mining Company. *Assemblée générale ordinaire du 7 juillet 1922: Rapports du conseil d'administration et du commissaire des comptes.* Paris: Imprimerie Chaix, 1922.

Arceo Pérez, Miguel. *Informe del Presidente de la Liga "Carlos Marx" relativo a su actuación en el año social de 1929.* Mérida: El Porvenir, 1929.

Ardant, Gabriel. "Financial Policy and Economic Infrastructure of Modern States and Nations." In *The Formation of National States in Western Europe*, edited by Charles Tilly, 164–242. Princeton, N.J.: Princeton University Press, 1975.

Arias, Patricia, and Lucía Bazán. *Demandas y conflicto: El poder político en un pueblo de Morelos.* Mexico City: Centro de Investigaciones Superiores del Instituto Nacional de Antropología e Historia, 1979.

Askinasy, Siegfried. *El problema agrario de Yucatán.* 2nd ed. Mexico City: Ediciones Botas, 1936.

Banco de la Nación. *50 años llevando la Banca a donde tú estás.* Lima: Banco de la Nación, 2016.

Basadre, Jorge. *Elecciones y centralismo en el Perú.* Lima: Centro de Investigación de la Universidad del Pacífico, 1980.

Basadre, Jorge. *Historia de la República del Peru, 1822–1933.* 17 vols. 6th ed. Lima: Editorial Universitaria, 1968–69.

Basadre, Jorge. *Reflexiones en torno a la Guerra de 1879.* Lima: F. Campodónico, 1979.

Batres, Carlos Milla. *Cartas a Piérola: Sobre la ocupación chilena de Lima.* Introduction and notes by Rubén Vargas Ugarte. Lima: Ediciones Milla Batres, 1979.

Beatty, Edward. *Institutions and Investment: The Political Basis of Industrialization in Mexico Before 1911.* Stanford: Stanford University Press, 2001.

Beckman, Ericka. *Capital Fictions: The Literature of Latin America's Export Age.* Minneapolis: University of Minnesota Press, 2013.

Beetham, David. *The Legitimation of Power.* Atlantic Highlands, N.J.: Humanities Press, 1991.

Beezely, William. "Kaleidoscopic Views of Liberalism Triumphant, 1862–1895." In *The Divine Charter: Constitutionalism and Liberalism in Nineteenth-Century Mexico*, edited by Jaime E. Rodríguez O., 167–79. Lanham, Md.: Rowman & Littlefield, 2005.

Belaunde, Víctor Andrés. *La crisis presente, 1914–1939.* 7th ed. Lima: Ediciones "Mercurio Peruano," 1940.

Benjamin, Thomas. *El Camino al Leviatán: Chiapas y el estado mexicano, 1891–1947.* Mexico City: Consejo Nacional para la Cultural y el Arte, 1990.

Benjamin, Thomas. *A Rich Land, a Poor People: Politics and Society in Modern Chiapas.* Albuquerque: University of New Mexico Press, 1989.

Bermúdez, Oscar. *Historia del salitre desde sus orígenes hasta la Guerra del Pacífico.* Santiago de Chile: Universidad de Chile, 1963.

Bess, Michael. *Routes of Compromise: Building Roads and Shaping the Nation in Mexico, 1917–1952.* Lincoln: University of Nebraska Press, 2017.

Blasco, Juan. "La industria aguarentera chiapaneca, 1900–1940." Manuscript in author's possession, n.d.

Blasco, Juan. "Producción y comercialización del aguardiente en los Altos de Chiapas en la segunda mitad del siglo XIX." Master's thesis, Universidad Autónoma de Chiapas, San Cristóbal de las Casas, 2001.

Bolio Ontiveros, Edmundo. *Pluma obrera: Cuestiones sociales.* Mexico City: n.p., 1918.

Bolio Ontiveros, Edmundo, ed. *El Partido Socialista del Sureste y el futuro gobierno del Prof. Bartolomé García Correa.* Mérida: Pluma y Lapiz, 1930.

Boloña, Carlos. *Políticas arancelarias en el Perú, 1880–1980.* Lima: Instituto de Economía de Libre Mercado, 1994.

Bonfil Batalla, Guillermo. *Mexico Profundo: Reclaiming a Civilization.* Austin: University of Texas Press, 1996.

Bonilla, Heraclio. *Guano y burguesía en el Perú.* 3rd ed. Quito: Facultad Latinoamericana de Ciencias Sociales, 1994.

Bonilla, Heraclio. *El minero en los Andes.* Lima: Instituto de Estudios Peruanos, 1974.

Bonilla, Heraclio. "The War of the Pacific and the National and Colonial Problem in Peru." *Past and Present*, no. 81 (1978): 92–118.

Bonin, Hubert. "The Political Influence of Bankers and Financiers in France in the Years 1850–1960." In *Finance and Financiers in European History 1880–1960*, edited by Youssef Cassis, 219–42. New York: Cambridge University Press, 1992.

Bonney, Richard. *The Rise of the Fiscal State in Europe, c. 1200–1815.* Oxford: Oxford University Press, 1999.

Boykin, V. I., and Boris Anan'ich. "The Role of International Factors in the Formation of the Banking System in Russia." In *International Banking, 1870–1914*, edited by Rondo Cameron and V. I. Boykin, 130–58. New York: Oxford University Press, 1992.

Brandenburg, Frank Ralph. "Mexico: An Experiment in One-Party Democracy." PhD diss., University of Pennsylvania, 1956.

Brewster, Keith. "Caciquismo in Post-revolutionary Mexico: The Case of Gabriel Barrios Cabrera in the Sierra Norte de Puebla." PhD diss., University of Warwick, 1995.

Buchenau, Jürgen. "Plutarco Elías Calles and Revolutionary-Era Populism in Mexico." In *Populism in Twentieth Century Mexico: The Presidencies of Lázaro Cárdenas and Luis Echeverría*, edited by Amelia M. Kiddle and María L. O. Muñoz, 38–57. Tucson: University of Arizona Press, 2010.

Buchenau, Jürgen. *Plutarco Elías Calles and the Mexican Revolution*. Lanham, Md.: Rowman and Littlefield, 2007.

Bulmer-Thomas, Víctor. *La historia económica de América Latina desde la independencia*. Mexico City: Fondo de Cultura Económica, 1998.

Burga, Manuel, and Alberto Flores Galindo. *Apogeo y crisis de la república aristocrática*. Lima: Rikchay Perú, 1979.

Bustamante, Juan. *Los indios del Perú*. Lima: Printed by J. M. Monterola, 1867.

Bustillos Méndez, Rafael. *El gran Kanxoc: José María Iturralde Traconis*. Mexico City: Fuentes Impresores, 1987.

Butler, Matthew. "Introduction: A Revolution in Spirit? Mexico, 1910–1940." In *Faith and Impiety in Revolutionary Mexico*, edited by Matthew Butler, 1–20. London: Palgrave Macmillan, 2007.

Camberos Vizcaíno, Enrique. *Francisco el Grande: Mons. Francisco Orozco y Jiménez, biografía*. 2 vols. Mexico City: Editorial Jus, 1966.

Campbell, John. "The State and Fiscal Sociology." *Annual Review of Sociology* 19 (1993): 163–85.

Cantón, Miguel. *En tiempos de conquista: Veinte años de accion socialista*. Mérida: Editora "Mayab" S.A., n.d.

Carballo, David. "Labor Collectives and Group Cooperation in Pre-Hispanic Central Mexico." In *Cooperation and Collective Action: Archaeological Perspectives*, edited by David Carballo, 243–74. Boulder: University Press of Colorado, 2013.

Cardoso, Fernando Enrique, and Enzo Faletto. *Dependency and Development in Latin America*. Translated by Marjory Mattingly Urquidi. Berkeley: University of California Press, 1979.

Carmagnani, Marcello. *Estado y mercado: La economía pública del liberalismo mexicano, 1850–1911*. Mexico City: Fondo de Cultura Económica, El Colegio de México y Fideicomiso Historia de las Américas, 1994.

Carrasco, Pedro. "La economía del México prehispánico." In *Economía política e ideologia en el México prehispánico*, edited by Pedro Carrasco and Johana Broda, 13–77. Mexico City: Nueva Imagen, 1978.

Centeno, Miguel Angel. "Blood and Debt: War and Taxation in Nineteenth-Century Latin America." *American Journal of Sociology* 102, no. 6 (1997): 1565–1605.

Chapman, Stanley. *The Rise of Merchant Banking*. Boston: Allen & Unwin, 1984.

Chiaramonti, Gabriella. *Ciudadanía y representación en el Perú (1808–1860)*. Lima: Universidad Nacional Mayor de San Marcos, 2005.

Chiaramonti, Gabriella. "Construir el centro, redefinir al ciudadano: Restricción del sufragio y reforma electoral en el Perú de finales del siglo XIX." In *Legitimidad, representación y alternancia en España y América Latina: Las reformas electorales, 1880–1930*, edited by Carlos Malamud, 230–61. Mexico City: Fondo de Cultura Económica, 2000.

Chiaramonti, Gabriella. "A propósito del debate Herrera-Gálvez de 1849: Breves reflexiones sobre el sufragio de los indios analfabetos." In *Historia de las elecciones en el Peru: Estudios sobre el gobierno representativo*, edited by Cristóbal Aljovín de Losada and Sinesio López, 325–58. Lima: Instituto de Estudios Peruanos, 2005.

Chiaramonti, Gabriella. "La redefinición de los actores y de la geografía política en el Perú a finales del siglo XIX." *Historia* 42, no. 2 (2009): 329–70.

Chowell, G., et al. "The 1918–1920 Influenza Pandemic in Peru." *Vaccine* 29 (Suppl. 2) (2011): B21–26.

Cirerol Sansores, Manuel. *Historia del transporte de pasajeros en Mérida*. Mérida: Talleres Gráficos del Sudeste, 1960.

Coatsworth, John. "Comment on 'The United States and the Mexican Peasantry.'" In *Rural Revolt in Mexico and U.S. Intervention*, edited by Daniel Nugent, 61–68. San Diego: Center for U.S.-Mexican Studies, University of California, San Diego, 1988.

Coatsworth, John. "Inequality, Institutions and Economic Growth in Latin America." *Journal of Latin American Studies* 40, no. 3 (2008): 545–69.

Coatsworth, John. "Obstacles to Economic Growth in Nineteenth-Century Mexico." *American Historical Review* 83, no. 1 (February 1978): 80–100.

Coatsworth, John. "Los orígenes del autoritarismo moderno en México." *Foro Internacional* 16, no. 2 (1975): 205–32.

Comité "Pro-Henequen." *Ante la ruina del henequen: Documentos relativos a las labores efectuadas en defensa de la industria henequera por un grupo de productores*. Mérida: Compañía Tipográfica Yucateca, 1933.

Confalonieri, Antonio. *Banca e industria in Italia, 1894–1906*. Vol. 3, *L'esperienza della Banca Commerciale Italiana*. Milan: Banca Commerciale Italiana, 1980.

Contreras, Carlos. *El aprendizaje del capitalismo: Estudios de historia económica y social del Perú republicano*. Lima: Instituto de Estudios Peruanos, 2004.

Contreras, Carlos. *Centralismo y descentralismo en la historia del Perú independiente*. Lima: Instituto de Estudios Peruanos, 2000.

Contreras, Carlos. *La economía pública en el Perú después del guano y el salitre: Crisis fiscal y elites económicas durante su primer siglo independiente*. Lima: Banco Central de Reserva del Perú; Instituto de Estudios Peruanos, 2012.

Contreras, Carlos. "El impuesto de la contribución personal en el Perú." *Histórica* 29, no. 2 (2005): 67–106.

Córdova, Arnaldo. *La ideología de la Revolución Mexicana: La formación del nuevo régimen*. Mexico City: Era, 1985.

Córdova y Urrutia, José María. *Estadística histórica, geográfica, industrial y comercial de los pueblos que componen las provincias del Departamento de Lima*. Lima: Imprenta de Instrucción Primaria, 1839.

Cornelius, Wayne. *Mexican Politics in Transition: The Breakdown of a One-Party-Dominant Regime*. San Diego: Center for U.S.-Mexican Studies, 1996.

Corrigan, Philip, and Derek Sayer. *The Great Arch: English State Formation as Cultural Revolution*. Oxford: Basil Blackwell, 1985.

Cotler, Julio. *Clases, estado y nación en el Perú*. Lima: Instituto de Estudios Peruanos, 1978.

Cottrell, Philip L. "Anglo-French Financial Co-operation, 1850–1880." *Journal of European Economic History* 3, no. 1 (1974): 75–86.

Cottrell, Philip L. "The Coalescence of a Cluster of Corporate International Banks, 1855–75." *Business History* 33, no. 3 (1991): 31–52.

Cowling, Mark, and James Martin, eds. *Marx's "Eighteenth Brumaire": (Post)Modern Interpretations.* London: Pluto Press, 2002.

Cramer, Christopher. *Violence in Developing Countries: War, Memory, Progress.* Bloomington: Indiana University Press, 2007.

Crehan, Kate. *Gramsci, Culture, and Anthropology.* Berkeley: University of California Press, 2002.

Crozier, Ronald. "Guano y salitre: Las causas económicas de la guerra de Perú y Bolivia contra Chile en 1879." Paper presented at the Congreso de Historia de la Minería, San Luis Potosí, 1997.

Cruz Cruz, Florencio. "Surgimiento de la escuela rural en la Sierra Juárez." In *Los maestros y la cultura nacional,* vol. 5, *Sureste,* 155–86. Mexico City: Dirección General de Culturas Populares, Secretaría de Educación Pública, 1987.

Cueto, Marcos. *Excelencia científica en la periferia: Actividades científicas e investigación biomédica en el Perú, 1890–1950.* Lima: Grupo de Análisis para el Desarrollo, 1989.

Cueto, Marcos. *El regreso de las epidemias: Salud y sociedad en el Perú del siglo XX.* Lima: Instituto de Estudios Peruanos, 1997.

Cushman, Gregory T. *Guano and the Opening of the Pacific World: A Global Ecological History.* Cambridge: Cambridge University Press, 2013.

Dagnino, Evelina. *Meanings of Citizenship in Latin America.* Sussex, UK: University of Sussex, 2006.

Dancuart, Pedro, and José Rodríguez. *Anales de la hacienda pública del Perú: Historia y legislación fiscal de la República.* 24 vols. Lima: Ministerio de Hacienda, 1902–1926.

Dargent, Eduardo. "Islas de eficiencia y reforma del Estado: Ministerios de Economía y de Salud 1990–2008." Report, Consorcio de Investigación Económica y Social, Lima, September 2008.

Dávalos y Lissón, Pedro. *La primera centuria: Causas geográficas, políticas y económicas que han detenido el progreso material y moral del Perú en su primera centuria.* 4 vols. Lima: Librería e Imprenta Gil, 1926.

Davis, Diane. *Discipline and Development: Middle Classes and Prosperity in East Asia and Latin America.* New York: Cambridge University Press, 2004.

Davis, Diane. "Uncommon Democracy in Mexico: Middle Classes and the Military in the Consolidation of One-Party Rule, 1936–1946." In *The Social Construction of Democracy, 1870–1990,* edited by George Reid Andrews and Herrick Chapman, 161–89. New York: New York University Press, 1995.

de la Fuente, Julio. *Yalàlag, una villa zapoteca serrana.* Mexico City: Museo Nacional de Antropología, 1949.

de la Peña, Moises. *Problemas sociales y económicos de las mixtecas.* Mexico City: Instituto Nacional Indigenista, 1950.

del Río, Manuel. *Memoria que presenta a las Cámaras reunidas en Sesiones Extraordinarias en 1849 por el Ministro de Hacienda [Manuel del Río] sobre la situación actual de esta y las causas que la han motivado.* Lima: Imprenta de Juan Masías, 1849.

Denegri, M. A. *Estadística minera del Perú en 1905.* Lima: Imprenta la Industria, 1906.

Deustua, José R. *The Bewitchment of Silver: The Social Economy of Mining in Nineteenth-Century Peru.* Athens: Ohio University Press, 2000.

Díaz Gálvez, Ali. "La política tributaria en el Perú de 1930 a 1948: De los impuestos indirectos a los impuestos directos." Undergraduate thesis, Pontificia Universidad Católica del Perú, Lima, 2007.

Domínguez, José Luis. "Situación política en el partido de Sotuta (1911–16)." In *Yucatán: Peonaje y liberación*, edited by Blanca Gonzalez R. et al., 178–205. Mérida: Fondo Nacional para Actividades Sociales, 1981.

Drake, Paul W. *The Money Doctor in the Andes: The Kemmerer Missions, 1923–1933.* Durham, N.C.: Duke University Press, 1989.

Drinot, Paulo. *The Allure of Labor: Workers, Race, and the Making of the Peruvian State.* Durham, N.C.: Duke University Press, 2011.

Drinot, Paulo, ed. *La Patria Nueva: Economía, sociedad y cultura en el Perú, 1919–1930.* Chapel Hill: University of North Carolina Press, 2018.

Drinot, Paulo. "Peru, 1884–1930: A Beggar Sitting on a Bench of Gold?" In *An Economic History of Twentieth-Century Latin America*, vol. 1, *The Export Age: The Latin American Economies in the Late Nineteenth and Early Twentieth Centuries*, edited by Enrique Cardenas, José Antonio Ocampo, and Rosemary Thorp, 152–87. Basingstoke: Palgrave Macmillan, 2000.

Dunkerley, James, ed. *Studies in the Formation of the Nation-State in Latin America.* London: Institute of Latin American Studies, 2002.

Eiss, Paul. *In the Name of El Pueblo: Place, Community, and the Politics of History in Yucatán.* Durham, N.C.: Duke University Press, 2010.

Eiss, Paul. "A Measure of Liberty: The Politics of Labor in Revolutionary Yucatán, 1915–1918." In *Peripheral Visions: Politics, Society, and the Challenges of Modernity in Yucatán*, edited by Edward Terry, Ben Fallaw, Gilbert Joseph, and Edward Moseley, 54–79. Tuscaloosa: University of Alabama Press, 2010.

Eiss, Paul. "Redemption's Archive: Remembering the Future in a Revolutionary Past." *Comparative Studies in Society and History* 44, no. 1 (January 2002): 106–36.

Fagen, Richard R., and William S. Tuohy. "Aspects of the Mexican Political System." *Studies in Comparative International Development* 7, no. 3 (1972): 208–20.

Fagen, Richard, and William S. Tuohy. *Politics and Privilege in a Mexican City.* Stanford: Stanford University Press, 1972.

Falcón, Romana. "Force and the Search for Consent: The Role of the Jefaturas Políticas de Coahuila in National State Formation." In *Everyday Forms of State Formation*, edited by Gilbert M. Joseph and Daniel Nugent, 107–34. Durham, N.C.: Duke University Press, 1994.

Fallaw, Ben. "Bartolocallismo: Calles, García Correa, y los Henequeneros de Yucatán." *Boletín del Archivo Plutarco Elías Calles* 27 (April 1998): 1–32.

Fallaw, Ben. "Bartolomé García Correa and the Politics of Maya Identity in Postrevolutionary Yucatán, 1915–1935." *Ethnohistory* 55, no. 4 (Fall 2008): 553–78.

Fallaw, Ben. *Cárdenas Compromised: The Failure of Reform in Postrevolutionary Yucatán.* Durham, N.C.: Duke University Press, 2001.

Fallaw, Ben. "Los fundamentos económicos del bartolismo: García Correa, los hacendados yucatecos y la industria del henequén, 1930–1933." *Unicornio* 7, no. 338 (October 19, 1997): 3–9.

Fallaw, Ben. *Religion and State Formation in Postrevolutionary Mexico.* Durham, N.C.: Duke University Press, 2013.

Fallaw, Ben. "Varieties of Mexican Revolutionary Anticlericalism: Radicalism, Iconoclasm, and Otherwise, 1914–1935." *The Americas* 65, no. 4 (2009): 481–509.

Fallaw, Ben, and Terry Rugeley, eds. *Forced Marches: Soldiers and Military Caciques in Modern Mexico.* Tucson: University of Arizona Press, 2012.

Ferrer de Mendiolea, Gabriel. "Historia de las comunicaciones." In *Enciclopedia Yucatanense*, vol. 3, 563–64. Mexico City: Gobierno de Yucatán, 1977.

Ficker, Sandra Kuntz. "The Import Trade Policy of the Liberal Regime in Mexico, 1870–1900." In *Constitutionalism and Liberalism in Nineteenth-Century Mexico*, edited by Jaime E. Rodríguez O., 308–13. Lanham, Md.: Rowman & Littlefield, 2005.

Fink, Leon, and Juan Manuel Palacio. *Labor Justice in the Americas.* Urbana: University of Illinois Press, 2017.

Flores Galindo, Alberto. *Dos ensayos sobre José María Arguedas.* Lima: Casa SUR, 1992.

Flores Galindo, Alberto. *Los mineros de la Cerro de Pasco: 1900–1930.* Lima: Pontificia Universidad Católica del Perú, 1974.

Franck, Harry A. *Vagabonding Down the Andes.* Garden City, N.Y.: Garden City Publishing, 1917.

Franz, David A. "Bullets and Bolshevists: A History of the Mexican Revolution and Reform in Yucatán, 1910–1924." PhD diss., University of New Mexico, 1973.

Fraser, Nancy. "Rethinking the Public Sphere: A Contribution to the Critique of Actually Existing Democracy." *Social Text* 25/26 (January 1990): 56–80.

French, William. *A Peaceful and Working People: Manners, Morals, and Class Formation in Northern Mexico.* Albuquerque: University of New Mexico Press, 2008.

Frías Conor, Bonifacio. *Divorcios célebres y amores fugaces: Historia auténtica de un famoso abogado especialista en divorcios.* Mexico City: Botas, 1939.

Fuentes, Hildebrando. *Curso de estadística.* Lima: Impr. de "La Revista," 1907.

Gálvez Montero, José Francisco. "Herrera y los Hermanos Gálvez." In *Bartolomé Herrera y su tiempo*, edited by Fernán Altuve, 237–48. Lima: Sociedad Peruana de Historia, 2010.

Gamboa Ricalde, Alvaro. *Yucatán desde 1910.* 3 vols. Veracruz: Imprente Standard, 1943.

Garcés Feliú, Eugenio, and Angela Vergara. "El Salvador: A Modern Company Town in the Chilean Andes." In *Company Towns in the Americas: Landscape, Power, and Working-Class Communities*, edited by Oliver J. Dinius and Angela Vergara, 178–97. Athens: University of Georgia Press, 2011.

García Cantón, Alberto. *Memorias de un ex-hacendado henequenero.* 3rd. ed. Mérida: Shared Pen, 2012.

García de León, Antonio. *Resistencia y utopía: Memorial de agravios y crónica de revueltas y profecías acaecidas en la provincia de Chiapas durante los últimos 500 años de su historia.* 2 vols. Mexico City: Era, 1985.

García Márquez, Gabriel. *The Autumn of the Patriarch.* New York: Harper & Row, 1976.

Gauss, Susan. *Made in Mexico: Regions, Nation, and the State in the Rise of Mexican Industrialism, 1920s–1940s.* College Station: Penn State University Press, 2010.

Gilley, Bruce. *The Right to Rule: How States Win and Lose Legitimacy.* New York: Columbia University Press, 2009.

Gillingham, Paul. "Force and Consent in Mexican Provincial Politics: Guerrero and Veracruz, 1945–1953." PhD diss., Oxford University, 2005.

Gillingham, Paul. "'We Don't Have Arms, but We Do Have Balls': Fraud, Violence, and Popular Agency in Elections." In *Dictablanda: Politics, Work, and Culture in Mexico, 1938–1968,* edited by Paul Gillingham and Benjamin T. Smith, 149–71. Durham, N.C.: Duke University Press, 2014.

Gobierno Federal. *Censo y división territorial del estado de Chiapas, año 1900.* Mexico City: Secretaría del Fomento, 1905.

Gómez Estrada, José Alfredo. *Lealtades divididas: Camarillas y poder en México, 1913–1932.* Mexico City: Instituto Mora, 2012.

Gonzales, Michael J. *Plantation Agriculture and Social Control in Northern Peru, 1875–1933.* Austin: University of Texas Press, 1985.

Gonzales, Osmar. *La academia y el ágora: En torno a intelectuales y política en el Perú.* Lima: Universidad Nacional Mayor de San Marcos, 2010.

González Navarro, Moisés. *Historia moderna de México.* Vol. 4, *El Porfiriato: La vida social.* Mexico City: Editorial Hermes, 1957.

González Prada, Manuel. *Pensamiento y librepensamiento.* Caracas: Biblioteca Ayacucho, 2004.

González y González, Luis. *San José de Gracia: Mexican Village in Transition.* Austin: University of Texas Press, 1982.

Gootenberg, Paul. *Imagining Development: Economic Ideas in Peru's "Fictitious Prosperity" of Guano, 1840–1880.* Berkeley: University of California Press, 1993.

Gootenberg, Paul. "Population and Ethnicity in Early Republican Peru: Some Revisions." *Latin American Research Review* 26, no. 3 (1991): 109–57.

Gosner, Kevin. *Soldiers of the Virgin: The Moral Economy of a Colonial Maya Rebellion.* Tucson: University of Arizona Press, 1992.

Gramsci, Antonio. *Selections from the Prison Notebooks of Antonio Gramsci.* Translated and edited by Quintin Hoare and Geoffrey Nowell-Smith. New York: International Publishers, 1971.

Graña, Francisco. *El problema de la población en el Perú: Inmigración y autogenia.* Lima: Tipografía El Lucero, 1908.

Grandin, Greg. *The Blood of Guatemala: A History of Race and Nation.* Durham, N.C.: Duke University Press, 2000.

Guardino, Peter. "Community Service, Liberal Law, and Local Custom in Indigenous Villages: Oaxaca, 1750–1850." In *Honor, Status, and Law in Modern Latin America*, edited by Sueann Caulfield, Sarah C. Chambers, and Lara Putnam, 50–66. Durham, N.C.: Duke University Press, 2005.

Guerra, François-Xavier. *México: Del antiguo régimen a la revolución*. Vol. 1. 3rd ed. Mexico City: Fondo de Cultura Económica, 1995.

Haber, Stephen. "Industrial Concentration and the Capital Markets: A Comparative Study of Brazil, Mexico, and the United States, 1830–1930." *Journal of Economic History* 51 (September 1991): 559–80.

Haber, Stephen. *Industry and Underdevelopment: The Industrialization of Mexico, 1890–1940*. Stanford: Stanford University Press, 1989.

Hamilton, Nora. *The Limits of State Autonomy*. Princeton, N.J.: Princeton University Press, 1982.

Helfgott, Federico M. "Transformations in Labor, Land and Community: Mining and Society in Pasco, Peru, 20th Century to the Present." PhD diss., City University of New York, 2013.

Henderson, Timothy. "Unraveling Revolution: Yucatán, 1924–1930." Master's thesis, University of Texas, 1988.

Hernández Chávez, Alicia. *Historia de la Revolución Mexicana, período 1934–1940: La mecánica cardenista*. Mexico City: Colegio de México, 1979.

Hinrichs, Harley. *Una teoría general del cambio de la estructura tributaria durante el desarrollo*. Mexico City: Centro de Estudios Monetarios Latinoamericanos, 1967.

Hirabayashi, Lane Ryo. *Cultural Capital: Mountain Zapotec Migrant Associations in Mexico City*. Tucson: University of Arizona Press, 1993.

Hirsch, Steven Jay. "The Anarcho-Syndicalist Roots of a Multi-Class Alliance: Organized Labor and the Peruvian Aprista Party, 1900–1933." PhD diss., George Washington University, 1997.

Holden, Robert. *Mexico and the Survey of Public Lands: The Management of Modernization, 1876–1911*. DeKalb: Northern Illinois University Press, 1994.

Holston, James. *Insurgent Citizenship: Disjunctions of Democracy and Modernity in Brazil*. Princeton, N.J.: Princeton University Press, 2008.

Hunt, Shane. *Growth and Guano in Nineteenth-Century Peru*. Princeton, N.J.: Princeton University Press, 1973.

Hunter, Wendy, and Robert Brill. "Documents, Please: Advances in Social Protection and Birth Certification in the Developing World." *World Politics* 68, no. 2 (2016): 191–228.

Irurozqui, Marta. *La ciudadanía en debate en América Latina: Discusiones historiográficas y una propuesta teórica sobre el valor público de la infracción electoral*. Lima: Instituto de Estudios Peruanos, 2004.

Jaffrelot, Christophe. "Voting in India: Electoral Symbols, the Party System and the Collective Citizen." In *The Hidden History of the Secret Ballot*, ed. Romain Bertrand, Jean-Louis Briquet, and Peter Pels, 78–85. Bloomington: Indiana University Press, 2006.

Jimenez, Carlos P. *Estadística minera del Perú en 1907.* Lima: Litografía y Tipografía Carlos Fabbri, 1908.

Jimenez, Carlos P. *Estadística minera del Perú en 1913.* Lima: Imprenta Americana, 1915.

Jimenez, Carlos P. *Estadística minera del Perú en 1914.* Lima: Imprenta Americana, 1916.

Jimenez, Carlos P. *Estadística minera del Perú en 1915.* Lima: Imprenta Americana, 1917.

Joseph, Gilbert M. *Rediscovering the Past at Mexico's Periphery: Essays on the History of Modern Yucatán.* Tuscaloosa: University of Alabama, 1986.

Joseph, Gilbert M., and Daniel Nugent, eds. *Everyday Forms of State Formation: Revolution and the Negotiation of Rule in Modern Mexico.* Durham, N.C.: Duke University Press, 1994.

Katayama, Roberto. "Bartolomé Herrera y su debate con los liberales." In *Bartolomé Herrera y su tiempo*, edited by Fernán Altuve, 223–35. Lima: Sociedad Peruana de Historia, 2010.

Katz, Friedrich. "The Agrarian Policies and Ideas of the Revolutionary Mexican Factions Led by Emiliano Zapata, Pancho Villa, and Venustiano Carranza." In *Reforming Mexico's Agrarian Reform*, edited by Laura Randall, 21–34. Armonk, N.Y.: M. E. Sharpe, 1996.

Katz, Friedrich. "The Liberal Republic and the Porfiriato, 1867–1910." In *Mexico Since Independence*, edited by Leslie Bethell, 49–124. New York: Cambridge University Press, 1991.

Katz, Friedrich. "Rural Rebellions After 1910." In *Riot and Rebellion: Rural Social Conflict in Mexico*, edited by Friedrich Katz, 521–60. Princeton, N.J.: Princeton University Press, 1988.

Katz, Friedrich. *The Secret War in Mexico: Europe, the United States and the Mexican Revolution.* Chicago: University of Chicago Press, 1981.

Keefer, Philip. "Protection Against a Capricious State: French Investments and Spanish Railroads, 1845–1875." *Journal of Economic History* 56, no. 1 (1996): 170–92.

Killingray, David, and Howard Phillips, eds. *The Spanish Influenza Pandemic of 1918–1919: New Perspectives.* London: Routledge, 2003.

Klarén, Peter F. *Modernization, Dislocation and Aprismo: Origins of the Peruvian Aprista Party, 1870–1932.* Austin: University of Texas Press, 1973.

Klarén, Peter Flindell. *Peru: Society and Nationhood in the Andes.* New York: Oxford University Press, 2000.

Klein, Naomi. *The Shock Doctrine: The Rise of Disaster Capitalism.* New York: Metropolitan Books / Henry Holt, 2007.

Klinge, Germán. *Estadística minera del Perú en 1906.* Lima: Imprenta la Industria, 1907.

Klubock, Thomas. *Contested Communities: Class, Gender, and Politics in Chile's El Teniente Copper Mine, 1904–1951.* Durham, N.C.: Duke University Press, 1998.

Knight, Alan. "Cardenismo: Juggernaut or Jalopy?" *Journal of Latin American Studies* 26, no. 1 (February 1994): 73–107.

Knight, Alan. "Habitus and Homicide: Political Culture in Revolutionary Mexico." In *Citizens of the Pyramid: Essays on Mexican Political Culture*, edited by Wil Pansters, 107–29. Amsterdam: Thela, 1997.

Knight, Alan. *The Mexican Revolution.* 2 vols. Lincoln: University of Nebraska Press, 1986.

Knight, Alan. "The Peculiarities of Mexican History: Mexico Compared to Latin America, 1821–1992." *Journal of Latin American Studies* 24, no. 1 (March 1992): 99–144.

Knight, Alan, and Wil Pansters, eds. *Caciquismo in Twentieth-Century Mexico.* London: Institute for the Study of the Americas, 2006.

Kristal, Efraín. *The Andes Viewed from the City: Literary and Political Discourse on the Indian in Peru, 1848–1930.* New York: Peter Lang, 1987.

Kruijt, Dirk, and Menno Vellinga. *Labor Relations and Multinational Corporations: The Cerro de Pasco Corporation in Peru (1902–1974).* Assen: Van Gorcum, 1979.

Landes, David. *Bankers and Pashas.* Cambridge, Mass.: Harvard University Press, 1958.

Landes, David. "The Old Bank and the New: The Financial Revolution of the Nineteenth Century." *Revue d'Histoire Moderne et Contemporaine* 3 (1956). Reprinted in *Essays in European Economic History, 1789–1919,* edited by F. Crouzet, W. H. Chaloner, and W. M. Stern, 112–27. London: Economic History Society, 1969.

Larson, Brooke. *Trials of Nation-Building: Liberalism, Race, and Ethnicity in the Andes, 1810–1910.* Cambridge: Cambridge University Press, 2004.

Lear, John. *Workers, Neighbors, and Citizens: The Revolution in Mexico City.* Lincoln: University of Nebraska Press, 2001.

Lewis, Oscar. *Life in a Mexican Village: Tepoztlán Restudied.* Urbana: University of Illinois Press, 1951.

Lockhart, James. *The Nahuas After the Conquest: A Social and Cultural History of the Indians of Central Mexico, Sixteenth Through Eighteenth Centuries.* Stanford: Stanford University Press, 1992.

Lombardo Toledano, Vicente. *El llanto del sureste.* 2nd ed. Mexico City: Centro de Estudios Históricos del Movimiento Obrero Mexicano, 1977.

López, Sinesio. *Ciudadanos reales e imaginarios: Concepciones, desarrollo y mapas de la ciudadanía en el Perú.* Lima: Instituto de Diálogo y Propuestas, 1997.

López, Sinesio, and Milagros Barrenechea. "Peru, 1930–1968: Competencia y participación en el estado oligárquico." In *Historia de las elecciones en el Peru: Estudios sobre el gobierno representativo,* edited by Cristóbal Aljovín de Losada and Sinesio López, 109–78. Lima: Instituto de Estudios Peruanos, 2005.

López-Alves, Fernando. *State Formation and Democracy in Latin America, 1810–1900.* Durham, N.C.: Duke University Press, 2000.

Loret de Mola, Carlos. *Confesiones de un gobernador.* Mexico City: Grijalbo, 1978.

Ludlow, Leonor. "El Banco Nacional Mexicano y el Banco Mercantil Mexicano: Radiografía social de sus primeros accionistas, 1881–1882." *Historia Mexicana* 39, no. 4 (1990): 979–1027.

Ludlow, Leonor. "La construcción de un banco: El Banco Nacional de México (1881–1884)." In *Banca y poder en México, 1800–1925,* edited by Leonor Ludlow and Carlos Marichal, 299–345. Mexico City: Grijalbo, 1986.

Ludlow, Leonor, and Carlos Marichal, eds. *La banca en México, 1820–1920.* Mexico City: Instituto Mora, 1998.

Ludlow, Leonor, and Carlos Marichal, eds. *Banca y poder en México, 1800–1925*. Mexico City: Grijalbo, 1986.

Macías, Carlos, ed. *Plutarco Elías Calles: Pensamiento político y social*. Mexico City: Fondo de Cultura Económica, 1988.

Mallon, Florencia. *The Defense of Community in Peru's Central Highlands: Peasant Struggle and Capitalist Transition, 1860–1940*. Princeton, N.J.: Princeton University Press, 1983.

Mallon, Florencia. *Peasant and Nation: The Making of Postcolonial Mexico and Peru*. Berkeley: University of California Press, 1995.

Manero, Enrique. *Hacia una económica henequenera racionalmente dirigida*. Mérida: Oriente, 1935.

Manrique, Nelson. *Campesinado y nación: Las guerrillas indígenas en la guerra con Chile*. Lima: Centro de Investigación y Capacitación, 1981.

Manrique, Nelson. "Desarrollo del mercado interior y cambios en la demarcación regional en los Andes centrales del Perú (1820–1930)." In *Estados y naciones en los Andes: Hacia una historia comparativa; Bolivia, Colombia, Ecuador, Perú*, 2 vols., edited by Jean-Paul Deler and Yves Saint-Geours, 1:245–67. Lima: Instituto de Estudios Peruanos, 1986.

Manrique, Nelson. *Mercado interno y región: La sierra central, 1820–1930*. Lima: Centro de Estudios y Promoción del Desarrollo, 1987.

Martínez, Luis de Guadalupe. *La lucha electoral del PAN en Oaxaca*. Vol. 1, *1939–1971*. Mexico City: n.p., 2002.

Martínez, María Antonia. *El despegue constructivo de la Revolución: Sociedad y política en el alemanismo*. Mexico City: Porrúa, 2004.

Martínez Gracida, Manuel. *Cuadros sinópticos de los pueblos, haciendas y ranchos del estado libre y soberano de Oaxaca*. Oaxaca: Imprenta del Estado de Oaxaca, 1883.

Marx, Karl. *The Eighteenth Brumaire of Louis Bonaparte*. 1852. Repr., New York: International Publishers, 1994.

Massolo, Alejandro. "Las políticas del barrio." *Revista Mexicana de Sociologia* 56, no. 4 (1994): 165–84.

Masterson, Daniel. *Militarism and Politics in Latin America: Peru from Sanchez Cerro to Sendero Luminoso*. Santa Barbara, Calif.: Praeger, 1991.

Mathew, William. *La firma inglesa Gibbs y el monopolio del guano en el Perú*. Lima: Banco Central de Reserva del Perú; Instituto de Estudios Peruanos, 2009.

Matthews, Michael. *The Civilizing Machine: A Cultural History of Mexican Railroads, 1876–1910*. Lincoln: University of Nebraska Press, 2014.

Maurer, Noel. "Banks and Entrepreneurs in Porfirian Mexico: Inside Exploitation or Sound Business Strategy?" *Journal of Latin American Studies* 31, no. 2 (1999): 331–61.

Maurer, Noel. *The Power and the Money: The Mexican Financial System, 1876–1932*. Stanford: Stanford University Press, 2002.

Maurer, Noel, and Stephen Haber. "Institutional Change and Economic Growth: Banks, Financial Markets, and Mexican Industrialization, 1878–1913." In *The Mexican Economy, 1870–1930*, edited by Jeffrey Borzt and Stephen Haber, 23–92. Stanford: Stanford University Press, 2002.

Mbembe, Achille. "Necropolitics." *Public Culture* 15, no. 1 (Winter 2003): 11–40.

McCoy, Alfred W. "Covert Netherworld: An Invisible Interstice in the Modern World System." *Comparative Studies in Society and History* 58, no. 4 (October 2016): 847–79.

McEvoy, Carmen. "Estudio preliminar, recopilación y notas." In *La huella republicana liberal en el Perú: Manuel Pardo; Escritos fundamentales*, edited by Carmen McEvoy, 217–48. Lima: Fondo Editorial del Congreso del Perú, 2004.

McMichael, Philip. *Development and Social Change: A Global Perspective*. 6th ed. Los Angeles: SAGE, 2016.

Mediz Bolio, Antonio, and José Castillo Torre. *La agonía de Yucatán: Exposición de la actual situación política, social y económica del estado*. Mexico City: Partido Socialista del Sureste, 1932.

Mehta, Uday S. "Liberal Strategies of Exclusion." *Politics and Society* 18, no. 4 (December 1990): 427–54.

Melgar, José Fabio. *Memoria que presenta á la Lejislatura Ordinaria del Perú del año de 1849, el Oficial Mayor del Ministerio de Hacienda encargado de su despacho*. Lima: Imprenta de Eusebio Aranda, 1849.

Mendiburu, José de. *Presupuesto calculado del producto de las Rentas de la República en un año, que forma la Dirección Jeneral de Hacienda, conforme a los datos que existen en ella*. Lima: Ministerio de Hacienda, 1849.

Menéndez, Carlos R. *En pos de la justicia: La clausura forzosa del "Diario de Yucatán."* Mérida: Compañía Tipográfica de Yucatán, 1932.

Meyer, Lorenzo. *Historia de la Revolución Mexicana, período 1928–1934: Los inicios de la institucionalización; La política del maximato*. Mexico City: El Colegio de México, 1978.

Meza Bazán, Mario. "Caminos al progreso: Mano de obra y política de vialidad en el Perú; La Ley de Conscripción Vial, 1920–1930." Master's thesis, National University of San Marcos, Lima, 1999.

Meza Bazán, Mario. "Estado, modernización y la Ley de Conscripción Vial en Perú." *Revista Andina* 49 (2009): 165–86.

Migdal, Joel S. *Strong Societies and Weak States: State-Society Relations and State Capabilities in the Third World*. Princeton, N.J.: Princeton University Press, 1988.

Miller, Rory. "The Making of the Grace Contract: British Bondholders and the Peruvian Government, 1885–1890." *Journal of Latin American Studies* 8, no. 1 (1976): 73–100.

Ministerio de Hacienda y Comercio [Peru]. *Censo nacional de población de 1940*. Vol. 9. Lima: Dirección Nacional de Estadística, República del Perú, 1942.

Mitchell, Timothy. "Society, Economy, and the State Effect." In *State/Culture: State Formation After the Cultural Turn*, edited by George Steinmetz, 76–97. Ithaca, N.Y.: Cornell University Press, 1999.

Montalvo Ortega, Enrique. *Yucatán: Sociedad, economía, política y cultura*. Mexico City: Universidad Nacional Autónoma de México, 1997.

Morelos Rodríguez, Lucero. "A peso el kilo: Historia del sistema métrico decimal en México." *Investigaciones Geográficas*, no. 69 (August 2009): 132–35.

Mücke, Ulrich. "Estado nacional y poderes provinciales: Aspectos del sistema político peruano antes de la Guerra con Chile." *Anuario de Estudios Americanos* 56, no. 1 (1999): 173–94.

Murra, John. *El "control vertical" de un máximo de pisos ecológicos en la economía de las sociedades andina*. Huánaco, Peru: Universidad Hermilo Valdizan, 1972.

Naranjo Morales, Baltazar. *El doctor Torre Díaz y su actuación*. [Mexico City?]: n.p., [1928?].

Nardelli, Albert. *Un hombre representativo: Bartolomé García Correa, sus ideas y su acción en pro de los anhelos populares de Yucatán*. Mérida: Basso, 1928.

Nugent, David. "Conclusion: Mexican State Formation in Comparative Perspective." In *Forced Marches: Soldiers and Military Caciques in Modern Mexico*, edited by Ben Fallaw and Terry Rugeley, 238–68. Tucson: University of Arizona Press, 2012.

Nugent, David. *The Encrypted State: Delusion and Displacement in the Northern Peruvian Andes*. Stanford: Stanford University Press, 2019.

Nugent, David. *Modernity at the Edge of Empire: State, Individual, and Nation in the Northern Peruvian Andes, 1885–1935*. Stanford: Stanford University Press, 1997.

Nugent, David. "Phantom Pathologies: Regulating Imaginary Threats to the Common Good in Northern Peru." In *Social Wellbeing: New Pathologies and Emerging Challenges*, edited by Angela Hobart, Robert Muller, and David Napier. Herefordshire, UK: Sean Kingston Publishing, forthcoming.

Nugent, David. "State and Shadow State in Turn-of-the-Century Peru: Illegal Political Networks and the Problem of State Boundaries." In *States and Illegal Practices*, edited by Josiah Heyman, 63–98. London: Berg, 1999.

Ochoca Espejo, Paulina. *The Time of Popular Sovereignty: Process and the Democratic State*. University Park: Penn State University Press, 2011.

Ong, Aihwa. *Flexible Citizenship: The Cultural Logics of Transnationality*. Durham, N.C.: Duke University Press, 1999.

Orosa Díaz, Jaime. *Legislación Henequenera en Yucatán*. 4 vols. Mérida: Universidad Autónoma de Yucatán, 1962.

Osten, Sarah. *The Mexican Revolution's Wake: The Making of a Political System, 1920–29*. New York: Cambridge University Press, 2018.

Ouweneel, Arij. "From 'Tlahtocayotl' to 'Gobernadoryotl': A Critical Examination of Indigenous Rule in 18th-Century Central Mexico." *American Ethnologist* 22, no. 4 (1995): 756–85.

Palma Castro, Efraim. *La cuestión henequenera: Ecos de un debate periodístico*. Mérida: Oriente, 1933.

Pansters, Wil, ed. *Violence, Coercion, and State-Making in Twentieth-Century Mexico: The Other Half of the Centaur*. Palo Alto: Stanford University Press, 2012.

Paré, Louise. "Diseño teórico para el estudio del caciquismo actual en México." *Revista Mexicana de Sociología* 34, no. 2 (1972): 335–54.

Parker, David. *The Idea of the Middle Class: White-Collar Workers and Peruvian Society, 1900–1950*. University Park: Pennsylvania State University Press, 1998.

Partido Socialista del Sureste. *Código del Partido Socialista del Sureste estudiado y decretado por el Tercer Congreso Obrero, reunido del 1º al 7 mayo de 1930.* Mérida: Pluma y Lápiz, 1930.

Partido Socialista del Sureste. *Convocatoria para el Tercer Congreso Obrero del Partido Socialista del Sureste, que se efectuará en esta ciudad del 1º al 6 de mayo de 1930.* Mérida: Gráficos "Basso," 1930.

Partido Socialista del Sureste. *Memorias del Cuarto Congreso del Partido Socialista del Sureste: Primero de carácter agrícola-ganadero celebrado en Mérida los días del 1º al 4 de mayo de 1931.* Mérida: Gobierno del estado, 1931.

Partido Socialista del Sureste. *Memoria del Quinto Congreso Obrero del Partido Socialista del Sureste, inspirado en las tendencias cooperativistas: Se celebró en la ciudad de Progreso los días del 10 al 6 del mayo de 1932.* Mérida: n.p., 1932.

Partido Socialista del Sureste. *Segundo Congreso Obrero de Izamal.* 2nd ed. Mexico City: Centro de Estudios Históricos del Movimiento Obrero Mexicano, 1977.

Passananti, Thomas. "Dynamizing the Economy in a façon irrégulière: A New Look at Financial Politics in Porfirian México." *Mexican Studies / Estudios Mexicanos* 24, no. 1 (Winter 2008): 1–29.

Passananti, Thomas. "Financial Conflict and Cooperation in the Belle Epoque: German Banks in Late Porfirian Mexico, 1889–1910." In *México y la economía atlántica (Siglos XVIII–XX),* edited by Sandra Kuntz Ficker and Horst Pietschmann, 173–203. Mexico City: Colegio de México, 2006.

Passananti, Thomas. "Nada de Papeluchos: Managing Globalization in Early Porfirian Mexico." *Latin American Research Review* 42, no. 3 (October 2007): 101–28.

Passananti, Thomas. "The Politics of Silver and Gold in an Age of Globalization: Mexico's Monetary Reform of 1905." *América Latina en la Historia Económica,* no. 30 (July–December 2008): 67–95.

Paxman, Andrew. *Jenkins of Mexico: How a Southern Farm Boy Became a Mexican Magnate.* New York: Oxford University Press, 2017.

Peck, Annie S. *Industrial and Commercial South America.* New York: Thomas Y. Crowell, 1927.

Peloso, Vincent C., and Barbara A. Tenenbaum, eds. *Liberals, Politics, and Power: State Formation in Nineteenth-Century Latin America.* Atlanta: University of Georgia Press, 1996.

Peralta, Víctor. "Los vicios del voto: El proceso electoral en el Perú, 1895–1929." In *Historia de las elecciones en el Perú: Estudios sobre el gobierno representativo,* edited by Cristóbal Aljovín de Losada and Sinesio López, 75–107. Lima: Instituto de Estudios Peruanos, 2005.

Peralta Hernández, Juan Carlos. *Cuyotepeji: Desde la época de las aldeas; Reseña histórica.* Oaxaca: Consejo Nacional para Cultura y las Artes, 2006.

Pereyra Chávez, Nelson. "Los campesinos y la Conscripción Vial: Aproximaciones al estudio de las relaciones estado-indígenas y las relaciones de mercado en Ayacucho (1919–1930)." In *Estado y mercado en la historia del Perú,* edited by Carlos Contreras and Manuel Glave, 334–50. Lima: Pontifica Universidad Católica del Perú, 2012.

Perry, Laurens B. *Juárez and Díaz: Machine Politics in Mexico*. DeKalb: Northern Illinois University Press, 1978.

Piel, Jean. "Las articulaciones de la reserva andina al Estado y al mercado desde 1820 hasta 1950." In *Estados y naciones en los Andes: Hacia una historia comparativa; Bolivia, Colombia, Ecuador, Perú*, 2 vols., edited by Jean-Paul Deler and Yves Saint-Geours, 1:323–36. Lima: Instituto de Estudios Peruanos, 1986.

Polanyi, Karl. *The Great Transformation: The Political and Economic Origins of Our Time*. Boston: Beacon, 1944.

Ponce, Luis. "Banca libre y empresas privadas de recaudación." *Revista Peruana de Ciencias Sociales* 3, no. 3 (1993): 9–41.

Porras Gallo, Maria-Isabel, and Ryan A. Davis, eds. *The Spanish Influenza Pandemic of 1918–1919: Perspectives from the Iberian Peninsula and the Americas*. Rochester: University of Rochester Press, 2014.

Postero, Nancy. *The Indigenous State: Race, Politics, and Performance in Plurinational Bolivia*. Berkeley: University of California Press, 2017.

Poulantzas, Nicos. *Political Power and Social Classes*. New York: Verso, 1975.

Quiroz, Alfonso W. *Banqueros en conflicto: Estructura financiera y economía peruana, 1884–1930*. Lima: Universidad del Pacífico, 1989.

Quiroz, Alfonso W. *La deuda defraudada: Consolidación de 1850 y dominio económico en el Perú*. Lima: Instituto Nacional de Cultura, 1987.

Quiroz, Alfonso W. *Domestic and Foreign Finance in Peru, 1850–1950: Financing Visions of Development*. Pittsburgh: University of Pittsburgh Press, 1993.

Rabasa, Emilio. *La evolución histórica de México*. Mexico City: Imprenta Franco-Mexicana, 1920.

Rabasa, Emilio. *La organización política de México: La constitución y la dictadura*. Madrid: Editorial América, 1920.

Ragas, José. "A Starving Revolution: ID Cards and Food Rationing in Bolivarian Venezuela." *Surveillance & Society* 15, nos. 3/4 (2017): 590–95.

Rath, Thomas. *Myths of Demilitarization in Postrevolutionary Mexico, 1920–1960*. Chapel Hill: University of North Carolina Press, 2013.

Redfield, Robert. *Tepoztlán: A Mexican Village; A Study of Folk Life*. Chicago: University of Chicago Press, 1930.

Redfield, Robert, and Alfonso Villa Rojas. *Chan Kom: A Maya Village*. Chicago: University of Chicago Press, 1962.

Reglamento Interior de la Liga de Baratilleros "Andrés Ortega" y Seción de Veladoras adscritas al Gran Partido Socialista del Sureste. 2nd ed. Mérida: n.p., 1929.

Reglamento Interior de la Liga Protectora de Chauffeurs del Estado adscrita al Gran Partido Socialista del Sureste. Mérida: n.p., 1925.

Reina, Ricardo Feijóo. "The Department of Amazonas Has Been Converted into a True Fief: Twenty Years of Prostration and Servilism," *Amazonas* 4, no. 19 (May 1929).

Rénique, José Luis. *La batalla por Puno: Conflicto agrario y nación en los Andes peruanos*. Lima: Instituto de Estudios Peruanos, 2004.

República del Perú. *Liquidación del presupuesto de 1911 al 31 de mayo de 1912: Anexo á la Cuenta general de la república*. Lima: Ministerio de Hacienda, 1912.

Ridgeway, Stan. "The Cooperative Republic of Tomas Garrido Canabal: Developmentalism and the Mexican Revolution." PhD diss., University of North Carolina at Chapel Hill, 1996.

Ridgeway, Stan. "Monoculture, Monopoly, and the Mexican Revolution." *Mexican Studies / Estudios Mexicanos* 17, no. 1 (Winter 2001): 143–69.

Riguzzi, Paolo. "From Globalisation to Revolution? The Porfirian Political Economy: An Essay on Issues and Interpretations." *Journal of Latin American Studies* 41, no. 2 (2009): 347–68.

Rippy, J. Fred. *British Investments in Latin America, 1822–1949: A Case Study in the Operations of Private Enterprise in Retarded Regions.* Minneapolis: University of Minnesota Press, 1959.

Rojas Rabiela, Teresa. *La organización del trabajo para las obras públicas: El coatequitl y las cuadrillas de trabajadores.* Mexico City: Instituto Nacional de Antropología e Historia, 1977.

Roseberry, William. *Anthropologies and Histories: Essays in Culture, History, and Political Economy.* New Brunswick, N.J.: Rutgers University Press, 1989.

Roseberry, William. "Hegemony and the Language of Contention." In *Everyday Forms of State Formation: Revolution and the Negotiation of Rule in Modern Mexico*, edited by Gilbert M. Joseph and Daniel Nugent, 355–66. Durham, N.C.: Duke University Press, 1994.

Roseberry, William. "Political Economy." *Annual Review of Anthropology* 17 (1988): 161–85.

Rugeley, Terry. *Rebellion Now and Forever: Mayas, Hispanics, and Caste War Violence in Yucatan, 1800–1880.* Stanford: Stanford University Press, 2009.

Salas, Miriam. *El presupuesto, el Estado y la Nación en el Perú decimonónico y la corrupción institucionalizada, 1823–1879.* Lima: Instituto de Estudios Histórico Marítimos del Perú, 2014.

Saragoza, Alex. *The Monterrey Elite and the Mexican State, 1880–1940.* Austin: University of Texas Press, 1988.

Sater, William. *Andean Tragedy: Fighting the War of the Pacific, 1879–1884.* Lincoln: University of Nebraska Press, 2007.

Schryer, Frans. *Ethnicity and Class Conflict in Rural Mexico.* Princeton, N.J.: Princeton University Press, 1990.

Seminario, Bruno. *El desarrollo de la economía peruana en la era moderna: Precios, población, demanda y producción desde 1700.* Lima: Pontificia Universidad Católica del Perú, 2015.

Sempat Assadourian, Carlos. *El sistema de la economía colonial: El mercado interior, regiones y espacio económico.* Mexico City: Nueva Imagen, 1983.

Sempat Assadourian, Carlos. "The Colonial Economy: The Transfer of the European System of Production to New Spain and Peru." *Journal of Latin American Studies* 24, S1 (March 1992): 55–68.

Sinkin, Richard. *Mexican Reform, 1855–1876: A Study in Liberal Nation-Building.* Austin: University of Texas Press, 1979.

Smith, Benjamin T. "Anticlericalism, Politics, and Freemasonry in Mexico." *The Americas* 65, no. 4 (2009): 559–88.

Smith, Benjamin T. "Building a State on the Cheap: Taxation, Social Movements, and Politics." In *Dictalanda: Politics, Work, and Culture in Mexico, 1938–1968*, edited by Paul Gillingham and Benjamin T. Smith, 255–76. Durham, N.C.: Duke University Press, 2014.

Smith, Benjamin T. "Who Governed? Grassroots Politics in Mexico Under the Partido Revolucionario Institucional, 1958–1970." *Past and Present* 225, no. 1 (November 2014): 227–71.

Sociedad Nacional Agraria. *La tributación directa en el Perú: La nueva legislación y las disposiciones legales anteriores*. Lima: Sociedad Nacional Agraria, 1935.

Spenser, Daniela. "Workers Against Socialism? Reassessing the Role of Urban Labor in Yucatecan Revolutionary Politics." In *Land, Labor, and Capital in Modern Yucatán: Essays in Regional History and Political Economy*, edited by Gilbert Joseph and Jeffrey Brannon, 220–42. Tuscaloosa: University of Alabama Press, 1991.

Stein, Steve. *Populism in Peru: The Emergence of the Masses and the Politics of Social Control*. Madison: University of Wisconsin Press, 1980.

Stein, William. *El levantamiento de Atusparia: El movimiento popular ancashino de 1885*. Lima: Mosca Azul, 1988.

Stern, Steve J., ed. *Resistance, Rebellion, and Consciousness in the Andean Peasant World, 18th to 20th Centuries*. Madison: University of Wisconsin Press, 1998.

Stevens, Donald. "Agrarian Policy and Instability in Porfirian Mexico." *The Americas* 39, no. 2 (October 1982): 153–66.

Sulmont, Denis. *El movimiento obrero en el Perú, 1900–1956*. Lima: Pontífica Universidad Católica del Perú, Fondo Editorial, 1980.

Tantaleán Arbulú, Javier. *Política económica financiera y la formación del estado: Siglo XIX*. Lima: Centro de Estudios para el Desarrollo y la Participación, 1983.

Tarrow, Sydney. *Power in Movement: Social Movements and Contentious Politics*. Cambridge: Cambridge University Press, 1998.

Távara, Santiago. *Emancipación del indio decretada en 5 de julio de 1854 por el libertador Ramón Castilla*. Lima: Printed by J. M. Monterola, 1856.

Taylor, Lewis. *Bandits and Politics in Peru: Landlord and Peasant Violence in Hualgayoc, 1900–30*. Cambridge Latin American Miniatures 2. Cambridge: Centre of Latin American Studies, University of Cambridge, 1986.

Taylor, Lewis. "Desarrollo económico y relaciones sociales en las haciendas Huacraruco y Sunchubamba, 1920–1939." In *Estructuras agrarias y cambios sociales en Cajamarca, siglos XIX–XX*, 193–292. Cajamarca: Asociación Obispo Martínez Compañón, 1994.

Taylor, Lewis. "The Origins of APRA in Cajamarca, 1928–1935." *Bulletin of Latin American Research* 19, no. 4 (2000): 437–59.

Taylor, William. *Magistrates of the Sacred: Priests and Parishioners in Eighteenth-Century Mexico*. Stanford: Stanford University Press, 1996.

Taylor, William. *Shrines and Miraculous Images: Religious Life in Mexico Before the Reforma*. Albuquerque: University of New Mexico Press, 2010.

Thobie, James. "European Banks in the Middle East." In *International Banking, 1870–1914*, edited by Rondo Cameron and V. I. Bovykin, 406–40. New York: Oxford University Press, 1991.

Thomson, Guy P. C. *Patriotism, Politics, and Popular Liberalism in Nineteenth-Century Mexico: Juan Francisco Lucas and the Puebla Sierra.* With David LaFrance. Wilmington, Del.: Scholarly Resources, 1999.

Thorp, Rosemary, and Geoffrey Bertram. *Peru, 1890–1977: Growth and Policy in an Open Economy.* New York: Columbia University Press, 1978.

Tilly, Charles. "War Making and State Making as Organized Crime." In *Bringing the State Back In*, edited by Peter B. Evans, Dietrich Rueschemeyer, and Theda Skocpol, 169–91. Cambridge: Cambridge University Press, 1985.

Topik, Steven. "When Mexico Had the Blues: A Transatlantic Tale of Bonds, Bankers, and Nationalists, 1862–1910." *American Historical Review* 105, no. 3 (2000): 714–38.

Torre Díaz, Álvaro. *Cuatro años en el gobierno de Yucatán, 1926–1930.* Mérida: Compañía Tipográfica Yucateca, 1930.

Tudela, Fernando, et al. *La modernización forzada del trópico: El caso de Tabasco.* Mexico City: Colegio de México, 1989.

Ugalde, Antonio. *Power and Conflict in a Mexican Community: A Study of Political Integration.* Albuquerque: University of New Mexico Press, 1970.

Urías Horcasitas, Beatriz. "Retórica, ficción y espejismo: Tres imágenes de un México bolchevique (1920–1940)." *Relaciones: Estudios de Historia y Sociedad* 26, no. 101 (2005): 261–300.

Vanderwood, Paul. *Disorder and Progress: Bandits, Police, and Mexican Development.* Lincoln: University of Nebraska Press, 1981.

Vaughan, Mary Kay. *Cultural Politics in Revolution: Teachers, Peasants, and Schools in Mexico, 1930–1940.* Tucson: University of Arizona Press, 1997.

Vaughan, Mary Kay, and Stephen Lewis, eds. *The Eagle and the Virgin: Nation and Cultural Revolution in Mexico, 1920–1940.* Durham, N.C.: Duke University Press, 2006.

Vega, Katia Bendezú. "Relación entre el Estado y las poblaciones vulnerables a través del acceso a los documentos de documentación e identificación (de cómo ven la identificación los sectores vulnerables)." *Nombres* 1, no. 1 (2013): 39–78.

Velasco Ortiz, M. Laura. *Mixtec Transnational Identity.* Tucson: University of Arizona Press, 2005.

Vincent, Joan. *Anthropology and Politics: Visions, Traditions, and Trends.* Tucson: University of Arizona Press, 1990.

Viotti da Costa, Emilia. "New Publics, New Politics, New Histories: From Economic Reductionism to Cultural Reductionism—In Search of Dialectics." In *Reclaiming the Political in Latin American History*, edited by Gilbert Joseph, 17–31. Durham, N.C.: Duke University Press, 2001.

Vizcarra, Catalina. "Guano, Credible Commitments, and Sovereign Debt Repayment in Nineteenth-Century Peru." *Journal of Economic History* 69, no. 2 (2009): 358–87.

Walker, David. "Porfirian Labor Politics: Working Class Organizations in Mexico City and Porfirio Diaz, 1876–1902." *The Americas* 37, no. 3 (January 1981): 257–89.

Walsh, Casey. *Building the Borderlands: A Transnational History of Irrigated Cotton Along the Mexico-Texas Borderland*. College Station: Texas A&M University Press, 2008.

Warren, Richard. *Vagrants and Citizens: Politics and the Masses in Mexico City from Colony to Republic*. Wilmington, Del.: Scholarly Resources, 2001.

Washbrook, Sarah. *Producing Modernity in Mexico: Labour, Race and the State in Chiapas, 1876–1914*. Oxford: Oxford University Press, 2012.

Wasserman, Mark. *Pesos and Politics: Business, Elites, Foreigners, and Government in Mexico, 1854–1940*. Stanford: Stanford University Press, 2015.

Waters, Wendy. "Re-mapping the Nation: Road-Building as State Formation in Postrevolutionary Mexico, 1925–1940." PhD diss., University of Arizona, 1999.

Weber, Max. *Economy and Society*. 2 vols. Berkeley: University of California Press, 1978.

Weber, Max. *From Max Weber: Essays in Sociology*. Edited by Hans Gerth and Charles Wright Mills. New York: Oxford University Press, 1958.

Weiner, Richard. *Race, Nation, and Market: Economic Culture in Porfirian Mexico*. Tucson: University of Arizona Press, 2004.

Wells, Allen, and Gilbert M. Joseph. *Summers of Discontent, Seasons of Upheaval: Elite Politics and Rural Insurgency in Yucatán, 1876–1915*. Stanford: Stanford University Press, 1996.

Wightman, Ann M. *Indigenous Migration and Social Change: The Forasteros of Cuzco, 1570–1720*. Durham, N.C.: Duke University Press, 1990.

Wilkie, James. *The Mexican Revolution: Federal Expenditure and Social Change Since 1910*. 2nd ed. Berkeley: University of California Press, 1970.

Wilkins, Mira, and Harm Schroter, eds. *The Free-Standing Company in the World Economy, 1830–1996*. Oxford: Oxford University Press, 1998.

Wilson, Fiona. "Leguía y la política indigenista." In *La Patria Nueva: Economía, sociedad y cultura en el Perú, 1919–1930*, edited by Paulo Drinot, 139–68. Raleigh: Editorial A Contra Corriente, 2018.

Wolf, Eric R. *Europe and the People Without History*. Berkeley: University of California Press, 1982.

Wolf, Eric R., and Edward C. Hansen. "Caudillo Politics: A Structural Analysis." *Comparative Studies in Society and History*, no. 2 (1967): 168–79.

Yepes, Ernesto. *Economía y política: La modernización en el Perú del siglo XX; Illusión y realidad*. Lima: Mosca Azul, 1992.

Zeveda, Ricardo. *Calles, el presidente*. Mexico City: Editorial Nuestro Tiempo, 1983.

CONTRIBUTORS

Carlos Contreras is a Peruvian historian born in Lima. He obtained his PhD at the Colegio de México and is a professor at the Department of Economics of the Pontificia Universidad Católica del Perú. His research has revolved around the economic history of Peru and Latin America, focusing on the problems that occurred for the formation of a national economy and a public economy after independence. Among his books are *La economía pública en el Perú después del guano y del salitre: Crisis fiscal y élites económicas durante su primer siglo independiente* (2012).

Paulo Drinot is an associate professor of Latin American history at the Institute of the Americas, University College London. He is the author of *The Allure of Labor: Workers, Race, and the Making of the Peruvian State* (2011), published in Spanish as *La seducción de la clase obrera: Trabajadores, raza y la formación del estado peruano* (2016); editor of *Che's Travels: The Making of a Revolutionary in 1950s Latin America* (2010) and *Peru in Theory* (2014), the latter published in Spanish as *El Perú en teoría* (2017); and co-editor of *Más allá de la dominación y la resistencia: Estudios de historia peruana, siglos XVI–XX* (2005), *The Great Depression in Latin America* (2014), also published in Spanish translation as *La Gran Depresión en América Latina* (2015), *Comics and Memory in Latin America* (2017), and *The Peculiar Revolution: Rethinking the Peruvian Experiment under Military Rule* (2017), also published in Spanish as *La revolución peculiar: Repensando el gobierno militar de Velasco* (2018). He is completing a book manuscript titled *The Sexual Question: A History of Prostitution in Peru, 1850–1956*.

Ben Fallaw is a professor of Latin American studies at Colby College, Maine. He is the author of *Cárdenas Compromised: The Failure of Reform in Yucatán* (2001) and *Religion and State Formation in Postrevolutionary Mexico* (2013). His research has been supported by the Mellon Foundation, the American Council of Learned Societies Ryskamp Fellowship, and the National Endowment for the Humanities. Fallaw is currently completing an ethnobiography of Bartolomé García Correa.

David Nugent is a professor of anthropology at Emory University. His works include *Modernity at the Edge of Empire* (1997), *State Theory and Andean Politics* (with Christopher Krupa, 2015), and *The Encrypted State: Delusion and Displacement in Northern Peru* (2019). His interests focus on the anthropology of political and economic life. Much of his fieldwork has been conducted in the Andean region of South America, but he has also done research in East Africa and among indigenous groups in North America.

Thomas Passananti earned his PhD at the University of Chicago and is an associate professor of history at San Diego State University. His research centers on the international and economic history of Mexico and Latin America, with a focus on globalization in nineteenth- and twentieth-century Mexico. Passananti has conducted archival work in Mexico, the United States, England, France, Germany, Holland, and Italy. Current projects include revising his manuscript, "Managing Globalization: The Politics of Banking, Finance, and Money in Porfirian Mexico," for publication.

José Ragas is a historian of technology and holds a PhD from the University of California, Davis. He is an assistant professor at the Instituto de Historia at the Pontificia Universidad Católica de Chile. Prior to this, he was a Mellon Postdoctoral Fellow at Cornell University and a lecturer in the Program in the History of Science and Medicine at Yale University. He is currently working on his book manuscript about the emergence of an early surveillance society in postcolonial Peru. His next project studies the ice trade routes along the Pacific Rim—between Alaska and Patagonia—on the eve of the global warming era in the late nineteenth century. His work has been featured in *Slate*, *Perspectives on History*, and *Harvard International Review*, among others.

Benjamin T. Smith is a professor of Latin American history at the University of Warwick. He has written widely on Mexican politics, journalism, Catholicism, and the drug trade. His latest book is *The Mexican Press and Civil Society: Stories from the Newsroom, Stories from the Street* (2019). When not teaching or writing, he acts as an expert witness for Mexican refugees fleeing drug violence and runs long distances exceptionally slowly.

Lewis Taylor is a senior lecturer at the Institute of Latin American Studies, University of Liverpool. He earned his PhD in rural sociology at the University of Liverpool. He has published widely on the history of Peru's northern highlands (agrarian change, interfactional conflict, banditry), in addition to contemporary Peruvian politics (rural social movements, electoral corruption, the Fujimori regime) and the insurgency mounted by Sendero Luminoso.

Sarah Washbrook completed a PhD at the University of Oxford on state building and export development in Chiapas, Mexico, during the Porfiriato, and was later appointed British Academy Postdoctoral Fellow at St Antony's College, Oxford. She has taught the history of modern Latin America at La Universidad Católica Andrés Bello, Caracas, Venezuela; the University of Manchester, United Kingdom; and University College London. Her doctoral and postdoctoral work on Mexico, Venezuela, and Peru examines unfree labor, including slavery, debt peonage, and indenture as a means to understand export development, nation-state building, modernization, social inequality, and relations of gender and race during the period 1830–1930. She is currently working on a research project at the University of Copenhagen, Denmark, that examines the development of literacy in Maya languages in Chiapas since the 1970s.

INDEX